BOOK TWO Fifth Edition

CENTURY 21

KEYBOARDING, FORMATTING, AND DOCUMENT PROCESSING

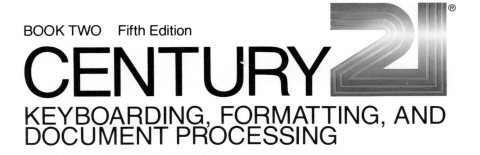

JERRY W. ROBINSON, Ed.D.
Senior Editor
South-Western Publishing Co.

JACK P. HOGGATT, Ed.D.
Professor of Business Education
and Administrative Management
University of Wisconsin,
Eau Claire

JON A. SHANK, Ed.D.
Professor of Administrative Management
and Business Education
Robert Morris College,
Coraopolis (PA)

ARNOLA C. OWNBY, Ed.D.
Professor of Office Administration
and Business Education
Southwest Missouri State University

LEE R. BEAUMONT, Ed.D.
Professor of Business, Emeritus
Indiana University of Pennsylvania

T. JAMES CRAWFORD, Ph.D.
Professor of Business/Education, Emeritus
Indiana University

LAWRENCE W. ERICKSON, Ed.D.
Professor of Education, Emeritus
University of California (LA)

 SOUTH-WESTERN PUBLISHING CO.

Contributing Authors

Several teachers prepared selected materials for this textbook and correlating laboratory materials and tests. Their names are listed here as evidence of our appreciation of their helpful participation.

Connie M. Forde, Ph.D.
Mississippi State University

John E. Gump, Ph.D.
Eastern Kentucky University

Donna M. N. Newhart, Ph.D.
Western Carolina University

Marilyn K. Popyk
Henry Ford Community College
Dearborn, Michigan

Photo Credits

COVER PHOTO:	© Geoff Gove/The IMAGE BANK © Steven Hunt/The IMAGE BANK
PHOTO, p. vi, top:	International Business Machines Corporation*
PHOTO, p. vi, bottom:	Brother International Business Machines Corporation*
PHOTO, p. vii:	
GLOSSARY PHOTOS, pp. xi–xiv:	
"Disk"	Courtesy BASF Corporation
"Facsimile"	Courtesy of AT&T Information Systems
"Sheet feeder"	Photo Courtesy Xerox Corporation
PHOTO, p. ix:	Apple Computer, Inc.**
PHOTO, p. 293:	Bob Daemmrich
PHOTO, p. 325:	Unisys Corp.
PHOTO, p. 337:	Hilton Hotels Corporation
PHOTO, p. 364:	© Wayne Michael Lottinville
PHOTO, p. 389:	Courtesy of ACCO World Corporation
PHOTO, p. 428:	© Michael Philip Manheim/The Stock Solution
PHOTO, p. 434:	© The Stock Solution
PHOTO, p. 443:	© 1989, Comstock
PHOTO, p. 449:	© Wayne Michael Lottinville
PHOTO, p. 464:	© 1987, Comstock
PHOTO, p. 471:	Courtesy of International Business Machines Corporation
PHOTO, p. 488:	© Royce Bair/The Stock Solution
PHOTO, p. RG13, "Offset printer":	Courtesy of A.B. Dick Company

* IBM is a registered trademark of International Business Machines Corporation.

** Apple and the Apple logo are registered trademarks of Apple Computer, Inc.

Any reference made to or use of any of these names or logos in this textbook refers to the foregoing credits.

Copyright © 1993
by SOUTH-WESTERN PUBLISHING CO.
Cincinnati, Ohio

ISBN: 0-538-60075-6

1 2 3 4 5 6 7 8 9 10 11 12 13 14 H 00 99 98 97 96 95 94 93 92

Printed in the United States of America

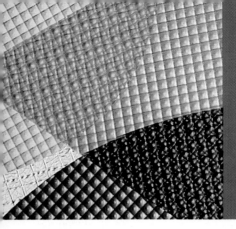

PREFACE

Century 21 Keyboarding, Formatting, and Document Processing—Book 2, Fifth Edition, continues the instructional activities of Book 1. Book 2 has been designed to serve as the capstone of a variety of keyboarding instructional programs. *Century 21* is an excellent instructional resource for high school programs regardless of the type or mix of keyboard equipment employed.

Century 21, Fifth Edition, focuses on three traditionally important components of keyboarding instruction that must be included in any program of keyboarding courses. The three areas of focus are these:

1. Keyboarding skills—fluent manipulation by "touch" of the letter keyboard, the figure/symbol keyboard, and the basic service keys. (This emphasis is the focus of Book 1. Book 2 strengthens and refines keyboarding skills.)

2. Formatting skills—arrangement, placement, and spacing of copy according to accepted practices. (Begun in Book 1, the emphasis on formatting skills is expanded in Book 2.)

3. Document processing skills—the combination of keyboarding and formatting skills needed to produce usable documents. (Book 2 focuses on this component of instruction.)

In addition to these historically important focal points, Book 2 gives frequent attention to two other areas—introduced in Book 1—that must be included in up-to-date keyboarding instruction:

1. Refining of language skills.

2. Increasing knowledge of word processing terminology, procedures, and equipment.

Century 21, Fifth Edition, gives proper treatment to each of these five important instructional areas at strategic times in the 150 lessons included in Book 2. The learning activities are structured, sequenced, and distributed so that learners move from the simpler to the more complex and less-often used. The amount of time and emphasis each learning area receives depends upon the difficulty of the learning task and the level of skill required for acceptable performance.

When combined with the expertise of a keyboarding teacher, Book 2, Fifth Edition, will contribute immensely to the development of document processors who have the attributes expected of beginning office workers.

Those individuals who have completed Book 2 will have made great strides in developing the keyboarding, formatting, production, language, and information technology skills expected of people working in offices. Additionally, the office simulations in Book 2 provide students with ample opportunities to develop the "hidden" job competencies that employers often report as deficient in entry-level workers (e.g., teamwork, problem-solving ability, listening skills, personal/career development, creative thinking, goal-setting/motivational strategies, and knowing how to learn).*

Text Organization/Content

Century 21, Book 2, is organized into two cycles (Cycles 3 and 4 of *Century 21, Complete Course,* Fifth Edition), plus a skills inventory, additional enrichment drills and timed writings, and a modern office-job simulation.

Cycle 3 (Lessons 151–225) and Cycle 4 (Lessons 226–300) each contains three phases of 25 lessons divided into units.

Every phase in Cycle 3 has at least one unit that focuses on each of the following goals:

1. To extend keyboarding/language skills.

2. To simulate an office environment.

3. To evaluate student performance.

The remaining units in each phase focus on extending the students' formatting and document production skills.

Each phase in Cycle 4 has at least one unit that extends keyboarding/language

---

*"What Basic Workplace Skills Training Will Cover, 1990–1992." *Training & Development Journal.* December 1989, 11.

skills and one that measures student performance. Phase 10 (Lessons 226–250) and Phase 11 (Lessons 251–275) have multiple-unit office-job simulations in which students are "employed" in different departments of a company — a large office supply company in Phase 10 and an international mail order firm in Phase 11. Phase 12 (Lessons 276–300) simulations are set in legal, medical, accounting, and travel offices.

Keyboarding Skills

Century 21, Book 2, like Book 1, recognizes the essential relationship between straight-copy skills and document processing skills. To provide the maximum effect from this relationship, Book 2 includes skill-building units so that students will have intensive practice periods to maintain and improve keyboarding speed and accuracy. Further, lessons designed to measure basic skill include timed writings typical of those used in pre-employment tests.

Language Skills

Besides continuing the word-choice activities begun in Book 1, Book 2 requires the application of language skills presented in Book 1. This application occurs in language check and evaluation activities, in simulations (embedded errors in rough drafts), and composition activities.

Formatting Skills

In relation to document formats, Century 21, Book 2, uses four conventions to improve students' retention and transfer of learning:

1. Each basic format and, then, each of its variations is presented and practiced one by one.
2. Drill is provided on document parts that emphasize the format features to be learned.
3. Each format is presented in arranged form followed by semiarranged, then, unarranged source copy in script and rough draft.
4. Each type of document (letter/memo, report, table, etc.) in its various formats recurs periodically.

The lessons in Phase 7, the first phase of Cycle 3, review widely used format features of letters, memos, reports, and tables. In Phase 8, students format special communications, including form letters on executive-size stationery, letters arranged in the simplified block letter style (a new letter style included in Century 21, Fifth Edition), electronic messages, and news releases. Phase 9 includes formatting features of business forms and tables, including tables with leaders and horizontal and vertical lines.

Phases 10, 11, and 12 include simulations that require the use of specified or previously learned format features to process in acceptable form a variety of business documents.

Document Processing

Students combine their keyboarding and formatting skills with language and word processing skills to process documents efficiently and effectively. Throughout Book 2, document processing skills are improved by having students repeatedly recall format features, build skill on these features, complete sustained production timings, and measure production skills. At each of these steps, students are alerted to the important role of planning work, handling work materials, working under time pressures, identifying and correcting errors, and dispensing of completed work in developing and maintaining high-level document processing skills. The numerous simulations in Book 2 provide realistic settings for students to integrate their keyboarding, language, formatting, and document processing skills.

Basic Computer Orientation

Word processing hardware and software have changed the language of keyboarding applications. Century 21 uses the vocabulary of word processing and a simple set of abbreviations that imitate computer commands in giving directions for practice activities. Many of its timed writings and documents are about computer and word processing technology. Word processing software and hardware can be used in meaningful ways to process the documents of Book 2.

In these and additional ways, Century 21 Keyboarding, Formatting, and Document Processing, Fifth Edition, provides the right material in the right amounts for keyboarding courses — whether microcomputer-based instruction is a distant possibility or a present reality. Students who successfully complete Century 21, Book 2 activities will be well-prepared for the modern workplace.

CONTENTS

KNOW YOUR EQUIPMENT: Typewriters

ELECTRONIC (Brother EM-811fx)

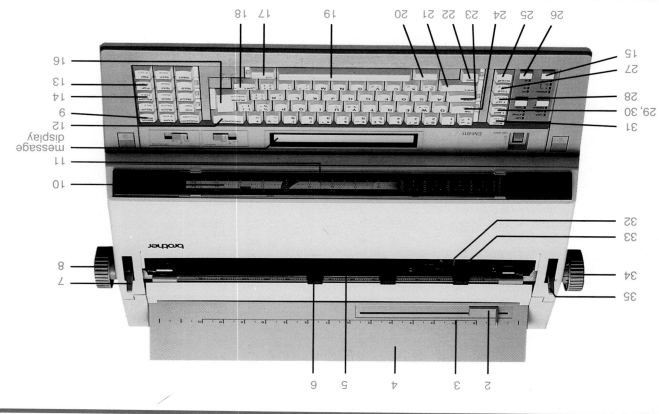

message display

ELECTRIC (IBM Selectric II)

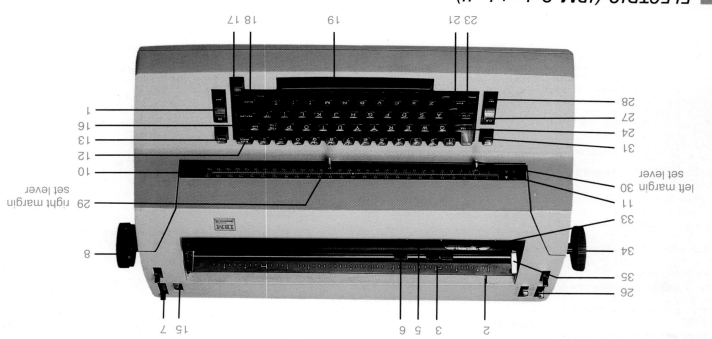

right margin set lever

left margin set lever

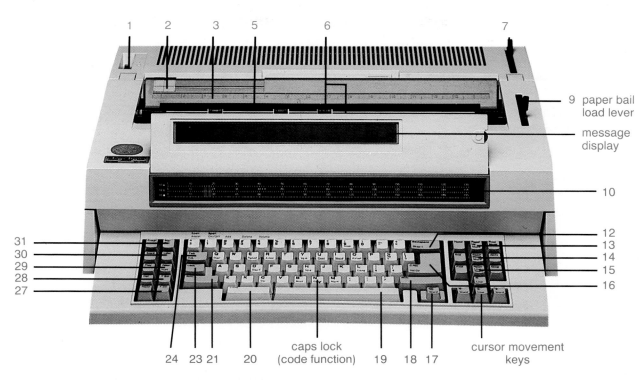

The diagram labels:
1, 2, 3, 5, 6, 7

9 paper bail load lever

message display

10

12, 13, 14, 15, 16

31, 30, 29, 28, 27

caps lock (code function)

cursor movement keys

24 23 21 20 19 18 17

■ *ELECTRONIC (IBM Wheelwriter 30 Series II)*

The diagrams above show the parts of an electric and two electronic typewriters. Illustrated on pp. viii-ix is an array of microcomputers to which your keyboarding skills will transfer.

Since all typewriters have similar parts, you will probably be able to locate the parts on your machine using one of these diagrams. However, if you have the User's Manual that comes with your machine, use it to identify the exact location of each machine part, including special parts that may be on one machine but not on another.

1 ON/OFF control--used to turn machine on or off (not shown on Brother EM-811--under left platen knob)

2 paper guide--used to position paper for insertion

3 paper guide scale--used to set paper guide at desired position

4 paper support--used to support paper in machine (not on IBM Wheelwriter or Selectric)

5 platen--used to feed paper into machine and to provide a hard surface for daisy wheel or element to strike

6 paper bail and **paper bail rolls**--used to hold paper against platen

7 paper release lever--used to adjust position of paper after insertion

8 right platen knob--used to turn platen manually (not on IBM Wheelwriter)

9 paper insert key--used to feed paper into machine and advance paper to proper position for keying (not on Selectric); some machines also have an eject key

10 line-of-writing or **format scales**--used to plan margin settings and tab stops

11 print point indicator--used to position print carrier at desired point (on Selectric--red piece behind left margin set lever; not visible on IBM Wheelwriter)

12 backspace key--used to move print point to the left one space at a time

13 paper up key--used to advance paper one-half line at a time; can be used for paper insertion and ejection; also called **page up key** and **index key**

14 paper down key--used to retract paper one-half line at a time (not on Selectric); also called **page down key**

15 line space selector--used to select line spacing, such as single spacing or double spacing

16 return key--used to return print carrier to left margin and to advance paper up to next line of writing

17 correction key--used to erase ("lift off") characters

18 right shift key--used to key capital letters and symbols controlled by left hand

19 space bar--used to move print carrier to the right one space at a time

20 code key--used with selected character or service keys to key special characters or to perform certain operations (not on Selectric)

21 left shift key--used to key capital letters and symbols controlled by the right hand

22 caps lock key--used to lock shift mechanism for *alphabet characters only* (not on Selectric)

23 shift lock key--used to lock shift mechanism for *all* keyboard characters

24 tab key--used to move print carrier to tab stops

25 repeat key--used to repeat the previous keystroke (IBM Wheelwriter and Selectric have a feature that causes certain keys to repeat when held down)

26 pitch selector--used to select pitch (type size); some machines (like the IBM Wheelwriter) adjust pitch automatically depending upon the daisy wheel inserted

27 tab clear key--used to erase tab stops

28 tab set key--used to set tab stops

29 right margin key--used to set right margin

30 left margin key--used to set left margin

31 margin release key--used to move print carrier beyond margin settings

32 print carrier--used to carry ribbon cassette, daisy wheel or element, correction tape, and print mechanism to print point (not visible on IBM Wheelwriter or Selectric)

33 aligning scale--used to align copy that has been reinserted (not visible on IBM Wheelwriter)

34 left platen knob--used to feed paper manually; also **variable line spacer** on machines with platen knobs (not on IBM Wheelwriter)

35 paper bail lever--used to move paper bail forward when inserting paper manually (Selectric has one at each end of the paper bail)

Tandy 1000
Personal Computer SX

IBM Personal System/2
Model 30

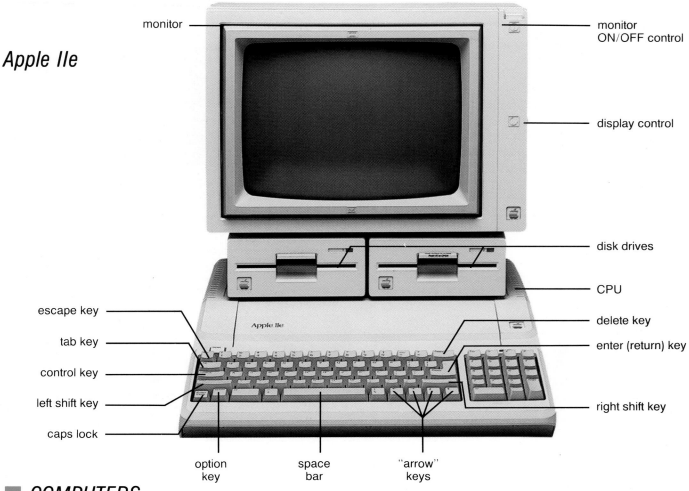

Apple IIe

monitor — monitor ON/OFF control
— display control
— disk drives
— CPU
escape key — delete key
tab key — enter (return) key
control key —
left shift key — right shift key
caps lock —
option key   space bar   "arrow" keys

■ COMPUTERS

The diagram above shows the parts of various microcomputers/ word processors with some examples of different types of machines.

Microcomputers/word processors have similar parts, though the names of these parts and their arrangement may differ. With the help of the User's Manual for your equipment, you should be able to identify each item labeled in the illustration above.

The particular word processing software that you use will determine the specific uses of so-called "function keys." Therefore, you must familiarize yourself with the User's Manual for your software as well as the one for your equipment.

The number in parentheses with some items in the alphabetized list at right refers to a comparable machine part on an electric or electronic typewriter (pp. vi-vii).

alternate (ALT) key--used with selected function keys to perform certain operations (called **option key** on Apple IIe)

"arrow" keys--used to move cursor in the direction of the arrow

caps lock key--used to lock shift mechanism for alphabet characters only (22)

control (CTRL) key--used with selected function keys to perform certain operations

CPU (Central Processing Unit)-- the piece of equipment that holds the hardware or "brain" of the computer

delete key--used to remove characters from the screen one by one

display control(s)--used to adjust contrast and brightness in display

disk drive--a device into which a disk is inserted so information can be either retrieved or recorded

enter (return) key--used to return cursor to left margin and down to the next line; also, to enter system commands (16)

escape (ESC) key--used to cancel a function or exit a program section

left shift key--used to key capital letters and symbols controlled by the right hand (21)

monitor--the piece of equipment used to display text, data, and graphic images on screen

ON/OFF control--used to "power up" or "power down" the system (1) (Apple IIe CPU control not shown--back of CPU, your left side)

right shift key--used to key capital letters and symbols controlled by the left hand (18)

space bar--used to move cursor to right one space at a time or to add space between characters (19)

tab key--used to move cursor to tab stops (24)

1 *Insert Paper*

Electronic Typewriters

1. Align **paper guide** (2) with *0* (zero) on the **paper guide scale** (3). Turn typewriter on using **ON/OFF control** (1).

2. With your left hand, place paper on **paper support** (4), left edge against **paper guide.**

3. With your right index finger, strike the **paper insert key** (9). Paper will feed to a preset point on the sheet.

4. If paper is not straight, pull **paper release lever** (7) toward you (or upward on some machines).

5. Straighten paper; then push **paper release lever** back.

6. Slide **paper bail rolls** (6) to divide paper into thirds (or fourths if there are three rolls).

Electric Typewriters

1. Align **paper guide** (2) with *0* (zero) on the **paper guide scale** (3) or **line-of-writing** or **format scale** (10).

2. Pull **paper bail lever** (35) toward you (or upward on some machines).

3. With your left hand, place paper on **paper support** (4), left edge against the **paper guide.**

4. With your right hand, turn the right **platen knob** (8) or strike the **index key** (13) until paper is about 1½″ above the **aligning scale** (33).

5. If paper is not straight, pull **paper release lever** (7) toward you or upward, straighten paper, and push lever back.

6. Slide **paper bail rolls** (6) to divide paper into thirds (or fourths if there are three rolls).

2 *Set Line Space Selector*

Many machines offer 3 choices for line spacing--1, 1½, and 2--indicated by bars or numbers on the **line space selector** (15).

Set the **line space selector** as directed for lines to be keyed in Phase 1:

- on (−) or 1 to single-space (SS)
- on (=) or 2 to double-space (DS)

To quadruple space (QS), set the **line space selector** on (−) or 1 to SS and strike the **return key** 4 times; alternatively, set the **line space selector** on (=) or 2 to DS and strike the **return key** twice.

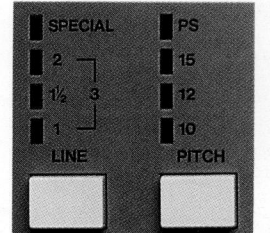

SPECIAL	PS
2	15
1½ 3	12
1	10
LINE	PITCH

1 Lines 1 and 2 are single-spaced (SS).
2 Lines 2 and 4 are double-spaced (DS).
3   1 blank line space
4 Lines 4 and 8 are quadruple-spaced (QS).
5
6   3 blank line spaces (2 DS)
7
8 Set the selector on "1" or "−" to SS.

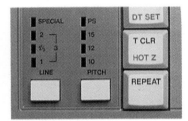

Character pitch

Continuous-feed paper

Control key (CTRL)

Cursor

Daisy wheel

ACCURACY degree of freedom from errors measured from zero--usually expressed as 1 error, 2 errors, etc.; sometimes as errors a minute (eam) or percent of error.

AUTOMATIC ADJUST a feature of automated equipment that automatically reformats the line endings to reflect changes caused by inserted/deleted text or margin changes.

AUTOMATIC CENTERING a formatting feature of automated equipment that places text at an equal distance from the right and left margin settings (equal copy on either side of the center point).

AUTOMATIC PAGE NUMBERING a formatting feature that automatically numbers the pages of a document as it is keyed and renumbers them during revision.

AUTOMATIC UNDERLINE a formatting feature that automatically underscores text.

AUTOMATIC WORD WRAP a formatting feature that places text on the next line without requiring the operator to strike the return key when the text reaches the right margin.

AUTOMATION the use of equipment and software programs to increase productivity and efficiency of procedures.

BACKSPACE to move the print carrier or print point (element, daisy wheel, or cursor) to the left one space at a time by striking the backspace ("back arrow") key once for each character or space.

BACKUP COPY a copy of an original storage medium such as a diskette.

BLOCK a word processing feature that defines a specific portion of text; used with the copy, move, and delete features.

BLOCK HEADING a column head that begins where the column begins.

BOILERPLATE stored text that can be merged with previously stored or new text to create new documents.

BOLD a formatting feature that prints the designated text darker than the rest of the copy to add emphasis.

BOOT to activate a central processing unit (CPU) by loading a disk operating system (DOS) into it.

CAPS LOCK a key that causes *all letters* to be CAPITALIZED without having to depress a shift key for each stroke; differs from the **SHIFT LOCK**, which causes *all shifted characters (letters and symbols)* to print.

CENTERED HEADING a heading that appears exactly centered over a column in a table or over document text.

CENTERING the placing of text so that half the copy is on each side of the center point.

CHARACTER PITCH type size expressed as the number (10, 12, or 15) of characters per horizontal inch: pica (10-pitch); elite (12-pitch); and 15-pitch. ("PS" for "Proportional Spacing" refers to a variable type size with a different number of characters per inch depending upon the particular characters.)

CONTINUOUS-FEED PAPER sheets of paper joined together for use in a printer but perforated for ease of separation.

CONTROL the power to cause the hands and fingers to make correct motions; also the ability to hold keystroking speed down so that errors (mistakes) are kept to an expected or acceptable number.

CONTROL KEY (CTRL) a special key that is pressed at the same time another key is struck, causing that key to perform a specific operation.

COPY a word processing feature that allows the operator to define text at one location and duplicate it in another location; also, material that has been or is to be keyed.

CPU (Central Processing Unit) the internal operating unit or "brains" of an electronic computer system.

CURSOR a lighted point on a display screen where the next character or space can be entered.

DAISY WHEEL a printing wheel shaped like a daisy used on some typewriters and electronic printers.

DECIMAL TAB a word processing feature that positions numbers in columns so that the decimal points are aligned (one under the other).

DEFAULT STANDARDS preset specifications in word processing software that control line length, tabs, etc.

DELETE to remove from text a segment of copy such as a character, a word, a line, a sentence, etc.; also, a word processing feature that allows the operator to eliminate a defined block of text.

DELETE EOL a word processing function that deletes text and codes from the cursor point to the end of the line.

DELETE WORD a word processing function that deletes the word at the cursor.

DESKTOP PUBLISHING using microcomputers, laser printers, and special software to create near typeset-quality documents.

GLOSSARY, continued

DIRECTORY a listing of documents filed on computer software.

DISK (DISKETTE) a magnetic, Mylar-coated record-like disk (encased in a protective cover) used for recording, reading, and writing by a central processing unit (CPU). Common sizes are 5¼" and 3½".

DISK DRIVE the unit into which a disk is inserted to be read or written on by the central processing unit (CPU).

DOCUMENT formatted information such as a letter, memo, report, table, or form.

DOS (Disk Operating System) a program recorded on a disk that causes a computer to operate or function.

DOUBLE-SPACE (DS) to use vertical line spacing that leaves one blank line space between printed lines of copy; equals 2 single-spaced lines.

EDIT to arrange, change, and correct existing text; editing includes proofreading but is not limited to it.

ELECTRONIC FILES information stored in machine-readable form.

ELECTRONIC MAIL information transmitted electronically from one computer to another without transmitting hard copy.

ELEMENT a ball-shaped printing device on the print carrier of many electric and electronic typewriters.

ELITE a type size that prints 12 characters per inch; see CHARACTER PITCH.

ENTER to input keystrokes; see KEY.

ENTER KEY see RETURN KEY.

ERROR any misstroke of a key; also any variation between source copy and displayed or printed copy; departure from acceptable format (arrangement, placement, and spacing).

ESCAPE KEY (ESC) a key that lets the user cancel a function or exit one segment of a program and go to another.

FACSIMILE the use of scanning devices and telephone lines to transfer text and images; a copy of such text/images; commonly abbreviated "FAX."

FINAL COPY copy that is free of error and ready for use or distribution.

FLUSH RIGHT to key copy so that it ends even with the right margin.

FONT a set of characters of a named type style.

FOOTER see HEADER/FOOTER.

FORMAT the style (arrangement, placement, and spacing) of a document; also to arrange a document in proper form or style.

FORMATTING the process of arranging a document in proper form or style.

FUNCTION KEYS special keys on computers and word processors that are used alone or in combination with other keys to perform special operations such as setting margins, centering copy, etc.

GWAM (Gross Words a Minute) a measure of the rate of keyboarding speed; GWAM = total standard 5-stroke words keyed divided by the time required to key those words.

HANGING INDENT a word processing feature that positions the first line of a segment of text at the left margin or other point and indents the remaining lines a specific number of spaces to the right; frequently used with enumerations.

HARD COPY typewritten or printed copy.

HARD DISK high-capacity storage medium measured in megabytes (millions of characters).

HARD RETURN (REQUIRED RETURN) a manually entered return to the left margin; used in letter addresses and closing lines and at the ends of paragraphs.

HARDWARE the physical equipment that makes up a computer or word processing system.

HEADER/FOOTER line(s) of copy keyed at the top (header) or bottom (footer) of each page of a multi-page document, usually the document title or chapter title and page number; also, a word processing feature for inserting header/footer lines automatically.

HELP SCREEN an on-screen list of instructions for using the features of word processing software.

HIGHLIGHTING identifying on-screen text by changing the color or light intensity.

HYPHENATION a word processing feature that overrides word wrap, allowing the operator to divide words at line breaks or to have words divided automatically.

INDENT to set copy farther to the right than the left margin; for example, the first line of a paragraph.

INFORMATION PROCESSING the task of putting text and data into usable form, as in letters, tables, and memos.

INPUT text and data that enter an information system; also the process of entering text and data.

INSERT (INSERTION) to add new text to existing text without rekeying the entire document; also the text that is added.

KEY to strike keys to print or display text and data; also called enter, key in, keyboard, input, and type.

Function keys

Facsimile

Element

Disk drive

Disk (diskette)

Menu

Monitor

Numeric keypad

Prompt

KEYBOARD an arrangement of keys on a "board" that is attached to a typewriter, computer, or word processor; also the act of keying or typing.

LOAD to retrieve a specified computer file or program.

MACRO a word processing feature that allows the operator to save a series of keystrokes--such as often-used phrases, paragraphs, and document formats--to be used repeatedly.

MARGINS specification of the number of spaces (or inches) at the left and right of printed lines; also the number of characters (inches) per line; also the number of line spaces above the page beginning (first line of type) or below the last line of type.

MEMORY data storage location in a computer, word processor, or electronic typewriter.

MENU a listing of available software options that appears on a display screen.

MERGE to assemble new documents from stored text such as form paragraphs; to combine stored text such as form letters with stored or newly keyed text (variables such as names and addresses).

MICROCOMPUTER a small-sized computer with a keyboard, screen, and auxiliary storage; its central processor is usually a single CPU chip.

MONITOR a TV-like screen used to display text, data, and graphic images; also called CRT, display screen, and video display terminal (VDT).

MOVE a word processing feature that allows the operator to define text at one location and shift it to another location.

NUMERIC KEYPAD an arrangement of figure keys and special keys, such as $+$, $-$, and $=$, to the right of most microcomputer keyboards; used for keying all-number copy and for calculations.

OPERATOR'S GUIDE (USER'S MANUAL) a set of instructions accompanying equipment or software that tells/shows how the hardware/software features are made to work.

ORPHAN the first line of a paragraph appearing alone at the bottom of a page; see **WIDOW/ORPHAN**.

OUTPUT data or documents that leave an information system, usually presented to the user as a screen display or a printout.

OVERSTRIKE a word processing feature that replaces existing text with newly keyed text; also, to key new text in place of existing text.

PAGINATION dividing text into segments that will print on a page; can be automatic or operator specified.

PICA a type size that prints 10 characters per inch; see **CHARACTER PITCH**.

POWER UP/DOWN to turn on/off a computer system by following established procedures for specific types of equipment.

PRINT to produce (using a printing device) a paper copy of information displayed on a screen or stored in computer, word processor, or typewriter memory.

PRINT COMMANDS software options for specifying the character pitch, margins, line spacing, justification, number of copies, page numbering, etc., of a document to be printed.

PRINTER a device attached to a computer or word processor that produces a paper (hard) copy of electronically stored text.

PRINTOUT the printed paper output of a computer, word processor, or electronic typewriter.

PROMPT a message displayed in the window of an electronic typewriter or on the screen of a computer or word processor telling the user that the machine is awaiting a specific response.

PROOFREAD to compare copy on a display screen or printout to the original or source copy and to correct errors (or mark them for correction); one of the steps in editing text.

PROOFREADER'S MARKS notations used to indicate changes and corrections needed to convert draft copy to final copy.

QUADRUPLE-SPACE (QS) to use vertical line spacing that leaves 3 blank line spaces between printed lines of copy; equals 4 single-spaced lines or 2 double-spaced lines.

RATE the speed of doing a task; keying or typing rate is usually expressed in gross words a minute (GWAM) or lines per hour.

RETRIEVE a software function that recovers information that has been stored (saved).

RETURN to strike the return or enter key to cause the print carrier or cursor to move to left margin and down to next line.

RETURN KEY (ENTER KEY) a key that when struck causes the print carrier or cursor to move to left margin and down to next line; also struck to enter system commands on word processors or computers.

RIGHT JUSTIFICATION a word processing feature that inserts extra spaces within and between words, causing printed copy to have an even right margin.

SAVE (STORE) a software function that records keystrokes on a magnetic medium (disk) so that the data may be retrieved later; on some software, STORE records text and removes it from the screen while SAVE records and leaves it on the screen.

SEARCH a word processing feature that locates a specified series of characters or words in a document for editing purposes.

SEARCH AND REPLACE a word processing feature that locates a specific block of text and replaces it with new text. When an entire document is searched in this manner, the feature is called GLOBAL SEARCH AND REPLACE.

SHEET FEEDER a device attached to some printers that feeds separate 8½" × 11" sheets of paper into the printer.

SHIFT KEY a key that is depressed as another key is struck to make capital letters and certain symbols.

SHIFT LOCK see CAPS LOCK.

SINGLE-SPACE (SS) to use vertical line spacing that leaves no blank space between printed lines of copy.

SOFTWARE instructions, or programs, that tell a computer or word processor what to do; may be contained on a disk or on computer hardware.

SOURCE DOCUMENTS original papers (documents) from which information (data and/or text) is keyed.

SPACE BAR a long bar at the bottom of a keyboard used to move the print carrier or cursor to the right one space at a time; also used to add space between on-screen characters.

SPACING the number of blank line spaces between printed lines--usually indicated as SS (0), DS (1), or QS (3).

SPELLING VERIFICATION SOFTWARE a program that identifies misspelled words in a document generated on a computer, word processor, or electronic typewriter.

SPLIT SCREEN software capability that permits more than one file to be displayed on the screen at the same time.

STORE see SAVE.

SUBSCRIPT a word processing/printing feature that allows a character to print below the line of writing; also, the character itself.

SUPERSCRIPT a word processing/printing feature that allows a character to print above the line of writing; also, the character itself.

TAB KEY a key that when struck causes the print carrier or cursor to skip to a preset position; used to indent paragraphs or other document parts.

TECHNIQUE a keyboard operator's form or keying style.

TEMPLATE a disk on which only text files (documents) and/or document formats--but no program--are stored.

TEXT EDITOR automatic equipment that permits easy keying, revising, storing, and printing of information or documents.

TEXT (DATA) ENTRY the process of transferring text (data) from the writer's mind or from a written or voice record into a word processing system.

UNDELETE (UNDO) a word processing function that restores text to its state prior to deletion.

USER'S MANUAL see OPERATOR'S GUIDE.

VARIABLES information (such as names, addresses, or financial data) in prestored files that is inserted in standard documents to personalize messages; see MERGE.

VDT (Video Display Terminal) see MONITOR.

WIDOW the last line of a paragraph appearing alone at the top of a page; see WIDOW/ORPHAN.

WIDOW/ORPHAN a word processing feature that prevents the occurrence of widows and orphans (see definitions above) during automatic paging.

WORD PROCESSING the act of writing and storing letters, reports, and other documents on a computer, electronic typewriter, or word processor; may also include printing of the final document.

WORD WRAP a word processing feature that permits information to be keyed on successive lines without having to strike the return key at the end of each line.

ABBREVIATIONS YOU SHOULD KNOW

BM	bottom margin
CH	center horizontally
CS	columnar spacing; space between columns
CV	center vertically
DS	double-space; double spacing
GWAM	gross words a minute
LL	line length
LM	left margin
LP	LabPac (workbook)
LS	line spacing
N-PRAM	net production rate a minute
PB	page beginning
PI	paragraph indent
QS	quadruple-space; quadruple spacing
RM	right margin
SM	side margins
SS	single-space; single spacing

User's Manual

Text (data) entry from a voice record

Source documents

Sheet feeder

Keyboarding, Formatting, and Language-Skills Inventory

This special section consists of 16 basic keyboarding, formatting, and language-skills assignments that all keyboard operators should be able to perform. Your performance on these tasks will reveal the levels of your knowledge and skills at the beginning of the vocational (advanced) keyboarding course. On the basis of your performance on these assignments, your teacher can help you decide those areas to which you should give the heaviest emphasis during the second-year program. Your long-range goals for developing vocational competence should be based on these tasks.

Machine Adjustments

1. Paper guide at *0* (for typewriters).

2. Ribbon control set to use top half of ribbon (for typewriters).

3. LL (line length): 70 spaces unless otherwise directed.

4. LS (line spacing): Double-space (DS) drills; DS paragraphs; as required for problems.

**Inventory 1:
Straight-Copy
Timed Writing**

two 3' timed writings; determine *gwam;* proofread, circle errors

| all letters used | A | 1.5 si | 5.7 awl | 80% hfw |

gwam 3'

In the years to come, quality office workers with good basic skills will continue to be in high demand. Employers in most organizations will seek out employees who have a good knowledge base in English grammar and usage, an ability to speak and write well, and accurate proofreading skills. Preference will be given to people who can think through a task, plan the best way to do it, and then complete it ably and skillfully.

Getting the job done in a cost-effective manner is a primary goal of all companies. Employees wanting to move up the ladder and advance in an office career must be efficient and productive. They must exhibit a good balance of skills. That is, office workers must be dependable, be able to work accurately under pressure, be very flexible in learning new things and ways of doing tasks, and be able to set priorities each day.

		5	62
		9	66
		14	71
		19	76
		24	81
		28	85
		33	90
		38	95
		43	100
		47	104
		52	109
		57	114

gwam 3' | 1 | 2 | 3 | 4 | 5 |

**Inventory 2:
Statistical-Copy
Timed Writing**

two 3' timed writings; determine *gwam;* proofread, circle errors

| all letters/figures used | A | 1.5 si | 5.7 awl | 80% hfw |

gwam 3'

The effects of inflation are being noticed in the costs of producing a letter in today's office. In 1930 when the first study was conducted, the average cost of a typical business letter was 29 cents. As amazing as it may seem, due to spiraling salaries and specialized equipment, a letter that cost about $7.60 in 1983 cost $10.26 in 1989.

Postage (like spiraling salaries and the cost of specialized equipment) has kept rising over the years, another factor related to the expense of a letter. In 30 years, the cost of mailing a first-class letter jumped from 4 cents in 1960 to 25 cents in 1990. The expense of transmitting a letter is one example of rising costs in today's offices.

		4	51
		9	55
		14	60
		19	65
		23	69
		27	74
		32	79
		37	83
		42	88
		46	93

gwam 3' | 1 | 2 | 3 | 4 | 5 |

Document 15 (continued)

WP Tip -- Search and Replace:
Before printing the report, study
procedures (p. A-16 or user's
guide) for using the search and replace feature. Search for the word
supervisor; if preceded by the
word **immediate**, replace with **superior**. Search for the word **doctor**; replace with **physician**.

be suspended for twenty-one days. ‸An lc Unexcused absence of six days will lead to immediate dismissal.

In the event of a death in your immediate family {parents, siblings, spouse, or children}, you will be permitted an absence of three days with pay. For the death of grandparents, aunts,‸ and uncles, you will be‸ ~~allowed time off for the funeral only.~~ *permitted an absence of one day with pay.*

(Insert paragraph numbered ⑤.)

① *Other employees depend upon the work you do in order to complete their jobs. You will gain their respect and enhance your reputation as a responsible, cooperative employee if you are on the job regularly. Keep in mind that attendance is a major factor when an individual is considered for promotion or a bonus.*

② *If your supervisor decides that the absence is unexcused, you have the right to appeal the decision to your next higher supervisor and to the Human Relations Board, if you so desire.*

③ *These actions are to ensure that you do not return to work before you are entirely well and to protect the well-being of your fellow workers.*

④ *counseled by your supervisor in an effort to discover the cause of your absence and to determine if problems exist that can be corrected. A record of the discussion will be placed in your employee file.*

⑤ *Any employee who maintains a perfect attendance record for a period of three consecutive months will be awarded an additional day of vacation with pay; for six consecutive months, two additional days; for one year of perfect attendance, four additional days.*

Inventory 3:
Rough-Draft
Timed Writing
two 3′ timed writings;
determine *gwam*; proof-
read, circle errors

Proofreader's Marks

⊏	move left
⊐	move right
∧	insert
ℓ	delete
↗	insert comma
/ or *lc*	lowercase
⌣	close up
∿	transpose
≡	capitalize
∨	apostrophe
___	underline
○ˢᵖ	spell out
SS	single space
# or /#	insert space
∨∨	insert quota- tion marks
DS	double space

all letters used | A | 1.5 si | 5.7 awl | 80% hfw |

gwam 3′

One of the ~~very~~ *most* important tools required in an *the* office — 4 | 65

of today is the telphone. It ~~permits~~ *allows* a busness firm to bring — 8 | 69

the out side world in to the office in a matter of ~~just~~ a few — 12 | 73

seconds. Numberous critical decisions are mdae over *the* a phone. — 16 | 78

The phone also ~~offers~~ *provides* a means for information to be given, — 20 | 82

good will to be created, and varous ideas to be exchanged. — 24 | 86

~~It~~ *The phone* saves time, and time is a quite scarce resource for — 28 | 90

todays typical business *firm*. — 30 | 92

With in a few seconds after a telephone is ansered, the — 34 | 96

caller ~~gets~~ *forms* an impresion about the business based on the — 38 | 100

employe answering the phone. The employee answering is an — 42 | 104

ambasador for the ~~company~~ *firm* and becomes *actually* the firm to the — 46 | 108

caller at the other end of the lien. Therefore, ~~it is very~~ — 49 | 111

~~essential that~~ all employees *must* realise *that* they are ~~building~~ *creating* a — 53 | 114

first impresion of the firm almost every time they pick up — 57 | 118

the reciever. A positive *public* image is a must for a succesful — 61 | 123

firm. — 62 | 123

Inventory 4:
Center Vertically
and Horizontally

1. On a full sheet, center the announcement DS vertically; center each line horizontally.

2. On a half sheet (long edge at top), center the announcement DS verti- cally; center each line horizontally.

words

DO YOU BELIEVE IN YOURSELF? — 6

Guest Speaker: Dr. Carolyn Barker — 11

Sponsored by — 13

National Honor Society — 18

CHS Auditorium — 21

October 14, 19-- — 24

11 a.m. to 12 Noon — 28

REQUEST FOR IP SERVICES
Originator: **Gail M. Turner, Administrative Assistant**
Document: L **M** R T F X
Date: **June 7**
To: **Aloysius L. Martin, Chief of Personnel**
Subject: **EMPLOYEE ABSENTEEISM**
Enclosures/Attachments: **1**
  Attach the table on employee absenteeism that was keyed on June 3.
Hard copy: **memo form, LP p. 223**
Special: ---
Code: **asd1113**

REQUEST FOR IP SERVICES
Originator: **Aloysius Martin**
Document: L **M** R T F X
Date: **June 7**
To: ---
Subject: ---
Enclosures/Attachments: ---
Hard copy: **plain sheets**
Special: **Numbered insertions are attached (next page).**
Code: **asd1132**

WP Tip -- Move: Key rapidly all report copy as it is given here and on p. 520, including numbers with the ¶s on p. 520.

Then use the move feature (see p. A-17 and/or user's guide) to move/insert each numbered ¶ in the proper place. (Delete the ¶ number before moving the next block.)

As usual, use spell check, thesaurus, macros, etc., to improve your productivity.

(¶) Mrs. Engles notes with some concern the increase in employee absenteeism during the past quarter. She plans an all-out campaign to reverse this trend. The enclosed table outlines the time lost in each department for the second and third quarters of this fiscal year.

(¶) As a part of the campaign, Mrs. Engles wishes you to review and revise our current absentee policies. She would like the policy to reflect a more positive approach. Please let us have a suggested revision within the next two weeks.

POLICY ON ABSENTEEISM

3 blank spaces

The absence of an employee from work has a serious effect upon the operations of *your* ~~any~~ work group. (*Insert material numbered ①* on the next page.) ~~The absence of a worker reflects a lack of dependability and respect for other employees.~~ ~~Furthermore,~~ absenteeism can also result in lower productivity which, in turn, may *affect the company's ability to increase pay and benefits.* ~~cause a great financial loss to the firm.~~

Absence from work is excusable only in the case of serious illness, death in the immediate family, or *an* ~~serious~~ emergency. In such cases, *please* ~~you will be expected to~~ notify your immediate supervisor at the earliest possible *time* ~~moment.~~ Upon your return to work, you will *be asked to* complete an *~~absentee~~* form giving the reason for your absence. Your supervisor has the *authority* ~~right~~ to determine whether the (*Insert material numbered ② on the next page.*) absence is excused or unexcused.

If you are absent because of illness, you will be expected to report to the company doctor *for a brief examination* prior to returning to your ~~desk~~ workstation. For an absence of three or more days, *please obtain* a certificate (*Insert material numbered ③ on the next page.*) from your physician. ~~will be needed.~~ ¶ If you are absent for three (*Insert material numbered ④ on next page.*) days with no acceptable excuse, you will be ~~given a verbal and written reprimand that will be placed in your personnel file.~~ If you are absent for five days with no acceptable excuse, you will

Inventory 5:
Format/Key
Business Letters

plain full sheets
LL: 1½" side margins
PB (page beginning): line 16
PI (paragraph indent): 5 spaces, when needed

Correct all errors: marked, unmarked, and those you may make as you key.

1. Format/key the letter in block style with open punctuation.

2. Format/key the letter in modified block style with open punctuation.

3. Format/key the letter in modified block style with indented ¶s and mixed punctuation.

(sp) Sept. 8, 19-- — 4

Ms. Mary Jo Lupino, Chair — 9
Red Bank High School Business Education —
Department — 19
3500 Red Bank Road — 23
Cincinnati, OH 45227-9076 — 28

Dear Ms. Lupino : — 31

¶ The office automation conference at the — 39
Sabin Convention Center involved many bene- — 48
fits. A highlight of the conference for me — 57
was the time I spent talking with to you. — 65
¶ Our discussion about the integration of — 73
word processing as part of a total office auto- — 82
mation system was timely, for this is precisely exactly — 91
what is happening today. As we move into — 99
the next decade, word processing will be inte- — 108
grated into every office environment. — 116
¶ For these this reasons, I endorse your proposed — 124
integrated word and data processing curriculum, which is — 136
designed to train young men and women for the — 145
automated office. In order for your school to — 154
provide relevant training, it is important that you should im- — 162
pliment this approach as quick ly as possible. — 172
¶ Please let me know how I may support you and — 181
Red Bank High School in this endeavor. — 188

Sincerely yours, — 192
Eldon R. Brookshire —
Information Systems Manager — 196

xx — 201
— 202

REQUEST FOR IP SERVICES
Originator: **Matt Stevens**
Document: **L M R T F X**
Date: **June 7**
To: **3 vendors in file (below)**
Subject: ---
Enclosures/Attachments: ---
Hard copy: **ETI PO forms,
LP pp. 221-223**
Special: **PO #s MT5893,
MT5894, MT5895. Order all
the items listed by stock
number on Order List
attached. Consolidate the
items on the PO's by
vendor, using the Low Bid
Register attached. Shipping
info shown in file (below).
Compute total price for
each item and total each
PO.**
Code: **icg1596...icg1598**

Booker Tool Co.
153 Elk Street
Biloxi, MS 39530-9402

Ship via **Trans-Am Shipping**

Long Industries, Inc.
320 East Street
Monroe, LA 71202-5940

Ship via **Allied Express**

Seaboard Tools, Inc.
1840 Frow Avenue
Miami, FL 33133-2364

Ship via **T & O Express**

ORDER LIST FOR METRIC TOOLS

(As of June 1, 19--)

Stock No.	Item	Quantity
3249	Chisel Set, 6 mm, 10 mm, 11 mm	100 sets
5836	Drill Set, 1-5 mm	200 sets
8965	Flexible Rule, 185 cm	20 ea.
6590	Micrometer w/Readings to .01 mm	50 ea.
7401	Rule, Steel, 0-.9144 m	120 ea.
5420	Ratchet, Flex-Head, 15 mm Drive	10 ea.
3604	Screwdriver Set, 1-3 mm	60 sets
7504	Socket Wrench Set, 10-24 mm, 30 mm	100 sets
0249	Thermometer, -40C to +150C	30 ea.
7458	Universal Box-End Wrench, 9-22 mm	100 ea.
4305	Wrench Set, 6 x 8 mm, 10 x 11 mm	20 sets

LOW BID REGISTER

STOCK NUMBER	LOW BIDDER	VENDOR STOCK NUMBER	TERMS	UNIT PRICE
3249	Booker Tool Co.	6384	Net	21.90/set
5836	Seaboard Tools, Inc.	5-691	2/10, n/30	27.20/set
8965	Long Industries, Inc.	721A	3/30, n/60	3.60/ea.
6590	Long Industries, Inc.	318C	3/30, n/60	31.20/ea.
7401	Long Industries, Inc.	901C	3/30, n/60	1.00/ea.
5420	Booker Tool Co.	1495	Net	5.30/ea.
3604	Seaboard Tools, Inc.	5-702	2/10, n/30	37.00/set
7504	Booker Tool Co.	850	Net	24.10/set
0249	Long Industries, Inc.	347D	3/10, n/60	8.20/ea.
7458	Booker Tool Co.	84	Net	3.20/ea.
4305	Seaboard Tools, Inc.	5-580	2/10, n/30	8.50/set

Inventory 6:
Format/Key a
Simplified Memorandum
plain full sheet
LL: as format requires
LS: as format requires

Correct all errors: marked,
unmarked, and those you
may make as you key.

   Format/key the rough-
draft copy as a simplified
memorandum.

words

September 9, 19--   4

All Workers Using Type Writers   10

MAINTAINANCE AND SERVICE OF TYPEWRITERS   17

Your typewriter is made of *highly sophisticated* mechanisms, so never attempt   33

to repair it yourself. Whenever repair *is needed* becomes necessary,   43

contact the vendor who holds the service contract on the ma-   55

chine after *you have* checking *ed* the following: 64

    1. The power cord is pluged into a socket.   73

    2. The power cord is *securely* connected.   82

    3. The power switch is turned on.   89

    4. The *printing device* element, ribbon cassete, and correction tape are   102
    properly installed.   106

The service contract on your typewriter does not include   118

cleanings for the housing. You should *occasionally* clean the housing,   132

using a *soft* cloth to remove dust, stains, and finger prints. *You should*   145

Never use water or solvents such as thinner or alcohol to   158

cleanse your machine. Further, never *attempt to* disassemble the machine.   173

When the top cover is open *ed* to replace the printing   183

device, *ribbon* cassette, or correcting *on* tape, be sure *not* to drop any   197

itmes such as pins, paper clips, or pins into the machine.   209

These items could cause damage to the typewriter, or an elec-   221

tricle *a* shock to the operator could result. Another precau-   233

tion is to turn the power off before opening the cover.   244

Etta Mae Williams, Manger *a*   249
Administrative Services   254

xx   254

Document 10

REQUEST FOR IP SERVICES
Originator: **Alicia Allen**
Document: **L M R T F X**
Date: **June 6**
To: ---
Subject: ---
Enclosures/Attachments: ---
Hard copy: **plain sheets**
Special: ---
Code: **pro1010**

WP Tip -- Search: Before you print this document, see p. A-16 and/or your user's guide before using the search feature. Search for the ¶ indentions in this document. (Do you have the right number of ¶s?) Then search for the character string "**SUPER-vision**." (Be sure the string occurs at least in the beginning and ending ¶s of the report. Also, edit a ¶ in which this string occurs more than once.)

WP Tip: Can you use thesaurus to find alternatives to the words **innumerable** (¶3) and **enhanced** (¶4)? **Reminder:** Let spell check identify words that contain spelling or keystroking errors; then, look carefully for the kinds of errors that spell check cannot detect.

PROJECT 34912 PROGRESS REPORT

Project {Code Name "SUPER-vision"} was initiated 18 months ago with the goal of applying the latest in electronic improvement to the development of a new generation of television receivers for mass production. This Project is now in the final stages and a prototype will be available soon.

"SUPER-vision" will be a television receivers with a large screen and a degree of clarity equal to the best moving picture film. Colors are truer and brighter. "Ghosts" and interference from outside sources will be eliminated. An integral program will monitor the operations of the set and will make needed adjustments to maintain high-quality performance.

These changes are made possible through the use of chips, similar to those used in computers, which will convert incoming visual and audio signals to numbers. When these signals are changed, innumerable machinations are possible.

Through the use of digital technology, the vertical and horizontal resolution of waves {currently set by federal regulations at 250 horizontal lines and 520 vertical lines} change changed to almost double. Impressive improvements in television reception is possible, without changing current regulat broadcast criteria.

As an "added extra attraction," "SUPER-vision" will be equiped with stereo sound which will provide high-fidelity audeo. Many television stations are all ready broadcasting in stereo and most will do so within a very short time.

Inventory 7:
Format/Key an Unbound
Report with Footnotes
plain full sheet
LL: as format requires
LS: as format requires
PB: as format requires
PI: as format requires
Correct all errors: marked, unmarked, and those you may make as you key.

Format/key as a 1-page unbound report the rough-draft copy shown at the right.

words

PREPARING FOR EMPLOYMENT
5

Business educations students recieve instruction on pre- 16
paring job ~campaign~ materials. Much time is ~~given~~ _devoted_ to units on prepar- 30
ing letters of application and personal data sheets. Discus- 42
sion _usually_ centers around making a good impression through written 56
communication and knowing what employers are looking for in _an_ 69
~~worker~~ _employee_. Students are ~~told~~ _informed_ that employers are interested in 82
knowing about their education _al background_ ~~history~~, honors and awards, 95
occupational experience, and membership in organizations.[1] 107

An important area that is often overlooked in these dis- 118
cussions is what to do to keep the job after ~~you have it.~~ _becoming employed_ In 131
a study conducted by Accountemps, Fortune 1000 company vice 143
presidents and personnel heads wer_e_ asked what employee behav- 155
ior disturbed them most. The five traits and attitudes that 168
were ~~listed~~ _given_ most often are listed below. 176

1. Dishonesty and lying. 181

2. Irresponsibility, goofing off, and attending to per- 192
   sonal business on company time. 199

3. Arrogance, ego problems, and excessive aggressiveness. 211

4. Absenteeism and lateness. 217

5. Not following instructions or ignoring company _policy._[2] ~~rules~~ 229

_____

[1]Carol W. Henson and Thomas L. Means, _Fundamentals of Business_ 233
Communication (Cincinnati: South-Western Publishing Co., 250
1990), p. 407. 265

[2]"How to Avoid Crashing in Your First Job," _Career World_, 268
May 1985, p. 18. 282
285

Document 8

August 15	Completion of Planning Directive 145-30.
September 15	Submission of replies to questionaires by branch and division chiefs.
September 16 to November 15	Analysis of data submitted by branch and division chiefs.
November 16 to December 5	Formulation of changes based on analysis of data.
January 6 to January 21	Discussion of changes with branch and division chiefs individually.
January 22 to February 10	Completion of final plans for reorganization.
February 11	Submission of plans for approval.
February 15	Implementation of plans for reorganization of Marietta headquarters.

Document 9

WP Tips: The new project named *"SUPER-vision"* likely will occur often in future documents. Name the macro **sv**.

Using thesaurus, try to find a suitable replacement for **complete** in ¶2 (*...who has a complete knowledge....*). **Reminder:** Enhance your proofreading with spell check.

(¶) Enclosed is a report of the progress we have made in the production of the next generation of television receivers to which we have given the development title of "SUPER-vision." If all goes well, we should have a working model of this transceiver in operation by October 1.

(¶) At this point, I suggest that representitives of the Director of Electronics Manufacturing and the Director of Marketing Operations become a part of our project team. I recommend Karen C. McKay, my assistant, who has a complete knowledge of all aspects of this project; Yoko Yukimura, our electronics engineer, who can provide any necessary technical information; and Gloria Rios, who can direct the testing phase of the project. With their assistance, we can plan for the manufacture and sale of "SUPER-vision" as soon as we have completed our exhaustive tests in the laboratory and in a selected marketing test area.

Inventory 8:
Format/Key a Leftbound Report with Internal Citations and a Reference Page

plain full sheet
LL: as format requires
LS: as format requires
PB: as format requires
PI: as format requires

Correct all errors: marked, unmarked, and those you may make as you key.

Format/key as a 2-page leftbound report the rough-draft copy shown at the right. Format the reference page as a separate sheet.

(Total words on the reference page: 43)

ADDRESSING FOR EFFICIENT MAIL HANDLING — 8

All who rely [depend] upon the United States [U.S.] Postal Seyvice [Service] to process, sort, and deliver their mail to proper destinations seek two benefits: speed and low cost. From Pony Express to modern jet planes, the speed of transporting mail form "here" to "there" has drastically increased; but at the same time, so has postage cost to the mailer. — 18 / 30 / 42 / 55 / 68 / 74

For [During] the past 25 years, efforts [major attempts] have been made to match the internal speed and efficiency of processing mail to the external speed of moving mail form place to place once it has been processed and sorted. These efforts include the use of Expanded ZIP Codes, bar-coding devices, OCR s, and a variety of other sorting devices. — 89 / 102 / 114 / 126 / 139 / 141

Determining the efficiency of the new systems is hard because of the increasing volume of mail that must be handled. According to the Postmaster General's Office, over one hundred fifty billion pieces of mail are processed annually (Letter from Mrs. Rita Moroney, Research Administration/Historian, Office of the Postmaster General, 1979). Further, according to some estimates, as much as 85 percent of the mail must be sorted by less efficient equipment than the OCR or by hand (DeRoche, W. Timothy, Jr. "Addressing Mail for the Eighties." The Balance Sheet, February 1981, 219-222.) — 152 / 164 / 177 / 188 / 188 / 192 / 204 / 215 / 228 / 240

To raise [increase] the per centage of mail that is processed [processable] by OCR and other mechanical equipment, and thus reduce the cost, the U.S. Postal Service suggests the following formats: [practices] — 251 / 264 / 275

1. Key all lines in block style with a unifrom [uniform] left margin. — 285 / 287

2. Use uppercase letters without punctuation. — 297

3. Key attention lines (when used) as the first line of the address, above the company-name line. — 310 / 316

4. Key the street address or box number on the second line from the bottom. — 329 / 332

5. Key apartment numbers (when used) immediately after the street address on the same lien [line]. — 345 / 351

6. Key the city name, the two-letter state abbreviation, and the ZIP Code together on the last line. (Addressing for Success, Notice 221, USPS, September 1988). — 362 / 371 / 386 / 388

OCR equipment can scan [read] ALL-CAP [unpunctuated] addresses more efficiently than those keyed in cap-and-lowercase letters with punctuation. Human sorters, however, read the latter more efficiently when hand sorting mail or precoding mail for subsequent mechanical processing. Therefore, cap-and-lowercase addresses likely will become acceptable for the U.S. postal service for several [some] years to cme [come]. — 400 / 412 / 424 / 436 / 448 / 459 / 465

Documents 4-7

Applicant 1:

**Miss Juanita L. Marietta
62 Orchard Street
Forest Park, GA 30050-6978**
Position: **WP Specialist**
¶s: B2, M1, E1

Applicant 2:

**Ms. Tracy R. Parkes
Box 33800 North
Decatur, GA 30031-4620**
Position: **WP Trainee**
¶s: B3, M3, E2

Applicant 3:

**Mr. Lu Huang
513 Fair Street
Atlanta, GA 30315-2685**
Position: **Administrative
Assistant**
¶s: B6, M4, E2

Applicant 4:

**Mr. Patrick K. Ridgewood
809 Mimosa Street
Riverdale, GA 30274-3811**
Position: **WP Supervisor**
¶s: B5, M2, E3

WP Tip -- Merge: Refer to
"merge" in your software user's
guide. Key (as shown) and store
each ¶ as a separate file named
B1, B2, etc. Make a reference file
of the ¶s.
   Format/key the date, address,
and salutation; retrieve each ¶ file
as needed. Use edit features to fill
in variables. Key the closing lines.

B1 Thank you for your recent telephone inquiry regarding vacancies for office personnel in Electro-Tech, Inc.

B2 Thank you for your recent letter in which you applied for a position as a/an (insert title of position). We appreciate your interest in Electro-Tech, Inc.

B3 Thank you for applying for the position of (insert title of position).

B4 We acknowledge, with thanks, your application for a position as a/an (insert title). We may have a position for which you are qualified.

B5 Several months ago, you applied for a position as a/an (insert title of position). At that time, we did not have a vacancy for which you were qualified. However, we may have an opening in the very near future.

B6 Recently, you were interviewed by a member of our staff for a position in the office of Electro-Tech, Inc. The competition for this job was very keen, and selecting the person to fill the position was quite difficult.

M1 Will you please complete the enclosed application blank and return it to us promptly. After we have had an opportunity to review your background, we shall be able to determine whether you have the qualifications necessary to fill the position.

M2 Will you please call our office at 555-8100, Ext. 410, and arrange for a personal interview so that we can discuss the position.

M3 At this time we do not have a position for which you are qualified. We shall keep your application on file for six months and if the need arises for someone with your skills, we shall contact you.

M4 We regret that you were not selected for the position. We shall keep your application on file for six months and shall call you if another vacancy occurs.

E1 Within ten days after we receive your application blank, we shall let you know whether we have a position for which you are qualified.

E2 Your interest in becoming an employee of our company is appreciated.

E3 If you are no longer interested in a position with our company, will you please call and let us know.

Inventory 9:
Format/Key Tables

LL: as format requires
LS: as format requires
PB: as format requires
PI: as format requires
Correct all errors.
   Format/key the tables at the right and lower right. Center each table vertically and horizontally.

Table A

half sheet, long edge at the top
LS: DS
CS (columnar spacing): 14 spaces

FIVE NEWEST STATES OF THE U.S.			words
FIVE NEWEST STATES OF THE U.S.			6
(With Date of Entry and Capital)			13
Hawaii	August 21, 1959	Honolulu	19
Alaska	January 3, 1959	Juneau	25
Arizona	February 14, 1912	Phoenix	32
New Mexico	January 6, 1912	Sante Fe	36
Oklahoma	November 16, 1907	Oklahoma City	47

Table B

half sheet, long edge at the top
LS: DS headings; SS body
CS: 10 spaces between longest items in columns
headings: blocked
Note: Key $ beside the first number in column (and with total figure in column, if used) in a position so it is one space to the left of the largest number in the column.

CHECKS OUTSTANDING			words
CHECKS OUTSTANDING			4
Week Ending (Aug.) 31 19--			9
Check #	Amount	Balance	17
997	$ 13.97	$2,972.33	22
998	408.58	2,563.75	27
999	306.10	2,257.65	31
1000	61.01	2,196.63	35
1001	102.27	2,094.36	39

Table C

full sheet
LS: DS
CS: 6 spaces
headings: centered
totals indent: 5 spaces

SALES SUMMARY				words
SALES SUMMARY				3
For the Month of August 19--				9
Region	Projected	Actual	Difference	23
Eastern	$1,250,000	$1,297,000	$ 47,000	31
Southern	994,500	999,200	4,700	38
North Central	2,483,000	2,598,500	115,500	47
Mountain-Pacific	928,300	973,600	45,300	55
Western	3,150,000	2,990,000	−160,000	68
Totals	$8,805,800	$8,858,300	$ 52,500	76

Document 3

REQUEST FOR IP SERVICES
Originator: **Cynthia Morris**
Document: **L M R T F X**
Date: **June 4**
To: ---
Subject: ---
Enclosures/Attachments: ---
Hard copy: **plain sheet**
Special: ---
Code: **rnd0805**

WP Tip: Note that the 5-digit numbers all begin with **349**; also, many of the amounts end with **,000**. Can you create macros for these often-used combinations?

OFFICE OF RESEARCH AND DEVELOPMENT

Projects Under Development as of June 1

Number	Manager	Funds Budgeted	Funds Expended
~~34899~~	~~Davidson~~	~~$2,850,000~~	~~$2,745,000~~
~~34900~~	~~Fredericks~~	~~1,475,000~~	~~1,480,500~~
34901	Matthews	#3,890,000	$2,970,460 ~~2,050,430~~
34902	O'Connor	950,500	685,740 ~~820,635~~
34903	Goldman	1,900,550	1,020,560 ~~874,500~~
34904	Hartley	750,000	592,300 ~~455,000~~
34905	Demalio	2,375,000	1,785,000 ~~1,249,000~~
34906	Parramore	4,500,000	3,691,600 ~~2,980,500~~
~~34907~~	~~Morton~~	~~875,000~~	~~873,500~~
34908	Henderson	1,250,000	1,000,000 ~~970,500~~
~~34909~~	~~Hernandez~~	~~3,850,000~~	~~1,320,000~~
34910	Vasserman	2,000,000	1,460,700 ~~850,500~~
34911	McNeil	900,000	336,700 ~~125,600~~
34912	Allen	5,970,000	4,930,600 ~~3,820,500~~
34913	Wallace	750,600	265,370 ~~300,250~~
34914	Martinez	1,530,500	1,370,500 ~~1,230,000~~
34915	Richardson	4,500,000	260,400
34916	Lee	960,000	50,300
34917	Carpenter	1,870,000	22,600
34918	Sukumo	2,590,500	17,200

Inventory 10:
Format/Key an Outline

full sheet
LL: 60 spaces
PB: line 10 (pica) or line 12 (elite)
Correct all errors.

1. Set tab stops to indent second-level (A.) and third-level (1.) headings (or reset left margin for second-level headings and backspace into left margin for the Roman numerals).

2. Format/key the outline with appropriate spacing between first-, second-, and third-level headings.

words

JOB
THE ⋀ APPLICATION PROCESS   6

I.   THE RESEARCH/PLANNING PHASE   12

     A. Locating Potential Employers   18
         1. Sources of potential employees   26
         2. Checking and selecting potential employers   35
     B. Analyzing Job Characteristics and Your Qualifi-   45
         cations   47

II. THE WRITING PHASE   51

     A. The Resume (Personal Data Sheet)   59
     B. The Letter of Application   64
     C. The Application Form (Company Data sheet)   73
     D. The Follow-Up Letter   78

III. THE SPEAKING PHASE (PERSONAL INTERVIEW)   87

     A. Preparing For the Interview   94
     B. During the Interview   98

Inventory 11:
Apply Word-Division Guides

full sheet
LL: 60 spaces
LS: DS
PB: line 10

1. Clear all tab stops.

2. Set a tab stop 23 spaces to the right of left margin; set another stop 25 spaces beyond the first tab stop.

3. Key the first word in Column 1 as shown; tab to Column 2 and key the word again with a hyphen between syllables; tab to Column 3 and key the word again, using a hyphen to show only acceptable points of division at line endings.

4. Key each of the other words in the same way.

CORRECT WORD DIVISION   4

Word	Syllables	Acceptable Division	
			7
			16
applicant	ap-pli-cant	ap-pli-cant	22
aren't			27
buttery			32
classify			38
contents			44
ideas			48
increased			54
medical			59
prompt			64
sitting			69
timely			73
variety			79

key | 9 | 14 | 11 | 14 | 11 |

Document 2 (continued)

2.³ We shall offer competetive wages and salaries together with other benefits ~~which~~ *that* will contribute to the well-being of all employees.

4. We shall apply all personnel *policies* ~~practices~~ in a fair, unbiased, and unprejudiced manner.

5. We shall promote communications with and between management and employees at all times.

5.⁶ We shall offer opportunities for all employees to develope their skills and abilities to the utmost extent so that they will enjoy the maximum satisfaction form their work.

Our Customers

Satisfied customers from the *foundation* ~~basis~~ of our success. We must always *endeavor* ~~try~~ to attract *an increasing* number of customers by providing superior products at competetive prices. *Every* ~~All~~ action$ we take must be concnetrated on satisfying *our* customer('s) needs. We msut always *stet* ~~try~~ to provide prompt, courteous service to insure confidence *and continued patronage*. In all relations with customers, we msut maintain our integrity.

Our Stockholders

Without the capitol *a* provided by stock holders, the company would not exist. We pledge *therefore* to achieve a rate of return on our stock ~~which~~ *that* equals or exceeds that of any of our *major* competitors. We (further pledge) to operate the company on sound financial *principals* ~~guidelines~~ and to keep stockholders informed *of our progress* on a quarterly basis.

The Public

Every corporation has social objectives as well as economic objectives. Social objectives include good citizenry *ship* and a concern for the *communities* ~~areas~~ in which *stet* we operate. We encourage *our* employees to engage in civic affairs and will assist *them* in ~~the~~ promoting social and educational *enterprises* ~~causes~~. Farther, we promise to promote environmental conservation and to conduct all operations in a manner ~~which~~ *that* will ~~provide an~~ *maintain the* ecological *equilibrium* ~~balance~~.

Inventory 12:
Format/Key Second Page of a 2-Page Letter

plain full sheets
LL: 1″ side margins
LS: SS
Correct all errors.

Letter A
Block Format
Format/key the copy as page 2 of a 2-page letter in block format.

Letter B
Modified Block Format
Format/key the copy in modified block format.

words

Mr. Martin L. Simms — 4
Page 2 — 5
September 12, 19-- — 9

After
~~When~~ you have ∧ ~~reviewed~~ *studied* the enclosed manuscript carefully — 21

r
pleas(e)s send me you∧ over all reaction in addition to your — 32

page-by-page
detailed ∧ comments and suggestions. ∧ # These comments will be — 47

helpful in deciding whether ~~or not~~ to proceed with this pub- — 57

lication. — 59

Miss
Sincerely yours ∧ Rhonda J. Ingram, Editor xx Enclosure — 70

Inventory 13:
Format/Key Second Page of a 2-Page Report

plain full sheets

Report A
Unbound Format
Format/key the copy in un-bound report format.

Report B
Leftbound Report
Format/key the copy in left-bound report format.

2

e
The forgoing summary leads to the unassailable conclu- — 11

and equipment   increasingly
sion that the use of electronic systems will become ~~more and~~ — 27

ten
~~more~~ wide spread in this decade. Further, in the next ~~the~~ — 37

years   students   come
~~decade~~, if ~~people~~ are to be effective workers, they must *be* ∧ — 50

trained   to
~~learn~~ to understand the functions of electron(i)c equipment and ∧ — 64

d
use it with knowl∧ege and skill (Clark et al., 1990, iii). — 75

QS
REFERENCES — 78

To   Wo
Clark, James, Warren Allen, and Dale Kooster. <u>Computers and</u> — 94
Hol
    <u>Information Processing</u>. 2d ed. Cincinnati: South- — 109
    Western Publishing Co., 1990. # — 115

Shelly, Gary B., Thomas J. Cashman, and Gloria Waggoner. — 127
    <u>Computer Concepts</u>. Cincinnati: South-Western Publish- — 142
    ing Co., 1990. — 144

Inventory 14:
Center On and Between Lines

plain full sheet

1. Key two 3″ underlines about 3 lines apart. Remove the paper from the machine; reinsert it; align the first underline with the alignment scale; center and key your name on the first line, your city and state on the second line.

2. Using your machine and a pencil or pen, draw two short vertical lines about 3″ apart. Remove the paper; reinsert it; center and key your name and city/state on two lines between the vertical rules.

Theron Carter

Lincoln, Nebraska

| Theron Carter |
| Lincoln, Nebraska |

REQUEST FOR IP SERVICES
Originator: **Susan Engles**
Document: **L M R T F X**
Date: **June 3**
To: ---
Subject: ---
Enclosures/Attachments: ---
Hard copy: **plain sheet**
Special: **Check accuracy of right-hand column. Hold table while Gail Turner prepares a memo to go with this table.**
Code: **exo1113**

ADMINISTRATIVE SUPPORT DIVISION

Employee Absenteeism for 2d and 3d Quarters of Year*

Department	2d	3d	+ or -
Mail	14%	16%	+ 2%
Telecommunications	8%	11%	+ 3%
Reprographics	10%	14%	+ 4%
Records	12%	17%	+ 5%
Personnel	9%	9%	0%
Training	10%	8%	+ 2%
Industrial Relations	9%	10%	+ 1%
Pay and Benefits	7%	12%	+ 5%
Forms Control	15%	16%	+ 1%
Office Supplies	11%	15%	+ 4%

*Time lost as a percentage of total work time.

REQUEST FOR IP SERVICES
Originator: **Martha Capelli**
Document: **L M R T F X**
Date: **June 3**
To: ---
Subject: ---
Enclosures/Attachments: ---
Hard copy: **plain sheets**
Special: ---
Code: **exo1114**

WP Tip -- Spell Check: If spell check is available, read your user's guide. Access spell check to highlight words throughout a document -- as you key or afterwards, depending on your software -- not in its dictionary. Follow on-screen directions to correct each spelling/keyboarding error, delete a double word, or skip to the next highlighted word.

Spell check will not highlight these errors: word usage (*its/it's*), similar words (*send/sent*), and misused proper nouns, top-row keys, punctuation, caps, and symbols.

Policy Statements: Human Resources — Center ALL CAPS

There are 4 groups of human resources that are indispensible to the continued success for Electro-Tech, Inc.

They are, our employees, our coustomers, our stock holders, and the general public. It is essential, we must ensure therefore, that our philosophy and attitude toward each of these groups be clearly defined delineated.

Our Employees

We believe strongly It is our philosophy that the propsperity of the company depends on a qualified dedicated group of employees. To that end, our company's firm's policy toward its employe relations can be expressed told in 6 vital statements:

1. First and formost, we shall consider each employee as an indicidual irregardless of gender, race, color, creed, religion, or age.

2. We shall maintain a safe, suitable work enviroment.

(continued, p. 513)

Inventory 15:
Language Skills
plain full sheet
LL: 70 spaces
LS: DS
PB: line 6

Capitalization and Number Expression

1. Center the heading over the line of writing on line 6; then DS.

2. Key lines 1-8, with the number and period, capitalizing words where necessary and expressing numbers in words or figures, as appropriate.

3. Check accuracy of work with teacher or by using RG 1.

Punctuation

1. Center the heading a DS below line 8; then DS.

2. Key lines 9-16, with the number and period, inserting punctuation where necessary.

3. Check accuracy of work with teacher or by using RG 3.

Spelling/Word Choice

1. Center the heading a DS below line 16; then DS.

2. Key lines 17-25, with the number and period, correcting errors in word choice and spelling.

3. Check accuracy of work with teacher or by using a dictionary.

Capitalization and Number Expression

1. i work for arno manufacturing company at one commercial boulevard.
2. did ms. miles say, "turn in your report on friday after halloween"?
3. jason grew up in anadarko, a town on the washita river in oklahoma.
4. nelda received over 60% of votes cast in the may election.
5. almost 2/3 of the spanish club members cast ballots for b. j.
6. only 2 of the eleven proposals ever left senator long's desk.
7. the quotation is in section two, page 15, of the anthology.
8. can you meet dr. simms and me at 4 o'clock on monday, may 8th?

Punctuation

9. Marsha Kevin and I are the planning committee for the party
10. If you have suggestions please submit them in writing by Friday
11. Do you believe that an ad hoc committee should be formed
12. I would rather not run the race however I will run if you will
13. All your arguments have been heard now it's time to take a vote
14. The choice is mine I see I choose to go with Evan's plan.
15. As soon as the bids come in assign the job to the lowest bidder.
16. The meeting was held on Thursday August 12 1991 at 2 30 pm

Spelling and Word Choice

17. As they past the bell tower, the bells began to peal.
18. At what point in the hike did they lose there way?
19. You should chose accounting as a career if its your preference.
20. In his talk, the principle listed several behavior principals.
21. I paid more for the stationary then the manager thought I should.
22. The word processing specialists asked that there salaries be razed.
23. The change in company policy effects a great number of employees.
24. We were told that the flew should be cleaned each Fall.
25. He tryed to make a lye of the fact that the building site was ready.

Electro-Tech, Inc.
A Modern Office Simulation

Simulation Goals

1. To prepare a typical variety of error-free documents in acceptable form.

2. To apply basic language skills.

3. To improve skill in processing documents from special sources and with minimal directions.

4. To demonstrate adaptability in office procedures.

Documents Processed

1. Tables

2. Reports

3. Letters from form paragraphs

4. Memos

5. Purchase orders

ELECTRO-TECH, INC. A MODERN OFFICE SIMULATION

Read the information at the right and below carefully, noting procedures, before beginning to process the documents on pp. 512–520.

Check all work requests for a particular due date. Set priorities for completing the day's documents. First, do requests marked RUSH; second, requests from **exo** group; third, other requests in order as given to you.

For word processor/microcomputer users, various, pertinent software features and tips for their use are described throughout this simulation. These features are described as *macro*, *spell check*, *thesaurus*, *merge*, *move*, *search*, and *search and replace*. If your machine is a word processor/microcomputer, you should use these features and apply the tips given to the appropriate documents.

WP Tip -- Macro: In your software user's guide, study procedures for storing a "macro" -- a set of (often-used) keystrokes/commands to be inserted in documents as needed by striking a function key. Create macros for *Electro-Tech, Inc.* and *We shall*.

Access the macro feature (define macro); name the macro (**eti**, **wsh**). Key the phrase you want to save; now, end the macro definition.

Prepare a list of macros/names so you can retrieve each macro quickly as needed. Note which function key(s) are used to "call up" a macro.

Work Assignment

Based in Marietta, Georgia, Electro-Tech, Inc. (ETI) is a multi-national organization that manufactures/markets electronic equipment. At ETI, you work as an Information Processing Specialist in one of four information processing groups (or "satellites"). The keyboard operators in your satellite serve these groups of the organization: Administrative Support Division (**asd**), Executive Office (**exo**), Inventory Control Group (**icg**), Production (**pro**), and Research and Development (**rnd**).

The documents you process come to you in the form of a *Request for IP Services*. The requests are seen first by your supervisor, Mrs. Joyce T. Witkowski, who sorts the requests and distributes them among the keyboard operators. Mrs. Witkowski reminds you to correct any language-skills errors that may not have been marked for correction.

Document Codes

Before distributing each request, Mrs. Witkowski enters it on a log and assigns a unique code to each document. She enters the document code, consisting of the three-letter group designation and several digits (for example, asd0266 for a document processed for the Administrative Support Division), on the Request form.

Aside from serving as the document "name" when the document is stored (on a microcomputer disk), the code is keyed for identification on all documents as follows:

Letters/memos. After reference initials on same line (example: rt asd0954).

Reports. A DS below last line of copy at left margin.

Tables. About 1″ from the bottom edge at left margin.

Forms. The lower-left corner.

Other documents. Format as appropriate.

Request for IP Services

Document originators fill out a *Request for IP Services* form as follows:

1. *Originator.* Enter originator's name as it is to appear on signed document. Enter position title if it is to appear.

2. *Document.* Underline letter to indicate document type: Letter, Memo, Report, Table, Form, **X** (other).

3. *Date.* Enter date to appear on dated document(s).

4. *To.* Enter name/address for letters/memos or indicate where to find.

5. *Subject.* Enter subject line for letters/memos only.

6. *Enclosures/Attachments.* Enter number of items included with a letter/memo.

7. *Hard copy.* Specify type of paper to be used for printed documents.

8. *Special.* List further details needed for filling request.

9. *Code.* Do not write in this space.

Document Format Guides

The block letter format (open punctuation) is used throughout ETI. Other document styles vary among work groups:

Memos. Use formal memos for the Executive Office and Administrative Support Division; the simplified format for other groups.

Reports. Prepare reports in leftbound format for Production. Block enumerations in these reports at the paragraph indention. For other units, use unbound format and "hang-indented" enumerations.

Tables. Use full sheets. DS most tables; SS if necessary to fit on one sheet. Except for Research and Development, center tables up and down and side to side; center column headings. For RND, use PB line 10; block column headings; center tables side to side.

Forms. Fill in every item. A "low bid register" contains several vendors' names. A purchase order (PO) is prepared for each vendor listed, with all items for that vendor compiled on one PO form. On the PO be sure to key the **vendor** stock number (as found on the low bid register), not the stock number found in the left-hand columns of the order list and low bid register.

1. Read the rough-draft letter at the right, noting unmarked as well as marked corrections.

2. Format and key the letter in modified block format with mixed punctuation. As you key the letter, make the indicated corrections; correct any unmarked errors you find and any errors you may make as you key.

words

Sp.

Sept. 2, 19--   4

Mr. Lionel Brooks *Wo*   8
4385 Grand Avenue   11
Omaha, NE   68111-2956   16

Dear Mr. Brooks   19

        Because we have *had* so many ~~inquiries~~ *questions* about charges and pay-   31
ments on *charge-card* ~~credit~~ accounts, we have modified our monthly bill-   44
ing statements. We hope our new *monthly* statement simplifies your   57
checking of your transactions with us. ¶ The *l*nclosed state-   69
ment provides a *complete* summary of all transactions effecting your   83
account for the month of August. The summary on the bottom   95
half of the statement shows the unpaid balance carried over   107
from the preceding month. Following the balance item is a   118
separate entry for each charge or payment during the month.   131
Buy identifing the *y* ~~firm~~ *business* from which you make each purchase *d* *you* ~~it~~ 144
can more easily ~~is easier for you to~~ check the statement entries with the 155
custamer copies of you're charge card reci*e*pts.   164

        Please let us know wether these changes in our billing   175
statement are helpful to you in checking the charges and   187
credits to you *r* account. We *shall* ~~will~~ appreciate your help.   198

Sincerely yours   201

Mrs. ~~Ms.~~ Elizabeth *a.* Seligman   207
Senior Credit Manager   211
Charge-Card Department   216

xx   216

Enclosure   218

Skill-Enrichment Drill: Improve Keyboarding Speed

LL: 70 spaces

1. Key a 1' writing on each line; calculate *gwam* on each writing.

2. Key another 1' writing on each of your three slowest lines to improve speed.

balanced-hand	1	Tory may fix the bicycle for the neighbor girl if she signs the forms.
double letters	2	Robb took his little sister to the zoo to see the baboons and parrots.
combination	3	Ana may wish to serve for them at a big union social in the town hall.
adjacent keys	4	Sophia said she spotted a lion sculpture in the ruins after the fires.
long reaches	5	Myra brought nuts and plum tarts to the gym party to celebrate my win.

| 1 | 2 | 3 | 4 | 5 | 6 | 7 | 8 | 9 | 10 | 11 | 12 | 13 | 14 |

Skill-Enrichment Timed Writing

LL: 70 spaces
LS: DS
PI: 5 spaces

1. Key a 1' writing on ¶ 1; calculate *gwam* to establish a base rate.

2. Add 2-4 *gwam* to your base rate to set a new goal rate.

3. Using the table below, pick the speed nearest your goal rate and note the quarter-minute intervals for that speed.

4. Key two 1' writings with your teacher's call of the quarter-minute guides.

5. Key ¶s 2 and 3 in the same way.

6. Key a 3' writing on ¶s 1-3 combined; calculate *gwam*, circle errors.

7. Key a 5' writing on ¶s 1-3 combined; calculate *gwam*, circle errors.

Quarter-Minute Checkpoints

gwam	¼'	½'	¾'	1'
32	8	16	24	32
36	9	18	27	36
40	10	20	31	40
44	11	22	33	44
48	12	24	36	48
52	13	26	39	52
56	14	28	42	56
60	15	30	45	60
64	16	32	48	64
68	17	34	51	68
72	18	36	54	72
76	19	38	57	76
80	20	40	60	80

all letters used | A | 1.5 si | 5.7 awl | 80% hfw

	gwam 3'	5'

One of the most essential documents found in an office today is the report. Reports are so vital because they have many uses. They are one of the prime means by which an executive at any level of an organization can keep informed. Reports also can establish a two-way channel of communication through which data essential to the efficient conduct of the firm can flow. Information today is vital to the dynamic growth of any enterprise. Without up-to-date data, no firm can survive.

To be efficient, a report must be complete, correct, clear, and concise. A report must contain all the pertinent information an executive needs to analyze the situation and reach a valid conclusion. Reports must be written in a fashion that leaves no doubt in the reader's mind about the cogent facts. Ideally, reports should be written in as few words as possible, not only for the sake of clarity, but to save the executive's time. The most useful report is usually the shortest one.

The overall appearance of a report is an important factor. The person who receives the report views it initially as a whole. A report that is not attractive may be just set aside and ignored. On the other hand, a report that is attractively placed on the page with clean, even type and no untidy erasures will certainly attract attention. A report of quality that is well written and well formatted reflects favorably on the secretary as well as on the executive who prepared it.

gwam 3'	4 9 14 19 24 29 32 37 41 46 51 56 61 65 69 74 79 84 89 94 97
5'	3 6 9 11 14 17 19 22 25 28 31 33 36 39 42 45 47 50 53 56 58
	61 64 67 70 73 75 78 80 83 86 89 92 95 97 100 103 106 109 112 114 117

gwam 3' | 1 | 2 | 3 | 4 | 5 |
5' | 1 | 2 | 3 |

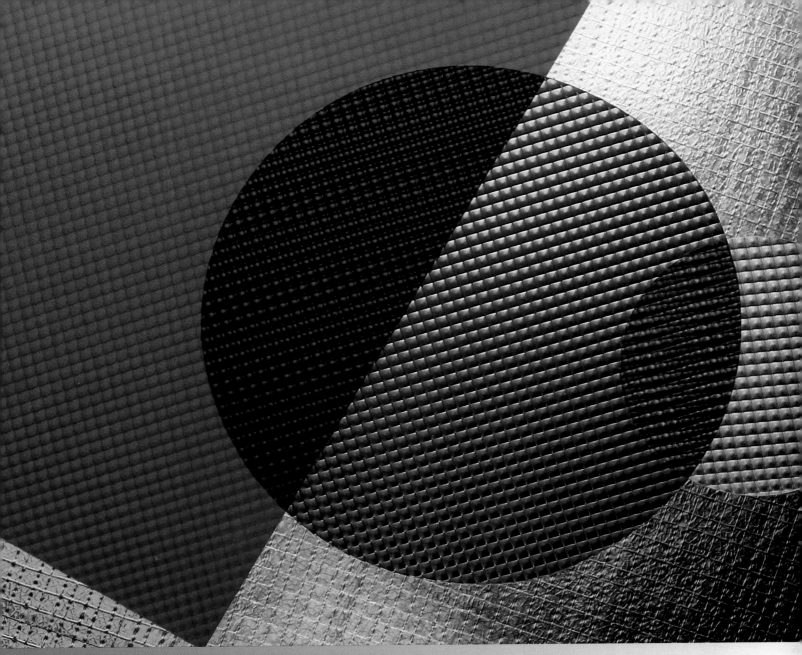

PHASE 7

ASSESS AND IMPROVE KEYBOARDING, FORMATTING, AND DOCUMENT PROCESSING SKILLS

The primary purpose of Phase 7 (Lessons 151-175) is to assess and improve previously learned keyboarding skills. The first unit concentrates on basic keyboarding and language skills. The next three units focus on formatting and processing correspondence, reports, and tables. These units are followed by a simulation designed to integrate keyboarding, formatting, and document processing skills. The last unit in Phase 7 is an evaluation unit.

The learning goals of Phase 7 are to improve the following competencies.

1. Techniques that contribute to keyboarding productivity.
2. Straight-copy keyboarding speed and control.
3. Keyboarding from script and rough-draft copy.
4. Formatting and processing letters, memorandums, reports, and tables.
5. Language skills.
6. Decision-making skills.

Skill-Enrichment Drill: Improve Keyboarding Skill

LL: 70 spaces

1. Key a 1' writing on each line; calculate *gwam* on each writing.
2. Key another 1' writing on each of your three slowest lines to improve speed.

balanced-hand	1	Nan and six of the firms may aid the auditor with the city work forms.
double letters	2	Todd carried the books from the classroom to the office at noon today.
combination	3	John is eager to go to the mill at eight to work on the antique chair.
adjacent keys	4	Lois says her sister made silk poppies for the new shop in the square.
long reaches	5	My deck is hung with many bright nylon banners and hundreds of lights.

`| 1 | 2 | 3 | 4 | 5 | 6 | 7 | 8 | 9 | 10 | 11 | 12 | 13 | 14 |`

Skill-Enrichment Timed Writing

LL: 70 spaces
LS: DS
PI: 5 spaces

1. Key a 1' writing on ¶ 1; calculate *gwam* to establish a base rate.
2. Add 2-4 *gwam* to your base rate to set a new goal rate.
3. Using the table below, pick the speed nearest your goal rate and note the quarter-minute intervals for that speed.
4. Key two 1' writings with your teacher's call of the quarter-minute guides.
5. Key ¶s 2 and 3 in the same way.
6. Key a 3' writing on ¶s 1-3 combined; calculate *gwam*, circle errors.
7. Key a 5' writing on ¶s 1-3 combined; calculate *gwam*, circle errors.

Quarter-Minute Checkpoints

gwam	¼'	½'	¾'	1'
32	8	16	24	32
36	9	18	27	36
40	10	20	31	40
44	11	22	33	44
48	12	24	36	48
52	13	26	39	52
56	14	28	42	56
60	15	30	45	60
64	16	32	48	64
68	17	34	51	68
72	18	36	54	72
76	19	38	57	76
80	20	40	60	80

all letters used | A | 1.5 si | 5.7 awl | 80% hfw

gwam 3' | 5'

What is word processing? Is it a novel concept? Is it laborious? — 5 | 3 | 62
The answer to the last two queries is "no." Ever since humans began to — 9 | 6 | 65
convey their ideas in writing, we have been processing words. In its — 14 | 8 | 68
simplest form, word processing is nothing more than forming a record — 19 | 11 | 70
of ideas. The function of word processing is not new to business or — 23 | 14 | 73
other enterprises because office workers have been processing words for — 28 | 17 | 76
many years. Thousands of people have proven that it is not a hard job. — 33 | 20 | 79

Some people believe that the pencil is the ultimate word processor. — 37 | 22 | 82
A pencil is easy to move from place to place, can produce documents in — 42 | 25 | 85
any language, can be fixed easily if it breaks, and needs only human — 47 | 28 | 87
power to make it work. Writing by hand, unfortunately, is very slow, — 51 | 31 | 90
often difficult to decipher, and very expensive in terms of time when — 56 | 34 | 93
it is used to produce business documents. Until the invention of the — 61 | 36 | 96
typewriter, though, all documents in an office were written by hand. — 65 | 39 | 98

The typewriter was hailed as the "amazing writing machine," and it — 70 | 42 | 101
did improve the speed and quality of work in the office. Unfortunately, — 75 | 45 | 104
even this machine was too slow to keep up with the large increase in — 79 | 47 | 107
data. This led to the birth of modern word processing, which is now a — 84 | 50 | 110
vital part of information processing. What is word processing? Word — 89 | 53 | 112
processing is simply a system of producing documents of all types at — 93 | 56 | 115
higher speeds, lower costs, and with less effort by the use of elec- — 98 | 59 | 118
tronic equipment. — 99 | 59 | 119

gwam 3' | 1 | 2 | 3 | 4 | 5
5' | 1 | 2 | 3

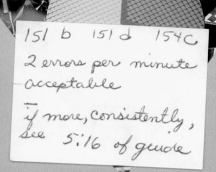

Assess/Improve Keyboarding and Language Skills

Learning Goals

1. To assess/improve keyboarding techniques.
2. To assess/improve straight-copy speed and control.
3. To assess/improve script-copy speed and control.
4. To assess/improve decision-making and language skills.

Format Guides

1. Paper guide at *0* (for typewriters).
2. LL (line length): 70 spaces.
3. LS (line spacing): Single-space (SS) word and sentence drills; double-space (DS) ¶s; or space as directed within an activity.
4. PI (paragraph indent): 5 spaces.

(handwritten note:) 151 b   151 d   154 c
2 errors per minute acceptable
if more, consistently, see 5:16 of guide

Lesson 151   Keyboarding/Language Skills

151a ▶ 5
Conditioning Practice

each line twice SS (slowly, then faster); DS between 2-line groups; if time permits, rekey selected lines

alphabet 1 Quen packed an extra big jar full of very zesty wild apples for Homer.
figures 2 Order color monitor 4103, printer 278-7, and CPU 3956 for this office.
fig/sym 3 The original PC-409 cost $1,325 while the new clone #6-8 costs $1,187.
speed 4 Pamela got the authentic antique handiwork by the giant island shanty.

| 1 | 2 | 3 | 4 | 5 | 6 | 7 | 8 | 9 | 10 | 11 | 12 | 13 | 14 |

151b ▶ 20 Assess Straight-Copy Skill

1. Three 1' writings on each ¶ for speed; find *gwam*.
2. Two 1' writings on each ¶ for control; circle errors.
3. Two 3' writings on ¶s 1-2 combined; find *gwam*, circle errors.
4. Record your better 3' *gwam* to compare with your 3' *gwam* in 153d.

all letters used | A | 1.5 si | 5.7 awl | 80% hfw

	gwam 3'	5'

Many aspects of a job present challenges to those who strive to do — 4 | 3 | 39
their best in all they do. One of the most critical challenges all — 9 | 5 | 41
workers face is being able to relate well with the many individuals with — 14 | 8 | 44
whom they have to work. It is common for workers to have daily dealings — 19 | 11 | 47
with bosses, peers, and subordinates. Also, most workers will interact — 24 | 14 | 50
with telephone callers and visitors from outside as well as inside the — 28 | 17 | 53
company. — 29 | 17 | 53

While it is critical to learn all you can about your job and com- — 33 | 20 | 56
pany, it is often just as critical to learn about the people with whom — 38 | 23 | 59
you will work and interact. Frequently you can rely upon experienced — 43 | 26 | 61
workers for information that will help you analyze the formal structure — 47 | 28 | 64
of the company and the informal structure the workers bring to the com- — 52 | 31 | 67
pany. What you learn may help you determine what an employer expects, — 57 | 34 | 70
likes, or dislikes, and will help you adjust. — 60 | 36 | 72

gwam 3' | 1 | 2 | 3 | 4 | 5 |
      5' | 1 | 2 | 3 |

Skill-Enrichment Drill: Improve Keyboarding Control

LL: 70 spaces

1. Key each line once SS; DS between 2-line groups.

2. Key a 1' writing on each of lines 2, 4, and 6; calculate *gwam* on each writing.

3. Key a 1' writing on each of your slowest lines to improve speed.

adjacent keys	1	ads opt ask oil quit post fire buys sort went says drop coil suit cash
	2	Coila asked if you dare to take the new post after they drop the suit.
long, direct reaches	3	ice sum nut fun spun must runt hymn stun trunk under curve grunt dance
	4	Cecilia must have spun on the ice to swerve and kill the smelly skunk.
outside reaches	5	adz split paper quest plaza power spots glass expose aisle soaps spark
	6	Max can zip the squad to a peak skill level if they will let him play.

| 1 | 2 | 3 | 4 | 5 | 6 | 7 | 8 | 9 | 10 | 11 | 12 | 13 | 14 |

Skill-Enrichment Timed Writing

LL: 70 spaces
LS: DS
PI: 5 spaces

1. Key a 1' writing on ¶ 1; calculate *gwam* to establish a base rate.

2. Add 2-4 *gwam* to your base rate to set a new goal rate.

3. Using the table below, pick the speed nearest your goal rate and note the quarter-minute intervals for that speed.

4. Key two 1' writings with your teacher's call of the quarter-minute guides.

5. Key ¶s 2 and 3 in the same way.

6. Key a 3' writing on ¶s 1-3 combined; calculate *gwam*, circle errors.

7. Key a 5' writing on ¶s 1-3 combined; calculate *gwam*, circle errors.

Quarter-Minute Checkpoints

gwam	¼'	½'	¾'	1'
32	8	16	24	32
36	9	18	27	36
40	10	20	31	40
44	11	22	33	44
48	12	24	36	48
52	13	26	39	52
56	14	28	42	56
60	15	30	45	60
64	16	32	48	64
68	17	34	51	68
72	18	36	54	72
76	19	38	57	76
80	20	40	60	80

all letters used | A | 1.5 si | 5.7 awl | 80% hfw

	gwam 3'	5'

As our society grows in size and complexity, a great need for in- 4 | 3 | 59
formation exists--data on which to base decisions. Many experts say we 9 | 5 | 62
are in the midst of an "information explosion" that will play a very 14 | 8 | 65
important role in the way we live and work. A wave of new electronic 18 | 11 | 68
equipment has given us new tools to produce, process, store, retrieve, 23 | 14 | 70
and utilize information so that work can be done better and faster. 28 | 17 | 73
One of the vital steps in this process, of course, is communication. 32 | 19 | 76

The value of office employees is rated, in large measure, on the 37 | 22 | 79
basis of their communication skills. The number of positions for those 41 | 25 | 81
who can operate a keyboard continues to grow, but the demand is for 46 | 28 | 84
those who can take the ideas of others and express them correctly. Many 51 | 30 | 87
accountants are in great demand, but they must be able to do more than 56 | 33 | 90
just enter figures in a column; they must be able to interpret clearly 60 | 36 | 93
and concisely the meaning of figures on a spreadsheet. 64 | 38 | 95

Business places a premium on individuals who are adept in the use 68 | 41 | 98
of language. People who are well trained to work in an office can earn 73 | 44 | 100
good salaries, but those who also have developed the talent to express 78 | 47 | 103
ideas quickly and concisely will gain success more rapidly. If you 82 | 49 | 106
have developed a high skill in communication, you will find your skill 87 | 52 | 109
rewarded in terms of better pay. If you excel in communication, you 92 | 55 | 112
can expect a better job in your future. 94 | 57 | 113

gwam 3' | 1 | 2 | 3 | 4 | 5 |
5' | 1 | 2 | 3 |

151c ▶ 10 Reinforce Word-Division Skills

1. Key in one column the words shown at the right, inserting hyphens between all syllables. Use a 1″ left margin and DS.

2. Review the first three word-division guides on RG 5.

3. In your copy, circle any hyphen that does not violate Guides 1-3.

central	furnished	eraser
staged	dozen	obesity
every	began	agency
coverage	universal	obedient

151d ▶ 15 Improve Straight-Copy Skill

Goal: Set a goal of *speed* if you did not exceed 6 errors on the 3′ writing in 151b; *control* if you made more than 6 errors.

1. Take three 1′ writings on each ¶ of 151b. Find *gwam* or circle errors, depending on your goal.

2. Take a 5′ writing on ¶s 1-2 combined. If you finish all copy before time is called, start over. Find *gwam* or circle errors.

3. Record your 5′ *gwam* to compare with your *gwam* in Lesson 154c.

Lesson 152	Keyboarding/Language Skills

152a ▶ 5 Conditioning Practice

each line twice SS (slowly, then faster); DS between 2-line groups; if time permits, rekey selected lines

alphabet	1	Zelda was quite naive to pack the four big boxes with just fresh yams.
figures	2	Try to call me before 10 a.m. at 952-3468; let the phone ring 7 times.
one hand	3	After I stated my opinion based on facts, fewer fees were agreed upon.
speed	4	Elsie and the neighbor got an authentic jai alai title with an emblem.

| 1 | 2 | 3 | 4 | 5 | 6 | 7 | 8 | 9 | 10 | 11 | 12 | 13 | 14 |

152b ▶ 20 Assess Script-Copy Skill

1. Three 1′ writings on each ¶ for speed; find *gwam*.

2. Two 1′ writings on each ¶ for control; circle errors.

3. Two 3′ writings on ¶s 1-2 combined; find *gwam* and circle errors.

Note: If you finish all the copy before time is called, start over.

all letters used | A | 1.5 si | 5.7 awl | 80% hfw

	gwam 1′	3′
Over the years, keyboard operators have used various meth-	12	4
ods to correct mistakes they made when using manual and elec-	24	8
tric machines. One of the early methods was to use an eraser	36	12
to remove errors from the paper. Other products that have come	49	16
into use in more recent years include correction tape or fluid	62	21
to cover up errors and lift-off tape to take errors from the	74	25
paper.	75	25
Various parts of the typewriter were used to squeeze words	12	29
into less space or spread a word to fill extra space when era-	24	33
sure, cover-up, and lift-off methods were used. When using ma-	37	37
chines that display electronic copy on a screen, workers can	49	41
correct errors just by inserting, deleting, moving, or writing	62	46
over before the final copy is printed on the paper.	72	49

Skill-Enrichment Drill: Improve Keyboarding Control

LL: 70 spaces

1. Key each line once SS; DS between 2-line groups.

2. Key a 1' writing on each of lines 2, 4, and 6; calculate *gwam* on each writing.

3. Key a 1' writing on each of your slowest lines to improve speed.

adjacent keys

1 art ore try buy well spot coin ruin open silk said hero stop soil owes
2 Lois was very sad when we opposed plans for selling juice at the pool.

long, direct reaches

3 ace any nub gum spun deck many gyms curb echo numb fume cent much nice
4 Myra sprinted at quick paces to win my team many county bronze medals.

outside reaches

5 as zoo pow ooze aqua zoom slap zone pool axle span flax axis quiz pass
6 Zoe wore an aqua blouse and a purple skirt to the tax audit last week.

| 1 | 2 | 3 | 4 | 5 | 6 | 7 | 8 | 9 | 10 | 11 | 12 | 13 | 14 |

Skill-Enrichment Timed Writing

LL: 70 spaces
LS: DS
PI: 5 spaces

1. Key a 1' writing on ¶ 1; calculate *gwam* to establish a base rate.

2. Add 2-4 *gwam* to your base rate to set a new goal rate.

3. Using the table below, pick the speed nearest your goal rate and note the quarter-minute intervals for that speed.

4. Key two 1' writings with your teacher's call of the quarter-minute guides.

5. Key ¶s 2 and 3 in the same way.

6. Key a 3' writing on ¶s 1-3 combined; calculate *gwam*, circle errors.

7. Key a 5' writing on ¶s 1-3 combined; calculate *gwam*, circle errors.

all letters used | A | 1.5 si | 5.7 awl | 80% hfw

gwam 3' | 5'

How well do my employees do their work? This is a question that a — 4 | 3 | 63
good supervisor often ponders. Supervisors are always observing the way — 9 | 6 | 66
in which their workers do their jobs and, in effect, are evaluating the — 14 | 8 | 69
work they do and their value to the organization. In some firms, this — 19 | 11 | 72
merit rating is done on a very informal basis, while in other firms there — 24 | 14 | 75
are formal procedures. In most large companies today, employees undergo — 29 | 17 | 78
periodic ratings of the work they have done. — 32 | 19 | 80

How can supervisors rate their employees? The simplest way is for — 36 | 22 | 82
the supervisor to rank each of the workers in comparison to others in — 41 | 24 | 85
terms of performance and value to the company. Some companies develop — 45 | 27 | 88
formal checklists, which include a number of items to be rated, that the — 50 | 30 | 90
supervisor must complete for each worker. After each item is a scale on — 55 | 33 | 94
which the exact degree of proficiency can be noted. The points are — 60 | 36 | 97
totaled and the results are used to measure performance to company stan- — 65 | 38 | 99
dard and to identify areas that are in need of improvement. — 68 | 41 | 102

What is the purpose of rating employees? The ratings are used to — 73 | 44 | 104
ascertain whether or not employees should be considered for a raise in — 78 | 47 | 107
pay, a bonus, a promotion, or if they should be let go. Further, most — 82 | 49 | 110
of us like to know how well we are doing. If the ratings are discussed — 87 | 52 | 113
with employees, they serve as a means for identifying weak points and — 92 | 55 | 116
establishing ways for improvement. If conducted properly, a rating sys- — 97 | 58 | 119
tem will help employees develop new goals for the next rating period. — 101 | 61 | 121

Quarter-Minute Checkpoints

gwam	¼'	½'	¾'	1'
32	8	16	24	32
36	9	18	27	36
40	10	20	31	40
44	11	22	33	44
48	12	24	36	48
52	13	26	39	52
56	14	28	42	56
60	15	30	45	60
64	16	32	48	64
68	17	34	51	68
72	18	36	54	72
76	19	38	57	76
80	20	40	60	80

gwam 3' | 1 | 2 | 3 | 4 | 5 |
5' | 1 | 2 | 3 |

152c ▶ 10 Reinforce Word-Division Skills

1. Key in one column the words shown at the right, inserting hyphens between all syllables. Use a 1″ left margin and DS.

manual p. 25

2. Review word-division Guides 1-6 on RG 5.
3. In your copy, circle any hyphen that does not violate Guides 1-6.

fitted
spinner
sunning
staffing

selling
classes
actually
manner

benefit
policies
association
evacuation

152d ▶ 15 Improve Script-Copy Skill

Goal: Set a goal of *speed* if you did not exceed 6 errors on the 3′ writing in 152b; *control* if you made more than 6 errors.

1. Take three 1′ writings on each ¶ of 152b, p. 270.
2. Take two 3′ writings on ¶s 1-2 combined; find *gwam* and circle errors.

3. Compare better 3′ *gwam* with 3′ *gwam* recorded in 151b.
4. Record the better *gwam* for use in 153d.

Lesson 153 — Keyboarding/Language Skills

153a ▶ 5 Conditioning Practice

each line twice SS (slowly, then faster); DS between 2-line groups; if time permits, rekey selected lines

alphabet 1 Six glazed rolls with jam were quickly baked and provided free to all.
fig/sym 2 The 0-384 MC costs $196.75, and the 300/1200 Baud modem costs $265.89.
shift key 3 Ronald Lee read "A Hard Road" and "Lead Us" for Spanish IV in January.
speed 4 The sixth autobus turns to visit the busy shantytown dock by the lake.

| 1 | 2 | 3 | 4 | 5 | 6 | 7 | 8 | 9 | 10 | 11 | 12 | 13 | 14 |

153b ▶ 10 Reinforce Word-Division Skills

1. Key in one column the words shown at the right, inserting hyphens between all syllables. Use a 1″ left margin and DS.

2. Review word-division Guides 1-9 on RG 5.
3. In your copy, circle any hyphen that does not violate Guides 1-9.

readily
comical
easily
sabbatical

cyclical
self-service
low-keyed
well-mannered

wouldn't
didn't
$535,987
Contract F-23-8765

153c ▶ 15 Assess Keystroking Response Patterns

each line twice SS; DS between 2-line groups; rekey difficult lines as time permits

Words
letter 1 ad in be ho as him age ill awe ion cabs hill daft jink ears milk tarts
letter 2 at my we on ax hip arc imp bad joy cage hook dare join east nook taste
word 3 ye us to so ox nap man lay ken jai ibid corn glem flam envy dory cubit
combination 4 an up by oh it era jam hop gob fad mend moon rich ever pane loll theme

Phrases
letter 5 you are | wade in | trade up | on target | on my raft | fast breeze | fewer awards
word 6 an oak | go half | so sick | make do | lent me | kept down | profit by | such sorrow
word 7 do rush | dial six | sight land | it's downtown | fish and fowl | fuel the flame
combination 8 the men | oak tree | melt down | queue up | right hand | rosy scarf | penalty fees

Sentences
letter 9 Rebecca served plump, sweet plum desserts on my east terraces at noon.
word 10 Diane is due to dismantle the antique chair when it is right to do so.
combination 11 The corn was in the burlap bag and the small beets were in nylon bags.
combination 12 The six beggars deserved a better neighbor than the neurotic busybody.

| 1 | 2 | 3 | 4 | 5 | 6 | 7 | 8 | 9 | 10 | 11 | 12 | 13 | 14 |

Skill-Enrichment Drill: Improve Keyboarding Speed

LL: 70 spaces

1. Key each line once SS; DS between 2-line groups.

2. Key a 1' writing on each of lines 2, 4, and 6; calculate *gwam* on each writing.

3. Key another 1' writing on your two slowest lines.

letter response
1 in my ads we saw him in my case you were ill oil tax data set upon him
2 You gave him a few facts on my union cards after you read my tax case.

word response
3 of us pay the man she owns it an auto firm fix the dial sign the proxy
4 She may sign the proxy to aid the chair of the panel to amend the bid.

combination response
5 as she was to see him bid on it we paid him if you are they are to get
6 I may fight him for the right to set the wages of the union agreement.

| 1 | 2 | 3 | 4 | 5 | 6 | 7 | 8 | 9 | 10 | 11 | 12 | 13 | 14 |

Skill-Enrichment Timed Writing

LL: 70 spaces
LS: DS
PI: 5 spaces

1. Key a 1' writing on ¶ 1; calculate *gwam* to establish a base rate.

2. Add 2-4 *gwam* to your base rate to set a new goal rate.

3. Using the table below, pick the speed nearest your goal rate and note the quarter-minute intervals for that speed.

4. Key two 1' writings with your teacher's call of the quarter-minute guides.

5. Key ¶s 2 and 3 in the same way.

6. Key a 3' writing on ¶s 1-3 combined; calculate *gwam*, circle errors.

7. Key a 5' writing on ¶s 1-3 combined; calculate *gwam*, circle errors.

Quarter-Minute Checkpoints

gwam	¼'	½'	¾'	1'
32	8	16	24	32
36	9	18	27	36
40	10	20	31	40
44	11	22	33	44
48	12	24	36	48
52	13	26	39	52
56	14	28	42	56
60	15	30	45	60
64	16	32	48	64
68	17	34	51	68
72	18	36	54	72
76	19	38	57	76
80	20	40	60	80

all letters used | A | 1.5 si | 5.7 awl | 80% hfw |

	gwam 3'	5'

Once you have found a job, keeping the job may be more difficult — 4 | 3 | 59
than it was to find. The criteria for selecting office workers are — 9 | 5 | 61
chiefly objective in nature. Workers are chosen on the basis of their — 14 | 8 | 64
ability to keyboard quickly and accurately, to prepare business docu- — 18 | 11 | 67
ments, to use standard office machines, and to pass a standardized — 23 | 14 | 70
language skills test. Based on the results of these tests, the person — 27 | 16 | 73
with the best skills is selected for a job. — 30 | 18 | 74

Only a small number of those who lose their jobs do so because they — 35 | 21 | 77
lack the proper skills to do a good job. A number of studies indicate — 40 | 24 | 80
that poor work patterns and bad personality traits are two of the major — 44 | 27 | 83
reasons given by employers for the firing of office workers. These in- — 49 | 29 | 86
clude the failure to adapt to the work situation, a lack of cooperation, — 54 | 32 | 89
the inability to get along with other employees, and frequent absences — 59 | 35 | 91
for reasons other than illness. — 61 | 36 | 93

Today, employers expect a great deal more from their office workers — 65 | 39 | 95
than secretarial skills. They seek employees who will display sincere — 70 | 42 | 98
interest in their jobs, who will take pride in their work, and who will — 75 | 45 | 101
persevere until all the tasks they have been requested to do have been — 80 | 48 | 104
completed. They also seek employees who can follow directions exactly — 84 | 51 | 107
and use their time to the best advantage, who are on the job unless they — 89 | 53 | 110
are ill, and who possess the ability to get along well with others. — 94 | 56 | 112

gwam 3' | 1 | 2 | 3 | 4 | 5 |
      5' | 1 | 2 | 3 |

Step 4 - skip
Step 5 - 3 1'
trying to reach new
goal rate
Speed - not circle errors

15...
K...
G...

1. ...
co...

2. A 1' writing on ¶ 1; find *gwam* to establish your base rate.

3. Add 2-6 words to Step 2 *gwam;* use this as your goal rate.

4. From the table below, find quarter-minute checkpoints; note these figures in ¶ 1.

5. Take three 1' speed writings on ¶ 1, trying to reach your quarter-minute checkpoints as the guides (¼, ½, ¾, time) are called.

6. Follow Steps 2-5 for ¶ 2.

7. Take another 3' writing on ¶s 1-3 combined; find and compare *gwam* with that achieved in Step 1.

8. Record your better 3' *gwam;* then compare it to the 3' *gwam* you made in 151b and 151d.

gwam	¼'	½'	¾'	1'
32	8	16	24	32
36	9	18	27	36
40	10	20	30	40
44	11	22	33	44
48	12	24	36	48
52	13	26	39	52
56	14	28	42	56
60	15	30	45	60
64	16	32	48	64
68	17	34	51	68
72	18	36	54	72
76	19	38	57	76
80	20	40	60	80
84	21	42	63	84
88	22	44	66	88
92	23	46	69	92
96	24	48	72	96
100	25	50	75	100

...rs used | A | 1.5 si | 5.7 awl | 80% hfw

	gwam 3'	5'

...ographics, a vital part of the information processing field, is | 5 | 3 | 49 |
a term that is used to describe all procedures and machines involved in | 9 | 6 | 52 |
making multiple copies. It is an area that has undergone many changes | 14 | 8 | 55 |
due to the many new machines and procedures that have been introduced. | 19 | 11 | 58 |
The vast changes have made it possible for businesses to make copies | 23 | 14 | 60 |
easier and faster and for less money than in the past. | 27 | 16 | 62 |

Two kinds of equipment are often used to make copies--duplicators | 31 | 19 | 65 |
and copiers. Duplicators use stencils or masters to make copies. The | 36 | 22 | 68 |
stencils and masters must, of course, be prepared before copies can be | 41 | 25 | 71 |
made from them. On the other hand, copiers use an image-forming process, | 46 | 28 | 74 |
much like that of a camera, to make an exact copy directly from the | 50 | 30 | 76 |
original. | 51 | 31 | 77 |

Most copiers use regular or coated paper for the copies. In recent | 56 | 33 | 80 |
years, fiber optic copiers have replaced many of the old mechanical | 60 | 36 | 82 |
models since they are often small, cost less to run, and are more reli- | 65 | 39 | 85 |
able because they have few parts that move. Intelligent copiers that | 69 | 42 | 88 |
bring together the power of a computer and the convenience of a copier | 74 | 45 | 91 |
have been emphasized in the past few years. | 77 | 46 | 92 |

gwam 3' | 1 | 2 | 3 | 4 | 5 |
5' | 1 | 2 | 3 |

Lesson 154   *Keyboarding/Language Skills*

154a ▶ 5
Conditioning Practice

each line twice SS (slowly, then faster); DS between 2-line groups; if time permits, rekey selected lines

alphabet 1 Five expert judges were asked to quickly analyze both new board games.

fig/sym 2 I should pay $1,825 on Models #04-6 and #73-9 by May 8 to get 15% off.

long words 3 Unexpected fluctuations in work load or personnel affect productivity.

speed 4 Did the big quake on the key island shake the autobus and the visitor?

| 1 | 2 | 3 | 4 | 5 | 6 | 7 | 8 | 9 | 10 | 11 | 12 | 13 | 14 |

Skill-Enrichment Drill: Improve Keyboarding Speed

LL: 70 spaces

1. Key each line once SS; DS between 2-line groups.

2. Key a 1' writing on each of lines 2, 4, and 6; calculate *gwam* on each writing.

3. Key another 1' writing on your two slowest lines.

letter response	1	a set you saw join safe pink fact pump save milk best upon refer nylon
	2	Asa set a fast rate on a union test after you gave him a few tax data.
word response	3	a box pan tie owns kept such maps fuel girl then hang they throw river
	4	The girls work with vigor to make the maps of the ancient city for us.
combination response	5	a fur tax | he saw us | as she ate | when you go | in the area | they were after
	6	Pamela may go to the union hall to get an award for aid she gave them.

| 1 | 2 | 3 | 4 | 5 | 6 | 7 | 8 | 9 | 10 | 11 | 12 | 13 | 14 |

Skill-Enrichment Timed Writing

LL: 70 spaces
LS: DS
PI: 5 spaces

1. Key a 1' writing on ¶ 1; calculate *gwam* to establish a base rate.

2. Add 2-4 *gwam* to your base rate to set a new goal rate.

3. Using the table below, pick the speed nearest your goal rate and note the quarter-minute intervals for that speed.

4. Key two 1' writings with your teacher's call of the quarter-minute guides.

5. Key ¶s 2 and 3 in the same way.

6. Key a 3' writing on ¶s 1-3 combined; calculate *gwam*, circle errors.

7. Key a 5' writing on ¶s 1-3 combined; calculate *gwam*, circle errors.

Quarter-Minute Checkpoints

gwam	¼'	½'	¾'	1'
32	8	16	24	32
36	9	18	27	36
40	10	20	31	40
44	11	22	33	44
48	12	24	36	48
52	13	26	39	52
56	14	28	42	56
60	15	30	45	60
64	16	32	48	64
68	17	34	51	68
72	18	36	54	72
76	19	38	57	76
80	20	40	60	80

all letters used | A | 1.5 si | 5.7 awl | 80% hfw

	gwam 3'	5'

What is an office? Thousands of years ago, the office was the — 4 | 3 | 60
site of the secrets of an organization. A secretary, in fact, was known — 9 | 5 | 63
as the one who kept the secrets because he or she wrote in a secret lan- — 14 | 8 | 66
guage. In the minds of many people, an office is just a place where you — 19 | 11 | 69
will find furniture, equipment, people, and papers of all kinds. The — 23 | 14 | 72
office is also said to be a place where administrative functions are — 28 | 17 | 75
performed, such as preparing, storing, and distributing documents. — 32 | 19 | 77

In today's business world, information is not only essential but — 37 | 22 | 80
critical to the success of any company. Executives spend most of their — 42 | 25 | 83
time making decisions that lead to the sale of goods and services to — 46 | 28 | 85
the public. If the goals of the company are to be accomplished, the — 51 | 30 | 88
decisions made must be based on current, precise information. Today, — 55 | 33 | 91
business thrives on data; and the lack of the facts and figures upon — 60 | 36 | 94
which to base decisions may well spell the failure of the company. — 64 | 39 | 96

An office is something more than just a place occupied by people, — 69 | 41 | 99
equipment, furniture, and documents. The people in an office assemble — 74 | 44 | 101
and analyze data in great amounts; they process, revise, store, print, — 78 | 47 | 105
and transmit a large volume of data. The office is the nerve center of — 83 | 50 | 107
any company; it runs a communication network through which vital data — 88 | 53 | 110
flow. This information makes it possible for all of the other parts of — 93 | 56 | 113
the firm to reach their goals so that success can be won. — 96 | 58 | 116

gwam 3' | 1 | 2 | 3 | 4 | 5
5' | 1 | 2 | 3

154b ▶ 15
Improve Keystroking Response Patterns

each line twice SS; DS between 2-line groups; as time permits, take a 1' writing on each of lines 9-12

Words

letter 1 as no ad up be hop are ink bag kin card hoop dart junk eats noun texts
letter 2 ax oh at in we ilk ate inn bar lip care hull data kiln ewes only vexed
word 3 am and bye doe eke fib irk jay ken lens make name ogle paid quay right
combination 4 ad he in go to hem lop ape rag irk upon fizz veer heir bass giro zebra

Phrases

letter 5 at ease | join in | ate beef | new facts | no opinion | act better | eager beavers
word 6 lay by | if when | got down | pen pals | rush to | city bus | visit with | by and by
word 7 to own | tow us | paid off | the theory | their goals | naughty man | hand and eye
combination 8 were we | held off | brave men | mangy dog | did better | deserve it | up and down

Sentences

letter 9 I'll get him a million jolly eager readers after my greatest act ever.
word 10 Keith and the busy girls did make a visit to the tidy chapel downtown.
combination 11 It was great to visit my neighbor and to get to see Zoe, my big puppy.
combination 12 Bret may gas the autobus and cars in the usual cycle at the city pump.

| 1 | 2 | 3 | 4 | 5 | 6 | 7 | 8 | 9 | 10 | 11 | 12 | 13 | 14 |

154c ▶ 15 Assess Straight-Copy Skill

1. Two 5' writings on ¶s 1-3 combined; find *gwam*, circle errors.

2. Record the better *gwam*.

3. Compare this *gwam* score with the score you recorded in 151d.

all letters used | A | 1.5 si | 5.7 awl | 80% hfw

	gwam 3'	5'
A dictionary is a good resource for a secretary and should be part	4	3	40
of every office library. Most secretaries use one to find how words are	9	6	43
spelled, to determine correct definitions of words, and to learn what	14	8	46
part of speech a word can be used as. Another frequent use is to learn	19	11	50
the pronunciation of an unfamiliar word such as zori.	22	13	51
Along with the few major uses listed above, a dictionary can give	27	16	54
secretaries much more. For example, most dictionaries have parts that	31	19	57
list the names of and basic information about famous people and places.	36	22	59
A list of abbreviations used to shorten frequently used words can be	41	25	62
found in quite a few.	42	25	63
In addition to improving spelling skills through dictionary use,	47	28	66
secretaries should know some of the other useful information a dictio-	51	31	68
nary has so they will be able to use it more. Those who know when and	56	34	71
how to use a dictionary will be able to finish most communication tasks	61	37	74
with more speed and accuracy.	63	38	75

gwam 3' | 1 | 2 | 3 | 4 | 5 |
5' | 1 | 2 | 3 |

LL: 70 spaces
Tabs: every 8 spaces

1. Key each line once SS; DS between 2-line groups.

2. Key a 1' writing on line 2, then on line 4; calculate *gwam* on each writing.

3. Key lines 5 and 6 again to improve tab technique.

space bar	1	is to own | the old urn | and they | by the firm | it is handy | an ivory emblem
	2	They may wish to buy the ivory urn if an emblem on it can be repaired.
shift keys	3	Narragansett | Martha's Vineyard | the Statue of Liberty | Sea Island cotton
	4	Appleby Brothers, Inc., is located at Epson Place and Las Palmas Road.
tab	5	open 9036 soap 2910 void 5983 just 7725 profit
	6	disk 3828 make 7183 risk 4828 rich 4836 island

| 1 | 2 | 3 | 4 | 5 | 6 | 7 | 8 | 9 | 10 | 11 | 12 | 13 | 14 |

Skill-Enrichment Timed Writing

LL: 70 spaces
LS: DS
PI: 5 spaces

1. Key a 1' writing on ¶ 1; calculate *gwam* to establish a base rate.

2. Add 2-4 *gwam* to your base rate to set a new goal rate.

3. Using the table below, pick the speed nearest your goal rate and note the quarter-minute intervals for that speed.

4. Key two 1' writings with your teacher's call of the quarter-minute guides.

5. Key ¶s 2 and 3 in the same way.

6. Key a 3' writing on ¶s 1-3 combined; calculate *gwam*, circle errors.

7. Key a 5' writing on ¶s 1-3 combined; calculate *gwam*, circle errors.

Quarter-Minute Checkpoints

gwam	¼'	½'	¾'	1'
32	8	16	24	32
36	9	18	27	36
40	10	20	31	40
44	11	22	33	44
48	12	24	36	48
52	13	26	39	52
56	14	28	42	56
60	15	30	45	60
64	16	32	48	64
68	17	34	51	68
72	18	36	54	72
76	19	38	57	76
80	20	40	60	80

all letters used | A | 1.5 si | 5.7 awl | 80% hfw

	gwam 3'	5'

The ability to use a keyboard quickly and efficiently is a helpful — 4 | 3 | 60
tool at any level of an organization. Office employees may use a key- — 9 | 5 | 63
board to take orders, make reservations, or check an account; a manager — 14 | 8 | 66
may use a keyboard to send and receive mail, obtain data, or plan for — 19 | 11 | 68
the future. A major use of the keyboard is to process documents. With — 23 | 14 | 71
a display, storage unit, and printer, it is relatively simple to enter, — 28 | 17 | 74
revise, and produce business documents of all types. — 31 | 19 | 76

A person who enters the office as a keyboard operator may find — 36 | 22 | 79
that the job can be a stepping-stone to bigger and better jobs. From a — 41 | 24 | 82
position as an operator, one can progress to a specialist or trainer and — 46 | 27 | 85
then to the job of a supervisor or manager. The manager is responsible — 50 | 30 | 87
for all the work completed in the center. He or she selects equipment, — 55 | 33 | 90
develops procedures, provides a favorable place to work, and supervises — 60 | 36 | 93
the people who process the documents. — 62 | 37 | 95

The specific duties of a manager differ from place to place. Most — 67 | 40 | 97
experts agree, in general terms, that all managers plan, organize, direct — 72 | 43 | 100
and control the activities of their units. Since a manager can attain — 77 | 46 | 103
goals only through others, her or his most basic function concerns per- — 81 | 49 | 106
sonnel. In simpler words, he or she must be skilled in the art of get- — 86 | 52 | 109
ting along with others, including the talent to communicate with others — 91 | 54 | 112
and to motivate them to do their jobs to the best of their abilities. — 95 | 57 | 114

gwam 3' | 1 | 2 | 3 | 4 | 5 |
5' | 1 | 2 | 3 |

154d ▶ 5 Improve Language Skills: Word Choice

1. Study the spelling and definitions of each pair of words.

2. Key the **Learn** line, with the number and period, noting the proper use of the often confused words.

3. Key the **Apply** line, with the number and period, using the words that complete the sentence correctly.

complement (n) something that completes or makes up a whole	**expend** (vb) to use up; consume
compliment (n) an expression of praise or congratulation	**expand** (vb) to open up or out; enlarge; unfold or extend

Learn 1. Jim's compliment to Mary was that her hat complemented her outfit.

Apply 2. My (complement/compliment) was that Di's blouse is a nice (complement compliment) to her suit.

Learn 3. Al may expend too much time if he tries to expand his sales region.

Apply 4. I will (expand/expend) my display area unless it (expands/expends) too much floor space.

154e ▶ 10 Assess Language Skills: Word Division

1. Review the word-division guides on RG 5.

2. Set left margin at 12; tab stops on 31 and 56; DS.

3. Key the first word at the right beginning at the left margin stop.

4. Tab to first stop and key the word with a hyphen after each syllable.

5. Tab to the second stop and key the word with a hyphen between syllables where the word can be divided without violating any word-division guides.

Example
Column 1: situation
Column 2: sit-u-a-tion
Column 3: situ-ation

radio	spared
reliable	expressive
evacuee	drilling
staffer	occurring
unanimous	well-being
radioactivity	Part #60-798
panning	insufficient

ENRICHMENT ACTIVITY: Assess Language Skills: Spelling, Punctuation, Capitalization, and Composing

1. Proofread each sentence for errors in spelling (lines 1-3), punctuation (lines 4-6), and capitalization (lines 7-9).

2. Key each sentence, with the number and period, correcting the language-skills errors. Also, correct any errors you make while keying.

Spelling
1. Henry Huxster mist the deadline for the reduced fair by three daze.
2. Susan Harris beet the throw to second base by fore steps at leased.
3. The front breaks on my car did not seam write when I tried to stop.

Punctuation
4. Prizes were given to bikers with the top two times: 4'11 and 4'15".
5. Sue had cheese and crackers peanuts and hot cider at the reception.
6. Ford High had first second and third place finishers in the race.

Capitalization
7. the osa conference is in the desmond building on eighth street north.
8. the senator will speak in spanish on his trip to mexico next january.
9. the answer to problem 2 on test 3 is in lesson 6, unit 7, on page 98.

Composing at the Keyboard

1. Compose at the keyboard in DS format; do not correct language-skills or keying errors; if necessary, x-out errors and continue.

2. Edit your copy; then rekey it in final form on a full sheet. Use a 2″ top margin, 1″ side margins, and DS.

3. Describe the most valuable activity in which you engaged last summer; indicate how it is valuable to you.

ENRICHMENT ACTIVITIES:
Drills and Timed Writings

This section of enrichment activities contains eight pages of skill-enrichment drills and timed writings.

Each page consists of a set of lines designed variously to improve keyboarding technique, to build keyboarding speed, or to improve keyboarding control. Each set of lines may be used as a warm-up before the timed writing.

Each skill-enrichment drill is followed by a paragraph timed writing of average difficulty, word counted for 1', 3', and 5' timings.

Each drill and timed writing is accompanied with a set of guides for effective practice. The materials may, however, be practiced in a variety of ways.

Skill-Enrichment Drill: Improve Technique

LL: 70 spaces
Tabs: every 8 spaces

1. Key each line once SS; DS between 2-line groups.

2. Key a 1' writing on line 2, then on line 4; calculate *gwam* on each writing.

3. Key lines 5 and 6 again to improve tab technique.

space bar	1	an am by en jam men jay pan ham urn jay man pen own hay form sign worn
	2	When did the man sign the form and pay for the worn urn at the market?
shift keys	3	United States of America | the Fourth of July | United States Marine Corps
	4	Eva Lopez, Maria Ruiz, Ana Cruz, and Mario Ortez are from Puerto Rico.

tab	5	form	4957	then	5636	work	2948	pane	0163	social
	6	they	5636	dorm	3947	slap	2910	hand	6163	sleigh

| 1 | 2 | 3 | 4 | 5 | 6 | 7 | 8 | 9 | 10 | 11 | 12 | 13 | 14 |

Skill-Enrichment Timed Writing

LL: 70 spaces
LS: DS
PI: 5 spaces

1. Key a 1' writing on each ¶; calculate *gwam,* circle errors on each writing.

2. Key two 5' writings on ¶s 1-3 combined; calculate *gwam,* circle errors on each writing.

3. Record better speed and error scores to use as goals for later writings on ¶s on pp. 504-510.

all letters used | A | 1.5 si | 5.7 awl | 80% hfw | | gwam 1' | 5'

	1'	3'	5'
As a result of technological advances in equipment and methods,	13	3	57
many changes are being made in the modern office. The use of the com-	27	5	60
puter continues to grow by leaps and bounds because of its ability to	41	8	63
process figures with amazing speed and accuracy. In a matter of sec-	55	11	65
onds or minutes the computer can process numerical data which, in the	69	14	68
past, took hours or days. These data, in turn, help people to make	82	16	71
judgments or decisions that a computer is unable to do.	93	19	73
New equipment is now available that will improve the processing of	13	21	76
words. Included are machines that permit a person to make modifica-	27	24	29
tions at the keyboard. Errors can be corrected merely by backspacing	41	27	81
and entering the correct information. As information is entered, it	55	30	84
is recorded in memory. After the text has been entered and edited, the	69	32	87
operator can insert a sheet of paper in the machine or printer, press	83	35	90
a key, and the copy will be printed at a high rate of speed.	95	38	92
Most of the new equipment for processing figures and words have one	14	40	95
thing in common--they are operated through the use of a typewriter key-	28	43	98
board. Although these keyboards may not be identical, the location of	42	46	101
the letter keys is almost always the same. As a result, an operator can	57	49	104
learn to run one of the new machines with little or no difficulty. For	71	52	106
the speedy and accurate operator, these machines open new horizons.	84	55	109

gwam 1' | 1 | 2 | 3 | 4 | 5 | 6 | 7 | 8 | 9 | 10 | 11 | 12 | 13 | 14 |
gwam 5' | 1 | | | 2 | | | 3 | |

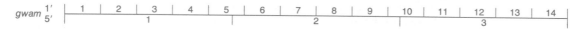

Assess/Improve Correspondence Processing Skills

Learning Goals

1. To assess/reinforce knowledge of letter and memorandum formats.

2. To improve productivity in processing letters and memorandums.

3. To reinforce production from script copy.

4. To rebuild/extend straight-copy skill.

5. To improve language-skills competency.

Format Guides

1. Paper guide at *0* (for typewriters).

2. LL (line length): 70-space line for sentence and ¶ drills, or as required for documents.

3. LS (line spacing): Single-space (SS) word and sentence drills; double-space (DS) ¶s; or space as directed within an activity.

4. PI (paragraph indent): 5 spaces.

FORMATTING GUIDES: LETTERS AND MEMORANDUMS

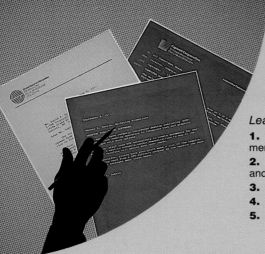

Block style letter;
open punctuation

Simplified memorandum

Guides for Letters

1. Letter length determines margin stops and date placement. Use the chart below or refer to RG 5 as a guide.

Length	Margins	Dateline
Short	2″	18
Average	1 ½″	16
Long	1″	14

Leave a quadruple space (QS) between the date and the letter address.

2. Include the person's name in the salutation when the letter is addressed to an individual. When a letter is addressed to a company, use the salutation "Ladies and Gentlemen." Use "Dear Sir or Madam" when the letter is addressed to an unidentified person such as "Office Manager." Leave a double space (DS) above and below the salutation.

3. Key the complimentary close a DS below the last line of the message.

4. Key the signer's name a QS below the complimentary close (or the company name if one is used).

5. Key the title of the signer on the line with the name separated by a comma, or on the next line (no comma), depending on the length of both the name and the title.

6. Key reference initials at left margin a DS below the signer's name or title. Use only the keyboard operator's initials (lowercase) when the signer's name is keyed in the closing lines.

7. Key the enclosure notation (if used) at left margin a DS below the reference initials.

8. Key the copy notation "c" a DS below the enclosure notation (or the reference initials if there is no enclosure).

Letter Styles

Block style. *Every* line begins at the left margin. Because of its efficiency, this style is highly recommended.

Modified block style. In this style, the date and the signature block begin at the horizontal center of the paper. (Set a tab stop at the center point to speed processing.)

Paragraphs may be blocked or indented 5 spaces from the left margin.

Punctuation Styles

Open. No punctuation follows the salutation or complimentary close.

Mixed. A colon follows the salutation, and a comma follows the complimentary close.

Either open or mixed punctuation may be used with block or modified block letters. Open punctuation, however, is typically used with block style and often used with modified block style.

Guides for Interoffice Memorandums

Formal style. Formal memos are prepared on full- or half-sheet forms with printed headings. Block style and 1″ side margins are used. The headings (TO:, FROM:, DATE:, and SUBJECT:) are printed in the left margin so that data used after the headings and message align at the 1″ left margin.

Memo headings are double-spaced, and a DS is left between the subject line and the first message line. The message is single-spaced; a DS is left between paragraphs. The keyboard operator's initials are keyed at the left margin a DS below the memo message.

Simplified style. Simplified memos are prepared on plain paper or company letterhead. They contain no preprinted or keyed headings. These memos are prepared in block format with 1″ side margins and follow these format guides:

Date: plain paper, line 10; letterhead, a DS below the last line of letterhead.

Addressee's name: a QS below the date; no personal title precedes name.

Subject: in ALL CAPS or cap-and-lowercase; a DS below the addressee's name.

Body: a DS below the subject line; single-spaced with a DS between paragraphs.

Writer's name: a QS below the last line of message.

Operator's initials: a DS below the writer's name.

Enclosure notation: "Enclosure" or "Attachment" a DS below operator's initials.

words

Document 2
Table with Horizontal Rulings

Format and key the table on a full sheet. Center the table horizontally and vertically. Center column headings; CS: 10.

THE ORIGINAL 13 STATES — 5

State	Order of Statehood	Date of Statehood
Connecticutt	5 6th	January 9, 1888
Deleware	1st	December 7, 1787
Georgia	4th	January 2, 1788
Maryland	7th	April 28, 1788
MassachusettS	6 5th	February 6, 1788
New Hampshire	9th	June 21, 1788
New Jersey	3rd	December 18, 1780
New York	11th	July 26, 1788
North Carolina	12th	November 21, 1789
Pennsylvania	2nd	December 12, 1787
Rhode Island	13th	May 29, 1790
South Carolian	8th	May 23, 1788
virginia	10th	June 25, 1788

Source: Fabulous Facts About the 50 States.

19
30
44
50
56
62
68
75
81
88
93
101
108
115
121
127
141
151

Document 3
Purchase Order

LP p. 193

Format and key the purchase order shown at the right with the changes that have been indicated.

Document 4
Table with Horizontal Rulings

Rekey Document 2 with the following changes:

DS the table; CS: 8; list the items in order of statehood (1-13).

Arlington Local School District
605 Baychester Avenue
Bronx, NY 10475-2294
(212) 638-7391

PURCHASE ORDER

Purchase Order No.: FM-3892-A — 2

LEARNING ESSENTIALS
1388 MONTGOMERY STREET
SAN FRANCISCO CA 94133-4611

Date: March 25, 19-- — 12

Terms: n/30 — 16, 24

Shipped Via: Arrow Express — 27

Quantity	Description/Stock Number	Price		Per	Total		
25	Essential Word Skills (6803-WS)	6	95	ea	173	75	37
25	Learn to Capitalize (2475-LC)	5	87	ea	146	75	47
10 5	Picture Punctuation (3820-PP)	6	25	ea	62	50	56
10 5	Reader Review (5970-RR)	5	10	ea	51	00	66
					434	00	68
	Less 10% discount	31	25		43	40	74
		25	50				
		377	25		390	60	75
		37	73		339	52	

By _____

155a ▶ 5
Conditioning Practice

each line twice SS (slowly, then faster); DS between 2-line groups; if time permits, rekey selected lines

alphabet	1	If Margie has extra help, a jigsaw puzzle can often be solved quickly.
fig/sym	2	BS & Sons used P.O. #708-A to buy 125 chairs (Style LE-64 and SSE-39).
3d row	3	Petite Terry used quite proper etiquette to outwit her poor tired pop.
speed	4	The ivory ornament and paisley handiwork make a rich pair of mementos.

| 1 | 2 | 3 | 4 | 5 | 6 | 7 | 8 | 9 | 10 | 11 | 12 | 13 | 14 |

155b ▶ 30 Document Processing: Letters

Review the formatting guides for letters on p. 275.

Letter 1
Short Letter

plain full sheet

1. Prepare a rough-draft copy in block style, open punctuation.

2. Proofread; identify errors with proofreader's marks; save copy for use in 155c.

Letter 2
Average-Length Letter

plain full sheet

modified block style, mixed punctuation; correct errors

Letter 3

plain full sheet

Reformat Letter 2 using block style, open punctuation; address to:

**Mr. James Q. Lento
Qualitech, Inc.
3300 Parallel Avenue
Kansas City, KS 66104-4397**

Supply appropriate salutation; correct errors.

	words	parts	total
September 5, 19--|Mr. Gene L. Howe|ATM Office Supplies|2300 Mission Street|Pasadena, CA 91108-1631|Dear Mr. Howe	14 / 22	14 / 23
I want to acknowledge receipt of your response to my Request for Proposal for 55 microcomputers, 17 laser printers, 2 file servers, and 3 optical scanners.	14 / 28 / 31	36 / 51 / 54
My staff will consider responses from all companies and make a recommendation by October 31 so the senior officers can make a decision by November 15. We plan to purchase no later than November 30. (words in body: 71)	46 / 60 / 11	68 / 83 / 94
Sincerely|Richard M. Pugliese|Administrative Manager|xx	22	105

---

	words	parts	total
September 5, 19--|Ms. Lynn S. Bost|Office Technology Associates|615 Miami Avenue|Kansas City, KS 66105-2187|Dear Ms. Bost	15 / 24	15 / 25
Your presentation at the Cedar Falls Office Systems conference on August 27, 19-- was excellent. Your expert system for configuring microcomputer networks might be invaluable to my staff as we network the micros in our office building.	15 / 30 / 44 / 48	40 / 55 / 69 / 72
As we discussed, I would like you to demonstrate your expert system to my staff on September 25, 19--. Please call to confirm this date or to set another and to select a time.	62 / 79 / 83	87 / 103 / 108
I will have one microcomputer (POS operating system) and a large-screen projection device for your demonstration. (106)	98 / 106	122 / 131
Sincerely|Charles H. Willy|Computer Systems Manager|xx	11	142

155c ▶ 10 Document Processing Drill: Letter Parts

Use the rough-draft copy of Letter 1 prepared in 155b and complete the following:

1. Three 1' writings in letter format on the opening lines (date through salutation) and as much of the message as time permits. Try to improve by 1 or 2 words with each timing.

2. Three ½' writings in letter format on the last line of the message and closing lines (complimentary close through initials).

Try to improve by 1 or 2 words each time.

3. A 3' writing on the entire letter. Use block style, open punctuation, plain full sheet.

300a ▶ 5
Conditioning Practice

Key each line twice. Then take two 30" writings for speed on line 4 followed by two 30" writings for control on line 1.

alphabet	1	Jack or Megan will buy the exquisite bracelet made of topaz in Denver.
figures	2	Their office buildings are at 2581 State, 7349 Dorbe, and 608 Sherman.
fig/sym	3	Kent & Sons donated $3,500 (Check #478) to the United Way on 12/16/91.
speed	4	They may both make the goals if they keep busy in their own cornfield.

| 1 | 2 | 3 | 4 | 5 | 6 | 7 | 8 | 9 | 10 | 11 | 12 | 13 | 14 |

300b ▶ 45
Evaluate Document Processing Skills: Tables/Forms

Time Schedule
Plan and prepare .... 5'
Timed production .... 30'
Proofread, compute *n-pram*... 10'

1. Arrange materials for ease of handling (LP p. 193 and 199).

2. Format and key Documents 1-4 for 30'. Proofread and correct errors before removing each document from machine or screen.

3. After time is called, proofread again and circle any uncorrected errors. Compute *n-pram*.

Document 1
Letter with Table
LP p. 199

Format and key the letter at the right in block format with mixed punctuation. Address the letter to

Mrs. Dorothy A. Romine
Arlington Grade School
605 Baychester Avenue
Bronx, NY 10475-2294

Date the letter **March 10, 19--** and supply any missing letter parts.

words

opening lines 24

Despite the fact that you are bringing another *school* year to a close, it is time to start planning for next year. Learning Essentials is eager to assist again in that planning.   37 / 49 / 62

You may be interested in the new products that we will have available in time for the start of the next school year. Our pilot-test schools have been very enthusiastic about the following ~~five~~ *six* products.   74 / 86 / 98 / 103

Product	Order No.	Unit Price	
Essential Word Skills	6803-WS	$6.95	116 / 124
Fun with Contractions	8319-FC	4.75	131
Learn to Capitalize	2475-LC	5.87	138
Picture Punctuation	3820-PP	6.25	144
Enhance Your Vocabulary	1024-EV	7.35	152
Reader Review	5970-RR	5.10	158

SS

Brochures *describing* ~~about~~ the products are enclosed. If you would like examination copies of any of these products, mail the card attached to each brochure.   170 / 182 / 188

Sincerely,   190

Jamison R. Cleworth
Sales Representative   194 / 201

A 10 percent discount will be given on orders totaling $100 or more that are received before June 15.   210 / 220

221/**239**

155d ▶ 5 Reinforce Script-Copy Skill

Three 1' writings for speed.
Goal: Improve rate by 1 or 2 words with each timing.
Note: If you finish ¶ before time is called, start over.

all letters used | A | 1.5 si | 5.7 awl | 80% hfw

gwam 1'

Applicants who seek a position in an office will be able   11
to increase their chances of getting the position if they can   24
just show that they have qualities for which employers are   36
looking. Applicants should emphasize experiences that show   48
they can work in a group with a great deal of enthusiasm and   60
pride.   61

Lesson 156   Letters and Memorandums

156a ▶ 5 Conditioning Practice

each line twice SS (slowly, then faster); DS between 2-line groups; if time permits, rekey selected lines

alphabet 1   Jaguars very quickly maximize to top speed when faced with big danger.
figures 2   Lenora served 438 hot dogs, 529 donuts, and 1,067 drinks at two games.
shift key 3   The nine vendors are from F & W Products, Cim & Co., and Kwynn & Sons.
speed 4   He or she may work with us to make a profit for the eighty city firms.

| 1 | 2 | 3 | 4 | 5 | 6 | 7 | 8 | 9 | 10 | 11 | 12 | 13 | 14 |

156b ▶ 20 Document Processing: Formal Memorandums

Memo 1
LP p. 9 or plain half sheet
1. Read the information about formal memorandums on p. 275.
2. Process a copy of the memo. Use formal style; block the ¶s; correct errors.
3. Process COMPANY MAIL envelope to:
Jim Torchek, Sales Manager
Sales Department
Note: If you do not have Lab Pac (LP) pages to use for the formal memo, follow these guidelines.
1. Set side margins at 1".
2. Beginning on line 10, key each heading flush with the left margin.
3. Space twice after the colon and key the information following each heading.
Memo 2 is on p. 278.

words

TO: Jim Torchek   2
FROM: Robert Elford   5
DATE: September 7, 19--   9
SUBJECT: RESPONSES TO REQUEST FOR QUOTATION (RFQ)   17

Enclosed are the responses to our RFQ from the companies that   29
met the deadline. Note that each addressed the requirements   42
we listed.   44

The enclosed spreadsheet gives each company's price for each   56
unit of equipment listed. I'll send a spreadsheet before   68
the September 14 meeting that shows each company's total   79
prices for all units.   84

x x   84

Enclosure   86

envelope **90**

Use the information given below to prepare the reference page.

Yukl, Gary A. Leadership in Organizations. 2d ed. Englewood Cliffs, NJ: Prentice-Hall, Inc., 1989.

Lundy, James L. Lead, Follow, or Get Out of the Way. San Diego: Slawson Communications, Inc., 1986.

References: 56 words.

Document 3
Unbound Report

plain full sheets

Rekey Document 2 as an unbound report.

words

Leadership styles | 141

A leadership style is the approach a person (leader) | 152

uses to get others to accomplish goals and objectives. | 163

Leadership styles can be classified as either authoritarian | 175

or participative. Styles are also classified as autocratic | 187

and

~~or~~ democratic. | 190

Authoritarian style. The authoritarian style of | 204

leadership allows for ~~very~~ little or no input from group | 214

members in the decision-making process. This style is also | 226

referred to as "autocratic." | 232

Participative style. The participative style of | 246

allows for   to

leadership ~~believes that~~ group members ~~should~~ be actively | 256

involved in the decision-making process and encourages input | 268

from the members of the group. "Democratic" is another name | 281

for this style. | 284

individual

In reality, ~~it is not uncommon for~~ a person's style to | 292

is often   styles   strictly

be a combination of ~~these~~ two rather than ~~totally~~ authori- | 305

strictly

tarian or ~~totally~~ participative. | 312

Characteristics of Respected Leaders | 327

Debate over which style of leadership is most effective | 338

#

has taken place for many years. Advantages and disadvantages | 350

of each are often discussed. However, most responses given | 362

in a survey that requested participants to list character- | 374

for

istics that contribute to their respect of leaders can be | 385

found in the participative style of leadership (Lundy, 1986, | 388

characteristics   the following

13-16). These include ~~such items as~~: | 409

1. Communicates, allows input, is willing to listen. | 419

2. Is objective, open-minded, tolerant, rational, rea- | 430
sonable, impartial, fair. | 435

DS   3. Delegates, trusts subordinates, allows room to | 446
achieve. | 447

DS   4. Motivates, challenges, inspires, is team-oriented. | 458
DS   5. Is available, approachable; provides feedback; | 469
trains, guides, coaches. | 473

156b (continued)

words

Memo 2

LP p. 11 or plain half sheet
Format and key in formal style the memo shown at the right; correct errors.

	words
TO: All Department Heads FROM: Director, Computer Operations	10
DATE: September 7, 19-- SUBJECT: COMPUTER DOWNTIME	17

The Major 9957 computer system will be shut down at 5:30 p.m. on September 15 for 48 hours so we can do preventative maintenance. | 32 / 44

If you need to access its files during this period, you should download the needed files to your microcomputer system. | 59 / 68

xx | 68/74

156c ▶ 15 Document Processing: Letters

Set margins and determine dateline position by judgment; proofread and correct errors. Review envelope addressing procedures (RG 7). Process envelopes.

Letter 1 LP p. 13
modified block with indented ¶s, mixed punctuation

Letter 2 plain full sheet
Reformat Letter 1 in block style, open punctuation.

	words	parts
September 8, 19--	Mr. David R. Lundy	X-TRA Corporation	16606 Grand River	15	15
Avenue	Detroit, MI 48227-1492	Dear Mr. Lundy	24	25
The facsimile machine (Model 3540) I purchased from you last May has been	15	39
out of service on five days during the last month.	25	49
Your service rep responded promptly to each service call, but on three occa-	40	64
sions the machine was out of service for more than 24 hours because he could	56	79
not get parts locally.	60	84
These delays disrupt my business, and I will have to seek service elsewhere	76	99
if your local inventory is not increased. (84)	84	108
Sincerely	Miss Jeanne L. Dixter	Communication Specialist	xx	12	120
		137

156d ▶ 10 Document Processing Drill: Letter Parts

plain full sheets

Use Letter 1, 156c, modified block with indented ¶s, mixed punctuation, to complete the following:

1. Three 1' writings in letter format on the opening lines and as many of the message lines as you can. Try to improve by 1 or 2 words on each timing.

2. Three ½' writings in letter format on the last line of the message and closing lines. Try to improve by 1 or 2 words on each

timing or complete the timing sooner each time.

3. A 3' writing on the entire letter. Use a plain full sheet.

| Lesson 157 | Letters and Memorandums |

157a ▶ 5 Conditioning Practice

each line twice SS (slowly, then faster); DS between 2-line groups; if time permits, rekey selected lines

alphabet	1	Seven lions were quietly caught just before they exited the park maze.
figures	2	The March 25, 1993 listing had 87 micros, 14 printers, and 60 copiers.
long words	3	Their powerful minicomputer features parallel processing capabilities.
speed	4	Their men may do the work for us and the city if she pays them for it.

| 1 | 2 | 3 | 4 | 5 | 6 | 7 | 8 | 9 | 10 | 11 | 12 | 13 | 14 |

157b ▶ 20 Document Processing: Simplified Memorandums

Memo 1

plain full sheet

1. Read the information about simplified memos on page 275.
2. Study the model memo on page 279.
3. Process a copy of the model memo on page 279; proofread/correct errors.

Memo 2

plain full sheet
Process a copy of the model memo on page 279 with the following changes.

Change the name/title of the addressee to:

Manual A. Santia
Marketing Promotions

Change "research" in ¶2 to "promotions."

299a ▶ 5
Conditioning Practice

Each line twice. Then take two 30″ writings for speed on line 4 followed by two 30″ writings for control on line 1.

alphabet 1 He was extremely helpful in moving the jazz band quickly to the stage.

figures 2 For more information on our rates, phone 615-889-2743, Extension 5077.

fig/sym 3 He bought 50 shares of BB&Q at $36.95 ($1,847.50) with 12% commission.

speed 4 If the firms do the tax audit, we may make the signs for their social.

| 1 | 2 | 3 | 4 | 5 | 6 | 7 | 8 | 9 | 10 | 11 | 12 | 13 | 14 |

299b ▶ 45
Evaluate Document Processing Skills: Reports/News Release

Time Schedule
Plan and prepare .... 5′
Timed production ....30′
Proofread; compute
  n-pram......................10′

1. Arrange materials for ease of handling (LP p. 197).

2. Format and key Documents 1-3 for 30′. Proofread and correct errors before removing each document from machine or screen.

3. After time is called, proofread again and circle any uncorrected errors. Compute n-pram.

Document 1
News Release

LP p. 197

Format and key the material to the upper right as a news release for release immediately with **Marsha G. Chen, 612-392-4219,** as the contact.

Document 2
Leftbound Report

plain full sheets

Format and key the material at the right as a leftbound report. Prepare a reference page on a separate sheet.

words
opening lines 8

(¶1) Minneapolis, MN, March 26, 19--. Gerald M. Richardson, Mall 20
Manager, announced today that construction of the new Oak Ridge Mall in 35
downtown Minneapolis is nearing completion and that stores will be opening 50
for business on May 1. The grand opening of the mall is scheduled for the 65
week of May 7. 68

(¶2) Richardson reported that 85% of the mall's 1.25 million square feet 82
of store space had been leased. "With the normal occupancy rate of a new 96
mall being 80% on opening day, we are confident that the mall is going to be 112
a huge success." The mall includes approximately 150 shops anchored by 126
three major department store chains. The fourth anchor is the Oak Ridge 141
Hotel which features a Supper Club & Dinner Theatre. 152

(¶3) Richardson stated that developers have focused on making the mall a 165
place that provides family entertainment as well as shopping. At the center 181
of the mall is a small amusement park for the children, featuring miniature 196
golf, a skating rink, and various food establishments. 207

LEADERSHIP 2

    The term leadership is very difficult to define. ∧ *Even* Those 14
who ~~do~~ *have done* ∧extensive research in the area∧ ~~find,~~ *have found* an abundance of 29
definitions∧ ~~with most,~~ *Many* of those definitions reflect~~ing~~ *e* the 39
individual perspectives of the person defining the term. 51
One researcher, after doing a comprehensive review of the 62
leadership literature, concluded that there are almost as 74
many definitions of leadership as there are persons who have 86
attempted to define the concept. (Yukl, 1989, 2)∧ Even 97
though one definition is difficult to∧ *agree on* ~~attain,~~ a greater un- 109
derstanding of leadership can be gained by looking at dif- 121
ferent leadership styles and characteristics of respected 132
leaders. 134

(continued, p. 500)

499

RŌLŌTRON CORPORATION

1351 East Allen Street, Springfield, IL 62703-7988

INTEROFFICE MEMORANDUM

		words
Side margins: 1″	DS (if printed form is used) Line 10 (if plain paper is used)	

Date   September 8, 19-- _{QS} — words 4

Addressee   Barbara M. Toland, Market Researcher _{DS} — 11

Subject   DESKTOP PUBLISHING SOFTWARE _{DS} — 17

Many vendors have recently introduced desktop publishing (DTP) — 29
software that enables operators to integrate text and graphics — 42
easier and with more options. _{DS} — 48

Body   Since your staff uses DTP extensively to create documents for re- — 61
search, I want to schedule vendor demonstrations to see if the — 74
upgraded versions will better meet your needs. _{DS} — 83

In preparation, please have your staff make a list of the require- — 96
ments they need from a DTP software package so the vendors can — 110
show how their packages meet these needs. _{QS} — 117

Gerri S. Yubath

Name of writer   Gerri S. Yubath _{DS} — 121

Reference
initials   xx — 121

Simplified Memo

157c ▶ 20 Document Processing: Letters

Letter 1

LP p. 15

Format in block style, open punctuation, the letter at the right; correct errors; prepare envelope.

Letter 2

plain full sheet

Format in modified block style, mixed punctuation, the letter at the right. Address the letter to:

**Mr. Dwight D. Miller
Architectural Services
70 Ship Street
Providence, RI 02903-4220**

   Supply an appropriate salutation; correct errors; prepare envelope.

	words
September 8, 19-- | Morris Design Group | 1086 Willett Avenue | Providence,	14
RI 02915-2098 | Ladies and Gentlemen	21

Enclosed is an update on the latest version of our personal computer work- — 36
station, which is very popular with architects. — 46

The ES/10 microcomputer has an 80286 microprocessor, has 3MB of user — 59
memory, and comes with advanced color and graphics capabilities. It sup- — 74
ports a full-page display monitor and the most sophisticated laser printers — 89
and scanners. — 92

When combined with state-of-the-art design software, this hardware gives — 107
architects an opportunity to use the most advanced technology throughout — 121
every phase in the design process. (107) — 128

Sincerely \| Mrs. Mary Ellen Rosowitz \| Sales Representative \| xx — 140

Enclosure — 142/155

Document 2
Formal Memorandum
LP p. 193

Format and key the material at the right as a formal memorandum to **Margaret Comstock, Personnel Manager** from **Thomas Salazar, Assistant Personnel Manager.** Date the memo **March 6, 19--.** Use **EMPLOYEE MORALE** for the subject line.

opening lines 22

After our meeting last week, I called Research Dynamics to discuss the possibility of their conducting the study for us on employee morale. I met with three of their research specialists to outline what we want from the research.

They are interested in working with us on the project, and I feel that they will be able to provide us with the information we need. They will present a proposal to us during the week of May 13. Let me know which day and time would best fit your schedule, and I will arrange for the meeting.

32
42
52
62
69
77
87
97
106
114
123
127/139

Document 3
Business Letter
LP p. 195

Format the material at the right as a modified block letter with mixed punctuation and blocked paragraphs. Use the **current date,** and address the letter to

Ms. Rosetta N. Johnson
2682 Gingham Court
Orlando, FL 32828-8461

Include an appropriate salutation and complimentary close.

The letter is from **Marcia G. Ogden, Studio Manager**

Special features:

Company name in closing lines:

SANDBERG PHOTOGRAPHY STUDIO

Supply any missing parts.

Document 4
Simplified Memorandum
plain full sheet

Rekey Document 2 as a simplified memorandum.

opening lines 20

Customer satisfaction is the primary goal of ours. In order to determine how we can improve our photography service, we rely on customer feedback.

Since you were a recent customer of our studio, we would like to solicit input from you regarding your perception of the service you received. The enclosed questionaire is divided into sections. The first section is to evaluate the receptionist; the second, the photographer; the third, the sales representative; and the last, the quality of your photos. Please take a few minutes to complete the questionaire, providing us with the information to better serve you in the future.

The enclosed Certificate for a 25 percent discount on your next sitting is a token of our apreciation for helping us to continue focusing on our primary goal--customer satisfaction.

33
47
53
66
77
81
92
113
127
138
149
162
174
185

closing lines 208/221

157d ▶ 5 Improve Language Skills: Word Choice

1. Study the spelling and definitions of each pair of words.

2. Key each **Learn** line with the number and period, noting the proper use of the often confused words.

3. Key each **Apply** line with the number and period, choosing the words that complete the sentence correctly.

defer (vb) put off until a future time; postpone

differ (vb) to be unlike or dissimilar

allowed (vb) past tense of allow, which means to let do or happen; permit

aloud (adv) with the voice; orally

Learn   1. Our solutions differ; so we must defer making the decision.
Apply   2. I will (differ/defer) building my model since it (defers/differs) from Jim's.

Learn   3. Lu-yin was allowed to give her response aloud to the class.
Apply   4. Al spoke (allowed/aloud) to each group as soon as he learned he was (allowed/aloud).

Lesson 158	Sustained Document Processing: Letters and Memorandums

158a ▶ 5 Conditioning Practice

each line twice SS (slowly, then faster); DS between 2-line groups; if time permits, rekey selected lines

alphabet 1 Jerry's big mistake was to list seven dozen xylophones for quick sale.

fig/sym 2 The 6% interest amounted to $190 on account #12-35-470 and #12-48-903.

LOCK 3 Use PAUL ELY of 103 LEMON PLACE in ALL CAPS in the new letter address.

speed 4 If they go to the city and sign the form, I may pay them for the work.

| 1 | 2 | 3 | 4 | 5 | 6 | 7 | 8 | 9 | 10 | 11 | 12 | 13 | 14 |

158b ▶ 35 Sustained Document Processing: Letters and Memorandums

Time Schedule

Plan and prepare .... 3'
Timed production .... 25'
Proofread; compute *n-pram* .... 7'

1. Make a list of documents to be processed:

page 276, 155b, Letter 2
page 278, 156b, Memo 2
page 278, 157b, Memo 1
page 279, 157c, Letter 1

2. Arrange full sheets, formal memo paper from LP p. 11, letterhead from LP pp. 17-19, and correction materials for easy access. Process as many documents as you can in 25'. Proofread and correct before removing each

document from the machine.

3. After time is called, proofread document in machine and circle errors.

4. Compute *n-pram*; turn in work arranged in order listed in Step 1.

158c ▶ 10 Paragraph Guided Writing

1. Three 1' writings for speed with quarter-minute checkpoints noted and guides called on 2nd and 3rd writings (See Table, p. 272).

Goal: 2-6 words faster on each writing.

2. Three 1' writings for control with quarter-minute checkpoints noted and guides called. Deduct 2-4 words from top speed; then note checkpoints.

Goal: 2 or fewer errors a minute.

| all letters used | A | 1.5 si | 5.7 awl | 80% hfw |

gwam 2'

Many office system experts think a sizable number of entry-level   7

office positions in this decade will go unfilled if there is a shortage   14

of qualified workers. They state that to get a position, a person must   21

show a good foundation in basic and technical skills. Employers will   28

hire only those people who can think, read, write, talk, and listen; have   35

balanced their studies with up-to-date technical skills; and show they   42

can relate to people on the job.   46

1' gwam | 1 | 2 | 3 | 4 | 5 | 6 | 7 | 8 | 9 | 10 | 11 | 12 | 13 | 14 |

298a ▶ 5
Conditioning Practice

Key each line twice. Then take two 30″ writings for speed on line 4 followed by two 30″ writings for control on line 1.

alphabet 1 Wayne Mazzilli very quickly expressed his own feelings on the subject.

figures 2 The call numbers for the last two books are HD52.7.L86 and SG40.9.L13.

fig/sym 3 Invoice #694 was billed to credit card #C17305 for $805.23 on 8/02/92.

speed 4 If they are too busy with work, the visitor may be a problem for them.

| 1 | 2 | 3 | 4 | 5 | 6 | 7 | 8 | 9 | 10 | 11 | 12 | 13 | 14 |

298b ▶ 45
Evaluate Document Processing Skills: Letters/Memos

Time Schedule
Plan and prepare .... 5′
Timed production ....30′
Proofread; compute
  n-pram ....10′

1. Arrange materials for ease of handling (LP pp. 191-195).

2. Format and key Documents 1-4 for 30′. Proofread and correct errors before removing each document from machine or screen.

3. After time is called, proofread again and circle any uncorrected errors. Compute n-pram.

Note: To find n-pram (net production rate per minute), deduct 10 words for each uncorrected error; divide remainder by 30 (time).

Document 1
Business Letter
LP p. 191

Format in block style with open punctuation the letter shown at the right. Address the letter to

**Mr. Robert T. Cline
Nagle College of Business
310 McDowell Avenue, S
Chicago, IL 60609-7395**

Use **March 4, 19--** as the date and prepare the letter to be sent **REGISTERED.**

Include the following postscript:

If you decide not to purchase the materials, please return them by June 4.

Supply any missing letter parts.

words

opening lines 27

Subject: Laura McKinzie Presentation Materials — 36

Here is the McKinzie material developed for improving presentation skills for your review. As I indicated to you during our conversation, the materials are comprehensive and include three videos, a text, transparencies, and a workbook. — 46 56 67 78 84

Once you have had the opportunity to review the materials, you will see how extremely helpful they are for instructing future businesspeople on the art of making an effective presentation. Several colleges in your area currently use this material. Also, many business organizations throughout the United States have purchased the materials and are using them for in-house training for their employees. — 94 104 115 126 136 147 156 165

If you have any questions after reviewing the materials, please call me at 1-800-639-6700. — 174 184

Sincerely — 187

EDUCATIONAL SPECIALISTS, INC. — 192

Marshall G. Pearson — 196

Sales Representative — 200

closing lines 218/**236**

Assess/Improve Report Processing Skills

Learning Goals

1. To improve your ability to produce unbound, topbound, and leftbound reports.

2. To improve your ability to document references by using internal citations/reference page; footnotes/bibliography; and endnotes.

3. To improve language-skill competency.

Format Guides

1. Paper guide at *0* (for typewriters).

2. LL: 70 spaces or as directed in document formatting guide.

3. LS: SS drill lines; DS ¶s; or as directed within an activity.

4. PI: 5 spaces unless otherwise directed.

FORMATTING GUIDES: REPORTS IN UNBOUND, TOPBOUND, AND LEFTBOUND FORMATS

REPORT FORMATS

PLACEMENT/SPACING		UNBOUND		LEFTBOUND		TOPBOUND	
		Pica	Elite	Pica	Elite	Pica	Elite
CENTERPOINT:		42	51	45	54	42	51
TOP MARGIN:	FIRST PAGE Place heading on .... QS below heading. No page number is necessary.	line 10	line 12	line 10	line 12	line 12	line 14
	SECOND AND SUCCEEDING PAGES Place page number on ...	line 6	line 6	line 6	line 6	line 62	line 62
		at right margin		at right margin		bottom center	
	Continue body of report on line	8	8	8	8	10	10
BOTTOM MARGIN:	ALL PAGES	1″	1″	1″	1″	1″	1″
		6 lines		6 lines		6 lines	
LEFT MARGIN:	ALL PAGES Inches .... Spaces	1″ 10	1″ 12	1½″ 15	1½″ 18	1″ 10	1″ 12
RIGHT MARGIN:	ALL PAGES	All report styles use a 1″ right margin.					
SPACING MODE:		Body of a report is usually DS, but may be SS.					

Footnotes and Explanatory Notes

To find the vertical line space on which to end text on a page with footnotes or explanatory notes, follow these guidelines:

1. Allow 3 lines for divider rule and the blank line space above and below it, 3 lines for each note, and 6 lines for the bottom margin.

2. Subtract the sum of these figures from 66 (number of line spaces on the paper). Text should not be keyed on a line lower than the resulting figure.

After completing the last line of text, DS above and below the 1½″ divider rule. Indent first line of a note 5 spaces and key a superscript number (raised ½ line space). Begin second line and succeeding lines at left margin. SS each note; DS between notes.

On a partially filled page, footnotes may immediately follow the text or may be placed at the foot of the page.

Note: If the equipment cannot print a superscript figure, follow these guidelines:

1. Key the footnote, endnote, or explanatory note reference figure in the text on the line of writing, preceded and followed by a diagonal (/) mark.

2. Key the endnote figure or the footnote or explanatory figure at the bottom of the page on the line of writing indented 5 spaces from the left margin and followed by a period and two spaces.

Reference Page or Bibliography

Use same margins and center point as for first page of report. SS references; DS between them. Begin first line of each entry at left margin; indent second line and succeeding lines 5 spaces.

Endnotes Page

Use same margins and center point as for first page of report. SS endnotes; DS between them. Indent first line of each endnote 5 spaces; key a superscript endnote number. If your equipment cannot print a superscript figure, indent first line of each note 5 spaces; key the note number on line of writing followed by a period and two spaces. Begin second line and succeeding lines of each note at left margin.

Table of Contents

Use same margins and center point as for first page of report. List side and paragraph headings in table of contents (TC). DS side headings beginning at left margin; SS paragraph headings with a DS above and below them. Key page number of TC entry at right margin; connect each entry to its page number by leaders.

Title Page

Use same side margins and center point as for first page of report. Center each line of copy horizontally. Key report title on line 16 in ALL CAPS. Space down 8 DS and key report writer's name. DS and key name of school or department; space down 8 DS and key report date.

LL: 70 spaces
LS: DS

1. The sentences at the right contain errors in capitalization, number expression, punctuation, grammar, and word choice.

2. As you key each sentence (with number and period), make all necessary corrections, including any keyboarding errors you may make.

3. After you key all sentences, proofread each one and mark each keyboarding error that was not corrected.

Capitalization/Number Expression

1. 9 fbla members from Utah may attend the Meeting in Washington, d.c.
2. they will arrive on flight 62 at ten thirty a.m. with president Chi.
3. She was invited to lunch at the Hotel lombardozzi on 5th avenue.
4. The singing statesmen will perform on friday, january 25, at 7 p.m.
5. Does the Mississippi river divide minneapolis and st. paul?
6. The united parcel service will still deliver on christmas eve.
7. The Roberts live at nine pacific view drive in San diego, california.

Punctuation

8. If we leave a week early we will go to Houston Dallas and Austin.
9. The man said "If you are staying for lunch please raise your hand."
10. The new president Jason Masters will take office in May.
11. I believe Dr. James you will be able to meet with him after lunch.
12. During the summer of 1991 10975 students attended the university.
13. The senator Sandra Myers is a charming intelligent person.
14. Tom my cousin was born on Friday July 2, 1976 in Oxford Maine.

Subject/Verb/Pronoun Agreement

15. Either Mr. Dixon or Ms. Jay were invited to be our guest of honor.
16. The executive committee have made arrangements for the next meeting.
17. Some of the report are finished. All of the boys are working on it.
18. The new desks that you ordered has arrived; the chairs have not.
19. Dr. Jones and Dr. Blassingame is in charge of the project.
20. Most of the administrators was pleased with his decision.

Word Choice

21. The two of them decided the report was too long too be acceptable.
22. They gave her a complement on the weigh she threw the baseball.
23. If they are write about the date, it does not make cents to weight.
24. The heir to the throne seams to be adapt at flying an airplane.
25. I am confidant that he will learn a good lessen from her advise.
26. The cereal number is written right at the bottom of the envelop.
27. They will let us know within the our if the site is acceptable.
28. He seems to recent the weigh they choose to cite his work.
29. She was told to be very implicit with her plans for paying the lone.
30. There mite be a big deference in the two types of stationery.

159a ▶ 5 Conditioning Practice

each line twice SS (slowly, then faster); DS between 2-line groups; if time permits, rekey selected lines

alphabet	1	Maxim just amazed the partial crowd by kicking five quick field goals.
figures	2	Order 97-341 for 215 Series 068 storm windows was shipped last May 28.
symbols	3	Susan's report had asterisks (*), pound signs (#), and ampersands (&).
speed	4	Claudia did lay the ivory memento and oak ornament by the enamel bowl.

| 1 | 2 | 3 | 4 | 5 | 6 | 7 | 8 | 9 | 10 | 11 | 12 | 13 | 14 |

159b ▶ 5 Improve Language Skills: Word Choice

1. Study the spelling and definitions of each pair of words.

2. Key the **Learn** line with the number and period, noting the proper use of the often confused words.

3. Key the **Apply** line with the number and period, choosing the words that complete the sentence correctly.

> **forward** (adj) going or moving to a position in front
>
> **foreword** (n) the preface or introductory pages of a book
>
> **forth** (adj) forward in time, place, or order
>
> **fourth** (adj) being number four in a countable series

Learn 1. The forward leap of technology was described in the book's foreword.

Apply 2. The (forward/foreword) of the text depicts society's (forward/foreward) trend.

Learn 3. Jim came forth to accept his trophy for finishing in fourth place.

Apply 4. The band marched back and (forth/fourth) during (forth/fourth) period.

159c ▶ 40 Document Processing: Reports

Review the formatting guides for unbound reports on p. 281 and the model report on RG 8.

Document 1
Unbound Report with Internal Citations

1. Format and key the copy given at the right and on p. 283 as an unbound report; DS.

2. Before you remove each page from the machine or screen, proofread it and correct any errors you may have made.

Formatting Enumerations:

1. SS each enumeration; DS between enumerations.

2. Key the number at the ¶ indention point used in the report.

3. Key lines to the right margin of the report.

4. Key the first stroke of "runover" line(s) flush with the number.

words

TELEPHONE SKILLS — 3

Next to face-to-face communication, the telephone is the most frequent — 18
method of exchanging information in business (Stout and Perkins, 1987, 87). — 33
It is important, therefore, that all employees realize that the business will — 49
be more successful if every employee can use the phone more efficiently — 63
and effectively. — 67

Telephone Techniques — 75

People who have good telephone techniques can turn complaining callers — 89
into satisfied ones; create a very good image for the business with its cus- — 104
tomers, clients, and suppliers; and get more done each day because they — 118
handle callers effectively and efficiently. — 127

Processing incoming calls. Incoming calls should be answered immedi- — 146
ately, "before the third ring" (Tilton, Jackson, and Popham, 1987, 287). The — 162
employee answering the call should identify himself or herself immediately — 177
and speak in a tone that is relaxed and low-pitched. A writing pad should — 192
be kept near the phone so that all important parts of the conversation can be — 207
recorded. The caller should be thanked at the end of the conversation. — 222

Processing outgoing calls. These techniques should be used to improve — 241
the process of placing calls: — 247

1. Group calls and make them during set times each day to reduce the — 261
amount of idle chatter. — 266

2. Place calls in order of importance or urgency. — 277

3. Identify yourself as the caller as soon as the call is answered. — 291

(continued, p. 283)

23:05

UNIT 71   LESSONS 297 – 300
Evaluate Keyboarding/Language/Document Processing Skills

Performance Goals

1. To measure your skill in keyboarding straight-copy material.
2. To evaluate your language skills.
3. To measure your document processing skill.

Format Guides

1. Paper guide at *0* (for typewriters).
2. LL: 70 spaces for drills and ¶s; as appropriate for documents.
3. LS: SS drills; DS ¶s; as required by document formats.
4. PI: 5 spaces for ¶s; as appropriate for document formats.

Lesson 297	Evaluate Keyboarding/Language Skills

297a ▶ 5
Conditioning Practice

Key each line twice. Then take two 30″ writings for speed on line 4 followed by two 30″ writings for control on line 1.

alphabet 1   Suzann gave the four new job descriptions to me to re-examine quickly.
figures 2   If you use F5-6091 rather than F25-7384, you can access the data file.
fig/sym 3   Kennedy & Nelson's last order (#2987), dated July 15, was for $31,640.
speed 4   Their problems with the forms may end when they go to see the auditor.

| 1 | 2 | 3 | 4 | 5 | 6 | 7 | 8 | 9 | 10 | 11 | 12 | 13 | 14 |

297b ▶ 15
Evaluate Straight Copy

Take two 5′ writings on the ¶s at the right. Record *gwam* and errors on better writing.

all letters used | A | 1.5 si | 5.7 awl | 80% hfw

gwam 1′ | 5′

You are nearing the end of your keyboarding classes. The skill — 13 | 3 | 53
level you have attained is much better than that with which you started — 27 | 5 | 55
when you were given keyboarding instruction for the very first time. — 41 | 8 | 58
During the early phase of your training, you were taught to key the let- — 55 | 11 | 61
ters of the alphabet and the figures by touch. During the initial period — 69 | 14 | 64
of learning, the primary emphasis was placed on your keying technique. — 83 | 17 | 67

After learning to key the alphabet and figures, your next job was — 13 | 19 | 69
to learn to format documents. The various types of documents formatted — 27 | 22 | 72
included letters, tables, and manuscripts. During this time of training, — 42 | 25 | 75
an emphasis also was placed on increasing the rate at which you were — 55 | 28 | 78
able to key. Parts of the lessons keyed at this time also were used to — 70 | 31 | 81
help you recognize the value of and to improve language skills. — 82 | 33 | 83

The final phase of your training dealt with increasing your skill — 13 | 36 | 86
at producing documents of high quality at a rapid rate. Directions were — 28 | 39 | 89
provided for keying special documents; drills were given to build skill; — 42 | 42 | 92
and problems were provided to assess your progress. You also were given — 57 | 44 | 94
a number of simulations to allow you to apply what you had learned. Now — 72 | 47 | 97
you have a skill that you will be able to use throughout your life. — 85 | 50 | 100

gwam 1′ | 1 | 2 | 3 | 4 | 5 | 6 | 7 | 8 | 9 | 10 | 11 | 12 | 13 | 14 |
5′ | 1 | | | 2 | | | 3 |

---

words

4. If necessary, determine the name and number of the person with whom you are speaking in the event a second call must be made. 305 316

5. Outline the major points of each call and have all needed reference material at hand before placing a call (Stout and Perkins, 1987, 91). 331 345

Telephone Procedures 353

Employees must know how to screen calls, transfer calls, and to place callers on hold properly if these calls are to be processed effectively. 367 382

Screening calls. Callers are screened by identifying who is calling and by asking the purpose of the call so the person answering the call can decide to process the call or transfer it to another person. 399 415 426

Transferring calls. Since having calls transferred can be an exasperating experience* for callers, the person transferring the call should be certain the caller is given the correct person on the first transfer. 444 459 473

Holding calls. Calls should be placed on hold only when necessary, for short periods of time, and in a courteous manner. If calls need to be put on hold for more than a minute or two, callers should be given the option of being called back (Oliverio and Pasework, 1988, 638). 489 505 520 531

535

*Repeated transfers may be exasperating because callers must explain the purpose of the call each time the call is transferred. 548 560

Learning cue: A single explanatory note in a report may be indicated by an asterisk with a matching asterisk preceding the note at the foot of the page.

If two or more explanatory notes occur in the report, matching superscript figures are used to number them.

Document 2
Reference Page
1. Reviewing formatting guides for references on p. 281 and the model on RG 8.
2. Format the references shown at the right for Document 1.

REFERENCES 2

Oliverio, Mary Ellen and William R. Pasewark. The Office: Procedures and Technology. Cincinnati: South-Western Publishing Co., 1988. 23 37

Stout, Vickie Johnson and Edward A. Perkins, Jr. Practical Management Communication. Cincinnati: South-Western Publishing Co., 1987. 55 71

Tilton, Rita Sloan, J. Howard Jackson, and Estelle L. Popham. Secretarial Procedures and Administration. 9th ed. Cincinnati: South-Western Publishing Co., 1987. 88 108 112

Document 3
Leftbound Report
1. Review the guides for leftbound reports on p. 281 and the leftbound models on RG 8.
2. If time permits, begin reformatting Document 1 as a leftbound report, substituting the copy at the right for ¶ 1. (Be sure to center the report heading over the line of writing.)

Spoken communication is powerful because through it images are created, emotions are affected, and listeners respond (Stout and Perkins, 1987, 82). It is important, therefore, that business people use the telephone correctly. 10 22 33 45

Document 10
Memorandum
plain sheet
This memo should go to **John C. Richardson;** I'll initial it.
Date: **February 8, 19--**

FYI ONLY

Conversation in the lunch room—

Did you read about the travel agency in La Jolla that closed because of a computer virus?

Do they know yet where the virus came from?

No, they're investigating their software vendors, former employees, and competitors—the virus, which "wiped out" the agency's data base, could have started with any of them.

Viruses are hard to track, aren't they?, because the virus code can be set to do its damage weeks—even months—in the future.

Exactly. Tracking is complicated by software swapping among users, which is all too common.

Besides rules for responsible use of computers, what can be done to protect Golden Gate?

Maybe...one of the new "vaccine" programs designed to locate and remove viruses.

Documents 11-13
Form Letters
LP pp. 185-189
Will you prepare these letters; I'll sign them. You'll find the addresses for Carlos, Kelley, and Vice in the February 3 telephone log. The variable information is shown on this note.

Document 11
V1 **$1,450**
V2 **Miss Carlos**

Document 12
V1 **$1,300**
V2 **Mr. Kelley**

Document 13
V1 **$1,350**
V2 **Mr. and Mrs. Vice**

Date: **February 9, 19--**

Your excellent promotion of the Rose Bowl Tour has resulted in a record accomplishment for GGTA. The table below compares last year's Football Pasadena tour with this year's Rose Bowl tour--and shows why I'm commending you.

	Football Pasadena	Rose Bowl Tour	Percent of Change
Students	90	126	40.0
Faculty and Staff	121	160	32.2
Berkeley Residents	42	46	9.5
Alumni Members	128	192	50.0
Other	26	16	(38.5)
Total	407	540	

A comparison of the two totals for the tours shows an increase of 133 participants (32.7 percent.) An increase is seen in all groups except the "Other" category. You increased the football tour number by one-third in just one year's time. Good work, John!

A detailed itinerary of your travel arrangements for April 1-8 is enclosed for your close review. Brochures describing our scheduled tours and optional tours plus tips on apropriate clothing for this climate are also enclosed. In addition, I have included several leaflets describing historical sites we will visit in New Zealand.

Your preregistration from for the New Zealand tour and check for (V1) was received today. You will be traveling to exciting New Zealand with a group of 75 people. I am delighted that I will be accompanying this tour group as its guide.

(V2), thank you for choosing GGTA; I look forward to serving you on you tour.

160a ▶ 5
Conditioning
Practice

each line twice SS
(slowly, then faster);
DS between 2-line
groups; if time permits,
rekey selected lines

alphabet 1 Alex passed the major keyboarding quiz when he got back from vacation.

fig/sym 2 Contract #41-23-76C (12/05/92) allowed 30% off on orders over $85,000.

long words 3 Reprographics and telecommunications are office administration topics.

speed 4 Their neighbor may fix the ivory dish and then keep it with the bowls.

| 1 | 2 | 3 | 4 | 5 | 6 | 7 | 8 | 9 | 10 | 11 | 12 | 13 | 14 |

160b ▶ 45 *Document*
Processing: Reports

Document 1
Leftbound Report with
Endnotes

1. Review formatting guides
for leftbound reports and endnotes on p. 281 and refer to
the leftbound models on RG 8.

2. Key the copy shown at the
right and on p. 285 in leftbound
report format; correct errors.

Note: The report copy contains 4 embedded (unmarked)
errors. Locate and correct them
as you key.

words

HEALTH SERVICES MANAGEMENT PROGRAM   7

This report gives information on opportunities in health services manage-   21
ment. It is expected that a proposal to have Heritage University develope   36
and offer a health services management curriculum at the undergraduate   50
level will be submitted within six months.   59

Employment Opportunities   69

Places of employment. People who are able to manage health services   87
are needed in a wide variety of work settings. The most common place   101
of employment for these individuals is hospitals, followed by the offices of   116
pyhsicians, dentists, and other health-related practioneers.[1]   129

Employment outlook. Careers in the health-care area are included in the   147
"Ten Best Careers for the '90's."[2] It is expected that the demand for health   163
services managers will be strong as the country's population ages and needs   178
increased health-care services. Also, demand for managers will increase as   193
the providers of health care become more oriented to the bottom line because   209
of competition.   212

Educational Opportunities   222

In 1984, about 100 colleges and unviersities offered bachelor's degree pro-   237
grams in health services administration. About 70 schools had pro-   250
grams leading to the master's degree in hospital or health services   264
administration. . . .[3]   269

Bachelor's degree programs. Health services managers are often re-   287
cruited from the college or university from which they were graduated.[4] In   302
larger hospitals, they are often recruited to fill assistant department head   318
positions. In smaller hospitals, they may be able to enter at the department-   333
head level.   336

Additional Information   345

The organizations listed below will be contacted to gather additional in-   359
formation about academic programs in health services management. These   374
organizations will be asked to recommend a curriculum design expert who   388
could assist in developing the courses in the major.   399

1. American College of Healthcare Executives, 840 North Lake Shore   412
Drive, Chicago, IL 60611.   418

2. Association of University Programs in Health Administration, 1911   432
Fort Meyer Drive, Suite 503, Arlington, VA 22209.   442

(continued, p. 285)

Document 8
Itinerary

plain sheet

Will you prepare this itinerary for a client, **CARL E. FILBECK**. Just refer to the itinerary for the dates of the trip and the destinations. Here's a model to follow.

ITINERARY FOR CARL E. FILBECK

February 24-26, 19--

Trip to Washington, D.C., and New York City

THURSDAY, FEBRUARY 24 (SAN FRANCISCO TO WASHINGTON, D.C.)

7:35 a.m.   Leave San Francisco International Airport on Nation-
            wide Flight 2533 (nonstop). Park automobile in long-
            term parking.

2:50 p.m.   Arrive Washington D.C. Take airport shuttle to Wash-
            ington City Inn, 299 North Circle Drive, Telephone:
            555-2111.

7:00 p.m.   Tickets to Washington Symphony. Take taxi to Wash-
            ington Concert Hall, 2991 H Avenue.

FRIDAY, FEBRUARY 25 (WASHINGTON, D.C. TO NEW YORK CITY)

8:00 a.m.   Washington City Tour with stops at Arlington National
            Cemetery, Washington Monument, and Lincoln, Jefferson,
            and Vietnam memorials.

2:25 p.m.   Leave Washington, D.C., on Eastrack--Train #788 for
            New York City.

5:05 p.m.   Arrive New York City. Take taxi to Grand Hotel, 232
            South Liberty Street. Telephone: 555-6961.

8:30 p.m.   Ticket to New York City Opera for the production of
            La Boheme.

SATURDAY, FEBRUARY 26 (NEW YORK CITY TO SAN FRANCISCO)

9:00 a.m.   Vintage Tour of Manhattan.

6:05 p.m.   Leave LaGuardia International Airport on Nationwide
            Flight 3222 (nonstop) to San Francisco.

7:20 p.m.   Arrive San Francisco International Airport.

THURSDAY, FEBRUARY 2~~3~~ 4 (SAN FRANCISCO TO WASHINGTON, D.C.)

7:~~2~~ 3 5 a.m.   Leave San Francisco International Airport ⌃on Nation-
                  wide Flight 2533 (nonstop). Park automobile in
                  long⌃-term parking.

2:50 ~~p~~ a.m.   Arrive Washington D.C. Take airport shuttle to
                  Washington City Inn, 299 North Circle Dr., Tele-
                  phone: 555-2111.   sp

7:00 p.m.   Tickets to ⌃Washington Symphony. Take taxi to Washington Con-
            cert Hall, 2991 H Avenue.

FRIDAY, FEBRUARY 25 (WASHINGTON, D.C. TO NEW YORK) City

8:00 a.m.   Washington City Tour with stops at Arlington Na-
            tional Cemetery, Washington Monument, Lincoln and
            Jefferson ~~Memorials~~⌃, and Vietnam Memorial⌃

2:25 p.m.   Leave Washington, D.C.,⌃ on Eastrack--Train #788 for
            New York City.

5:05 p.m.   Arrive New York City. Take taxi to Grand Hotel,
            232 South Liberty St. sp   Telephone: 555-6961

8:30
~~8:00~~ p.m.   Ticket to New York City Opera for the production
                of "La Boheme."

SATURDAY, FEBRUARY 26 (NEW YORK CITY TO SAN FRANCISCO)

9:00 a.m.   Vintage ~~Liberty~~ Tour of ~~New York City~~ Manhattan.

6:05 p.m.   Leave LaGuardia⌃ International Airport on Nationwide flight 3222
            (nonstop) to San Francisco.

7:20 p.m.   Arrive San Francisco International Airport.

Document 9
Letter Composition

plain sheet

Use these notes to draft a letter to

Coastal Airlines
2999 Southwood Drive
San Francisco, CA 94112-0933
I'd like to review your rough draft.

Date: February 8, 19--

1. Ask on behalf of our client, Ms. Alice B. Fulton, to have the price ($632.38) of her unused airline ticket (round-trip to Charleston, West Virginia) refunded to us.

2. Explain that the client's physician admitted her to a hospital on February 7, the day of her planned departure.

3. State that the airline ticket and a letter from the client's physician about her condition are enclosed.

words

3. National Health Council, Health Careers Programs, 70 West 40th   456
Street, New York, NY 10018.   462

4. American College of Health Care Administrators, P.O. Box 5890, 8120   476
Woodmont Avenue, Suite 200, Bethesda, MD 20814.   486

Document 2
Endnotes Page
Using the same margins as for p. 1 of report, format and key the endnotes on a separate page.

Document 3
Unbound Report with Endnotes
Begin reformatting Document 1 in unbound report format; correct errors you make as you key.

ENDNOTES   2

[1]U.S. Department of Labor, Bureau of Statistics, <u>Occupational Outlook</u>   20
<u>Handbook</u>, 1986-1987 ed. (Washington, D.C.: U.S. Government Printing Office,   37
April 1986), p. 29.   41

[2]John Stodden, "Ten Best Careers for the '90's," <u>Business Week Careers</u>,   59
1988 ed., p. 5.   63

[3]U.S. Department of Labor, Bureau of Statistics, p. 30.   74

[4]Myron D. Fottler, Robert Hernandez, and Charles Joiner, eds., <u>Strategic</u>   91
<u>Management of Human Resources in Health Services Organizations</u> (New   117
York: John Wiley & Sons, 1988), p. 256.   125

Lessons 161-162   *Reports with Footnotes*

161a-162a ▶ 5 *(daily)*
Conditioning Practice

each line twice SS (slowly, then faster); DS between 2-line groups; if time permits, rekey selected lines

alphabet	1	Seven quick scores and five extra points just amazed both weary girls.
figures	2	Call 375-4682, Extension 590, by 9 o'clock to set a 3:15 p.m. meeting.
LOCK	3	The YMCA will give away copies of PLAY TENNIS FOR FUN at today's game.
speed	4	The giant dirigible in the air is to land downtown by the island mall.

| 1 | 2 | 3 | 4 | 5 | 6 | 7 | 8 | 9 | 10 | 11 | 12 | 13 | 14 |

161b ▶ 15 *Review Footnote Formatting*

1. Review information on formatting footnotes on p. 281.

2. Using the copy shown at the right, determine the line on which to begin keying the last line of the report body to have at least a 1″ bottom margin below the last footnote.

3. Set a left margin of 1½″ and right margin of 1″.

4. Key the last line of report body, dividing line, and footnotes. Use a page line gauge from LP p. 8 or the line indicator on the screen to determine footnote placement.

words

marketability of B.A. degree holders in the marketplace.3   12

———————— DS   16

[1] S. Griffith, "Majors Lean to Business Track," *The New*   28
York Times, 12 April 1987, Education Life, p. 18. DS   40

[2] Ernest E. Boyer, <u>College: The Undergraduate Experience</u>   59
<u>in America</u> (New York: Harper & Row, 1987), p. 45. DS   72

[3] R. L. Jacobsen, "Group of Executives Wants to Make Lib-   83
eral Arts Part of the Preparation for Business Careers," <u>The</u>   96
<u>Chronicle of Higher Education</u>, 10 September 1985, p. 42.   113

Polynesian Cultural Center Dinner and Show

~~This tour includes~~ the play "Polynesia: Our Way of Life,"

a visit to four Polynesian villages, bountiful buffets, and is-

land music by live musicians. ~~Authentic~~ island handicrafts

await the tourists on this truly memorable side trip.

can be purchased at the numerous gift shops.

Pearl Harbor and U. S. S. Arizona Memorial

This historical ~~tour~~ excursion includes a guided tour of Pearl Har-

bor and the U.S.S. Arizona Memorial. Tourists will be able to board the U.S.S. Arizona Memorial

and pay tribute to the service men who were aboard ~~the U.S.S.~~

~~Arizona~~ during the bombing of Pearl Harbor.

Document 7
Table

plain sheet

I've developed this price list of optional side trips for the Baseball Hawaii Tour. I need the table for my meeting at 2 with the SHC Alumni Association officers. Oh, alphabetize the list please, and title it **OPTIONAL EXCURSIONS FOR BASEBALL HAWAII TOUR.**

Excursion	Price per Person
Sea Life Tour	$ 20.00
~~Big Island Luau~~	~~40.00~~
Oahu Cultural Dinner and Show	85.50
Catamaran dinner Sail	35.00
~~Polynesian Show + Dinner~~	~~75.00~~
Snorkeling / Beach Picnic	42.00
Diamond head Crater Tour	30.00
~~Roundtop Park Tour~~	~~25.00~~ 30.00
Nuuanu Valley Tour	~~25.00~~
National Memorial Cemetery Tour	15.00 20.00
Honolulu Whaling Museum	~~15.00~~
Pearl of the Pacific Tour	100.00
Waikiki Museum	12.50
Honolulu City Tour	20.00

Document Processing: Reports

Use leftbound format for the first four documents below and on p. 287; topbound for Document 5.

Document 1
Leftbound Report with Footnotes
1. Begin formatting the documents below and on p. 287. You will have two class periods to complete them.

2. There are 9 embedded (unmarked) errors in the report body. Find and correct them and any keying errors you may make as you key.

3. When you complete the first 4 documents, assemble them in proper order and then complete Document 5.

	words
LEADERSHIP SEMINAR PROGRESS REPORT	7

The development of the leadership seminars for supervisors and first-line managers are progressing on schedule. One seminar will be conducted at each of the 4 Indiana plant sights. The primary objective of the seminars is to have the participants understand the following: — 16, 25, 34, 44, 53, 62

1. The importance of having leaders at all levels of the corporation. — 71, 77

2. The definition of leadership and how leadership traits are developed for use within the corporation and the community. — 85, 94, 102

3. That various styles of leadership exist and that there is no one best leadership style. — 111, 120

Seminar Presenter — 127

Selection. Derme & Associates, Inc., a local consulting firm specializing in career enhancement seminars, has been selected to develop and conduct the four seminars. — 138, 147, 156, 163

Reason. One reason for selecting Derme & Associates is that they will develop the content of the seminars around Smith and Baker's definition of leadership,[1] which we want to emphasize with employees. — 172, 182, 191, 200, 204

Seminar Development — 212

We have had two meeting with representatives of Derme & Associates since the signing of the agreement two weeks ago. — 220, 229, 236

Meeting #1. This meeting was held so we could learn about the contnet of leadership seminars Derme & Associates has presented for other clients. — 246, 256, 264, 267

Meeting #2. The specific content for the four seminars was identified at this meeting. Also, it was decided to use the same content for each seminar except for the changes we suggest. — 278, 287, 297, 307

— 310

[1]Caroline Reynolds, Dimensions in Professional Development, 3d ed. (Cincinnati: South-Western Publishing Co., 1988), p. 278. — 322, 332, 340

These suggestions will be based on the feedback we get from the participants' evaluations at the end of each seminar. — 349, 359, 364

Seminar Dates — 369

The first seminar will be on October 15, at the Logansport Plant; the second will be at the Muncie Plant on October 22; the third meets at the Fort Wayne Plant on October 29; and the fourth will be at the Evansville Plant on November 5. The 85 employees who are to attend will be notified of the dates and times by the end of this week. Instructions will be given for arranging coverage during the attendees' absence. — 378, 387, 397, 405, 414, 422, 432, 441, 449, 453

Seminar Content — 459

The seminars will focus on leadership traits and styles that are applicable to most work and community environments. — 468, 478, 483

Traits. While all seven traits which Stout and Perkins[2] consider important will be included in the seminars, the following four will be targeted for development emphasis. — 493, 501, 511, 518

1. Understanding the feelings, problems, and needs of others. — 527, 531

2. Allowing others to particpate in decsisions that affect them. — 540, 544

3. Dealing with others in an objective, unemotional manner. — 553, 557

4. Adapting to a constantly changing environment. — 565, 567

Styles. Styles of leadership ranging from the autocratic to the democratic leader will be presented and then role-played in the seminars. It will be emphasized that there is no one best leadership style that all should use. Much — 577, 586, 595, 605, 615

— 618

[2]Vickie Johnson Stout and Edward A. Perkins, Jr., Practical Management Communication (Cincinnati: South-Western Publishing Co., 1987), p. 8. — 627, 643, 652, 653

(continued, p. 287)

Document 6
Report
plain sheet
This report describes the Baseball Hawaii Tour and is to be enclosed with the form letters you just completed.

BASEBALL HAWAII TOUR

College beautiful
Baseball, exciting travel, islands, and delicious food are all attractions of the Baseball Hawaii tour, the first tour of this type made available by Golden Gate Travel Agency. This tour is scheduled for May 12-16 in conjunction with the invitational baseball tour of the Sidney Hillman College baseball team in Hawaii. Baseball Hawaii includes round-trip airfare, hotel acommodations, a guided tours of Pearl Harbor/U.S.S. Arizona Memorial, and a dinner-show at the Polynesian Cultural Center. of course an added attractive on is 5 college baseball tickets to the SHC invitational games. Rates per person are $1,450.00 for single, $1,350.00 for double, and $1300.00 for triple.

Hotel Acommodations

The tour will begin in Honolulu on the island of Oahu. You will have delux e accommodations at the fabulous Hotel Waikiki for two nights. On the Big Island of Hawaii, you will be entertained at the Aloha Resort for two nights. The Kona Palace is the lodging place for the final night of this five-day tour.

Baseball Games

The top ranked SHC Warriors will play the third ranked Pacifica University Whales for two exciting action-packed games. To The highlight of the baseball activties in Honolulu will be a luau for the Baseball Hawaii Tour group.

The next two games will be played in Hilo, located on the Big Island of Hawaii. The grand final e game will be played on the spectacular Kona coast.

FYI ONLY

In Golden Gate Newsletter—Golden Gate has obtained rights to distribute three sports games in the Video Olympics series manufactured by Tronics, Inc. As promotional items, computer games named Front Four (football), Slam Dunk (basketball), and Ace It (tennis) will enable us to capitalize on the public's renewed interest in sports and leisure-time use of computers.

In these personal-use games, realistic sports action is made possible by high-level laser graphics.

(continued, p. 492)

words

of this material will be based on the work of 662
Manning and Curtis who concluded: 669

> There is no universally effective style of 678
> leading and following. Sometimes it is best 687
> for the leader to tell subordinates what to 695
> do; sometimes it is best for leaders and sub- 704
> ordinates to make decisions together; and 713

words

sometimes it is best for the subordinates to 722
direct themselves.[3] 726

  730

[3]George Manning and Kent Curtis, *Leader- 739
ship* (Cincinnati: South-Western Publishing Co., 749
1988), p. 56. 752

**Document 2
Bibliography**

1. Review formatting guides for preparing a bibliography on p. 281 and RG 9.

2. Format the references shown at the right as the bibliography for Document 1.

words

BIBLIOGRAPHY 3

Manning, George, and Kent Curtis. *Leadership*. Cincinnati: South-Western 20
    Publishing Co., 1988. 24

Ray, Charles, and Janet Palmer. *Office Automation: A Systems Approach*. 47
    Cincinnati: South-Western Publishing Co., 1987. 57

Reynolds, Caroline. *Dimensions in Professional Development*. 3d ed. 78
    Cincinnati: South-Western Publishing Co., 1987. 88

Stout, Vickie Johnson, and Edward A. Perkins, Jr. *Practical Management* 107
    Communication. Cincinnati: South-Western Publishing Co., 1987. 122

**Documents 3 and 4
Title Page and Table of Contents**

1. Review the formatting guides on p. 281 for preparing a title page and a table of contents.

2. Prepare a title page for Document 1; use your name, school, and today's date.

3. Prepare a table of contents for Document 1. Use side and ¶ headings as entries; insert leaders by alternating periods and spaces, noting whether the first period is on an odd or even space.

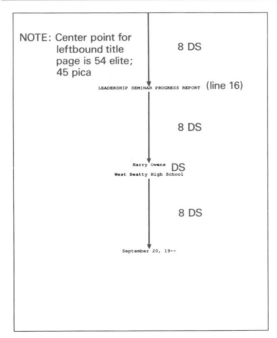

Leftbound title page

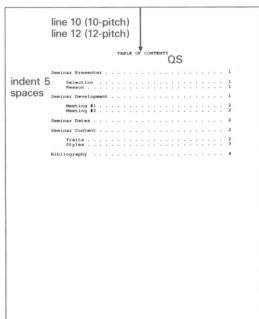

Leftbound table of contents

**Document 5
Topbound Report**

Topbound reports differ from unbound reports in only two ways: (1) the first item keyed on each page is 2 lines lower than for unbound reports; (2) page numbers are centered at the bottom of the page on line 62.

1. Reformat Documents 1-4 as a topbound report. Begin text on line 12, pica (10 pitch) line 14, elite (12 pitch).

2. On page 2, begin text on line 10, pica (10 pitch) line 10, elite (12 pitch).

3. Center page numbers on line 62 from top edge of the paper.

4. Begin title, bibliography, and contents pages 2 line spaces lower than for unbound reports to allow for binding.

Documents 2-5
Form Letters

LP pp. 177-183

I need to have this form letter processed for my signature. Send the form letter to the four clients who called about the Baseball Hawaii Tour. Their names and addresses are listed on the Telephone Log for February 3.

Date: **February 5, 19--**

FYI ONLY

Announcement at company meeting—

Golden Gate will install a videotex system. The system will involve a data base of airline schedules, hotel information, our special tours, and so on.

Customers who buy the service can make travel arrangements from home or office using their personal computers. It'll be interactive—like an automated teller machine, an ATM.

The system will be available first to on-campus users; we intend to have it in place by late next year. But the middle of the following year, we'll extend the service throughout the city.

We expect the system to increase volume by roughly 20%.

The Golden Gate Travel Agency is proud to announce the Baseball Hawaii Tour for the Sidney Hillman College baseball team, students, facutly, and alumni. This unique tour is scheduled for May 12-16. It features five exciting SHC baseball games to be played on two beautiful islands.

The five-day tour will start in Honolulu at the magnificent Hotel Waikiki. For 2 days you can enjoy Waikiki beach, sight-seeing, shopping, and 2 baseball games at Pacifica University. After the last ballgame, you will then fly to Hilo, located on the big island of Hawaii. There you will be staying at the beautiful Aloha Resort, known for its gracious hospitality and delicious food. Two baseball games and a delectable luau are planned just for the Baseball Hawaii tour are special highlights.

No ¶ The final stop of the tour is Kona Coast and the Kona Palace. Waterfalls, grand architecture, famous Hawaiian restaurants and the last baseball game awaits you. ¶ Join the baseball team, faculty, students, and alumni for a spring break never too be forgotten. Please read it carefully, share it with friends and family, and then sign up today. Simply call (916) 555-1238 and begin your plans planning for a spring break filled with relaxation, enchanting scenery, and SHC baseball.

A detailed description of the Baseball Hawaii Tour is enclosed.

Learning Goals

1. To assess and reinforce knowledge of table format.

2. To improve ability to process tables.

3. To improve language-skill competency.

Format Guides

1. Paper guide at *0* (for typewriters).

2. LL: 70 spaces or as directed.

3. LS: SS word and drill lines; or as directed within an activity; space tables as directed.

4. CS: (columnar spacing) as directed.

FORMATTING GUIDES: TABLES

Full sheet

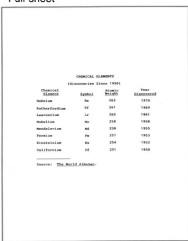

Half sheet, long edge at top

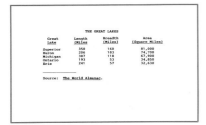

Half sheet, short edge at top

To format tables, you must know how to center vertically and horizontally.

Vertical Centering (top to bottom)

Tables are keyed on sheets so that the top and bottom margins are approximately equal. Approximately half of the lines of the table are placed above vertical center and approximately half are placed below the vertical center.

To determine the line on which to key the main heading, take the following steps:

1. Count the total lines needed in the table, including internal blank line spaces.

2. Subtract the total lines needed from lines available (66 for full sheet; 33 for half sheet, long edge at top; 51 for half sheet, short edge at top).

3. Divide the remainder by 2 to determine the number of the line on which to start. If a fraction results, disregard it. If an even number results, space down that number of lines from the top edge of the paper. If the number is odd, use the next lower number.

By dropping fractions and using even numbers, tables are placed a line or two above the exact center--in what is called "reading position."

Horizontal Centering (side to side)

Tables should be placed horizontally so that an equal number of blank spaces appears in the left and right margins. Half the number of characters and spaces in the lines of the table should be to the left of the horizontal center point of the paper, and half should be to the right of the horizontal center point.

Spacing between columns of tables varies, depending upon the number of columns to be centered. For ease of centering, leave an even number of spaces between columns. Use these steps to center horizontally:

1. Clear all margin and tab stops.

2. To find exact horizontal center, add the typewriter or format scale reading at the left and right edges of the paper and divide the total by 2.

3. Backspace from center point once for every 2 strokes in the longest item of each column, whether the longest item is a column heading or column entry. Carry over to the next column any extra stroke at the end of a column but ignore any extra stroke at the end of the last column. Then backspace once for every 2 spaces between columns. Set left margin stop.

4. Space forward once for each stroke in the longest item in the first column plus once for each space between Columns 1 and 2. Set a tab stop at this point for Column 2; continue the procedure for the remaining columns.

Centering Column Headings

Take the following steps to center column headings over their respective columns.

Note: When backspacing or spacing forward in the following procedures, do not backspace or space forward for any odd or leftover stroke at the end of any column entry or column heading.

When Column Heading is Shorter than Longest Column Entry

1. Determine the center point of the column by spacing forward once for every 2 characters and spaces in the longest column entry.

2. From the center point of the longest entry, backspace once for every 2 characters and spaces in the column heading.

3. Begin keying the column heading where the backspacing stops.

When Column Heading is Longer than Any Column Entry

1. Determine the center point of the column heading by spacing forward once for every 2 characters and spaces in the column heading.

2. From the center point of the column heading, backspace once for every 2 characters and spaces in the longest column entry.

3. The longest column entry should begin where the backspacing ends. Reset tab stop at this or other appropriate point to key the column entries.

292a-296a ▶ 5 (daily)
Equipment Check
each line twice SS; DS
between 2-line groups

alphabet	1	Tim quarreled with the angry zookeeper about the five jackal exhibits.
figures	2	On May 27, 1991, she reported 3,468 professional and 150 life members.
fig/sym	3	Wails & Simms offered 37,850 shares of common stock at $14.62 (up 9%).
speed	4	Jane is to pay a neighbor at the lake to fix their auto and a bicycle.

| 1 | 2 | 3 | 4 | 5 | 6 | 7 | 8 | 9 | 10 | 11 | 12 | 13 | 14 |

292b-296b ▶ 45 (daily)
Document Processing

Key as many of the following documents as you can during each daily session. Watch for unmarked errors in source documents. Proofread and correct each document before you remove it from the machine or print a copy.

Document 1
Table

plain sheet

Use my telephone log to compile an alphabetical list of clients interested in the New Zealand tour. Use the information on this sheet.

Main heading:
PROSPECTS FOR NEW ZEALAND TOUR
Secondary heading:
Date of the telephone log
Column heads:
Name Address Telephone

TELEPHONE LOG FOR February 3, 19--

NAME	ADDRESS	TELEPHONE	INQUIRY
Miss Maria R. Carlos	200 Jackson St. Oakland, CA 94607-0101	361-9661	New Zealand
Dr. Miriam J. Harrison	2604 College Ave. Berkeley, CA 94704-1374	236-9830	Baseball Hawaii
Mr. & Mrs. Joseph F. Vice	5 Panoramic Way Berkeley, CA 94704-6016	236-1100	New Zealand
Ms. J. Tracy Kavanagh	106 Eton Ave. Berkeley, CA 94705-1696	231-7661	New Zealand
Mr. & Mrs. Lance D. Abbott	1907 Bonita Ave. Berkeley, CA 94704-1562	235-2698	Baseball Hawaii
Miss Amber C. Kent	P. O. Box 615 Berkeley, CA 94701-0615	469-0168	New Zealand
Mr. Iyabode O. Adamou	605 Peralta Ave. Berkeley, CA 94707-2277	235-3361	Baseball Hawaii
Dr. & Mrs. W. S. Duff	3165 Telegraph Ave. Berkeley, CA 94705-3626	246-9987	Baseball Hawaii
Mr. Tom C. Kelly	P. O. Box 1096 University, CA 94707-1096	259-8163	New Zealand

163a ▶ 5
Conditioning
Practice

each line twice SS
(slowly, then faster);
DS between 2-line
groups; if time per-
mits, rekey line 3

alphabet	1	This bright jacket has an amazing weave and is of exceptional quality.
figures	2	Flight 679 will leave on Runway 28 at 10:45 p.m. with 13 crew members.
shift key	3	Mary Smith, Robert Kwon, and F. T. Pax work for MacDougal & O'Connell.
speed	4	Iris held half the land for the endowment for the ancient city chapel.

| 1 | 2 | 3 | 4 | 5 | 6 | 7 | 8 | 9 | 10 | 11 | 12 | 13 | 14 |

163b ▶ 15 Processing Tables:
Blocked Column Headings

Table 1
Format on full sheet; DS data; CS:
8; block column headings; correct
errors.

Table 2
Reformat Table 1 on half sheet,
long edge at top; SS data; CS: 6;
block column headings; correct
errors.

Learning cue: Key $ beside the
first number in column (and
with total figure in column, if
used) in a position so it is one
space to the left of the largest
number in the column.

words

BUSINESS EDUCATION BUDGET	5
Fiscal Year Starting June 1, 19--	12

Account Name	Budget	
Dues and Subscriptions	$ 225	26
Supplies General	975	32
Instructional Equipment	24,637	36
Instruction_al_ Supplies	2,_6_450	43
Other Services	1,895	48
Faculty Salaries	110,139	53

(Account Name / Budget line = 20)

163c ▶ 5 Formatting
Column Headings

1. Review centering of column
headings in formatting guides on
p. 288.
2. Center the column headings
and entries at the right by the

longest line, whether heading or
entry. Key the headings on line 12
on a half sheet of paper, long
edge at top; CS: 6; DS data; do
not correct errors.

Model Number	Capacity	Cost
625.348	Low	$347.99
625.3481	Medium	374.65
625.34811	High	396.44

163d ▶ 20 Processing Tables:
Centered Column Headings

Table 1
Format on full sheet; DS data; CS:
6; correct errors.

Table 2
Reformat Table 1 on half sheet,
long edge at top; SS data; CS: 8;
arrange column entries in alphabetical order by subject; do not
correct errors.

ANN MAY'S SUBJECT SCHEDULE			5
Subject	Period	Room	13
Business Dynamics	1	East-118	19
World History	2	South-135	24
Algebra	3	West-126	28
English Composition	4	North-109	34
Physical Education	5	North-Gym	40
Document Processing II	6	East-114	47
Science and Technology	7	West-129	54

Production Goals

1. To process a variety of documents from various kinds of source copy.
2. To compose a business letter.
3. To use information from several sources in processing documents.
4. To reinforce proofreading and language skills.

Documents Processed

1. Tables
2. Form letters
3. Report
4. Itinerary
5. Letter
6. Memorandum

GOLDEN GATE TRAVEL, INC.

Before you begin the work of this simulation, read the material and study the format guides at the right.

This simulation contains information not directly related to your job. Read—but do not key—copy under the FYI (For Your Information) ONLY heading.

FYI ONLY

A coworker, Ann, tells you that soon she will work at home. Golden Gate will install equipment so that she can send work into the office electronically.

Ann decided to work at home when her elderly mother became ill. Now she will be able to work for Golden Gate while attending to her mother.

Telecommuting, Ann explained, is what these work-at-home arrangements are called. "Would you like 'going to work' by turning on your personal computer at home?"

Work Assignment

You have notified Cal-Temp that you will assume a full-time position in two weeks. Your final temporary assignment is at Golden Gate Travel, Inc., a travel agency that caters to college students, professors, and other campus personnel. The agency is located in Berkeley at 2144 Shattuck Avenue.

Mrs. Linda T. Mitchell manages the agency, and she will originate most of the documents you process. Mr. John C. Richardson, one of the seven travel agents, will also ask you to prepare a document. Usually Mrs. Mitchell and Mr. Richardson will talk with you rather than write directions for you to follow. (Linda Mitchell's words are printed in blue; John Richardson's, in red.)

Mrs. Mitchell has developed communication guidelines that include rules for composing letters and for formatting various documents. Use your previously acquired knowledge when you're not given specific instructions. Review these communication guidelines now and refer to them as needed during your time at Golden Gate Travel.

Rules for Composing Letters

1. Make letters short, uncomplicated. If two or three sentences are enough to make your point, don't write more.

2. Plan each letter--no matter how short--before you draft it. Decide the steps (inform, explain, ask, apologize, etc.) to be taken in the letter and the order of the steps.

3. Include the C qualities: Make the letter courteous (express goodwill), considerate (show respect for reader), clear (state exact meaning), concise (omit unnecessary words), concrete (refer to specific things and actions), complete (say whatever is needed to fulfill purpose of the letter), and correct (accurate in content, language, and format).

4. Edit and revise. Add, delete, or move sentences and paragraphs in a draft as needed. Proofread for errors in grammar, punctuation, capitalization, number expression, spelling, and keystroking; and check for errors in format. Use standard proofreader's marks.

Format Guides

Letters. Block format, open punctuation; agency letterhead; standard complimentary closing--**Sincerely**. Sender's name and title on one or two lines depending upon length:

Sincerely

Linda T. Mitchell, Manager

Sincerely

John C. Richardson
Travel Agent

Memos. Simplified format; titles omitted following recipient's and sender's names; plain full-size sheets.

Tables. Center vertically (DS) and horizontally (CS: 6-10) on plain full-size sheets. Column headings are centered over columns. Two-line entries are keyed SS, with a DS between entries. Within letters, memos, or reports, DS above/below table and SS the items; center between side margins of the document.

Reports and Other Documents. Unbound format; page number at upper-right margin, except on page 1 (not numbered); plain full-size sheets.

163e ▶ 5 Improve Language Skills: Word Choice

1. Study the spelling and definitions of each pair of words.

2. Key the **Learn** line with the number and period, noting the proper use of the often confused words.

3. Key the **Apply** line with the number and period, choosing the words that complete the sentence correctly.

canvas (n) a heavy, coarse, tightly woven fabric	**cereal** (n) an edible grain, such as wheat, corn, or oats
canvass (vb) to conduct a survey on a given topic; to poll	**serial** (adj) of, forming, or arranged in a series

Learn   1. The man waiting near the canvas awning was to canvass all walkers.

Apply   2. I will (canvas/canvass) all designers on the use of (canvas/canvass) as a wall covering.

Learn   3. Serial numbers are assigned to farmers who grow grain for cereal.

Apply   4. Each box of (cereal/serial) had a different (cereal/serial) number.

Lesson 164   Tables

164a ▶ 5 Conditioning Practice

each line twice SS (slowly, then faster); DS between 2-line groups; if time permits, rekey line 3

alphabet   1   Gwen moved quickly to pack the extra dozen lanyards Freda just bought.

figures   2   The library has 95,468 books, 1,209 periodicals, and 3,735 references.

3d row   3   Porter worked quietly to prepare to fire the pretty pottery for Terry.

speed   4   When the auditor works in the city, he is to handle their big problem.

| 1 | 2 | 3 | 4 | 5 | 6 | 7 | 8 | 9 | 10 | 11 | 12 | 13 | 14 |

164b ▶ 40 Processing Tables: Various Paper Sizes (Centered Column Heads)

Table 1

Format on full sheet; DS data; CS: 10; correct errors.

Table 2

Reformat Table 1 on half sheet, long edge at top; SS data; CS: 6; do not correct errors.

Table 3

Format on full sheet; DS data; CS: 12; correct errors.

Learning cue: Add the line-of-writing scale readings at the left and right edges of the paper and divide the sum by 2 to determine the center point.

Table 4

Reformat Table 3 on half sheet, short edge at top; DS data; CS: 4; do not correct errors.

Learning cue: The line of underscores indicating total should be as long as the longest item in the column.

words

PRINCIPAL RIVERS OF THE WORLD   6

River	Continent	Kilometers	
			16
Nile	Africa	6,680	20
Amazon	South America	6,400	25
Yangtze	Asia	5,800	29
Hwang	Asia	4,873	32
Zaire	Africa	4,700	36
Amur	Asia	4,500	39
			43
Source: Collier's Encyclopedia.			54

MARY MORRIS' TEACHING ASSIGNMENT   7

(Fall 19-- Semester)   11

Course	Credits	Enrollment	
			21
Accounting I	1	28	24
Business Law	.5	24	28
Computer Applications	.5	20	34
Document Processing I	1	32	39
Document Processing I	1	29	44
Study Hall	---	45	49
Totals	4	178	52

Document 13
Statement of Change in Financial Condition
plain sheet
This statement of change in financial condition is for **OLYMPIC MUSEUM** and covers the fiscal year ended December 31, 19-- (*previous year*).

Sources of working capital:

Excess of support and revenue before capital additions	$ 12,500	
Capital additions	67,200	
Excess of support and revenue after capital additions		$ 79,700
Depreciation		45,800
Deferred revenue and restricted gifts received in excess of expenses incurred		220,600
Investments sold		835,900
		$1,182,000

Uses of working capital:

Fixed assets purchased	$ 98,700	
Investments purchased	901,400	
		1,000,100
Increase in working capital		$ 181,900

Changes in working capital:

Cash	($ (2,750)	
Receivables	10,300	
Investments	480	
Inventories	139,700	
Prepayments	10,600	
Accts. Pay. & Accrued Expenses	(3,500)	
Deferred revenue and restricted gifts, current portion	27,070	
		$ 181,900

FYI ONLY

Bulletin

Attorneys at Bayview Legal Services say that the number of software piracy cases has increased 12% in the past year. They are reminding their business clients of these ethical facts about software copies:

1. One backup copy only is allowed.
2. More than one copy violates copyright law, and more vendors than ever before are prosecuting violators.
3. Most vendors now offer a multiple-copy discount or site license to reduce piracy.

Needless to say, these laws apply to *What If, Formatics,* and other popular software used here.

K.C.

Document 14
Collection Form Letter
plain sheet
Prepare this collection letter to be added to the series in the office procedures manual. Identification: **Stage 4 Ultimatum.**

¶ A copy of your account is enclosed. Your cooperation is required to settle the long-overdue balance. Please notify me within 10 days of the date of this letter, telling me of your plan for payment. ¶ If we do not receive payment or a response from you within 10 days, we will have to assume that you do not intend to settle the account voluntarily. In that case, we will be forced to use other means of collecting the amount due.

164c ▶ 5 Improve Language Skills: Word Choice

1. Study the spelling and definitions of each pair of words.

2. Key the **Learn** line with the number and period, noting the proper use of the often confused words.

3. Key the **Apply** line, choosing the words that complete each sentence correctly.

confidant (n) one to whom secrets are confided

confident (adj) having assurance or certainty, as of success

envelop (vb) to surround; encircle

envelope (n) a flat, folded paper container for a letter

Learn 1. Ada is confident that her confidant will protect the mission's goals.
Apply 2. The (confidant/confident) is not (confidant/confident) in his ability.

Learn 3. The wrapper was placed so it would envelop the stack of envelopes.
Apply 4. Jim's large hand could (envelop/envelope) the small (envelop/envelope).

Lesson 165 | Tables

165a ▶ 5 Conditioning Practice

each line twice SS (slowly, then faster); DS between 2-line groups; if time permits, rekey line 3

alphabet 1 Zeb checked the liquid oxygen just before moving down the sizable pad.

figures 2 Deb's new stock fell 4.50 points to 86.75 on Tuesday, August 31, 1992.

long words 3 An electronic time sheet can be used in project-oriented environments.

speed 4 The visitor also saw six big turkeys in the field by the lake at dusk.

| 1 | 2 | 3 | 4 | 5 | 6 | 7 | 8 | 9 | 10 | 11 | 12 | 13 | 14 |

165b ▶ 5 Reinforce Formatting of Multiple-Line Column Headings

1. Multiple-line column headings are SS and the last line of each heading should be keyed on the same horizontal line.

2. Center the multiple-line column headings by longest item, whether it is one of the column-heading lines or column-entry lines. Key the first line of the headings on line 12 on a half sheet of paper, short edge on top; SS data; CS: 6; do not correct errors.

Distribution Center	Center Manager	Quota Last Year
East	Mary McKaiser	125,000
South	Tom Ridgewood	97,000

165c ▶ 40 Processing Tables

Table 1

Format on full sheet; DS data; CS: 8; center headings; correct errors.

Table 2

Reformat Table 1 on half sheet, long edge at top; SS data; CS: 6; center headings; correct errors; arrange lakes in order of size, listing the one with the largest area first, the second-largest area second, etc.

Table 3 and Table 4 are on p. 292.

words

THE GREAT LAKES				words
Great Lake	Length (miles)	Breadth (miles)	Area (Square Miles)	3 / 8 / 22
Erie	241	57	32,630	26
Huron	206	183	74,700	30
Michigan	307	118	67,900	35
Ontario	193	53	34,850	39
Superior	350	160	81,000	44
				48
Source: The World Almanac.				55

Document 10
Memorandum

plain sheet

Date this memo **January 20, 19--** and send it to **Randall Collins, Chair; Roberta Osborne; and Eugenia Rodriguez. Karl Coppersmith** will initial it. Use **Mission Statement of Our Firm** as the subject.

We are
~~Our firm is~~ in the process of preparing an Employees' Handbook. You have been assigned to the committee responsible for ~~devel-oping~~ writing the philosophy or mission statement of our firm. I have asked Randall to chair this ~~sessions~~ committee, and he will ~~inform you of~~ call the first meeting.

Listed below are some topics that I ~~feel~~ *believe* should be ~~included~~ addressed in our philosophy. Please do not feel that you must confine your thinking to this list. 1. Concern for the general public interest 2. Concern for the financial well-being of ~~all~~ our clients 3. Reinvestment of profits in the training and advancement of partners and ~~other~~ staff 4. Growth plans 5. Development of specialties such as auditing governmental units or concentration in ~~particular~~ certain fields 6. Extent of autonomy for partners

As the publication *date* for the handbook is early April, may I please have your report by March 1. xx

---

Document 11
Proposal Resume

plain sheet

When accounting firms submit bids for jobs, resumes of the key staff members who may be involved are included with each bid. Prepare the proposal resume at the right.

Document 12
Engagement Letter

LP p. 175

Prepare an engagement letter (refer to Document 6) for **Mr. Coppersmith** to sign. Here is the information you will need.

V1 **January 21, 19--**
V2 **Mr. Umeki Yoshino**
   183 Stoneyford Drive
   Daly City, CA 94015-2264
V3 **Mr. Yoshino**
V4 **January 17, 19--**
V5 *(Insert previous year)*
V7 **Umeki Yoshino**

EUGENIA RODRIGUEZ, CPA

Certification   <u>Certified Public Accountant</u>, licensed, state of California. Member: (CA) Society of CPAs.

Experience   <u>Bouchard & Roberson</u>, Oakland, California.

1990-1991 -- Senior <u>a</u>ccountant

1987-1989 -- Staff <u>a</u>ccountant

Prepared ~~annual tax~~ *financial* statements and federal and state *tax* returns for individuals and small businesses. planned, coordinated, and ~~conducted~~ *stet* certified audits.

EDUCATION   B.S. in Business Administration, San Mateo University, 1987. *with high honors,* M.B.A., Oakland University, 1989.

COMMUNITY
SERVICE   (Pres.), ~~The~~ Business and Professional Woman's Club, 1990-1991, Oakland.

165c (continued)

Table 3

Format on full sheet; DS data; CS: 6; center headings; correct errors.

Learning cue: To indicate a total, underline the last entry the full length of the total figure; DS; key the total figure.

THIRD QUARTER ANALYSIS				
Department	Cost of Goods Sold	Operating Expenses	Operating Profits	
Hardware	$ 3,758	$ 2,753	$ 1,655	33
Lawn & Garden	5,785	4,595	1,858	39
Toys	2,987	1,758	1,369	44
Clothing	15,878	6,549	7,337	50
Appliances	7,650	2,876	4,735	60
Totals	$36,058	$18,531	$16,954	68

THIRD QUARTER ANALYSIS — 5; 10; 25

Table 4

Format on full sheet; DS data; CS: 6; center headings; correct errors.

CHEMICAL ELEMENTS			
(Discoveries Since 1950)			
Chemical Element	Symbol	Atomic Weight	Year Discovered
Hahnium	Ha	262	1970
Rutherfordium	Rf	261	1969
Lawrencium	Lr	260	1961
Nobelium	No	258	1958
Mendelevium	Md	258	1955
Fermium	Fm	257	1953
Einsteinium	Es	254	1952
Californium	Cf	251	1950

CHEMICAL ELEMENTS — 4; 9; 13; 21; Hahnium 25; Rutherfordium 30; Lawrencium 35; Nobelium 39; Mendelevium 44; Fermium 48; Einsteinium 53; Californium 58; 61

Source: The World Almanac.   70

Lesson 166 — Sustained Document Processing: Tables

166a ▶ 5
Conditioning Practice

each line twice SS (slowly, then faster); DS between 2-line groups; if time permits, rekey line 3

alphabet	1	Visitors did enjoy the amazing water tricks of six quaint polar bears.
figures	2	Bea Day flew 3,580 miles in January, 1992 and 4,976 in December, 1991.
symbols	3	I used the search/locate key to find each @, #, &, and * in my report.
speed	4	Lena is proficient when she roams right field with such vigor and pep.

| 1 | 2 | 3 | 4 | 5 | 6 | 7 | 8 | 9 | 10 | 11 | 12 | 13 | 14 |

166b ▶ 45 Sustained Table Processing

format/key each table as directed; proofread; correct errors

Time Schedule

Plan and Prepare.................. 5′
Timed Production.................. 35′
Proofread/Compute *n-pram*..... 5′

1. Make a list of the tables to be processed:

p. 289, 163d, Table 1
p. 290, 164b, Table 1
p. 290, 164b, Table 3
p. 291, 165c, Table 1
p. 292, 165c, Table 3

2. Arrange paper and correction materials for efficient handling.

3. At the signal to begin, process as many tables as you can in 35′. Correct errors as you key. Proofread each table before removing it from machine.

4. Determine *n-pram;* turn in tables in the order given in Step 1.

287b–291b (continued)

**Document 8
News Release**

plain sheet

Prepare the news item at the right for immediate release. Suggest this title: **RODRIGUEZ JOINS REGENCY AGENCY.** Give **Mr. Coppersmith**'s name and telephone number (**213-555-6879**) as the contact.

Daly City, January 19, 19--. Regency Acctg. Services, Inc., is pleased to announce that Ms. Eugenia Rodriguez, CPA, has recently joined the agency. Ms. Rodriguez received her bachelor's degree in business administration from San Mateo Univ. and her master's degree from Oakland Univ. She passed the CPA exam in May. For the past 3 years Ms. Rodriguez has been associated with Bouchard & Roberson in Oakland where she specialized in tax services for small businesses and for individuals.

Regency Acctg. Services, Inc., Currently has a staff of 12 employees, including 2 CPAs. The agency's offices are located at 400 Serramonte Blvd. in Daly City. # # # center

---

**Document 9
Balance Sheet**

plain sheet

Key the balance sheet for **Robert and Kathy Pearson** for the period ending **December 31, 19--.** Add leaders.

Assets

Cash	DS	$ 3,500
Bonus Receivable		10,000
Stock Options		4,646
Cash Value of life insurance		55,500
Residence		83,000
Personal Effects		45,000
Total Assets		$151,554 (66)

Liabilities

Income Taxes--Current Yr. Bal.	DS	$ 4,400
Mortgage Payable		44,000
Total liabilities		$ 48,400 (52,136)

Net Worth

Robt. & Kathy Pearson, Net Worth	DS	103,264 (99,528)
Total Liabilities And Net Worth		$151,664
Car Loan Payable		2,910
Credit Card Bal.		826

Madison GOLD Baseball Club
(An Office Simulation)

Performance Goals

To demonstrate your ability to integrate the knowledge and skills reviewed and acquired in Phase 7.

1. Processing letters, reports, and tables.

2. Detecting language-skills and keyboarding errors.

3. Making decisions in appropriate situations.

Documents Processed

1. Letters/Simplified Memorandum

2. Tables

3. Report with Explanatory Notes

4. Report with Internal Citations

5. Reference Page, Title Page, and Table of Contents

MADISON GOLD BASEBALL CLUB: AN OFFICE SIMULATION

Unit 39 (Lessons 167-171) is designed to give you the kinds of experiences you are likely to have when you are working in an office. Assume you are enrolled in a second-year document processing course at your high school and have been doing general office work for Madison GOLD Baseball Club (the official corporate name) as a participant in your school's cooperative education program. Madison GOLD is a minor league baseball team in Madison, Tennessee. You have been answering the telephone, filing, photocopying, and processing routine letters, reports, and tables for various people since you started your co-op education assignment.

Miss Mary L. Ross (the full-time secretary assigned to Ms. Susan M. Demmet, Director, Promotions and Marketing) is scheduled for vacation this coming week, and you have been asked to do Miss Ross's work while she is away. Ms. Demmet is glad to have you because her colleagues have spoken highly of the quality of your work and your work ethic and habits. You are eager to have this assignment because it could lead to a full-time position when you are graduated, if you show that you can perform well.

Since this is the off-season for baseball, most of the activities in the Promotions and Marketing area focus on promoting next year's team and schedule.

Specific promotional activities include such things as having members of Madison GOLD Baseball Club remain active in the communities from which the Club draws its fans; developing marketing strategies; planning specific promotions for the up-coming season and planning various other activities designed to enhance the image of the baseball team so attendance can be increased in the coming season.

You are familiar with the general office policies, procedures, and routines used by the Club. To help you learn the specific preferences of Susan Demmet, her secretary left you these directions and tips. Follow the guidelines below. If a formatting guide is not given, use your previously acquired knowledge to decide the format features for a document.

Correspondence

1. Prepare all letters in block format with open punctuation; supply an appropriate salutation and complimentary close (if you cannot determine the appropriate title for a woman, use Ms.); use your reference initials; supply enclosure and copy notations as needed.

2. Prepare memorandums in simplified style with appropriate margins and vertical line spacing.

Tables

1. Center all tables horizontally and vertically on full sheets.

2. Determine the number of spaces to leave between columns and whether items within a column should be single- or double-spaced.

3. Center all headings.

Reports

1. Reports should be formatted as unbound.

2. Cited works should be formatted as internal citations with references.

Other

1. Be particularly alert to correct errors in punctuation, capitalization, spelling, word usage, and consistency (for example, "GOLD" appears in all caps when referring to the baseball team).

2. Susan Demmet always uses the title "Ms." before her name and her position title in the letters she sends. Also, she insists that you use the personal titles of the people to whom she sends letters.

Document 5
Balance Sheet
plain sheet
Key this balance sheet; add leaders. Use these headings:
MARY'S COUNTRY CRAFTS
Balance Sheet
December 31, 19--

Assets
DS

Cash — $16,735

Accts. Receivable — 753

Mdse. on hand — 3,243

Total Assets — $20,731

Liabilities
DS

Accts. Payable — $417

Utilities — 190

Wages Payable — 625

Total Liabilities — $1,232

Owner's Equity
DS

Mary Castleton, Capital — 19,499

Total Liabilities and Owner's Equity — $20,731

Document 6
Engagement Letter
plain sheet
Key the engagement letter at right for inclusion in the Office Procedures Manual. The identification of this form letter is **Engagement Letter for Representing Client Before the IRS.**
Key **V1, V2,** etc., to show where variable information will be inserted.

Format the closing lines, including an "approval" line and date line according to the document format guides in the Manual. (You will use Document 6 to prepare Documents 7 and 12.)

Document 7
Engagement Letter
LP p. 173
Prepare an engagement letter (Document 6) for **Mr. Coppersmith**'s signature. Use the following information.
V1 **January 17, 19--**
V2 **Mr. and Mrs. Robert Pearson**
    One Park Manor Drive
    Daly City, CA 94015-2265
V3 **Mr. and Mrs. Pearson**
V4 **January 16, 19--**
V5 (*Insert previous year*)
V7 **Robert Pearson**
    Kathy Pearson
    Include two approval lines and two date lines; DS between the two sets of lines.

This letter summarizes our discussion of (V4), concerning the terms of our engagement. If the letter does not accurately reflect your understanding of ~~them~~ these terms, call us for clarification. ~~of the terms.~~

We will represent you before the Internal Revenue Service and exert our best efforts to obtain a ~~settlement~~ satisfactory settlement of any issues that may arise in the examination of your (V5) income tax return. We will not audit or otherwise ~~verify~~ attempt to verify the information you have submitted, although we may ask ~~you~~ for clarification or further details on some matters.

Our fee, charged at standard billing rates for tax work plus out-of-pocket expenses, will be based upon the amount of time required for our services. A copy of our current fees ~~issue~~ and billing policies ~~are~~ is enclosed.

If this ~~agreement~~ letter accurately sets forth your / (and date) understanding of the engagement, ~~sign below~~ please sign below in the spaces provided and return ~~it~~ the letter to us. Retain a copy for your files.

167a-171a ▶ 5 (daily)
Conditioning Practice

each line twice SS (slowly, then faster); DS between 2-line groups; if time permits, rekey selected lines

alphabet	1	Jun quickly wrapped the five dozen big macaroons and the six cupcakes.
fig/sym	2	Ben sold 132 at $34 less 15%; 98 at $87 less 20%; & 56 at $76 less 8%.
shift key	3	RLS is pushing Part #196-74 for their PC's named QuikNet and QuikWork.
speed	4	The giant icicle did melt in the big right hand of the ensign on duty.

| 1 | 2 | 3 | 4 | 5 | 6 | 7 | 8 | 9 | 10 | 11 | 12 | 13 | 14 |

167b-171b ▶ 45 (daily)
Simulation:
Madison GOLD

Study the information on p. 293 before starting the simulation and refer to it as needed throughout the processing of the jobs in this unit. Correct any errors you make.

While Miss Ross is on vacation, Ms. Demmet will give you instructions for the following jobs.

Job 1
Letters
LP pp. 21-25

Message from
SUSAN DEMMET

Mary Ross was unable to send letters to the three people named on the cards clipped to the bottom of the letter at the right.

Use the letter at the right and the information on the cards to prepare a letter for each person. Use January 5 for the date; insert the appropriate ad size in the body of the letter.

SD

Madison GOLD is pleased to report that sales of its program book, GOLD Program, have increased in each of the last five seasons. Another increase is predicted for the coming season since the club expects to draw fans in record numbers.

A copy of the (ad size) page advertisement you placed in last year's program is enclosed for you to review. If you want to change your ad, revise the enclosed copy or send new copy.

Write the ad size you want in the upper left corner of the copy you return; you will receive an invoice in February. The prices for the ads are listed below.

Ad Size	Rate
Quarter Page	$ 125
Half Page	225
Full Page	400

Madison GOLD appreciates your support and is pleased that the GOLD Program helps promote your business.

```
Henry L. Yu
West Chevrolet
207 Mann Road
Madison, TN  37115-4219
Quarter-page ad
```

```
Mary T. Salter-Day
Valley Office Supplies
501 Marthonna Road, N
Madison, TN  37115-4507
Full-page ad
```

```
James E. Covic
C & F Construction
625 Vista Drive
Memphis, TN  38114-2323
Half-page ad
```

Document 2
Memorandum
plain sheet

Prepare this memo for **Karl Coppersmith** to initial. Leave the TO: line blank; names will be keyed in later.

Date the memo **January 16, 19--**, and use **UNITED WAY FUND DRIVE** as the subject.

¶ Yesterday marked the beginning of the ^current^ fund drive for the United Way of San Mateo County. ¶It ^The United Way.^ is an organization that addresses the needs of people ^in our area^ through financial support and volunteer work. ¶ The attached literature lists the ^organizations^ ~~groups~~ receiving financial aid and includes an (env.) ^sp^ for your contribution. If you wish to give ^to the United Way^ through a payroll deduction, simply see Marie Getz. You may ~~indicate~~ ^request^ that your gift go to a specific ^organization^ ~~group~~. xx Attachment

Document 3
Income Statement
plain sheet

Format this income statement. The heading is

MARY'S COUNTRY CRAFTS/ Income Statement/For the Year Ended December 31, 19-- (*previous year*).

Note: To key the double underline on a typewriter, first underline the total in the usual way. Then roll the paper up ½ line space and key the second underline. If your equipment will not permit you to key a double underline, use a ruler and pen or pencil to draw the second underline.

Income:
Sales $46,764
Craft Classes   2,503

Total Income $49,267

Operating expenses: *Add remaining leaders*
Rent Expense $12,000
Wages Expense   8,320
Advertising ^Expense^   295
Depreciation ^Expense^   1,440
Utilities expense   2,368
^sp^ (Mdse.) Expense   3,815
Supplies Expense   380 ~~280~~
Total ^Operating^ expenses   28,618
Net Income For The (Yr.) ^sp^ $20,649

Document 4
Statement of Owner's Equity
plain sheet

Key the Statement of Owner's Equity at the right.

MARY'S COUNTRY CRAFTS
Statement of Owner's Equity
For the Year Ended December 31, 19--   } DS
                    QS

Mary Castleton , Capital
    January 1, 19-- (*previous year*) $18,350

    Add:
        Net Income for (Yr.) ^sp^   20,649
                                                        <DS
                                                    $ 38,999
                                                        <DS
    Less:
        Capital Withdrawn during (Yr.) ^sp^   19,500
                                                        <DS
Mary Castleton , Capital
    December 31, 19-- $ 19,499

Job 2
Table

Message from SUSAN DEMMET

Please prepare a final copy of the GOLD Caravan schedule from the rough draft at the right while I compose a letter to send with it.

SD

Job 3
Letters
LP pp. 27-31

Message from SUSAN DEMMET

Here's a rough-draft copy of a letter that will be sent to the manager and players taking part in the caravan on January 15 and 16. Their names are listed at the bottom of the Caravan schedule.

Prepare a letter and envelope for each; date each letter January 6. The addresses are as follows:

Manager:
609 Menees Lane
Madison, TN 37115-5807

Chuck:
317 Adair Road
Jackson, TN 38305-2912

Jim:
6700 Forest Road
Columbus, GA 31907-3011

SD

MADISON GOLD CARAVAN SCHEDULE*

January 15 and 16, 19--

January	Time	Location	Store
15	1:00 p.m. ~~11:45 a.m.~~	Green City Mall	Altmants ~~Harvey's~~
15	4:00 p.m.	Crestmont Village	The Sport Spot
15	7:30 p.m.	East Shopping Mall	Everetts
16	11:30 a.m. ~~1:00 p.m.~~	Five Points	Athlete's Wear
16	2:30 p.m.	Westend Village	Oscar's Corner
16	5:45 p.m.	High Point Center	D & J Clothing ~~The Wilson Co.~~
16	8:00 ~~7:45~~ p.m.	Southland Mall	Big League's

_____

*The members of the caravan are Manager, Al S. Rojah and players, Chuck H. Mravic and Jim R. Alberti. The driver is Ted S. Botts. ss

_____

Dear _____:

The ~~itinerary~~ schedule for this month's Gold Caravan has been set for January 15 and 16, the two days you have agreed to represent the ~~club~~ GOLD baseball team. I have ~~(ne)~~closed a copy of the schedule for the two days ~~so you can see the~~ and have listed the locations and stores at which you will appear.

Please ~~report come to~~ be in my office by ~~11:30~~ 11:15 a.m. on January 15 so we can have a ~~short~~ luncheon meeting to review the purpose of the public appearances ~~caravan~~ and the schedule.

We ~~plan to~~ will all leave the stadium in one car at 12:30 p.m. to drive to the first location ~~appearnace~~.

Sincerly

287a-291a ▶ 5 (daily)
Equipment Check
each line twice SS; DS
between 2-line groups

alphabet	1	Lack of oxygen caused dizziness for Jeb who quickly moved up the hill.
figures	2	Please verify the $3,679 total on Invoice No. 4802 dated September 15.
fig/sym	3	K & S (6948 Loretta Street) is having a 50% sale from September 17-23.
speed	4	Iris did key in the surname and title of the auditor on the amendment.

| 1 | 2 | 3 | 4 | 5 | 6 | 7 | 8 | 9 | 10 | 11 | 12 | 13 | 14 |

287b-291b ▶ 45 (daily)
Document Processing

Process as many of the following documents as you can during each work period. Proofread and correct each document before you remove it from the typewriter or print a copy.

Document 1
Partial Audit Report
plain sheet
Key this rough draft as page 12 of a report (leftbound).

Organization and Facilities) header
DS

Sufficiency of Working Capital

As a result of our audit of your financial statements for the year ended December 31, 19--, we offer these suggestions concerning the status of your working capital. Our audit reveals that the corporation has been operating with insufficient working capital. Effective Long-range plans must be made to insure that the corporation has a sufficient amount of working capital in the future. The best from of working capital is still cash in the bank.

Providing for adequate record storage

A few number of record-storing inadequacies were discovered during our examination.

1. In our tests of the perpetual inventory records, we could not locate the records from Sept. 19--.

2. General ledgers, journal entry books, and other records are not clearly marked.

3. Record-storage area is cluttered; records are stacked on top of or in front of other records.

Since we found it time-consuming and often frustrating to locate the necessary records, we recommend that the records area be cleaned, organized, and efficiently maintained. All records must be clearly and marked and should be easily accessible.

FYI ONLY
Memo

Can you help me find more information about these ways of authorizing computer users to access company data bases: *audit trail* (tracks the user's actions), *data encryption* (scrambles data sent between computers over telephone lines), *callback verification* (pairs a password with a specific telephone), and *biotechnics* (identifies users by fingerprints, etc.).

These topics related to information privacy/responsible use of computers will be discussed at the Chamber of Commerce seminar this month.
K.C.

Job 4
Report

**Message from
SUSAN DEMMET**

*Mary processed this
draft for me to review
before she left. I re-
viewed it; it looks good.
You will have to find and
correct spelling and key-
ing errors; I didn't mark
them when I reviewed the
report. Also do the
following:*

*1. Key GOLD in all caps
when it refers to the
baseball club.*

*2. Delete WMMG Radio
from the sponsor list
in paragraph 2.*

*3. Key "giveaway" as
"give-away" when it ap-
pears in paragraph 5.*

*4. Key "homerun" as
two words in para-
graph 6.*

*5. Place each explana-
tory note at the bottom
of the page on which it
appears.*

SD

SPECIAL PROMOTIONS -- A PROGRESS REPORT
as of December 31, 19--

The marketing staff has lined up numerous promotions that should promote the Madison Gold Baseball Club and increase attendance at home games this coming season.

Preseason Promotions

Pocket schedules. Sponsors have been lined up to pay for, print, and distribute over one million pocket schedules, starting late January. The sponsors are Parkway Autos, Taco Haven, First City Bank, WMMG Radio, Scanlon Soft Drinks, Foodmarket, and local Quick Stop Marts.

Promotional video. A vidoetape of highlights from last year's season has been produced under the direction of Promo Video, Inc., and is available for distribution to professional, civic, and other community groups.*

GOLD Caravan. Players and other field personnel are scheduled to participate in the Gold Caravan during the month of January. Appearances are scheduled in over 45 stores within a 50-mile radius of Madison.

In-Season Promotions

Giveaway promotions. The giveaway items and schedule for May, June, and July will be finalised by the middle of January. Five such events are planned for this threemonth period, and four more are to be planned for the remainder of the season.

Chili homeruns. If one of our players hits a homerun in the ninth inning, the Chili Palace will give a free bowl of chili to everyone with a valid ticket stub from the game.

GOLD Program certificates. One of the players will autograph 15 programs before each game, and certificates from local restaurants will be awrded to those having autogrphed programs.

Special Promotions

Madison Area Chamber of Commerce Family Night. For $25 the Gold offers a mail order package of four tickets, soft drinks, hot dogs, and one parking pass. The Chamber prints and distributes coupons that publicize the game and offer.

Little League Night. The Gold offers community Little League associations discounted tickets good for admission, hot dog, and soft drink, provided the association places a minimum order of 100 tickets. Each league will promote the offer to its players.

Senior Citizen GOLD Cards. The Gold provides senior citizens with wallet-size GOLD cards that entitle them to a 10% discount on up to four tickets for each game and free parking in Lot A at day games. The Madison Senior Citizen Association will promote this offer to all of its members in a February mailing.

---

*Six copies of the 30-minute videotape are available for distribution; two copies always will be kept for staff to use.

Production Goals

1. To format formal memos on plain paper.
2. To process letters commonly written by accountants.
3. To format financial statements and other specialized documents.

Documents Processed

1. Partial audit report
2. Memorandums
3. Financial statements
4. Engagement letters
5. News release
6. Proposal resume
7. Collection letter

REGENCY ACCOUNTING SERVICES, INC.

Before you begin the work of this simulation, read the introductory material and study the format guide summary at the right.

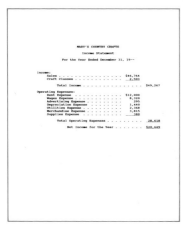

Income Statement

News Release

This simulation contains copy that is for your information (FYI) only. Read such information, labeled FYI ONLY; but do not key it.

You are assigned to work as a temporary replacement for one of the office assistants at Regency Accounting Services, Inc., 400 Serramonte Boulevard, Daly City, CA 94014-1820. Regency consists of two Certified Public Accountants (CPAs), four assisting accountants, and an office support staff.

Most of your work will be for Karl Coppersmith, CPA, whose job title is senior accountant; but you report directly to Roberta Osborne, office supervisor. Miss Osborne has given you an office procedures manual to review. More form letters are to be added to the manual in the near future.

While reviewing the office procedures manual, you note the following:

1. Letters are formatted attractively on letterhead in the modified block format (blocked paragraphs) with mixed punctuation. Name of the firm is keyed in ALL CAPS in the closing lines. The preferred complimentary closing is **Very truly yours.**

2. Memos, prepared on plain paper, have the guide words TO, FROM, DATE, and SUBJECT keyed and blocked 1" from the left edge. Enumerated items are listed in "hang indent" format. SS 2-line entries; DS between enumerated items.

3. Financial statements, such as balance sheets, statements of financial condition, and income statements, are compiled in leftbound report style (1½" left margin and 1" right margin). The page beginning ranges from line 6 to line 12 depending upon the length of the statement. One-page statements are preferred. Leaders are used in all financial statements.

4. Reports of 5 pages or more typically include headers at the top of each page. To create a header, place the title at the left margin on line 6 (same line as the page number).

5. Abbreviations, often used in handwritten drafts, are not used in final documents. Common abbreviations include

accts.	accounts	mdse.	merchandise
bal.	balance	mo.	month(s)
cr.	credit	qtr.	quarter(ly)
dr.	debit	stmt.	statement
ins.	insurance	yr.	year(s)

6. Accuracy is essential on all documents; financial statements MUST be error-free.

Document Format Guides

Form Letters. The form or standard part of a form letter is arranged on plain paper. Each form letter has a title or identification keyed on line 12. Variables are indicated by V1 (date), V2 (letter address), V3 (salutation), etc. The closing lines are formatted normally, except that the sender's name is variable information.

The engagement letter, used to clarify the accounting tasks to be performed for clients, includes an "approval" line (3") for the client's signature and a line (1½") for the date. These lines are arranged below the closing lines of the letter as shown here:

```
          Very truly yours, DS
          REGENCY ACCOUNTING SERVICES, INC.
                                  QS

          Karl Coppersmith, CPA
          Senior Accountant
                      DS
xx DS
Enclosures DS
Approved: DS
_____          _____
Umeki Yoshino              Date
```

Financial Statements. All financial documents have a 3-line heading, DS, containing the client's name, title of the statement, and the date or period the statement covers. Recommended: CS--4 spaces between amount columns. Long items should be keyed on two lines--not extended into the intercolumn space. Leaders are used to make statements more readable. Periods and spaces must align vertically. A leader must end at least two spaces to the left of the figures.

News Releases. PB: line 10; SM: 1"; DS. **For Release:** is keyed at the left margin followed by the release date. The suggested title of the article is keyed at the left margin in ALL CAPS. **Contact:** followed by a name, address, and telephone number is keyed at the left margin below the symbols ###.

Radio Station WMMG Pregame Party. Station WMMG will provide free refreshments (soft drinks and hot dogs), a disc jockey, and music from 6:00 p.m. to 7:00 p.m. before an August game. The date will be selected by mid-July and WMMG will publicize the party and the game.*

Additional Efforts

The marketing staff will continue to plan promotional events for strategic times in the season. These events will be consistent with the objectives of the marketing plan that we discussed and is almost ready for distribution.

---

*The decision is being delayed until mid-July so we can determine the date that our nearest competitor in the standings will be playing us at home.

Job 5
Report with Internal Citations

Message from SUSAN DEMMET

Here's the most recent draft of the marketing strategy report I have cut and pasted together. Process a final draft for me. SD

A MARKETING STRATEGY

This marketing strategy plan is based upon the marketing staff's extensive statistical analysis of (1) the responses to surveys which have been completed by over 7,500 fans during each of the last three years and (2) the information available as a result of the data base information system installed two years ago. It uses an innovative marketing orientation where "the commercial leisure service business adjusts its products and services to meet the needs of the customer" rather than the traditional selling orientation that focuses "on products or services that the business produces." (Bullaro and Edginton, 1986, 212). The plan

Assumptions

The plan has been constructed upon the following assumptions:

1. Madison Gold is a mature sports organization with an established base market.

2. Madison Gold's marketing strategy should be based on the results of the market research conducted from 1989-1991.

3. Existing fans can account for the majority of increases in attendance in the next year period.

Internal Marketing

DS recommends

The staff believes that internal marketing as described in Lewis and Appenseler (1985, 157-175) should be adopted during the next three years. Internal marketing is a technique used to

---

286a ▶ 5
Conditioning Practice

each line twice SS (slowly, then faster); then a 1′ writing on line 4

alphabet	1	Gladyce bought two dozen quarts of jam and five extra jars of pickles.
figures	2	The team batting average went from .389 on June 16 to .405 on June 27.
bottom row	3	Dr. Betz gave him an extensive physical examination on Monday morning.
speed	4	When they fix the chair by the door, they may also work on the mantle.

| 1 | 2 | 3 | 4 | 5 | 6 | 7 | 8 | 9 | 10 | 11 | 12 | 13 | 14 |

286b ▶ 15
Improve Language Skills

LL: 70 spaces
LS: DS

1. The sentences at the right contain errors in spelling, punctuation, capitalization, and grammar.

2. As you key each sentence (with number and period), make all necessary corrections, including any key-stroking errors you may make.

3. After you key all sentences, proofread each one and mark each error that was not corrected.

1. The Jay cooperation has a divers product line.
2. It seams to me that they should be farther than lesson 5.
3. The jefferson memorial was Dedicated on April 13 1943.
4. The implemintation of the Knew policy were succesful.
5. The misissippi and colorodo is two rivers in the us.
6. The recent events wayed heavily n his conscious.
7. Toms' resent promotion was the bases of Jack's resentment.
8. It is important too decrease expenditers on Foreign Oil.
9. Did dr. Sanchez enjoy her trip to south america in july?
10. His recomendation was to by the Knewer vehicle.
11. The Mark Twain museum are located in Hannibal Missour.
12. Will president Chi deliver the Keynote Address on friday may 23.
13. Ten of the sixteen computers was damaged during shipment.
14. The new desks are three ft. wide and five ft. long.
15. King louis XVI was executed in paris on january 21 1793.

286c ▶ 10
Improve Keyboarding Technique

Key each sentence twice; once for speed, then slower for accuracy; key difficult sentences again as time permits.

Balanced-hand	1	Diana may make the girls keep the lamb and fowl down by the city dock.
Double letters	2	Warren better have the three drill books when Annette arrives at noon.
Combination	3	Their box with the forms in it was left in my room by the old dresser.
3d row	4	Terri requested Peter to report your errors to the proper authorities.
Adjacent-key	5	News of a lower oil and crop production created very serious problems.
Shift key	6	Jana lived in New York City before moving to Salt Lake City in August.
Figures	7	I showed homes at 1856 Hatch, 297 Wren, and 403 Elm Street on July 30.

286d ▶ 20
Improve Basic Keyboarding Skills

1. Take a 1′ writing on each paragraph of 285d; determine *gwam* and errors on each writing.

2. Take two 5′ writings on 285d. Record *gwam* and errors of the better writing.

480

focus marketing efforts on existing customers first. . . . Internal marketing has shown to be cheaper and more effective at increasing total attendance and/or participation levels. In turn, more satisfied existing customers attract more non-consumers so that internal marketing has added benefits (Lewis and Appenzeller, 1985, 174).

An important aspect of the internal marketing approach is that it relies on making existing fans who are good fans into avid fans, making avid fans into our best fans, and maintaining the fans who will not or cannot increase their attendance. Madison GOLD will still need to attract some new fans who will attend a few games during the season.

Madison GOLD Fans

Existing attendance. Based on the information we have gathered during the past three years, it has been determined that Madison GOLD fans fall into the following categories:

Fan Category	No. of Fans in Category	Average No. of Games Attended	Computed Total Attendance
Best Fans	500	23	11,500
Avid Fans	1,050	14	14,700
Good Fans	14,500	3.5	50,750
Computed Total Attendance			76,950

Projected attendance. The following methods can be used to increase attendance for the coming season.

1. "Move" 10% of the avid fans into the best fans category; move 5% of the good fans into the avid category; and attract new fans to replace those who are "moved" or stop attending.

2. Increase the average number of games attended in each category by 10%.

If these goals are realized, the total attendance would climb almost 25 percent to 95,928, as shown in the table below.

Fan Category	No. of Fans in Category	Average No. of Games Attended	Computed Total Attendance
Best Fans	605	25.3	15,306
Avid Fans	1,775	15.4	27,335
Good Fans	14,500	3.675	53,287
Computed Total Attendance			95,928

(continued, p. 299)

Improve Keyboarding Technique

1. Key lines 1-10 once as shown.

2. Take a 1' writing on lines 2, 4, 6, 8, and 10. Try to maintain your line 2 rate on the other writings.

3. Compute *gwam* and compare rates on each writing.

Balanced-hand

1 and fix elf hair jams sick pays quay ruby fuzz vigor works towns sight
2 Lana may make the proficient girls handle the problems with the forms.

Double letters

3 add book tree offer dinner accept bottle pepper yellow message command
4 Debbie usually corrects all the keying errors in her business letters.

Combination

5 sir see man kept were them kind key very best social audit within have
6 If she is able to leave the downtown area by noon, she may be on time.

3d row

7 up put top pop two your yoyo were tire quite quote quiet teeter terror
8 They were quite polite to the witty reporter who requested your story.

Adjacent-key

9 as we buy open milk over save newer power union ponder return reporter
10 Broken sewer pipes created havoc prior to the popular fashion exhibit.

| 1 | 2 | 3 | 4 | 5 | 6 | 7 | 8 | 9 | 10 | 11 | 12 | 13 | 14 |

285d ▶ 20

Improve Basic Keyboarding Skills

1. A 1' writing on each paragraph; determine *gwam* and errors on each writing.

2. Two 5' writings on the ¶s. Record *gwam* and errors of the better writing.

all letters used | A | 1.5 si | 5.7 awl | 80% hfw

gwam 1' | 5'

All students should ponder the advantages of continuing their edu- 13 | 3 | 58
cation after finishing high school. A greater number of jobs than ever 28 | 6 | 61
before require post high school training in order to meet the minimum 42 | 8 | 63
standards of entry level. Many jobs that were previously open to indi- 56 | 11 | 66
viduals who had a high school diploma no longer exist, or technology has 71 | 14 | 69
changed the duties of the job to such an extent that some type of train- 85 | 17 | 72
ing after high school is now required in order to be qualified. 98 | 20 | 75

The secretarial position is an example of a job that has changed a 13 | 22 | 77
great deal by improved technology. Years ago, one of the major duties for 28 | 25 | 81
this type of work was to be able to use a manual typewriter with a 42 | 28 | 83
great deal of skill. Today the position has changed into one that re- 56 | 31 | 86
quires competence in operating word processing equipment and the ability 71 | 34 | 89
to utilize the computer as well as deal with customers and clients in 85 | 36 | 92
a skillful manner. 88 | 37 | 92

These changes are examples of how the current job market has made 13 | 40 | 95
it important for people to contemplate attending college in order to be 28 | 43 | 98
considered for some of the higher paying jobs. Advocates of more school- 42 | 46 | 101
ing also mention having a richer and more rewarding life as a reason 56 | 48 | 104
for continuing school. These factors are just a few of the reasons why, 71 | 51 | 106
over the years, young people, as well as old, have enrolled in some form 85 | 54 | 109
of advanced schooling. 90 | 55 | 110

gwam 1' | 1 | 2 | 3 | 4 | 5 | 6 | 7 | 8 | 9 | 10 | 11 | 12 | 13 | 14 |
5' | 1 | | 2 | | 3 |

Specific promotions [cap]

DS { The ideas mentioned below are based on listings in Lewis and Appenzeller (1985, 164-168) and an article that appeared in Time (Rudolph, 1987, 38-39).

Good fans. Since fans in the good category are not likely to be as near their satiation point as those in the avid and best categories, most of the [this year's] promotion efforts will be aimed at this group. The efforts include a continuation of the product give-away promotions already in place, the addition of quasi-price promotions (2 for 1's, half price days, ladies days), and special attractions (fireworks, circus acts, parties).

Avid fans. While most of the promotions targeted for the good fans will also work for avid fans, a new multiple-ticket plan will be started help move the avid fans to the higher group. This plan will be named "the GOLDen 25" and will allow fans to buy mini-season tickets for 25 games. The only restriction on choice is that the tickets purchased must include at least one game with each opponent.

Best fans. Increasing the games attended is the primary objective for fans in the best fans category. To help accomplish the goal, 30 free parking passes will be given to a person ordering two season tickets this coming year. In addition, season ticket holders will be given special discounts on extra tickets purchased during the season.

Conclusion

If the marketing efforts result in the addition of 25,000 fans, the GOLD will have made a good market better. This better base will provide the financial base needed to field a competitive team in a first-rate facility.

Improve Keyboarding and Language Skills

Learning Goals

1. To improve/refine technique and response patterns.
2. To increase keystroking speed and to improve accuracy on straight copy.
3. To improve language skills.

Format Guides

1. Paper guide at *0* (for typewriters).
2. LL: 70 spaces.
3. LS: SS drills; DS ¶s.
4. PI: 5 spaces.

Lesson 285   *Keyboarding/Language Skills*

285a ▶ 5
Conditioning Practice

Key each line twice. Then take two 30″ writings for speed on line 4 followed by two 30″ writings for control on line 1.

alphabet	1	James very quickly placed the two extra megaphones behind the freezer.
figures	2	The 120 computers were purchased in 1987; the 34 typewriters, in 1965.
shift keys	3	Terra McKinney and Margo Norton are new initiates of Delta Pi Epsilon.
speed	4	When we do the work for him, we may also fix their neighbor's bicycle.

| 1 | 2 | 3 | 4 | 5 | 6 | 7 | 8 | 9 | 10 | 11 | 12 | 13 | 14 |

285b ▶ 15
Improve Language Skills

LL: 70 spaces
LS: DS

1. The sentences at the right contain errors in spelling, punctuation, capitalization, and grammar.
2. As you key each sentence (with number and period), make all necessary corrections, including any keystroking errors you may make.
3. After you key all sentences, proofread each one and mark each error that was not corrected.

1. The united states tennis open will begin in new york next week.
2. There baby was born on the fifteenth of november at three thirty p.m.
3. When the alarm went off at the christmas party the crowd disbursed.
4. Tom and nancy Selby's vacationed in Denmark switzerland and Holland.
5. Mary has received her exceptance letter; Tom and Bob has not.
6. All of the homes on Vine street was damaged by the terrible whether.
7. The business professionals of America will meet on tuesday, May 15.
8. Some of the lone payments was received before the do date of may 1.
9. The federal reserve bank of minneapolis is on Marquette avenue.
10. They will spend independence day at their cottage in south Dakota.
11. The advise she recieved encouraged her to move foreward with the job.
12. The lincoln center is between amsterdam and columbus avenues.
13. They should apreciate the principle for the job she has dun.
14. please duplicate twelve copies of Page 4 and 15 copies of Page 5.
15. The office is located on the corner of 3rd Avenue and Maple lane.
16. You will find the answer to you question in section 9 on page 406.
17. Only 1 of the teachers are planning to attend the Senior play.
18. your Biology test will cover chapter 12 which starts on Page 256.
19. Gehrig ruth and mantle are just a few new york, yankee idles.
20. Pedro c. Ramirez immerged as the leading Presidential candidate.

Job 6
Reference Page, Title Page,
and Table of Contents

Message from
SUSAN DEMMET

*Process the reference page
as the last page of the report; prepare a title page
using my name and position
and the club name. Lastly,
prepare a table of contents
using all side and para-
graph headings.* *SD*

Job 7
Table

Message from
SUSAN DEMMET

*Here's a promotion schedule
from last year. Process one
for this year by making
these changes.*

*1. Add TENTATIVE to the
heading.*
*2. Change Actual to Esti-
mated.*
*3. Add 1 day to each June
date.*
*4. Change Calendar to
Umbrella.*
5. Increase $ amount by 5%.
*6. Do not use horizontal
lines except to underline
column heads and to place
divider line properly.* *SD*

Job 8
Memo

Message from *SD*
SUSAN DEMMET

*Prepare this memo that
I composed at my typewriter.
Address it to all staff; use
PLAYER APPEARANCE
GUIDELINES as the subject.*

REFERENCES

Bullaro, John J., and Christopher R. ~~Edgington~~ Edginton.
 <u>Commercial Leisure Services</u>. New York: ~~MacMill~~ Mac-
 millan Publishing Company, 1986.

Lewis, Guy, and Herb Appenzeller, eds. <u>Successful Sport Man-
 agement</u>. Charlottesville, VA: ~~Law Publishers~~ The
 Michie Company, 1985.

Rudolph, Barbara. "Bonanza in the Bushes." <u>Time</u>, 1 August
 1988, 38-39.

PROMOTION SCHEDULE FOR MAY, JUNE, AND JULY 19--

Date	Promotion	Actual Cost to Club	Item to Be Given to
May 5	Bat Night	$6,000	All fans under 16
May 18	Sportsbag Day	None*	First 5,500 fans
June 15	Cap Night	$5,000	All fans
June 30	Calendar Day	None*	All fans
July 15	Jersey Day	$3,000	First 5,500 fans

*Sponsor pays for promotion item.

To avoid ~~most of~~ last year's problems relating to player appearances that ~~caused~~ resulted in confusion, embarrassment,
and ~~bad~~ poor public relations, please follow these guidelines when you ~~are asked~~ receive a request for a player appearance.

1. All player appearance requests must be made in writing ~~a
minimum~~ at least ~~10~~ ten days in advance of the appearance date.

2. ~~Check~~ Refer to the Player Appearance Chart to determine
if a player (or the player requested) is available.

3. Once a player's availability has been confirmed, complete a~~n Appe~~ Player Appearance Form. Send two copies of
this form to the player (one ~~is ta~~ mailed to his home and
~~the~~ another delivered to him via interoffice mail). Send
the third copy to me; keep the fourth copy for your files.

4. Call the player making the appearance the day before the
appearance date to remind him of his commitment and to give
him information about the people he is to meet.

5. After the appearance, call the group to find out if they
were satisfied with the appearance, and then relay these
comments to the player who made the appearance.

Documents 10-11
Job Descriptions

2 plain sheets

Until now, Gateway has had one job description for all medical assistants, who performed both administrative (office) and clinical (medical) tasks. An increase in our patient load indicates a need to divide job duties between two types of medical assistants. From the job description at the right, prepare two separate job descriptions in report format.

Prepare a job description for **Medical Assistant--Administrative.** For the **Job Summary** key **The medical assistant--administrative performs typical office procedures.** Under **Job Duties** list items 1, 2, 9, 11, 12, and 15-18 (renumber the items, beginning with 1).

Prepare a job description for **Medical Assistant--Clinical.** For the **Job Summary** key **The medical assistant--clinical helps patients** (copy remainder of sentence from original). Under **Job Duties** list items 3-8, 10, 13, and 14 (renumber the items, beginning with 1).

L. Sanchez

Documents 12-13
Continuation Sheets

2 plain sheets

Dr. Lloyd made the notes at the right as he examined two of his young patients. Copy the notes to separate sheets, one for each patient's file. Center the words **CONTINUATION SHEET** on line 6; DS. Key the examination date in the six-digit format at the left margin; reset the margin 4 spaces to the right to key the notes single-spaced.

On Alexa Beerman's sheet, add the following note you recorded when Alexa's mother called in this morning (key your initials at end of note).

12/17-- TC axillary temp. 97.6 F w/i 6 hrs. after last dose. Stopped Tylenol. xx

L. Sanchez

JOB DESCRIPTION

Job Title: Medical Assistant

Job Summary: The medical assistant performs typical office procedures, helps patients prepare for examinations, assists physicians as requested, and performs basic clinical procedures.

Job Duties:

1. Greet patients.
2. Inspect patients' records for accuracy and completeness.
3. Gather essential patient information, prepare/drape patients, measure temperature, height, weight, blood pressure, etc.
4. Administer all injections and maintain accurate record of each.
5. Sterilize instruments and maintain quality of instruments.
6. Maintain examination rooms, workstations, and equipment.
7. Obtain and process specimens and attach Holter monitor and electrocardiograph.
8. Complete lab request forms.
9. Perform patient education activities.
10. Assist physician upon request.
11. Screen patients' telephone calls to determine need for/urgency of appointments.
12. Order medical supplies and prescription medications.
13. Obtain samples from pharmaceutical suppliers.
14. Organize and control pharmaceutical samples on sample shelves.
15. Maintain detailed records of all prescriptions filled in the office.
16. Maintain the supply closets.
17. Keep the patient information booklets and other handouts up to date.
18. Set up examination rooms each afternoon, including patients' charts, for the next day.

12/16--
CARL D. JOHNSON. Age--6 mos. Hgt. 26" Wt. 16 lbs., 10 oz. Head circum. 44 2/3 cm. Immunizations--DTP, OPV. Denver Developmental passed.

12/16-- ALEXA K. BEERMAN. Age--10 weeks. Hgt. 17½" Wt. 10 lbs., 2 oz. Head circum. 35½ cm. Axillary temp. 99.3 F. Rx for fever, 0.4 ml. Tylenol, q.i.d. /24 hrs. only.

Evaluate Keyboarding/Document Processing Skills

Measurement Goals

1. To measure/evaluate your competency in processing letters, reports, and tables in acceptable format under time pressure.

2. To measure the speed at which you can key straight copy with a reasonable degree of accuracy.

3. To evaluate your ability to apply your language skills as you key.

Format Guides

1. Paper guide at *0* (for typewriters).

2. LL: 70 spaces for drills and paragraphs.

3. LS: SS drill lines; DS ¶s; space documents as directed.

4. PI: 5 spaces, unless otherwise indicated.

Lesson 172   *Evaluate Correspondence Processing Skills*

172a ▶ 5
Conditioning Practice

each line twice SS (slowly, then faster); DS between 2-line groups; if time permits, rekey selected lines

alphabet	1	The fight crowd began to exit quickly just as the prize sum was given.
figures	2	The truck with License No. A987-135 is assigned to Space 240 in Lot 6.
long words	3	Two new software packages from nuSofttech are protechNet and safeWork.
speed	4	A key goal of the sorority tutor is to shape or form the right theory.

| 1 | 2 | 3 | 4 | 5 | 6 | 7 | 8 | 9 | 10 | 11 | 12 | 13 | 14 |

172b ▶ 9 *Evaluate Straight-Copy Skill*

1. Take a 5′ writing on the ¶s at the right.
2. Find *gwam* and number of errors.
3. Record score on LP p. 4.

all letters used | A | 1.5 si | 5.7 awl | 80% hfw

	gwam 1′	5′
A job description often lists the education, training, experience,	13	3 | 41
and personal qualities required of people who hold the job being de-	27	5 | 44
scribed. A job description is commonly used to list the major functions	42	8 | 47
of a job and to outline the main duties the person in the job should be	56	11 | 50
able to perform in a suitable fashion.	64	13 | 51
Another major function of a job description is to specify the rela-	77	15 | 54
tionship of the job to other jobs in the business. To do this, the job	91	18 | 57
description should have a section that names the supervisor of the job	·106	21 | 60
being described and lists the jobs supervised by the person in the job	120	24 | 62
being described.	123	25 | 63
It is important that all jobs be analyzed from time to time because	137	27 | 66
many jobs are likely to change. They change because the duties of the	151	30 | 69
job often change. Some are dropped and other duties are added. If	164	33 | 71
changes in a job occur and the job description is not revised, the job	179	36 | 74
description becomes obsolete because its information is not correct.	192	38 | 77

gwam 1′ | 1 | 2 | 3 | 4 | 5 | 6 | 7 | 8 | 9 | 10 | 11 | 12 | 13 | 14 |
5′ | 1 | 2 | 3 |

172c ▶ 36 *Evaluate Document Processing Skills: Letters/Memos*

Time Schedule
Plan and Prepare.................. 3′
Timed Production..................25′
Proofread/Compute *n-pram*...... 8′

Format and key as many of the letters/memos on p. 302 as you can in 25′.

Compute *n-pram* and turn in your work arranged in document number order.

n-pram =
  wds. keyed − (10 × errors) ÷ 25′

No family history of cardiac disease exists. (Her mother died of breast cancer at the age of 87.)

Pyhsical examination revealed that pateints' neck is supple without jvd. Breathe is even with a few scattered rhonchi. Heart had regular rhythm without murmur, gallop, or click. PMI was not palpable; S 1 and S 2 were normal. Pulse was 2 + and regular in carotids and radials, and carotid up strokes were normal. Blood pressure was 110/60 in her right arm, seated and standing. Juguler venus pulse pressure was 5 centimeters of water and normal in contuor. The lungs were clear. The left ventricle impulse was within the midclavicular line. All of her heart sounds were normal. Review of her electrocardiagram of March 17, 19-- revealed a normal sinus rhythm and a normal PR interval of 0.18.

In summary, Mrs. Johnson is a pleasant woman, in relatively good health, who is satisfied with her presented life style. Her history of occassional chest discomfort and prier occurrence of subendocardial myocardial infraction do not indicate cardiac diseases. I advice no further cardiac evaluation for 1 year unless the patient should expereince an increase in frequency or a change in character of the chest discomfort. Under either circumstance farther evaluation, including an in-hospital rest and an exercise first pass study, is advised. No cardiac treatment is recommended now other than prn sublingual nitroglycerin.

I would like to evaluate the patient again in 10-12 months. Thank you for refering Mrs. Johnson to me.

172c (continued)

Document 1
Letter

LP p. 37 or full sheet
block format; open punctuation; proofread/correct errors; process envelope

Current date Dr. Henrietta L. Mateer California College of Business 2806 15
Belden Street Sacramento, CA 95815-1731 Dear Dr. Mateer 26

I'm sending your official membership certificate for the Society for Super- 41
visors and Curriculum Developers. Please display it in your office or 55
classroom so other educators and administrators will identify you as par- 70
ticipating in an organization that is shaping the future of our schools. 85

As a new member in the Society, you will receive a free subscription to 99
Leadership in the Nation's Schools, which is published each month, Sep- 120
tember through May. Members receive a large discount on texts that the 134
organization publishes each year. Further, as a member you will be able 149
to register for next year's conference at a reduced rate. 161

I'm glad that you have decided to join the Society for Supervisors and 175
Curriculum Developers, and I hope you will be an active member. (161) 181

Sincerely Ms. Martha E. Ipolito Executive Director xx Enclosure 200/**220**

Document 2
Formal Memo

LP p. 39 or full sheet
Note: If you are using a plain sheet, refer to the note on p. 277 for help in setting up the form.

heading 24

TO: Jim Kohl, Information   FROM: Angela Roski, Vice President
      Management Director   for Administration
DATE: Current date   SUBJECT: ACCESS RIGHTS

You are authorized to give Ray Allan access to these files on the NuTech com- 39
puter system: GET.BIO.DATA, CLASS.ROST, GRADES, and LOCATE. 51

Mr. Allan is authorized to access this information on the terminal in his office. 68
His authorization is limited to access; he is not permitted to change or print 84
the information stored in the files. 91

Please make the necessary changes to the security program so Ray will be 106
able to access this material beginning on the first of next month, the effec- 121
tive date of his promotion to director of nursing certification. 134

xx 135/**153**

Document 3
Simplified Memo
full sheet
proofread/correct errors

Document 4
Letter

Reformat Document 1 on a plain sheet as a modified block letter with mixed punctuation; proofread/correct errors.

Current date Editorial Staff and Managers APPOINTMENT OF ASSOCIATE 14
EDITOR 15

I am pleased to announce that Jane L. McManis has accepted an offer to join 30
the International Association of Facility Managers as associate editor for the 46
publication, Managing Facilities. 57

Ms. McManis brings to our association a wealth of experience in facilities 72
management. She has managed seven theaters for Cinimex, Inc., in Pensa- 86
cola, Florida; the Dayton Civic Center in Dayton, Ohio; and the Preston Hotel 102
and Conference Center in Dallas, Texas. Jane was graduated from Orlando 116
College where she studied management and communications. She has taught 131
facilities management courses at three colleges. 141

Ms. McManis will begin her editorial duties at the beginning of the month and 157
will be located in the office next to mine. 166

Leona Q. Swartz, Editor xx 171

Documents 6-8
Form Letters
plain paper and
LP pp. 167-169
Dr. Liebman revised this form letter advising his patients about a lab test (urinalysis). First, format the letter on plain paper, omitting the date, letter address, salutation, and complimentary close, and keying **V1** and **V2** as shown. Then prepare a letter to the two patients named on these cards. Variable information (date, time) is shown on the cards. Date the letters **December 16.**

L. Sanchez

```
Ellison, Suzy B. (Miss)

4292 El Camino, Apt. 16
Palo Alto, CA  94306-8372

V1  December 22
V2  9:00 a.m.
```

```
Luebber, Richard M. (Mr.)

16 Thunderbird Ct.
Oakland, CA  94605-7127

V1  December 23
V2  9:30 a.m.
```

Document 9
Letter to Referring Physician
LP p. 171
1 plain sheet
Dr. Myers dictated the letter at the right following her evaluation of a patient referred to her by Dr. Lopez. One of your coworkers transcribed the dictation, producing this rough draft. Prepare the letter for Dr. Myers' signature, using this address:

Dr. Barbara M. Lopez
Bayside Professional Building
2000 Bay Street
San Francisco, CA 94213-6008

Date the letter **December 16, 19--.**

L. Sanchez

In order to obtain accurate results from urinanalysis, you should (1) maintnain a normal in take of liquids during the 24-hour specimen collection & (2) take the entire specimen to the lab the morning the collection is taken. In adition, these following substances should be avoided four at least 24 hours prier to beginning the collection: (Alphabetize each list below.)

coffee/tea	aspirin
chocolate	chlorpomazine
citrus fruits	serotonin
vanilla/chocolate	resperine
	pentobarbital

Remember, your lab apointment is on V1 at V2. The lab is in the Gateway Medical Center building. on the ground floor

---

The Evaluation of Carol Johnson has been completed. As you know she is a 69 year old white female who states that she had heart attack 15 years ago. A review of her clinic chart shows a history of sub-endocardial myocardial infraction. The pateint experiences episodes of chest discomfort that she describes as a "sharp to aching" sensation over the upper left quadrant. The sensation occurs suddenly and seems to be unrelated to activities. She reported that releif typicaly is gained by taking sub-lingual nitroglycerin. The patient reported no significant limitations in her usual activity. No orthopnea, PND, or petal edema was reported. Ms. Johnson reported that 2 years ago she discontinued smoking cigaretes after smoking a pack daily for over 25 years.

(continued, p. 476)

173a ▶ 5
Conditioning Practice

each line twice SS (slowly, then faster); DS between 2-line groups; if time permits, rekey selected lines

alphabet 1 Margy expected pop quizzes on the new books and five journal articles.

fig/sym 2 Tom's cancelled checks (#398 & #401) showed he paid for Model #25-769.

shift lock 3 MRS. MARY SMITH, 1234 BAKER ROAD, ALIQUIPPA, PA 15001, is to be added.

speed 4 To their dismay, the townsman kept the fox and the dog in the kennels.

| 1 | 2 | 3 | 4 | 5 | 6 | 7 | 8 | 9 | 10 | 11 | 12 | 13 | 14 |

173b ▶ 9 Evaluate Language Skills

As you key the ¶, correct errors in punctuation, capitalization, number expression, and correct any keying errors you find or make.

in 2 weeks it will be announced that professor tom wargo will visit 4 cities in the ussr to lecture to university students. professor wargo author of <u>friendship among nations</u> will be accompanied on the 2 week tour by his wife 2 daughters and 3 sons. the wargo family plans to leave the usa on thanksgiving and return in time for the professor to administer final exams at evergreen university.

173c ▶ 36 Evaluate Document Processing Skills: Tables

Time Schedule
Plan and Prepare.................. 3'
Timed Production..................25'
Proofread/Compute *n-pram*...... 8'

Document 1
3-Column Table with Block Column Headings

half sheet, long edge at top; DS data; CS: 8; correct errors

		words
FIVE MAJOR BATTLES OF THE CIVIL WAR		7

Battle	State	Estimated Casualties	
			9 / 18
Gettysburgh	Pennsylvania	40,000	24
Seven Days	Virginia	36,000	30
Petersburg	Virginia	30,000	35
Chickamauga	Georgia	28,500	41
The Wilderness	Virginai	28,000	47
_____			51
Source: <u>The World Book Encyclopedia</u>.			63

Document 2
3-Column Table with Centered Column Headings

full sheet, short edge at top; SS data; CS: 6; correct errors

Documents 3 and 4 are on p. 304.

SALES AND COMMISSION REPORT			6
Third Quarter, 19--			10
Salesperson	Sales	Commission	21
Jim Mullen	$ 35,540	$ 7,108	27
Sandra Lawton	41,250	8,250	32
Roberta Tessell	53,680	10,736	39
Bill Campbell	34,230	6,846	44
Paula Perfett	47,116	9,423	52
Totals	$211,816	$42,363	58

280b-284b (continued)

Documents 3 and 4
Statements of Account
LP pp. 163-165

Will you prepare statements of account from these patients' Accounts Receivable Ledger sheets. Wherever a zero balance appears, key only the lines *below* the zero balance.

Add the current year to the six-digit date; for example, 12/13/92. Key **.00** following all amounts.

Key the codes in the Service column as shown. For your information, a list of Gateway's codes is attached.

L. Sanchez

Service Codes

HC--Hospital Care
OC--Office Care
PRO--Procedures
INJ--Injections
OS--Lab, X-Ray, or
　　Other Service
INS--Insurance Payment
ROA--Received on
　　Account

ACCOUNTS RECEIVABLE LEDGER

Mr. Angelo Patti, 3740 San Bruno Ave., San Francisco, 94134-1833

DATE	PROFESSIONAL SERVICE	CHARGES	PAYMENTS	CURRENT BALANCE
11/22	OC	125	0	125
11/29	INJ	10	0	135
11/30	INS		25	110

ACCOUNTS RECEIVABLE LEDGER

Miss Lena M. Moss, 67 Eddy St., San Francisco, 94102-3331

DATE	PROFESSIONAL SERVICE	CHARGES	PAYMENTS	CURRENT BALANCE
10/01	OC, PRO	120	0	120
10/18	INJ	8	0	128
10/30	ROA		128	0
12/02	OC	40	0	40
12/09	INJ	8	0	48

Document 5
Partnership Contract

plain paper

This document, revised by Mr. Beard, is page **8** of Gateway's partnership contract, prepared as a leftbound report. Prepare a final draft for Mr. Beard.

On the same line as the page number key this *header* at the left margin: **Articles of Partnership--Gateway Medical Center.** The main heading (line 10 or line 12) is **ARTICLE XIX--COVENANT AGAINST COMPETITION**, followed by a QS. (In all articles of the contract, paragraphs are numbered as shown.)

L. Sanchez

P19.01 Each shareholder in Gateway Medical Center agrees **covenants and** that ~~if he chooses to withdraw~~ in the event of his **or her** withdrawal, volun**a**try or involuntary, he **or she** will not engage in the practice of medicine in ~~any county in the State of~~ **San Francisco County,** California, for a period of ~~one~~ **two 2** (1) year**s** from the time of such withdrawal.

P19.02. The former shareholder will not practice medicine **either or indirectly** directly, for his **or her** own account or for others, during the ~~one~~**two**-year period. Furthermore, during said period of ~~one~~ **two** year**s** from the date that he **or she** leaves the employment of Gateway Medical Center, he **or she** will not engage in **any** business in ~~any county in the State of~~ **San Francisco County,** California that competes in any manner with the business of the Corporation.

173c (continued)

Document 3
4-Column Table with Multiple-Line Column Headings
full sheet, short edge at top; DS data; CS: 4; center column headings; correct errors

Document 4
Reformat Document 1, p. 303, on a half sheet, short edge at top; DS data; CS: 4; center column headings; correct errors

COLLEGE OF BUSINESS

Expenditure Comparison

Department	Last Year	This Year	Percent Difference	
Accounting	$ 512,789	$ 537,614	4.84	33
Administrative Management	325,827	341,906	4.93	42
Business Teacher Education	85,401	89,723	5.06	52
Computer Information Systems	317,962	345,098	8.53	62
Economics and Finance	217,906	237,458	8.97	71
Logistics Management	95,763	102,948	7.5	79
Marketing	410,216	395,978	−3.48	85
Management	728,364	750,912	3.09	92
Sport Management	72,165	74,943	3.84	99
Quantitative Methods	174,269	193,058	10.78	112
Totals	$2,940,662	$3,069,638	4.38	121

(COLLEGE OF BUSINESS = 4, Expenditure Comparison = 9, Last Year = 12, This Year = 12, Percent Difference = 24, Accounting = 33)

Lesson 174 | *Evaluate Report Processing Skills*

174a ▶ 5
Conditioning Practice
each line twice SS (slowly, then faster); DS between 2-line groups; if time permits, rekey selected lines

alphabet 1 Jean may use twelve quart tins for packaging the extra zucchini bread.

symbols 2 Here & Now (Vol. 17, No. 12) was rated the #1 magazine in a 1992 poll.

first row 3 Vance named his baby Zina, Ben named his Maxine, and I named mine Nan.

speed 4 Their field hand works in the cornfield down by the lake by the docks.

| 1 | 2 | 3 | 4 | 5 | 6 | 7 | 8 | 9 | 10 | 11 | 12 | 13 | 14 |

174b ▶ 9 Evaluate Language Skills
As you key each sentence, with the number and period, correct errors in spelling and word usage. Correct keying errors you find or make. DS between sentences.

1. She is confidant she will be aloud to buy the stationary this year.

2. They were adviced to paint a picture of a sandy desert on the canvass.

3. Your overdo for sum good weather to pour concrete at a job sight.

4. I wont be build for the flew cleaning until he halls away the durt.

5. I aloud the hiring of for workers to expand the personal role.

174c ▶ 36 Evaluate Document Processing Skills: Unbound Report

Time Schedule
Plan and Prepare.................. 3'
Timed Production....................25'
Proofread/Compute *n-pram*...... 8'

1. Process the copy on p. 305 as an unbound report with footnotes.
2. If time permits, format a bibliography page from the report's footnotes.

3. Proofread/correct errors as you key.
4. Compute *n-pram* and turn in your work in document number order.

TIME SAVED BY AUTOMATION

Task	Time Required Current Method	Time Required Medic 1000
Appointment scheduling	1 hour	15 minutes
Monthly billing	2 days	30 minutes
Proving a daysheet	15 minutes	2-5 minutes
Processing claim forms	4-5 hours	10 minutes
Patient checkout	5 minutes	10 seconds

Document 2
Software Options Table

plain paper

Use these MEDIC 1000 menus, printed from my computer screen, to create a four-column table. Use these main and secondary headings:

MEDIC 1000 SOFTWARE
Basic Options Available*

Use the first four Main Menu options as column headings; block the submenu options under the column heads as shown by arrows. Don't key the option numbers. Key a divider line; then, this note: ***Custom options available in six upgrade modules.**

L. Sanchez

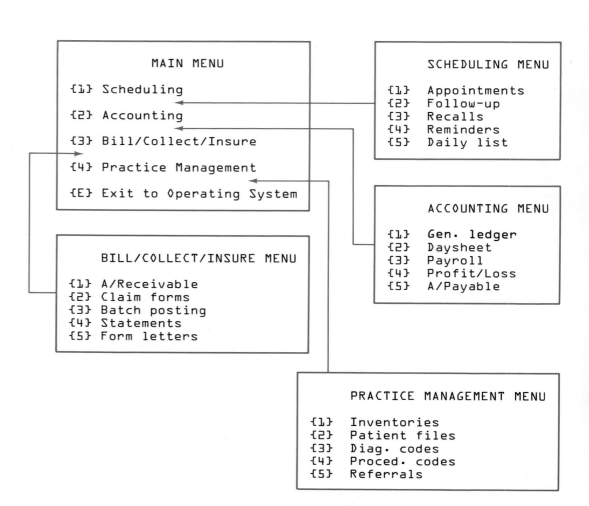

174c (continued)

Document 1
Unbound Report
with Footnotes

2 full sheets; correct errors as you key; proofread and make any additional corrections before removing a page from the machine or screen

INTERNATIONAL TRADE

A Report on Common Trade Restrictions

INTERNATIONAL TRADE	4
A Report on Common Trade Restrictions	12

It is important that employees of companies that market goods in foreign markets have a basic understanding of restrictions a nation can impose to reduce or eliminate goods being imported into the country.

26 / 41 / 53

Common Trade Restrictions

63

Before marketing goods to a foreign country, the exporting company should know the trade restrictions it is likely to face.

77 / 88

Tariff. The most common device a government uses to restrict trade between its nation and another is the tariff.

103 / 112

A tariff is a tax levied upon goods as they cross national boundaries usually by the government of the importing country. The words tariff, duty, and customs are generally used interchangeably. Tariffs may be levied either to raise revenue or to protect domestic industries.[1]

126 / 141 / 155 / 168

Quota. A quota is used by governments to set a limit on the amount of goods that can be imported in certain product categories. "The purpose of the quota is to conserve on foreign currency and protect local industry and employment."[2]

183 / 198 / 214 / 217

Other Trade Restrictions

226

Although the foregoing restrictions are the most commonly used, nations can discourage international trade through other means.

241 / 252

1. Reducing the amount of foreign currency available to buy imports and setting exchange rates at levels that make imports more costly.

266 / 280

2. Using nontariff barriers, such as discriminating against the bids of certain exporting countries or setting high product standards.

294 / 307

3. Establishing an embargo to eliminate imports coming into the country. Giordano defines embargo as "a government order stopping the import or export of a particular commodity or commodities."[3]

321 / 335 / 346

350

[1]The New Encyclopaedia Britannica, 15th ed., 1985, s.v. "Tariffs."

370

[2]Philip Kotler, Marketing Essentials, (Englewood Cliffs, New Jersey: Prentice-Hall, Inc., 1984), p. 428.

388 / 396

[3]Albert G. Giordano, Concise Dictionary of Business Terminology, (Englewood Cliffs, New Jersey: Prentice-Hall, Inc., 1981), p. 53.

417 / 430

Document 2
Bibliography

full sheet, correct errors

Document 3

If time permits, reformat Document 1 as an unbound report with internal citations; prepare a REFERENCE list on the last page of the report text; correct errors.

BIBLIOGRAPHY

3

Giordano, Albert G. Concise Dictionary of Business Terminology. Englewood Cliffs, New Jersey: Prentice-Hall, Inc., 1981.

26 / 36

Kotler, Philip. Marketing Essentials. Englewood Cliffs, New Jersey: Prentice-Hall, Inc., 1984.

54 / 60

"Tariffs." The New Encyclopaedia Britannica. Vol. 26. Chicago: Encyclopaedia Britannica, Inc., 1985, 430.

81 / 88

280a-284a ▶ 5 (daily)
Equipment Check
each line twice SS;
DS between 2-line
groups

alphabet 1 This quiet but perky jazz dancer will give fox-trot lessons on Monday.

figures 2 A total of 2,574 people attended the ball games on September 30, 1986.

fig/sym 3 Inventory list No. 182 included these stock numbers: #3597 and #6463.

speed 4 Both of the neurotic men did sue for the right to air the title fight.

| 1 | 2 | 3 | 4 | 5 | 6 | 7 | 8 | 9 | 10 | 11 | 12 | 13 | 14 |

280b-284b ▶ 45 (daily)
Document Processing
Key as many of the following
documents as you can during
each daily session. Watch for
unmarked errors in these original
documents. Proofread and correct each document before you
remove it from the machine or
print a copy.

Document 1
Software Selection Memo
2 plain sheets
December 12, 19--

Prepare this memo to **All Staff
Members;** I'll initial it. For the
subject line use **MEDIC 1000 WINS
HANDS DOWN.** The table to be
inserted is on page 473.

L. Sanchez

The software selection commitee completed it's feasibility study with input from many of you, and the results indicate that Medic 1000 is best suited to Gateways needs. All members agreed that of the three medical software package studied, Medic 1000 represents the best combination of funtion & price.

All of Members of the commitee spent 3 working days at the vendors location using the software to determine the time required to complete their jobs. particular tasks The table below "tells the story." Insert table.

Medic 1000 is to will be installed on our computer net work for a three-month trial within three weeks. Inhouse training will be offered by the vendor next month (dates to be announced). In the meantime, stop by Brook Sloan's office any Tuesday or Thurs-day to and see the video presentation of Medic 1000 to and skim the user manuals. The attachment shows the wide varelity of menu options available.

The initial training will involve a two-hour hands-on work-shop in the training room, plus 4 hours of vendor assistance at each workstation. The first group of trainees will also be able to assist the individuals trained later.

During the trial period, all of you will be asked to provide feed-back. Then if the Medic 1000 installation is not to be made permanant the other two options, Caduceus II and Hippocrates will be studied farther.

175a ▶ 5 Conditioning Practice

each line twice SS (slowly, then faster); DS between 2-line groups; if time permits, rekey selected lines

alphabet	1	Mary's five quaint, prized jugs and their six bowls broke into pieces.
fig/sym	2	Di (5/19/74) is my oldest sister; Lea (6/30/82) is my youngest sister.
one hand	3	Barbara beat Garrett in a debate on greater taxes on assessed acreage.
speed	4	He may sign the usual form by proxy if they make an audit of the firm.

| 1 | 2 | 3 | 4 | 5 | 6 | 7 | 8 | 9 | 10 | 11 | 12 | 13 | 14 |

175b ▶ 9 Evaluate Straight-Copy Skill

1. Take a 5' writing on the ¶s at the right.
2. Find *gwam* and number of errors.
3. Record score on LP p. 4.

| all letters used | A | 1.5 si | 5.7 awl | 80% hfw |

gwam 1' | 5'

Many people support the notion that a worker with a healthy body and mind is a valued worker. Healthy employees often have a greater chance for professional growth, produce more on the job, are happier with their lives, and are likely to be more successful than those who are in poor physical health or are not mentally alert.

If you want to have a healthy body, you should try to perform appropriate activities during your leisure time or try to find ways to enhance the level of your physical activity during your regular school day or workday. Brisk walking is a great way to bring exercise into daily activities with amazing ease and quick results.

Fast walks from your home to the bus stop, from the bus stop to your class, or from one class to another are very good ways to reap the benefits of exercise while you carry out your daily routine. Doing isometric exercises as you study, read, or watch television will produce excellent results. You should, of course, do only exercises that will not disrupt others.

	1'	5'
	14	3	44
	28	6	47
	43	9	49
	57	11	52
	65	13	54
	79	16	57
	94	19	60
	108	22	62
	122	24	65
	131	26	67
	145	29	70
	159	32	73
	174	35	76
	189	38	79
	203	41	82
	205	41	82

gwam 1' | 1 | 2 | 3 | 4 | 5 | 6 | 7 | 8 | 9 | 10 | 11 | 12 | 13 | 14 |
5' | 1 | 2 | 3 |

175c ▶ 36 Evaluate Document Processing Skills: Leftbound Report

Time Schedule

Plan and Prepare .... 3'
Timed Production .... 25'
Proofread/Compute *n-pram* ...... 8'

3 full sheets; correct errors

Document 1

Reformat the report in 174c as a leftbound report; but instead of using footnotes for documentation, use the endnotes shown at the right. Place them on a separate page.

Proofread and correct each page before removing a page from the machine or screen.

After you compute *n-pram*, turn in your work in document number order.

words

ENDNOTES   2

[1]The New Encyclopaedia Britannica, 15th   16
ed., 1985, s.v. "Tariffs."   22

[2]Philip K *at completion of* 'Engle-   35
wood Cliffs *Unit 40 – keep* , Inc.,   44
1984), p. 428 *43 gwam ≤ 10 or*   47

[3]Albert *fewer errors on 5'* ary of   59
Business T *writing* s, New   72
Jersey: Pi   81

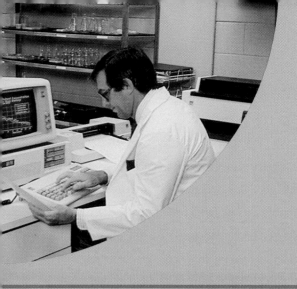

Gateway Medical Center (A Health Services Simulation)

Production Goals

1. To adapt previously acquired formatting and language skills to documents processed in medical offices.

2. To improve your ability to use judgment in the absence of specific directions.

3. To improve your ability to organize work and materials.

Documents Processed

1. Simplified memorandum with table
2. Four-column table
3. Statements of account
4. Partnership contract
5. Form letters
6. Block format letter
7. Job descriptions
8. Continuation sheets

GATEWAY MEDICAL CENTER

Read the "Work Assignment" before beginning the documents on pages 472-477. When processing documents in this simulation, refer to the format guides and other information provided here.

Work Assignment

Gateway Medical Center welcomes a new "temp"--you. As a temporary medical assistant at Gateway, you'll apply many of the document production skills you acquired at Bayview Legal Services and in school.

Gateway Medical Center is a corporation of 15 physicians, who offer primary care specialties including family practice, internal medicine, and cardiology. Office support is provided by three small support teams, each with a supervisor. An office manager, Mr. Charles W. Beard, oversees all office support personnel.

Your supervisor is Ms. Louise M. Sanchez. The physicians supported by your team--Dr. Janice Myers, cardiologist; Dr. Matthew W. Lloyd, family practitioner, and Dr. Kyle A. Liebman, internist--request document processing services from Ms. Sanchez, who then assigns the documents to someone in your support team.

During your initial meeting Ms. Sanchez emphasizes the importance of complete accuracy in a medical office, noting that patients' health--even their lives--are at stake when errors occur in medical documents. In particular, Ms. Sanchez cautions you always to transcribe a doctor's hand-written notes or dictation *verbatim;* that is, word for word and with the exact punctuation. In addition, of course, she stresses that careful proofreading is a *must* in this office.

Your supervisor says she usually will give you directions in writing, because she realizes that temporary medical assistants may need to "go over" the directions more than once. Until you become familiar with the office procedures and materials, she'll provide additional information you'll need, such as patients' address cards, with her written directions.

Ms. Sanchez then provides you with a copy of "Procedures Manual for Medical Assistants" and suggests that you take time to read carefully the document format guides that she has highlighted.

Procedures Manual for Medical Assistants

The following is a description of the standard document formats used at Gateway Medical Center.

Memorandums--Simplified Format

Stationery: plain sheets.
PB: line 10.
SM: 1". All memo parts begin at LM.
LS: QS below date and last line of body; DS below other parts; SS paragraphs.

Letters--Block Format/Open Punctuation

Stationery: Gateway letterhead.
PB: line 12.
SM: 1". All letter parts begin at LM.
LS: Same as memorandums.
Signature Line: Key the doctor's medical title (M.D.) on the same line following his/her name.

Tables

Stationery: plain sheet, unless in body of letter or memorandum.
CV: center vertically.
CH: center horizontally.
Column Headings: blocked.
CS: determined by operator.
LS: DS below main, secondary, and column headings, and between items; in body of letter or memorandum, DS above and below table.

Reports--Medical and Nonmedical

Stationery: plain sheets.
PB: line 10 or line 12 (page 1); line 6 (other pages).
SM: 1" unless "leftbound" is specified; then, 1½" LM, 1" RM.
LS: QS below main heading; DS elsewhere.
Enumerations: SS; DS between items; hang indent.
PE: at about line 60.

PHASE 8

ENHANCE SKILL IN DOCUMENT PROCESSING

Employees in a modern office are called upon to prepare many different kinds of communications. In Phase 8, you will learn how to prepare some special communications, including memorandums and letters with special features. At the same time, special drills are included to increase your efficiency at the keyboard and to improve your communications skills.

Specifically, the objectives of Phase 8 are as follows:

1. To develop skill in formatting special communications, including memorandums and letters with special features.

2. To improve your ability to plan, organize, and prepare communications quickly and efficiently.

3. To increase your basic keyboarding and language skills.

Document 7
List of Pending Cases

plain full sheet

Miss Lee has requested an updated list of cases that are pending. She will need this list tomorrow for the meeting of staff attorneys.

She has revised last week's list of pending cases (shown at the right). She has numbered the cases, putting them in alphabetical order for you. To save time, use blocked column headings.

Add a two-line main heading:

LIST OF PENDING CASES
JUNG JIN LEE

For the secondary heading, use **November 11, 19--.**

Arrange names in alphabetical order

	Client Name	~~Client~~ Number *Case No.*	Matter
6	Thomas P. Smothers	14,865	Divorce
	~~Watson & Watson, Inc.~~	~~16,521~~	~~Tax Planning~~
3	Bor-Rung Ousmane	15,313	Loan Closing
2	Follin, Follin & Guest, Inc.	15,989	Estate *and Tax* Planning
4	E. Jon and ~~Connie~~ *Constance* M. Qualles	15,231	House Closing
7	Jose *J.* Vinicki	13,775	Bankruptcy
1	*Helga A. Fitz*	*15,128*	*Personal Injury*
5	*Sims Company, Inc.*	*15,001*	*Proof of Claim*

Document 8
Acknowledgment of Signature by Notary Public

LP p. 161

Process the acknowledgment for Case No. 14,865. In the first paragraph, replace the blanks; insert client's name (from Document 7); insert the appropriate pronoun (her or his).

In the other paragraphs, key 1½" lines where indicated; the day and month will be written in by the notary public.

STATE OF CALIFORNIA

COUNTY OF ALAMEDA

     Personally appeared before me, the undersigned authority in and for the jurisdiction aforesaid, the within named _____, who being by me first duly sworn, states on _____ oath that all facts and matters contained in the above complaint are true and correct as therein stated and that the complaint is not filed by collusion with the defendant.

     Witness my signature this the _____ day of _____, 19--,

_____
(INSERT NAME OF CLIENT)

     SWORN TO and subscribed before me on this the _____ day of _____, 19--.

_____
NOTARY PUBLIC

MY COMMISSION EXPIRES:

_____

(SEAL)

Learn to Format Special Communications

Learning Goals

1. To learn how to process letters on executive-size stationery.

2. To learn how to format and process a Simplified Block Letter.

3. To learn how to produce form letters from form paragraphs.

4. To build production skill on special communications.

Format Guides

1. Paper guide at *0* (for typewriters).

2. LL: 70 spaces for drill copy; as directed for documents.

3. LS: SS drill lines with DS between groups; space documents as directed or required.

STANDARD FORMATTING GUIDES: SPECIAL COMMUNICATIONS

Caption: Executive-size letter 7¼″ × 10½″

Caption: Simplified Block Letter

Standard Formatting Guides

Executive-size Stationery (7¼″ × 10½″)

Format. Any letter format may be used.

Margins. 1″ side; at least 1″ bottom

Dateline. Line 12

Spacing. QS below dateline and complimentary close; DS above and below salutation, above complimentary close, below name of sender or title of writer, and above and below any special parts.

Simplified Block Letter

Dateline. Line 12

Letter Address. ALL CAPS with no punctuation

Format. Block

The salutation and complimentary close are omitted. A subject line in ALL CAPS is always included. Writer's name and title are keyed in ALL CAPS.

Margins. 6-inch line (12-72+, 10-pitch; 15-87+, 12-pitch)

Spacing. QS below date; DS above and below subject line; QS below letter body; DS between special parts.

Form Letters

A standardized letter that can be sent to numerous addressees is known as a form letter or "boilerplate." A form letter (or paragraphs which can be used to make up a letter) can be stored in memory on a diskette or an electronic typewriter and retrieved when needed. Address lists can be stored on the same diskette or on a separate diskette. Through text merging, a form letter and the addresses can be merged to provide an original letter to each addressee.

Format. Any letter format can be used.

5. The said ingestion of Kwell lotion by the ward and resulting injuries to the ward was a direct result of the gross negligence of the Tseng Pharmacy, Inc., its agents and employees, in the following particulars:

A. By failing to properly dispense medication pursuant according to a prescription therefor;

B. By negligently substituting a toxic substance for the prescribed medicine with total disregard for the consequences of its use by a small child;

C. By failing to properly label medication;

6. As a direct and proximate result of the negligence of defendant, its agents and employees aforedescribed, plaintiff's ward was painfully and seriously injured. Injuries sustained by plaintiff's ward include, but are not limited to burns and blisters of the face, lips, mouth, and tongue. Likewise, as a result, plaintiff's ward was severely nauseated for an extended period of time and required treatment not only for nausea and the burns and blisters but also for the internal effects of ingestion of Kwell lotion. All of said injuries are the direct and proximate result of the negligence of the said defendant.

Wherefore, Premises Considered, plaintiff demands judgement of and against said defendant in such amount sufficient to compensate plaintiff's ward for all losses and damages sustained by ward, which amount is in excess of the minimum jurisdiction limitations of the Circuit Courts of the State of California, together with costs of court.

Respectfully submitted by

Begin the closing lines at the center of the line of writing. Below Submitted by, QS and key a blank line for the signature; SS and key the following:

Kelly Q. Janqusek
Attorney for Plaintiff

176a ▶ 5
Conditioning Practice

each line twice SS (slowly, then faster); if time permits, take 1' writings on line 4

alphabet	1	James quickly analyzed and reviewed the usage of the complex keyboard.
figures	2	The pamphlet published in 1991 has 432,500 entries and 6,870 pictures.
fig/sym	3	The discount on Invoice #3196-91V should be $171.22 (4% of $4,280.50).
speed	4	Rosie may go with them by bus to the city and to the dock by the lake.

| 1 | 2 | 3 | 4 | 5 | 6 | 7 | 8 | 9 | 10 | 11 | 12 | 13 | 14 |

176b ▶ 45
Learn to Format Letters on Executive-size Stationery

LP pp. 53-57

1. Study and follow the formatting guides for executive-size stationery on p. 308.

2. Use modified block format, open punctuation, for Letters 1 and 2; address envelopes; circle errors.

Letter 1
Key the first letter in the proper format.

Letter 2
Key the script letter with a date of May 20, 19-- to

Mr. Arthur T. Ashby
58 Marietta Street N.W.
Atlanta, GA 30303-1248

for the signature of Lee T. Levy, executive vice president. Use an appropriate salutation and complimentary close.

Letter 3
Rekey Letter 2 in block format, open punctuation to

Mrs. Keith C. Thomas
260 Peachtree Street N.E.
Atlanta, GA 30303-1020

for the signature of Mr. Levy. Use an appropriate salutation and complimentary close.

	words
September 1, 19-- Mr. Samuel T. Ortega, President Ortega Office Machines	15
Distributors, Inc. 210 St. James Avenue Boston, MA 02116-4985 Dear	28
Mr. Ortega	30
Are you interested in becoming a regional distributor for a new word proces-	46
sor we are currently developing? Tentatively called the TELEWRITER, this	60
word processor will extend beyond the current state-of-the-art machines and	76
will offer features never before found in a low-cost machine.	88
The TELEWRITER will be a lightweight, portable machine with a detachable	103
keyboard and a combined CRT and printer. The printer will utilize inter-	117
changeable daisy wheels which will permit the use of many type styles. With	133
the built-in software, most operators will be able to perform basic editing	148
functions at high rates of speed after an hour of training. There are no com-	163
plex codes or commands to memorize.	171
We plan to introduce this machine at the National Office Systems Confer-	185
ence to be held in New York in April of next year. If you are interested in be-	201
coming the distributor of this machine in the New England area, please	215
write to Ms. Joan Winston, our sales manager, at the address above.	229
Sincerely yours Mrs. Jessica C. Madison Director of Marketing xx	241/**263**

---

opening lines 20

(¶1) As one of our favored customers, you are cordially	30
invited to attend a special preview of our exhibit at	41
the American Electronics Trade Show to be held at The	52
Omni June 10-12. (¶2) Your preview will begin at 6:30 p.m.	63
on June 9 in the V.I.P. Lounge. After the reception, you	75
will view our presentations of the new JANUS Optical	85
Character Reader and the amazing new ZEUS Facsimile	96
Machine. (¶3) So that we may complete our plans, will	106
you please call my executive assistant, Frank King,	116
at 555-7484 and let him know if you can join us.	126

closing lines 137/**150**

Document 6
Complaint--Personal Injury

plain full sheets

Kelly Q. Janqusek spoke recently with a new client, Helga A. Fitz, who is the guardian of James P. Cox. Ms. Janqusek will file a complaint against Tseng Pharmacy (defendant) in **Alameda** County circuit court for Mrs. Fitz on behalf of her ward, James P. Cox.

Although the complaint cannot be finalized until additional information is received from the attending physician at Alameda County Hospital, Ms. Janqusek requests that you prepare a first draft on plain paper for her review.

The case (No. **15,219**) is styled as follows: **HELGA A. FITZ** (PLAINTIFF) V. **TSENG PHARMACY, INC.** (DEFENDANT). Do not key the underlines; simply insert the appropriate information in the blanks.

IN THE CIRCUIT COURT OF _____ COUNTY

STATE OF CALIFORNIA

_____, GUARDIAN OF THE ESTATE   PLAINTIFF

V.   NO. _____

_____   DEFENDANT

COMPLAINT

          Comes now _____, guardian of the estate of _____, unmarried minor, plaintiff in the above styled and numbered cause, by and through her attorneys of record, and files this complaint against _____, defendant, and for cause of action would show unto the Court the following facts, to-wit:

          1. Plaintiff is an adult resident citizen of _____ County, California, and is the duly appointed and acting guardian of the estate of _____, an unmarried minor and present citizen of _____ County, California. Plaintiff was duly appointed guardian of the estate of her ward by a decree of the Chancery Court of _____ County, California.

          2. _____ is a corporation, organized and existing under the laws of the State of California, and whose registered agent for service of process is Victoria P. Lane, 1305 Franklin Street, Oakland, CA 94612-2033.

          3. On or about January 13, 19--, plaintiff's ward had a cold and was treated by his personal physician, Dr. Emily J. Long. Dr. Long prescribed medication, *and the plaintiff had the prescription* filled by Tseng Pharmacy, Inc. The plaintiff administered *pursuant to bottle directions* the prescription to the ward. Immediately the ward began to vomit and heave.

¶4. Approximately 45 minutes thereafter, an agent or employee of Tseng Pharmacy, Inc., appeared at *the* plaintiff's residence, and took aforesaid prescription, presented another bottle of medicine, and *advised* her to take the ward to the emergency room. The ward had ingested Kwell Lotion, a toxin not intended for internal use. Plaintiff immediately took her ward to the emergency room of Alameda *County* Hospital where he was treated.

(continued, p. 469)

177a ▶ 5
Conditioning Practice
each line twice SS (slowly, then faster); if time permits, take 1' writings on line 4

alphabet	1	Zack may request we adjust gross profits on big items except vehicles.
figures	2	In June, 5,498 units were processed; in July, 7,215; in August, 8,603.
fig/sym	3	The balance (as of May 1, 1991) was $36,450,700 -- an increase of 28.6%.
speed	4	To the dismay of the girls, he kept the key to the shanty by the lake.

| 1 | 2 | 3 | 4 | 5 | 6 | 7 | 8 | 9 | 10 | 11 | 12 | 13 | 14 |

177b ▶ 45
Learn to Format Simplified Block Letter

Letter 1
plain full sheet
1. Study the formatting guides for the Simplified Block Letter on p. 308 and the model letter on p. 311.
2. Key the Simplified Block Letter on p. 311 in the proper format.
3. Proofread; circle errors; check copy for correct format.

Letter 2
LP p. 59
1. Key the letter shown at the right in the Simplified Block Letter format. List the enumerated items.
2. Proofread; circle errors; check copy for correct format.

words

July 5, 19-- GLOBAL SALES INC 33 BROAD STREET NW ATLANTA GA 30303- 13
2108 ZEUS FACSIMILE MACHINE 19

When you want to send a document quickly, why spend hours at a cost of 33
dollars when you can send the document in minutes for a few cents with a 48
ZEUS Facsimile Machine. Consider these facts. 1. The ZEUS can transmit 63
documents, including drawings and photographs, at the speed of light any- 77
where in the country or the world--wherever there is a telephone. As a 91
multipurpose machine, the ZEUS can receive as well as transmit messages. 106
2. You can transmit documents to just one person or location or to almost 121
100 addressees simultaneously. 3. The ZEUS is small enough to set on a 136
desktop and merely plugs into the nearest electrical outlet and telephone 151
line. 4. Personnel can be trained to use the ZEUS in just a few minutes. 166
5. Errors in messages are completely eliminated. The document received 180
is an exact copy of the document transmitted. 6. Continuous (24-hour) op- 195
eration is possible which solves communications problems caused by the dif- 210
ferences in time throughout the country and the world. 221

Let us show you how you can save time and money with a ZEUS Facsimile 235
Machine. Call Lisa Dent at 555-7442 for a demonstration in your office. 250

JAMES M. TAYLOR, SALES DIRECTOR xx 257/**269**

Letter 3
LP p. 61
1. Key the letter shown at the right in the Simplified Block Letter format.
2. Proofread; circle errors; check copy for correct format.

July 1, 19-- MISS JULIA C REED DIRECTOR OF ADMINISTRATION JOHN- 12
SON & SONS INC 120 EAST HANCOCK AVENUE ATHENS GA 30601-1203 25
JANUS OPTICAL CHARACTER READER 31

For years, the United States Postal Service has been able to process mail with 47
phenomenal speed through the use of Optical Character Readers (OCR) 60
to scan ZIP Codes. Using OCR equipment, banks process checks and deposit 75
slips electronically by "reading" magnetic ink characters to sort the docu- 90
ments and post all necessary data to the proper account. 101

Thanks to the JANUS Optical Character Reader, you too can process docu- 115
ments with great speed. The JANUS has the ability to read printed or type- 130
written characters from almost any document. In a matter of minutes, the 145
JANUS will "read" and enter a document into a word processor for revision 160
or storage. Think of the time and money this can save. 171

The JANUS Optical Character Reader can be installed in minutes. For a 185
demonstration of this machine, simply call Jeff Barnes at 555-7430 to arrange 201
for a demonstration in your office at your convenience. 212

JAMES M. TAYLOR, SALES DIRECTOR xx 219/**241**

Document 4
Labor and Materials Statement
plain full sheet

Mr. Gonzales' client, Mr. Sims, gave him this copy of Exhibit A, which will be attached to the Proof of Claim (Document 3). This table provides supporting evidence in the Sims case.

1. Verify the accuracy of amounts in the last column (for example, for the first item, multiply 20 × 40.00) and make needed corrections.

2. Verify the accuracy of the total.

3. Process the table DS.

Labor and Materials Statement
For Overton Inn, Ltd.
September 1, 19--

Description	Unit Cost	Total
Labor, 20 hours	$ 40.00	$ 800.00
Carpet, 450 sq. yd.	18.99	8,545.50
Padding, 450 sq. yd.	1.00	45.00
3/4" molding, 500 ft.	.75	375.00
Paneling, 5 sheets	18.00	90.00
Nails, 2 lbs.	1.73	34.60
Paint, 15 gallons	19.59	293.85
Total		$10,557.81

Document 5
Form Letters
LP pp. 157-159

I need to have this form letter processed for my signature, **Jose B. Arias, Office Manager.** I drafted the message hurriedly, so you may need to correct errors in spelling and grammar. Use the date, addresses, and variables (V) listed below.

November 10, 19--
Mr. J. K. Randall
Randall Cablevision, Inc.
One Westwood Court
Oakland, CA 94611-2788
V1: **two years**
V2: **Subchapter S Corporation**
V3: **Mr. Randall**
V4: **Randall Cablevision, Inc.**

Mrs. Carmen G. Anglin
Cottage Crafters, Ltd.
1624 Jackson Street
Oakland, CA 94612-3205
V1: **year**
V2: **partnership**
V3: **Mrs. Anglin**
V4: **Cottage Crafters, Ltd.**

The professional staff at Bayview Legal Services, Inc., feels priviledged to have ~~had the opportunity to~~ provide legal services to your organization *for the past (V1)* ~~this year.~~ Our top priority have been to provide up-to-date, timely information as a basis for accurate advise about your *(V2)* ~~(type of organization)~~.

In anticipation of our continuing this business relationship, I have enclosed a proposal for next years retainer of legal services. Bayview would like to serve your legal needs in the ~~coming year~~ *future* stet. To better serve you we have implemented a sophisticated telecommunication system, which will be in place ~~January 1.~~ stet *by the first of next month*. Also, each member of our staff is committed to serving you in the most professional and competent manner.

(V3) ~~(Title and last name)~~, please consider our proposal carefully and call me at 555-3129 to discuss continuing our legal service to *(V4)* ~~(name of company)~~.

Communication ✕ Concepts Inc.

178 S. Prospect Avenue ■ San Bernardino, CA 92410-4567 ■ (714) 586-7934

words in parts   total words

4   4

Dateline   September 15, 19--   _{QS}   line 12

MISS MICHELLE T LAWSON	8	8
DEL AMO SECRETARIAL SERVICE	14	14
21200 HAWTHORNE AVE	18	18
LOS ANGELES CA 90058-2820 _{DS}	23	23

Subject line   SIMPLIFIED BLOCK LETTER FORMAT _{DS}   29   29

Body of letter   This letter illustrates the features that distinguish the   12   41
Simplified Block Letter format from the standard block format. _{DS}   24   54

1. The date is placed on line 12 so that the letter address   37   66
will show through the window of a window envelope when used. _{DS}   49   78

2. The letter address is keyed in the style recommended by   61   90
the U. S. Postal Service for OCR processing: ALL-CAP letters   73   103
with no punctuation. Cap-and-lowercase letters with punctua-   85   115
tion may be used if that is the format of the addresses stored   98   127
in an electronic address file. Personal titles may be omitted. _{DS}   111   140

3. A subject line replaces the traditional salutation which   123   153
some people find objectionable. The subject line may be keyed   136   165
in ALL-CAP or cap-and-lowercase letters. A double space is   148   177
left above and below it. _{DS}   153   182

4. The complimentary close, which some people view as a need-   165   195
less appendage, is omitted. _{DS}   171   200

5. The writer's name is placed on the fourth line space below   184   213
the body of the letter. The writer's title or department name   196   226
may appear on the line with the writer's name or on the next   208   238
line below it. The signature block may be keyed in ALL-CAP or   221   250
cap-and-lowercase letters. _{DS}   227   256

6. A standard-length line is used for all letters. A six-inch   239   269
line is a common length (60 pica or 10-pitch spaces; 72 elite   252   281
or 12-pitch spaces). _{DS}   256   286

The features listed and illustrated here are designed to bring   269   298
efficiency to the electronic processing of mail. _{QS}   278   308

Omit complimentary close   *Maria J. Lopez*

Writer's name and title   MRS. MARIA T. LOPEZ, DIRECTOR _{DS}   6   314

Reference notation   tms   7   314

shown in pica type
six-inch line

Simplified Block Letter

Document 3
Proof of Claim

LP pp. 153-155

Using the information provided below by Joseph W. Gonzalez, the attorney handling the case, process a Proof of Claim for the Sims case. Format and key the Proof of Claim given at the right, replacing the details with Mr. Gonzelez' information.

RE: OVERTON INN, LTD.
A PARTNERSHIP COMPOSED OF
STEPHEN P. GODDARD
GENERAL MANAGER
NO. 15,001

Changes in ¶s:

¶1: Matthew K. Sims, who resides at 901 Fairhaven Way, Oakland, CA 94947-3366, is President of Sims Company, Inc.

¶2: sum of ten thousand five hundred fifty-seven and 81/100 dollars ($10,557.81).

¶3: labor performed and materials furnished to the Overton Inn, Ltd., renovation project.

Special Notes:
Place the dateline a QS below the last line of the document. The dateline should be 1½" long. Use the Sims company name and replace the name under the By line. Key the "penalty" ¶ as shown.

IN THE UNITED STATES BANKRUPTCY COURT

NORTHERN DISTRICT OF CALIFORNIA

IN RE: RESEARCH TECHNOLOGY, INC.
A LIMITED PARTNERSHIP COMPOSED OF
SANDRA F. GIACHELLI
GENERAL PARTNER   NO. ~~88-0013702 BKS-EEL~~

PROOF OF CLAIM

DS the #s

    1. The undersigned, ~~Howard D. Delk, who resides at 5302 Estates Drive, Oakland, CA 94618-4172,~~ is President of ~~In-novative Software, Inc.~~, a corporation organized under the laws of the State of California, with its principal place of business in Oakland, California, and is duly authorized to make this Proof of Claim on behalf of said corporation.
    2. The debtor was at the time of the filing of the petition initiating this case, and is still indebted to this claimant in the ~~sum of ($12,331.99)~~.
    3. The consideration for this debt is as follows: ~~li-censed software and 40 hours of support supplied to Research Technology, Inc.~~
    4. A true and correct copy of the statement of account upon which this claim is founded is attached hereto as Exhibit A.
    5. No judgment has been rendered on the claim of ~~In-novative Software, Inc.~~
    6. The amount of all payments on this claim has been credited and deducted for the purpose of making this proof of claim.
    7. This claim is not subject to any set off or counterclaim.
    8. This claim is a general unsecured claim except to the extent that a lien, if any, described herein is sufficient to satisfy the claim.

Dated: _____

                 ~~INNOVATIVE SOFTWARE, INC.~~

                 BY: _____
                 HOWARD ~~D.~~ DELK, PRESIDENT

PENALTY FOR PRESENTING FRAUDULENT CLAIM: FINE OF NOT MORE THAN $5,000.00 OR IMPRISONMENT FOR NOT MORE THAN FIVE YEARS, OR BOTH. TITLE 18 USC. SECTION 152.

178a ▶ 5
*Conditioning
Practice*

each line twice SS
(slowly, then faster);
if time permits, take
1′ writings on line 4

alphabet	1	Jack said he filled the boutique with bizarre and very expensive gems.
figures	2	Note carefully the footnotes on pages 19, 32, 46, 57, 68, 83, and 107.
fig/sym	3	Barr & Derry paid the balance ($852.93) on September 6 by Check #7410.
speed	4	Ruth paid for both of the mementos of their visit to the ancient city.

| 1 | 2 | 3 | 4 | 5 | 6 | 7 | 8 | 9 | 10 | 11 | 12 | 13 | 14 |

178b ▶ 45
*Learn to Produce
Letters from Form
Paragraphs*

LP pp. 63-67

1. Prepare form letters
below in block format, open
punctuation to be signed by
Jan T. Scott, Chief, Software
Division.

2. Use current date (on
line 16) and 1½″ side margins.
Supply an appropriate salutation and complimentary
close; address envelopes;
circle errors.

Letter 1
Prepare letter to

**Miss Rose T. Chase
223 W. Jefferson Street
Louisville, KY 40202-3001**

Use ¶s 1.2 (product: IDEAL-
WORD), 2.1, and 3.3.
Total words: 177/**190**

Letter 2
Prepare letter to

**Mr. John P. Powers
913 Main Street
Kansas City, MO 64105-2750**

Use ¶s 1.1 (product: DB III),
2.3, and 3.1.
Total words: 191/**203**

Letter 3
Prepare letter to

**Ms. Nicole P. White
129 Madison Avenue
Memphis, TN 38103-3475**

Use ¶s 1.3 (name: David
Mays; product: ABC ARRAY),
2.2, and 3.2.
Total words: 179/**191**

¶ 1.1 At a recent trade show, you requested that we provide additional information about (insert product). We are pleased that our demonstration at the show prompted you to write for more information.

¶ 1.2 Thank you for your recent letter requesting information about (insert product). We are always pleased to receive requests of this nature which reflect an interest in one of our products.

¶ 1.3 We are pleased to learn that (insert name) suggested that you write to us about (name of product). It is always satisfying to learn that we have been recommended by one of our customers.

¶ 2.1 IDEALWORD 2.1 is one of the most advanced word processing programs available. In addition to the usual editing functions, IDEALWORD includes a thesaurus, spell checking, and outlining features. It also permits you to create personalized letters, forms, and tables, and to merge text through automated routines. Of paramount importance, IDEALWORD 2.1 is flexible, speedy, and easy to learn.

¶ 2.2 ABC ARRAY is a spreadsheet program which offers a great deal more than automatic calculations. Templates are included which permit you to perform typical data processing tasks such as analyzing, projecting, and forecasting statistical data. For greater flexibility, individual cells can be moved from one location to another and entire rows and cells can be rearranged. For ease of comprehension, the data can be displayed as charts and graphs.

¶ 2.3 DB III is a data base program which opens up the world of information to you. With DB III you can create files, store and retrieve data, and build reports quickly by following a few simple directions. If you want information on a specific topic, simply key in the topic and the computer will conduct an electronic search. The Structured Query Language (SQL) incorporated into DB III permits you to interface with different programs and systems to broaden your data base.

¶ 3.1 Thank you for your inquiry. If you would like any additional information, please call or write us and we will be happy to provide it.

¶ 3.2 If you would like a demonstration of this program, please call us at 1-800-555-7400 and we will be pleased to arrange it.

¶ 3.3 Your inquiry has been forwarded to our regional representative in your area who will call you in a few weeks to see if we can be of any further service.

276a-279a ▶ 5 (daily)
Equipment Check
each line twice SS; DS
between 2-line groups

alphabet	1	Dez will have to get a jet flight back to Rio to my unique exposition.
figures	2	At 6:30 p.m. on June 27, 1991, 458 guests attended the garden wedding.
fig/sym	3	A May 5, 1992, sales increase of $7,068 (43%) was praised by everyone.
speed	4	The girl paid a visit to the downtown auto firm to sign the work form.

| 1 | 2 | 3 | 4 | 5 | 6 | 7 | 8 | 9 | 10 | 11 | 12 | 13 | 14 |

276b-279b ▶ 45 (daily)
Document Processing

Mr. Jose B. Arias, the office manager, hands you a series of eight documents to be formatted and keyed. Using the notes given with each document, process as many documents as you can in each work session. Proofread and correct each document before removing it from your machine or printing a copy. Be alert for any unmarked errors that need to be corrected.

Document 1
Letter

LP. 151

Process, for **Miss Jung Jin Lee's** signature, the letter at the right. Miss Lee's title is **Attorney-at-Law.**

Date: **November 8, 19--**

Letter address:
The Honorable S. Troy Adams
Judge of the Chancery Court
Oakland Courthouse
1225 Fallon Street
Oakland, CA 94612-1038

Reference line:
RE: Chancery Court #169008

Salutation:
Dear Judge Adams

Subject line:
Jordan v. Jordan

Document 2
Memo

plain full sheet

I want the memo addressed to **All Attorneys and Paralegal Staff.** Use **November 8, 19--** as the date. Supply a subject line. Use my name, **Jose B. Arias,** as the writer of the memo.

The case, *indicated* shown above is ready for trail. I have discussed court dates with the attorney of the other party, and we have agreed that both parties can be available for a court appearance on November 28 or 30 or December 5, 8, or 15.

If you are unavailable on anyone of these dates, *please* let us know. Then we can make final plans to appear in your court on that date.

Judge Adams, you should be aware of an important *settlement* problem. The parties have been unable to agree on child custody arangements. Mr. Jordan is considering relocating in Pittsburgh; therefor, weekend visitation rights would not be possible. We hope to reach an agreement before appearing in court.

We look forward to recieving confirmation of one of these suggested dates.

A *special* staff meeting for attorneys and para legal staff will be held on Friday, november 12, at 10 a.m. in Conference Room C.

With the implimentation of the new telecomunication system in our office we must develop procedures that will continue to safeguard confidential information. In preparation for this meeting on Friday, please review the enclosed draft of new procedures concerning record protection. These new procedures will supersede procedures currently printed in the Office Procedures Manual.

During the past years Bayview has *gained* earned an outstanding reputation for confidential handling of legal services. Our clients continue to depend upon us to keep their private matters in confidence. If we are to maintain our reputation, problems of confidentiality must be a major concern. I look forward to your contributions at this meeting on Friday.

179a ▶ 5
Conditioning Practice

each line twice SS (slowly, then faster); if time permits, take 1' writings on line 4

alphabet 1 Jane found that good executives were able to analyze problems quickly.

figures 2 Of the 18,907 computers, 16,853 were accepted and 2,054 were rejected.

fig/sym 3 Read pages 245-306 in Infosystems by Ray & Dorr (Third Edition, 1987).

speed 4 The rich men may wish to amend the title of the firm when they own it.

| 1 | 2 | 3 | 4 | 5 | 6 | 7 | 8 | 9 | 10 | 11 | 12 | 13 | 14 |

179b ▶ 45
Sustained Production: Special Communications

letterheads, LP pp. 69-75 plain full sheets

Time Schedule
Plan and prepare .... 5'
Timed production .... 30'
Proofread; compute *n-pram* .... 10'

1. Make a list of letters to be processed:
p. 310, 177b, Letter 2
p. 309, 176b, Letter 1
p. 309, 176b, Letter 2
p. 312, 178b, Letter 2
2. Arrange letterheads and plain paper for efficient handling.

3. Key the documents for 30' when directed to begin. Proofread each letter carefully before removing it from the machine. Correct errors neatly. Address envelopes. If you finish before time is called, begin with Letter 1 and rekey on plain sheets as many documents as possible in the time remaining.

4. Compute *n-pram*:

$$\frac{\text{total words} - \text{penalty*}}{\text{time (30')}}$$

*penalty is 15 words for each uncorrected error.
5. Turn in letters arranged in the order given in Step 1.

180a ▶ 5
Conditioning Practice

each line twice SS (slowly, then faster); rekey selected lines if time permits

alphabet 1 Shares of the Wexcom stock took a sizable jump in quite heavy trading.

figures 2 The panel met on June 1, 24, 27, and 30 and on July 5, 6, 7, 8, and 9.

fig/sym 3 Ross & Lawler offered a discount of $437 (10% and 2%) on Order #56891.

speed 4 The visitor to the island paid for a ruby and a pair of antique bowls.

| 1 | 2 | 3 | 4 | 5 | 6 | 7 | 8 | 9 | 10 | 11 | 12 | 13 | 14 |

180b ▶ 45 *Measure Production Skills: Special Communications*

letterheads, LP pp. 77-83 plain full sheets
Refer to Time Schedule in 179b.
Letter 1
Letter on Executive-size Stationery

LP p. 77

modified block format, open punctuation

1. Arrange letterheads and plain sheets for efficient handling.
2. Key for 30' the letters below and on page 314. Correct errors neatly; address envelopes.

Proofread each letter carefully *before* you remove it from the machine. If you finish before time is called, begin with Letter 1 and rekey on plain sheets as many

letters as possible in the time remaining.
3. After the timed production, proofread and circle any errors you may have missed; compute *n-pram.*

words

April 24, 19-- Mr. Michael C. Evans Vice President CMC Industries, 13
Inc. Suite 6452 World Trade Center New York, NY 10048-3326 Dear 26
Mr. Evans 28

Alpha Electronics is offering a one-day seminar entitled "Analyzing Informa- 43
tion Needs" for managers at all levels. This seminar will be held in several 59
Eastern cities during the month of June. 67

The first meeting will be held in Philadelphia at the William Penn Room of 82
the International Inn on June 6. On June 13, the seminar will be held in the 98
Crystal Suite of the Boston Concord Shelley Hotel. The seminar will be re- 113
peated in the Rodney Room of the Concord Hotel in Wilmington, Delaware, 127
on June 20 and in the Petite Ballroom of the Chatham Hotel in Baltimore, 142
Maryland, on June 27. 146

(continued, p. 314)

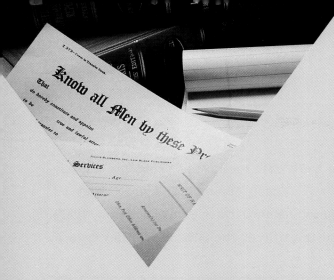

Bayview Legal Services, Inc.
(A Legal Office Simulation)

Production Goals

1. To prepare, in an acceptable form with all errors corrected, documents processed in a legal office.

2. To improve your document processing skills by keying from rough-draft and script source documents.

3. To improve proofreading skills by detecting and correcting errors.

Documents Processed

1. Block format letter
2. Simplified memo
3. Proof of Claim
4. Tables
5. Form letter with variables
6. Complaint
7. Acknowledgment of Signature

BAYVIEW LEGAL SERVICES, INC. (A Legal Office Simulation)

Before you begin the work of this simulation, read the introductory material and study the Format Guides for Legal Documents, Letters, Memos, and Tables at the right.

Your first temporary work assignment is in the office of Bayview Legal Services, Inc., 1540 San Pablo Avenue, Oakland, CA 94612-9475. Bayview consists of a group of five attorneys and a paralegal staff who share an on-site information processing center (IPC). Your position is in Bayview's IPC, preparing a variety of documents for the office manager, Jose B. Arias, and three attorneys: Miss Lee, Mr. Gonzalez, and Ms. Janqusek.

This legal firm is committed to following standard operating procedures. Its personnel have found that the organization is more effective when everyone follows these procedures. Therefore, review carefully the following guidelines taken from the <u>Office Procedures Manual</u> of Bayview Legal Services, Inc. If a formatting guide is not given, use your previously acquired knowledge to decide the format features for a document.

Accuracy

To serve the intended purpose, a legal document must be free of errors. In particular, the names of people and places and all figures must appear without error or obvious correction. Correct any errors made by the originator of a document; check spelling, punctuation, and grammar (a court case may rest on a misplaced comma).

Stationery

Legal documents and interoffice memos should be prepared on 8½″ × 11″ paper. (If ruled paper is to be used, it will be specified.) Letters are processed on the firm's letterhead.

Format Guides for Legal Documents

Margins. Each page should have a left margin of 1½″ and a right margin of ½″. On ruled paper, set the left margin 2 spaces to the right of the double rule; set the right margin 3-5 spaces to the left of the single rule. The standard page beginning (PB) is line 12; the bottom margin (BM) may be 1″ to 2″. (At least two lines of the body of a document must appear on the same page as the signatures.)

Titles. The title of a legal document (example, PROOF OF CLAIM) is keyed in all capital letters. A single line that extends from margin to margin is keyed above and below the title of the document. (See model below.)

```
          IN THE UNITED STATES BANKRUPTCY COURT
               NORTHERN DISTRICT OF CALIFORNIA

IN RE:  OVERTON, INN, LTD.
        A PARTNERSHIP COMPOSED OF
        STEPHEN P. GODDARD
        GENERAL MANAGER          NO.  88-0026500-EEL  SS
                                                      DS
              PROOF OF CLAIM                          SS
                                                      DS
        1.  The undersigned, Matthew K. Sims, who resides at
```

Paragraph indention and spacing. Paragraphs should be indented 10 spaces. The body of a legal document, including numbered paragraphs, generally should be double-spaced.

Page numbers. A page number should be centered at the bottom of each page, including the first, a DS below the last line of text and preceded and followed by a hyphen (example, -2-).

Signature lines. Lines for signatures should be about 3″ long. When more than one signature is needed, DS between the lines.

Format Guides for Letters, Memos, and Tables

Letters. Prepare letters in block format with open punctuation. Use 1½″ side margins and begin approximately a DS below the letterhead. If a letter is about a client's case, key a reference line a DS above the salutation and a subject line a DS below the salutation. For the reference line, key RE: followed by the court case number. For the subject line, key the case "style"; that is, the name of the case (example, Humphrey v. Gow). For the complimentary close, use Sincerely yours.

Memos. Prepare interoffice memos in simplified format. Omit all titles with recipients' and senders' names.

Tables. DS tables on plain full sheets, centered vertically and horizontally with 6-10 spaces between columns.

words

We cordially invite the managers in your various branch offices to attend | 161
this informative and instructive seminar. Simply have your administrative | 176
assistant complete the enclosed form giving the names and titles of the indi- | 191
viduals who will attend each of the seminars, and return it to me no later | 206
than May 10. | 209

Sincerely yours   Christina F. LaMonica   Director of Public Relations   xx | 223
Enclosure | 225/**246**

Letter 2
Simplified Block Letter

LP p. 79

Prepare the letter shown at the right in the simplified block format. List the enumerated items.

September 8, 19-- MS LINDSAY M SAXE CHAIRPERSON ELECTRONICS TRADE | 13
SHOW SAXE RESEARCH ASSOCIATES INC 351 FIFTH AVENUE NEW YORK | 25
NY 10016-7820 SECOND ANNUAL ELECTRONICS TRADE SHOW | 36

As Chairperson of the panel discussion "The Electronic Office--Today and | 50
Tomorrow," to be presented at the Electronics Trade Show next June 12 to 14, | 66
I have chosen the following individuals to be panel members. 1. Ms. Yoko | 81
Lee, assistant director of the Atlantic Institute, has had 15 years of expe- | 96
rience in word processing, office automation, and information process- | 109
ing. During that time, she has held positions in research, product planning | 125
and design, training, marketing, and managing information systems. 2. Dr. | 140
Ira Colton, senior associate of Colton, Rollins & Schmitt, Inc., has been | 155
involved with electronics in the business office for more than 18 years. | 170
As a consultant, he has assisted federal agencies and Fortune 500 corpo- | 184
rations in designing integrated information systems, installing electronic | 199
equipment, and developing specialized software to meet specific and unique | 214
requirements. 3. Mrs. Lila T. Alverez, information systems officer at Elec- | 229
tronics International, Ltd., has recently completed the installation of a world- | 245
wide information system which links all elements of Electronics Interna- | 259
tional on three continents. Mrs. Alverez earned her doctorate at MIT and has | 275
written and lectured extensively on electronics in the office. | 288

Each of the panel members will speak for 20 minutes, leaving 30 minutes for | 303
questions from the audience. With panel members of such high caliber, I | 317
feel certain that this panel discussion will be an exciting and informative one. | 334

KEITH T. KONA, PRESIDENT   xx | 339/**363**

Letters 3 and 4
Letters from Form Paragraphs

LP pp. 81-83

1. Prepare letters for Mr. Scott's signature in block format with open punctuation from form ¶s on p. 312.
2. Place current date on line 16 and use side margins of 1½".

3. Provide an appropriate salutation and complimentary close.
4. Copy the addresses and ¶ numbers in Letters 3 and 4 for the letters you are to format.

Letter 3
Prepare letter to
Miss Jennifer T. Franklin
577 Memorial Drive
Boston, MA 02139-4051
Use ¶s 1.1 (product: ABC ARRAY), 2.2, and 3.1.
Total words: 187/**200**

Letter 4
Prepare letter to
Mr. David C. Adams
2330 Alamo Street
Dallas, TX 75201-6452
Use ¶s 1.3 (name: Elizabeth Reita; product: IDEALWORD), 2.1, and 3.3.
Total words: 174/**185**

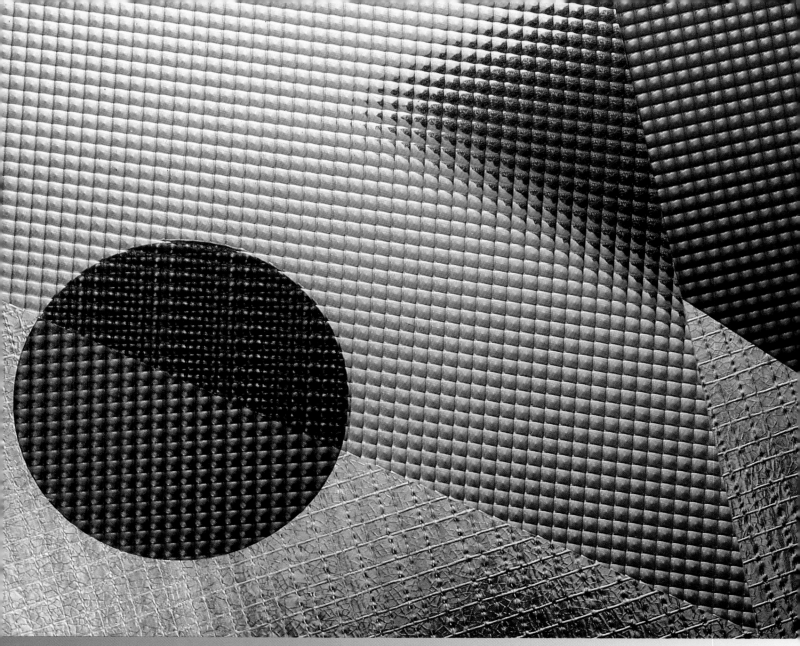

CAL-TEMP OFFICE AIDS, INC., PROFESSIONAL OFFICE SITUATIONS

You have opted for employment with Cal-Temp Office Aids, Inc., a temporary service agency in Oakland, California. As a Cal-Temp employee, you will be assigned to several professional offices in the San Francisco Bay area, including Bayview Legal Services, Inc., in Oakland; Gateway Medical Center in San Francisco; Regency Accounting Services, Inc., in Daly City; and Golden Gate Travel, Inc., in Berkeley.

As you move from one office to another, your position title will change; but in each office your primary duty will be to process the documents. Mostly, you will process the types of documents that are familiar to you--letters, reports, memos, tables, forms, etc. You also will prepare documents peculiar to the professions represented; at first, these types of documents may be unfamiliar to you.

Naturally, you will need to apply the language skills you have learned in school and on previous jobs; plus you will continue to polish and assess these skills by using special drills at home between your job assignments. The specialized vocabulary of each profession adds a new area of language-skill development.

No two offices anywhere are exactly alike. As a Cal-Temp employee, you will be challenged to become more self-reliant in adapting to differences and changes--a valuable trait not only in simulated work settings, but, especially, in *real* ones.

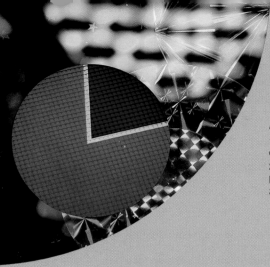

Improve Keyboarding and Language Skills

Learning Goals

1. To improve basic keyboarding skills with emphasis on figures and symbols.
2. To increase keystroking speed and to improve accuracy on straight copy.
3. To improve communications skills.

Format Guides

1. Paper guide at *0* (for typewriters).
2. LL: 70 spaces for drills, paragraphs, and language skills.
3. LS: SS sentence drills with DS between sets; DS paragraph writings; DS language skill sentences.

Lesson 181 | *Keyboarding and Language Skills*

181a ▶ 5
Conditioning Practice

each line twice SS (slowly, then faster); if time permits, take 1′ writings on line 3

alphabet	1	Jacques knew I might receive sizable rebates for taxes paid last year.
figures	2	Stereo music can be heard on 82.1, 96.5, 104.3, and 105.7 on the dial.
fig/sym	3	Costs in 1990 (based on final reports) rose $147,865 or 23% over 1989.
speed	4	The cubicle held a giant map of the world and a big map of the Orient.

| 1 | 2 | 3 | 4 | 5 | 6 | 7 | 8 | 9 | 10 | 11 | 12 | 13 | 14 |

181b ▶ 20 Improve Language Skills: Commonly Confused Words

1. Study the spelling and definitions of each pair of words.

2. Key the **Learn** line (with number and period) noting the proper use of the often confused words.

3. Key the **Apply** lines (with number and period), choosing the word that completes the sentence correctly.

disburse (vb) to pay out
disperse (vb) to cause to break up

emerge (vb) to become evident
immerge (vb) to plunge oneself into something

recent (adj) the very near past
resent (vb) to feel displeasure

elusive (adj) tending to evade grasp or pursuit
illusive (adj) misleading or deceptive

precede (vb) to go or come before
proceed (vb) to go on or to continue

ware (n) manufactured items or goods
wear (vb) to bear or to have on the person

Learn 1. The crowd will disperse when we disburse the paychecks.
Apply 2. We can (disburse, disperse) free samples at the meeting.
Apply 3. The chemicals will cause the oil slick to (disburse, disperse).

Learn 4. A clean boy may emerge if Andrew will immerge himself in the bath.
Apply 5. The swimmers like to (emerge, immerge) themselves in the pool.
Apply 6. As the facts (emerge, immerge), the truth will become evident.

Learn 7. Did Mark resent the remarks made at the recent meeting?
Apply 8. Jessica was elected mayor during the (recent, resent) election.
Apply 9. Arturo may (recent, resent) the terms of the contract.

Learn 10. An illusive tip misled me in my search for the elusive men.
Apply 11. Scientists searched years for the (elusive, illusive) virus.
Apply 12. The magician performed several amazing (elusive, illusive) acts.

Learn 13. If they precede us, we will not proceed with the parade.
Apply 14. After a short break, we will (precede, proceed) with the meeting.
Apply 15. He earned the right to (precede, proceed) them at the ceremony.

Learn 16. The wares at the bazaar were mostly items that people wear.
Apply 17. Did she (wear, ware) a wig for her role in the play?
Apply 18. A favorite birthday (wear, ware) for a man is a necktie.

Document 3
Job Description
LP p. 131
Key a job description in the proper format from the rough draft shown at the right.

words

JOB TITLE: Director, Public Relations; UNIT: Public Re- — 8
lations Office; REPORTS TO: Exexcutive Vice President; SUB- — 16
ORDINATE STAFF: Six Section Chiefs; DATE: May 2, 19--; — 22
D.O.T: 165.067-010 — 24

GENERAL STATEMENT OF THE JOB

Under the supervision of the Executive Vice President, — 35
plans, organizes, and ~~supervises~~ directs a public relations — 45
program ~~intended~~ designed to promote goodwill, ~~inspire~~ de- — 53
velop confidence, and create a favorable public image for — 65
the company. — 67

SPECIFIC DUTIES OF THE JOB

1. Plans and directs development and comunication of ~~data~~ — 78
information designed to keep the public informed of the com- — 90
pany's ~~deeds~~ accomplishments and point of view. 3 2. Estab- — 101
lishes policies and procedures for all official contact with — 113
the public by any employee. 2 3. Supervises the development — 125
and conduct of promotional activities such as exhibits, — 136
films and tours. 5 4. Represents the company at public, so- — 148
cial, and business events. 6 5. Conducts periodic surveys to — 160
determine the public's ~~concept~~ perception and opinoin of the — 170
company. 4 6. Coordinates the participation of company — 181
~~agents~~ representatives in community improvement, welfare, — 190
and social-beterment ~~activities~~ programs. — 198

Document 4
Table
Center the table vertically and horizontally; DS the items.

BOUTIQUES INTERNATIONAL, LTD. — 6

Pension Benefits by Years of Service — 13

Average Salary*	20 Years	25 Years	30 years**	
				15
$25,000	$ 9,175	$11,450	$ 13,750	28
35,000	12,854	16,300	19,250	36
45,000	16,115	20,610	24,750	41
55,000	20,185	25,290	30,250	47
65,000	23,854	29,779	35,750	53
75,000	27,525	34,450	41,250	59
85,000	31,295	38,930	46,750	64
95,000	43,865	43,510	52,250	70

— 75

*Highest 3 consecutive years out of final 10. — 88

**Benefits increase 2.5% per year for every year — 98
after 30 years. — 101

Take two 5' writings on
the ¶s at the right. Re-
cord *gwam* and errors.

Note: In the broadest
sense, the word *telecom-
munications* describes
the transmission of data
by any electronic means.
A computer can send
messages to other com-
puters provided that the
computers are on the
same network or system.

all letters used | A | 1.5 si | 5.7 awl | 80% hfw

	gwam 1'	5'

In the field of word processing, there are a number of levels of — 13 | 3 | 61

jobs. A trainee, for example, is an entry-level position which calls — 27 | 5 | 63

for good keyboarding and communications skills. The person must also be — 42 | 8 | 66

able to follow directions, have the ability to use reference materials — 56 | 11 | 69

of many kinds, and get along well with others. A trainee must be pre- — 70 | 14 | 72

pared to produce documents in the proper format, to proofread all work — 84 | 17 | 75

carefully, and to maintain a record of production each day or week. — 97 | 19 | 77

A word processing operator is the next step up in the organiza- — 13 | 22 | 80

tion. An operator is one who has been on the job a year or two and is — 27 | 25 | 83

able to key text-editing functions quickly in order to turn out many — 41 | 28 | 86

types of documents. A word processing specialist, on the other hand, — 55 | 30 | 88

is one who can format, revise, and produce complex papers such as long — 69 | 33 | 91

technical or scientific reports from many sources. Further, a special- — 83 | 36 | 94

ist may process mail by means of a telecommunications system. — 95 | 39 | 96

A word processing supervisor must be a very versatile person. He — 13 | 41 | 99

or she must have the ability to make work schedules, assign work to the — 28 | 44 | 102

operators, keep in touch with users, check all work for errors, keep a — 42 | 47 | 105

record of work completed, and make changes in procedures when they are — 56 | 50 | 108

needed. A word processing manager, at the top level, must plan, orga- — 70 | 53 | 111

nize, control, and direct the overall activities of the center to insure — 85 | 55 | 113

that all work is accomplished in a timely and efficient manner. — 97 | 58 | 116

gwam 1' | 1 | 2 | 3 | 4 | 5 | 6 | 7 | 8 | 9 | 10 | 11 | 12 | 13 | 14
5' | 1 | 2 | 3

Key each sentence twice *by
touch.* Proofread and circle
errors; then repeat the sentences in which you made the
most errors in figures, if time
permits.

1 The special committee will meet on May 14, 17, 19, 25, 26, 28, and 30.

2 Please correct the errors on pages 10, 61, 94, 105, 127, 132, and 189.

3 On June 28, we made 5,714 units, but on June 29 made only 3,806 units.

4 Place these figures in Column 1: 987, 1,605, 2,734, 3,806, and 5,192.

5 In 1987, they had only 2,653 employees; in 1989, 7,146; today, 10,540.

6 Locate cars with serial numbers 16328, 20597, 37546, 48190, and 52460.

7 Items 639510, 748029, 762513, 842501, and 963874 are not now in stock.

8 The population of the city grew from 934,575 to 1,860,273 in 20 years.

| 1 | 2 | 3 | 4 | 5 | 6 | 7 | 8 | 9 | 10 | 11 | 12 | 13 | 14 |

Time Schedule
Plan and prepare .... 5′
Timed production .... 30′
Proofread; compute *n-pram* ..... 10′

1. Arrange materials for ease of handling. Use LP pp. 129-131.
2. Key Documents 1-4 for 30′. Proofread and correct errors before removing documents from machine.

3. After time is called, proofread again and circle any uncorrected errors. Compute *n-pram*.

Document 1
Grievance Statement
LP p. 129
Key the formal grievance statement with 1″ side margins. Use **your name** as that of the steward.

	words
FORMAL STATEMENT OF GRIEVANCE	
EMPLOYEE *Joan T. Clark* I.D. NO. *43725* CLOCK NO. *891*	5
JOB TITLE *Data Entry Operator* DEPARTMENT *Administrative*	12

STATEMENT OF GRIEVANCE

Before my previous supervisor, James Friel, retired, he (23)
promised me that I would receive a merit raise on October (35)
16, after two years of service. Even though I received a (46)
performance rating of excellent, my new supervisor, Mrs. (58)
Mary Robb, refuses to recommend me for a merit raise because (70)
she says she is not familiar with my work. I feel that this (82)
is unfair treatment and that I should receive my raise (93)
immediately. (96)

Employee Signature   Steward Signature   Date *11/30/19--* (98)

Document 2
Table
Center the table vertically and horizontally. DS the items.

Documents 3 and 4 are on p. 462.

	BOUTIQUES INTERNATIONAL, LTD.		6
	Bonus for Employees Program		12
Job No.	**Title**	**Bonus***	18
169.167-014	Administrative assistant	$ 500	28
247.387-010	Advertising ~~Clerk~~ Specialist	200	36
162.117-018	Contract Specailist	4~~3~~00	43
186.117-014	~~Financial manager~~ Controller	1,000	49
249.131-014	Customer Services Supervisor	500	58
166.167-033	Employment Manager	8~~5~~00	65
166.267-018	Job Analyst	300	71
189.167-022	Management Trainee	300	78
161.116-014	Records Management Director	1,000	88
201.362-030	Secretary I, II	300	95
189.118.117-010	Research Director *tr*	1,000	103
922.687-058	Wharehouse Worker	100	109
203.362-022	Word Processer Operator	300	117
			121

*Fifty percent payable when hired; 50% payable ~~six~~ three (132)
months after satisfactory job performance. (140)

182a ▶ 5
Conditioning Practice

each line twice SS (slowly, then faster); DS between 2-line groups; if time permits, take 1′ writings on line 3

alphabet	1	Jen is working very hard to examine and publicize quotes from my book.
figures	2	The group will meet on June 28 to discuss Articles 10, 36, 75, and 94.
fig/sym	3	Of Lot #4763A, 25% (180 units) was rejected at a total cost of $2,390.
speed	4	If they wish me to do so, I may rush the hen turkeys and ducks by air.

| 1 | 2 | 3 | 4 | 5 | 6 | 7 | 8 | 9 | 10 | 11 | 12 | 13 | 14 |

182b ▶ 20 Improve Language Skills: Proofread/Correct

1. In each sentence at the right, items have been underlined. The underlines indicate that there *may* be an error in spelling, punctuation, capitalization, grammar, or word/figure usage.

2. Study each sentence carefully, then key the line (with number and period). If an underlined item is incorrect, correct it as you key the sentence. Also, correct any keyboarding errors you may make.

1. She said, "the committee did not follow it's agenda."
2. There will be adequate accomodations in our office in the south.
3. You're Doctor reported that nearly 1/2 of the group has the virus.
4. The delegates at the womens' conference past the rules unanimously.
5. Neither man are elligible to be chief of the personel division.
6. He declared; "The employee don't want to make a serious commitment."
7. At an apropriate time, we will review the book "Office Automation."
8. In my judgement, Joe was quite adapt in his work, he was fast to.
9. The pole showed that about 6% of the participants were absent.
10. We thought it was a posibility that Adams's study would win.
11. Prier to the meeting, we must impliment project X for there benefit.
12. In the absence of the jury panal, the Judge reviewed the calender.
13. Each of the men have their annual commission reports to prepare.
14. The subject of the correspondance was the currant 5 year plan.
15. Pursuent to her memo, new carpet was layed in rooms 986 and 1,020.

182c ▶ 10 Improve Keystroking Skills: Figures and Symbols

Take four 1′ writings on each ¶. Work for accuracy, especially when keying figures/symbols.

gwam 1′

The Consumer Price Index (CPI) measures changes in our buying power. 14
For comparison purposes, the cost of 400 items in 1967 was used as the 28
base and given a value of 100. Prices are collected monthly in 85 areas 43
from over 25,000 tenants, 20,000 owners, and about 32,400 establishments. 57

As an historic example, the CPI in 1980 was 246.8--an increase of 13
146.8% since 1967. In 1986, the CPI was 331.1--an increase of 84.3% 27
in just 6 years. In terms of dollars, the items that cost $100 to buy 41
in 1967 rose to $331.10 in 1986--an increase of 231.1%. 52

gwam 1′ | 1 | 2 | 3 | 4 | 5 | 6 | 7 | 8 | 9 | 10 | 11 | 12 | 13 | 14 |

182d ▶ 15 Improve Basic Keyboarding Skills

1. Two 1′ writings on each ¶ of 181c, p. 316. Find *gwam* and circle errors on each.

2. One 5′ writing on the three ¶s combined. Find *gwam* and circle errors; record scores.

Goals: To increase speed on 5′ writing by at least 2 *gwam* with fewer errors when compared with 181c.

Document 2
Unbound Report

Key this report in the unbound format. Correct all marked and unmarked errors. Heading:
REPORT OF OPEN HOUSE

words

heading 4

The annual Open House of Boutiques International in the — 15

New Orleans ~complex~ office was held on July 15, 19--. During the — 27

hours of 9 a.m. and noon, 126 people toured our ~company;~ *facilities,* dur- — 40

ing the hours of 1 p.m. and 4 p.m., 237 ~more~ *additional* people took the — 53

tour. Note should be ~made~ *taken* of the *big* increase ~in~ *during* the afternoon — 67

hours. At the 2 p.m. and 2:30 p.m. tours, the meeting room — 79

was unable to accomodate the number of people present, *and* we — 91

were forced to asked some people to wait for the ~following~ *next* tour. — 103

The tour of the mail room went smoothly; and the expla- — 114

nation of our order processing system was a highlight of the — 126

tour, thanks in great measure to the interesting presentation — 139

given by Maria Rodriques, *one of our machine operators.* — 150

en route to the shipping department The tour through warehouse B was not a success. The — 168

noise of the equipment prevented any explaination of the op- — 179

erations. Further, the *continuous* stream of people through the — 192

warehouse tended to disrupt *operations* ~work.~ — 200

The refreshments served in the employee's dining room — 211

were welcomed by all visitors. The group ~just~ *immediately* before and — 224

after the noon hour, however, disrupted operations). *of the kitchen personnel* — 240

The following recomendations are made. *to improve future tours of this nature* — 256

DS

1. Backup accomodations should be provided for the over- — 267

flow during the afternoon hours. *SS* — 273

3 2. The refreshments at the close of the tour should be — 285

served in a location other than the employee's dining room. — 297

2. The tour through Warehouse B should be eliminated. — 309

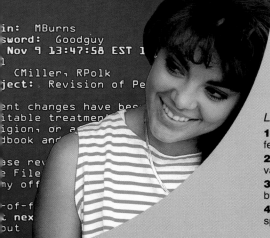

Learn to Format Messages with Special Features

Learning Goals

1. To learn how to process letters with special features.

2. To learn how to process form letters with variables.

3. To learn how to format messages to be sent by electronic mail.

4. To build production skill on messages with special features.

Format Guides

1. Paper guide at *0* (for typewriters).

2. LL: 70 spaces for drill copy; as directed for documents.

3. LS: SS drill lines with a DS between groups; space documents as directed or required.

4. PI: 5 spaces, when appropriate.

FORMATTING GUIDES: MESSAGES WITH SPECIAL FEATURES

Letter with Special Features

Electronic Mail

Letters with Special Features

Features which serve special purposes may be used in a letter as follows.

Mailing notations. A mailing notation such as CERTIFIED MAIL or SPECIAL DELIVERY is placed at the left margin a DS below the date, followed by a DS.

Attention line. The attention line is used to call the letter to the attention of a specific person, department, or job title (Attention Ms. Barr). It is keyed as the first line of the address.

Subject line. A subject line identifies the content of the letter and may be placed at the left margin, indented as the ¶s, or centered a DS below the salutation.

Company name in closing lines. A company name is keyed in ALL CAPS a DS below and aligned under the complimentary close, followed by a QS.

Listed enclosures. Enclosures are placed at the left margin a DS below the reference initials. Key the word "Enclosures" and then list each enclosure below SS, three spaces from the left margin, or key a colon after the word "Enclosures," space twice, and list each enclosure one beneath the other.

Copy notation. A copy notation is indicated with a "c" for either a carbon copy or a photocopy, and is placed at the left margin a DS below the reference initials (or enclosures), followed by the person's name. If more than one name is shown, list them SS one under the other or on the same line separated by a comma.

Postscript. A postscript is a message added at the end of a letter. It is placed a DS below the last reference line in the same manner as the ¶s in the body of the letter. (The abbreviation P.S. is no longer widely used.)

Electronic Mail

Electronic mail is any method of communication that involves sending text or facsimiles of documents electronically.

E-Mail can be transmitted from one computer to another in the same system.

There are many different mail systems, and few of them use exactly the same procedures in processing electronic mail. Most systems provide or respond to "prompts" which indicate information required or action to be taken.

The steps below illustrate, in a general way, a simple E-Mail system. (See illustrative screen on page 321.) The system prompts are shown in italics.

1. The system prompts the sender to *login* which may be done by entering the sender's first initial and last name: "MBurns."

2. The sender is then prompted to enter his or her *password.* This may be any combination of characters or a nickname, such as "Goodguy." For security reasons, the password, when keyed, does not appear on the screen.

3. The system now shows the day, date, and time of login: "Mon Nov 9 13:47:58 EST 1992." Note: For time, the 24-hour clock is used in which the hours are numbered from 0100 (1 a.m.) to 2400 (midnight). 13:47:58, therefore, is 1:47 and 58 seconds p.m.

4. The sender then keys in a prompt, such as *mail,* to indicate that he/she wishes to send a message.

5. The system prompts *To* and the sender indicates the name or names: "CMiller, RPolk."

6. The system then prompts *Subject* and the sender enters the subject of the message: "Revision of Personnel Handbook."

7. After the message has been keyed, the sender enters *end-of-file.*

8. The system then prompts *What next?* The sender can now edit the message, delete it, or send it by keying *send.*

9. To complete the session, the sender enters *logout* to log off the system.

Time Schedule
Plan and prepare .... 5'
Timed production .... 30'
Proofread; compute *n-pram*... 10'

1. Arrange materials for ease of handling.

2. Key Documents 1-2 for 30'. Proofread and correct errors before removing each page from the machine. If you complete both documents before time is called, rekey the report in Document 1 in the topbound format.

3. After time is called, proofread again and circle any uncorrected errors. Compute *n-pram*.

Document 1
Leftbound Report with Textual Citations

1. Key this unedited manuscript in the form of a leftbound report. Correct all errors, including unmarked ones.

2. The complete reference information has been included in the text of the report. As you prepare the report, insert the proper textual citation.

3. Place an alphabetized reference list on the final page (at the end of the report).

Document 2 is on p. 460.

words

ANNUAL REPORT OF THE HUMAN RESOURCES DEPARTMENT   10

<u>Employment</u   14

The company employed an average of 4,657 people during   25
the ~~last~~ past fiscl year. A total of 389 employees were ~~found~~   35
hired during the year. Of this number, 174 were replacements   48
for ~~those~~ employees who had left the company ~~and~~ while 215   58
were hired as additional personel. One of the major problem   70
areas has been the shortage of managerail and administrative   82
personnel. Despite ~~continued~~ increased recruiting efforts, we   93
have had difficulty finding qualified ~~individuals~~ people. As   103
forcast by the Bureau of Labor Statistics⌐Kutscher, Robert E.,   114
"An Overview of the Year 2000," <u>Occupational Outlook Quarter-</u>   114
<u>ly</u>, Spring 1988, p. 9⌐, these occupations are among the fastest   124
growing and, therefore, will continue to be a recruitment   135
problem. An analysis of the individuals employed ~~by~~   145
under our BONUS FOR EMPLOYEES PROGRAM ~~verifies~~ proves the   155
well-established belief that "(employee) referrals can be a   167
very good source of job applicants." ⌐Cunningham, William H.,   177
Aldag, Ramon J., and Swift, Christopher M., <u>Introduction to</u>   180
<u>Business</u>, Cincinnati: South-Western Publishing Co., 1984, p.   182
158.⌐   183

<u>Employee Benefits</u>   190

Without cost to employees, the company ~~offers~~ provides   200
health insurance, life insurance, retirement ~~pay~~ benefits,   211
liberal vacations, ~~five~~ six holidays, sick ~~leave~~ and jury duty   221
leave, and a profit sharing plan. A national survey⌐Bates,   233
Judith K., "A Survey of Desired Employee Benefits," Glick As-   233
sociates, February 1989, p. 19⌐ indicates that the desire for a   242
child care center (or compensation for child care) is growing,   254
~~indicating~~ reflecting an increase in the number of house   263
holds in which both parents work. We anticipate that child   275
care will be a major issue when we ~~discuss~~ negotiate our next   286
labor contract. In preparation for this ~~probability~~   295
eventuality, we have initiated a study to ~~find~~ determine the   306
feasibility and cost of providing this care benefit.   317

<u>Human Relations</u>   323

The company had a good human relations record this year.   335
We had ~~but~~ only six complaints filed under Title VII of the   346
Civil Rights act of 1964, as amended. All but two of these   358
have been resolved. A total of 32 greivances were filed under   370
the terms of our labor contract. Of these, 18 were resolved   383
at the supervisory level, 10 were resolved by the appeals com-   395
mitte, and 4 were referred to an arbitrator. Through mutual   407
agreement with our unions, ~~discussions~~ negotiations for the   417
next master contract will ~~start~~ begin at an earlier date than   428
previously ~~set~~ scheduled. It is hoped that the longer period   440
allowed for considering the issues by both sides ~~may~~ will help   452
prevent any work stop pages.   457

references   536

183a ▶ 5
Conditioning Practice

each line twice SS (slowly, then faster); if time permits, take 1' writings on line 1

alphabet	1	Vic asked him to take the job of awarding prizes for quality exhibits.
figures	2	Items 72, 465, 825, 934, 1068, and 1739 were removed from the catalog.
fig/sym	3	Their 1987 rates ranged from 6 3/4% to 10 1/5% (an average of 8 1/2%).
speed	4	If the firm pays half of the penalty, the men may also pay their half.

| 1 | 2 | 3 | 4 | 5 | 6 | 7 | 8 | 9 | 10 | 11 | 12 | 13 | 14 |

183b ▶ 45 Format Letters with Special Features

Letter 1
plain paper

1. Study the guides on p. 318 for formatting letters with special features.

2. Key the letter on p. 320 with 1" side margins, and key the date on line 12. Correct errors.

Letter 2
LP p. 89
block format; SM: 1"; PB: line 14

1. Key the letter shown at the right. Use open punctuation.

2. Send the letter by **SPECIAL DELIVERY** to the attention of **Miss Rose M. Chan** with the subject line: **YOUR ORDER 45821A.** Provide an appropriate salutation and complimentary close. Correct errors.

Letter 3
plain paper
SM: 1"; PB: line 14

1. Key the letter at the right in modified block format, open punctuation. Provide an appropriate salutation and complimentary close. Correct errors.

2. Use the company name in the closing lines: **ASSOCIATION OF OFFICE MANAGERS,** list the enclosures, and indicate that a copy of the letter has been sent to **Mrs. Carla F. Fernandez.**

3. Add the following postscript: **If you have received these publications previously, please accept these copies with our compliments.**

words*

March 28, 19-- Bronson Jewelers, Inc. 702 Broadway Street Denver, CO	23
80203-4117	33

The silver ornaments you ordered on February 15 have been delayed because	48
the special silver alloy required for these ornaments has not been received	63
from our supplier. We now anticipate that the silver will be received no	78
later than April 10.	82

Normally, a special order of this nature requires at least ten days to process.	98
In view of the situation, however, we will expedite the manufacture of your	114
ornaments and will complete your order in a maximum of five days after	128
receipt of the silver.	133

Thank you for your patience in this matter. If all goes well, we will ship	148
your ornaments by air express no later than April 15.	159

Ms. Lisa T. Scott	164
Marketing Manager	168/190

September 26, 19-- Mr. Frank P. Dalton 90 Spring Street Portland, ME	14
04101-7430	19

It has come to my attention that several of the publications you ordered in	34
August may not have arrived as yet. According to the enclosed copy of your	50
order, Items 3765A, 4890B, and 5021X have not yet been shipped.	63

Normally, orders received by the Association of Office Managers are pro-	77
cessed within 10 days of receipt. Because of a computer problem, however,	92
it appears that some orders in August may not have been completed.	105

A copy of Item 3765A is enclosed. Copies of 4890B and 5021X will be sent	120
priority mail within the next few days by Mrs. Carla F. Fernandez, chief of	135
special orders.	139

We appreciate your interest in our publications and thank you for your	153
patronage.	155

Brian E. Miller	168
Director of Publications	204/216

***Note:** Words in letter parts added to the letter are included in the word count at the right of the letter.

273b (continued)

Document 3
News Release

LP p. 127

Key the news release for immediate release with **Michelle T. Worthington, 504-565-6459,** as the contact.

Document 4
Simplified Memorandum

If time permits, rekey Document 1, p. 456, as a simplified memo.

Total words: 237

words

heading 10

NEW ORLEANS, LA, September 1, 19--. Mark E. La Grande, chairperson of Boutiques International, Ltd., announced today, that the management of the company will recommend that the Board of Directors increase the quarterly cash dividend on its common stock from 54 cents to 60 cents a share. The recommendation will be made at the next regular meeting of the board scheduled for September 15.

The increased dividend, if approved by the board, will be effective with the regularly scheduled third-quarter dividend payment, payable September 30. Annualized, the cash dividend will be $2.40 a share, an 11.1% increase over the present $2.16 a share.

Mr. La Grande stated that the increased dividend was the result of the company's policy of sharing the profits with its stockholders. He noted that the net income of the company had increased 22.9% over the previous fiscal year.

Boutiques International, Ltd., sells fine wares from all over the world by direct mail and in shops located throughout the U.S. The company has branch offices in London, Paris, Rome, and Hong Kong.

# # #

payable September 30.

19
30
39
49
60
70
79
87
97
109
125
135
138
148
158
167
177
184
195
205
217
226
227

REVERE SILVERSMITHS
1242 Delaware Avenue • Buffalo, NY 14209-6358 • (716) 438-7400

		words in parts	total words
	February 8, 19-- _{DS}	3	3
Mailing notation	CERTIFIED _{DS}	5	5
Attention line	Attention Mr. Arnold Bishop	10	10
	King Department Store	15	15
	800 Broad Street	19	19
	Chattanooga, TN 37402-1905 _{DS}	24	24
	Ladies and Gentlemen _{DS}	29	29
Subject line	SILVER FOR WEDDINGS _{DS}	32	32

We are pleased to announce a special sale of silver items espe-   12   45
cially for weddings. The sale includes personal gift items for   25   58
attendants such as money clips and perfume bottles as well as tra-   38   71
ditional gift items for the bride and groom. You will find an   51   83
interesting array of merchandise in the enclosed catalog. _{DS}   63   95

As one of our preferred customers, we are offering you a special   76   108
discount of 10% on all silver wedding items ordered no later than   89   121
April 15. This discount is in addition to the regular discounts   102 134
we offer for payment of invoices within 10 or 30 days. _{DS}   113 145

The enclosed special order blank identifies you as a preferred   126 158
customer. After you have reviewed the outstanding bargains we   138 171
offer, complete the order blank and return it without delay. Miss   152 184
Marylou Simpson of our Shipping Department has been alerted to   164 197
process your order immediately upon receipt. _{DS}   173 205

Sincerely _{DS}   2   207

Company name in closing lines   REVERE SILVERSMITHS _{QS}   6   211

E. Martin Bronson

E. Martin Bronson   10 215
Sales Manager _{DS}   12 218

mb _{DS}   13 218

Listed enclosures   Enclosures _{SS}   15 221
    Catalog   17 222
    Special Order Blank _{DS}   21 226

Copy notation   c Marylou Simpson _{DS}   24 230

Postscript   If you need additional order blanks, please call my office and we   38 243
will mail them to you promptly.   44 249

Letter with Special Features

words

We will ~~escalate~~ [intensify] our recruiting efforts (thru)[sp] our normal · 103

channels. In addition, I ~~suggest~~ [recommend] that we begin recruiting · 115

qualified persons through our ~~current~~ [present] employees by [initiating] a bonus · 129

program. Under this program, employees will be encouraged to · 142

"earn money and ~~to~~ [do] a fre~~i~~nd a favor" by ~~suggesting~~ [recommending] individuals · 155

for specific jobs. For th~~i~~e[i]r efforts, employees will be paid · 167

a bonus as ~~indicated~~ [shown] on the enclosed BONUS FOR EMPLOYEES PRO- · 178

GRAM. Experience ~~indicates~~ [has shown] that present employees can be · 190

~~greatly~~ [highly] effective in recruiting people and that employee[i] ~~sug-~~ [referrals] · 203

~~gestions~~ are often of a ~~better~~ [higher] quality than those obtained · 213

through other sources. · 218

[DS]

If you approve, we will ~~put~~ [announce] this program in the next edi- · 230

tion of our [lc]Employee [lc]Newsletter. · 237/253

Document 2
Form Letter
LP p. 125

Key the letter dated **August 14** for the signature of **Harold J. Peterson, Director, Customer Service Center,** to the address below. Use block format with open punctuation.

Mrs. Vicki T. Goldblum
1638 Park Avenue
New York, NY 10035-4442

opening lines 20

Because you are one of our most valued customers and a col- · 31
lector of fine crystal, we are pleased to offer you a preview · 44
of some special items that will be included in our next catalog. · 57
You are among a select few to receive this opportunity to ob- · 69
tain unusual items at reduced prices. · 77

You will find many new and exciting items in the enclosed leaf- · 89
let. Please note these extraordinary crystal items: · 100

   **Galway Irish Crystal in a Fleur-de-lis Pattern · 110
   **Cavan Irish Crystal Flower Bowls · 117
   **Waterford Crystal's new "Essex Suite" · 125
   **Austrian Crystal Lamps · 130
   **Swarovsky's Crystal Circus Animal Collection · 139

Many of these items are "special editions" and are available · 151
in limited quantities. Our next catalog will be mailed to the · 164
general public on September 15. Prior to that date, you will · 176
have the opportunity to order the items you desire; and, to · 188
show our appreciation for your continued patronage, we offer · 200
you a discount of 10% on your order. · 208

Be sure to send your order on or before September 15 to take · 220
advantage of this singular offer. · 227

Document 3 is on p. 458.

closing lines 244/256

```
login:  MBurns
password:  Goodguy
Mon Nov 9 13:47:58 EST 1992
mail
To:  CMiller, RPolk
Subject:  Revision of Personnel Handbook

Recent changes have been made in the laws regarding fair and
equitable treatment of employees regardless of race, sex,
religion, or age.  As a result, we must review our Personnel
Handbook and make necessary changes.

Please review the new regulations which are located in Data
Base Files 231.2 and 247.5 in preparation for a conference
in my office at 1500 hours on November 23.


end-of-file
What next?  send
logout
```

Electronic Message

Lesson 184	Electronic Messages

184a ▶ 5
Conditioning
Practice

each line twice SS
(slowly, then faster);
if time permits, take
1′ writings on line 1

alphabet	1	Five boys and six girls worked hard to equip and customize the jalopy.
figures	2	Model No. 539077 will be manufactured in sizes 10, 12, 14, 16, and 18.
fig/sym	3	The invoice shows that Brogan & Co. shipped #869 on 3/24/91, not #570.
speed	4	Blanche kept both of the keys to the auto with the maps of the island.

| 1 | 2 | 3 | 4 | 5 | 6 | 7 | 8 | 9 | 10 | 11 | 12 | 13 | 14 |

184b ▶ 45 Format
Electronic Messages

Note: A "data base" is an electronic encyclopedia in which important information is stored in computer memory.

Message 1
LP p. 91
PB (page beginning): line 7;
LL: 60 spaces

1. Key the electronic message shown above. If you make an error, backspace and strike the correct key.

2. When you have completed the message, refer to the directions on p. 318. Underline, in pencil, those prompts which were provided by the system; circle the prompts the sender used; and draw a line through the item which, although keyed, would not appear on the screen.

For those using plain paper:
Key the electronic message above exactly as shown, including the prompts provided by the system. Then follow the directions given in Step 2.

Message 2
LP p. 93
PB: line 7; LL: 60 spaces

1. Assume that you have received the electronic message above and find that you have another meeting scheduled at 1500 hours on November 23.

2. Compose a reply to MBurns. Use your name to login and a nickname as the password. Prompt the system to mail a message to MBurns with the subject: Meeting to Revise Personnel Handbook.

3. In the message, tell MBurns that you have an important meeting of the Executive Committee at

1500 hours on November 23 and will not be able to attend his conference to discuss changes in the Personnel Handbook. Ask him if he can set another date and time.

4. Close the message (end-of-file), instruct the system to send it, and then logout.

5. If you make an error, backspace and strike the correct key.

For those using plain paper:
Key the prompts as shown in the model above as you compose the message to MBurns. Follow the directions given in Steps 2 through 6.

Take two 5' writings on the ¶s at the right. Record *gwam* and errors on the better writing.

all letters used | A | 1.5 si | 5.7 awl | 80% hfw

gwam 1' | 5'

The system for processing documents in an office varies depending 13 | 3 | 62
upon the size of the office, the number of employees, the types of equip- 29 | 6 | 64
ment, and other factors. There are some major steps, though, which are 42 | 8 | 67
found in most offices. In the first step, the author of a document sub- 57 | 11 | 70
mits it in some manner. The words are then keyboarded, usually in rough- 71 | 14 | 73
draft form, and sent back to the author. The author edits the document, 86 | 17 | 76
makes any changes he or she wants, and returns it for final copy. 99 | 20 | 79

Many executives believe that they can best organize their ideas by 112 | 22 | 81
putting them on paper with pen or pencil. This may explain why many 126 | 25 | 84
documents are written by hand initially. Since no equipment is required, 141 | 28 | 87
this might be considered as a cost-effective way of producing documents. 156 | 31 | 90
On the other hand, the time involved by a highly paid person adds consid- 170 | 34 | 93
erably to the cost. Furthermore, much that is written by hand is dif- 184 | 37 | 96
ficult to read, which adds to the time and cost of keying the document. 198 | 40 | 99

Some executives who know how to key may provide rough drafts of 211 | 42 | 101
their material. A more effective means of preparing documents, however, 226 | 45 | 104
is machine dictation. The author can dictate at any time and at any con- 240 | 48 | 107
venient place, and the operator can key the material quickly in a timely 255 | 51 | 110
manner. The cost of the equipment, though, may be a drawback. Further, 269 | 54 | 113
the time required in training both the authors and the operators in the 284 | 57 | 116
proper use of the equipment may be a negative factor. 294 | 59 | 118

gwam 1' | 1 | 2 | 3 | 4 | 5 | 6 | 7 | 8 | 9 | 10 | 11 | 12 | 13 | 14
    5' | 1 | 2 | 3

Time Schedule

Plan and prepare .... 5'
Timed production .... 30'
Proofread; compute *n-pram*.... 10'

1. Arrange materials for ease of handling. Use LP pp. 123-131.

2. Key Documents 1-3 for 30'. Proofread and correct errors before removing documents from machine. If you complete the documents before time is called, key Document 1 in the simplified memo format.

3. After time is called, proofread again; circle any uncorrected errors; compute *n-pram*.

Document 1
Formal Memorandum LP p. 123

words

TO: Lucille K. Phillips, Vice President of Administration   11

FROM: Henry K. O'Brian, Director of Human Resources   20

DATE: August 7, 19-- SUBJECT: Bonus for Employees Program   29

We are *presently* ~~currently~~ faced with a shortage of manager all,   39
administrative and office personnel. Through our ~~normal~~ *usual*   51
(source of recruitment)--advertising, private *and public* employment agen-   64
cies, educational institutions, and *lc* Professional organi-   75
zations--we have not been able to fill a number of vacancies   88
in *key* ~~some~~ areas.   91

(continued, p. 457)

185a ▶ 5
Conditioning Practice

each line twice SS
(slowly, then faster);
if time permits, take
1' writings on line 1

alphabet 1 Jose Ruiz quickly taped very wild shows for a big festival next month.

figures 2 Send 15 copies of Form 6749, 20 copies of 8159, and 30 copies of 8321.

symbols 3 Use the "and" sign (&) in company names: C & D Autos; Sheehan & Sons.

speed 4 Did the maid mend the pale paisley formal gown for the sorority girls?

| 1 | 2 | 3 | 4 | 5 | 6 | 7 | 8 | 9 | 10 | 11 | 12 | 13 | 14 |

185b ▶ 45 Format Form Letters

LP pp. 95-99
modified block format with
indented ¶s; open punctuation;
SM: 1½"; PB: line 14

1. Key the form letter given at the right below, dated **October 30, 19--**, to the persons listed below.

2. Provide an appropriate salutation and complimentary close. The letters will be signed by **Sara C. Mills, Senior Vice President**.

3. Insert the personalized data in the appropriate spaces; correct errors.

Letter 1
Ms. Maria C. Fuentes
1501 Bay Avenue
Chelsea, MA 02150-4362
(A) **six-month** (B) **4057128**
(C) **November 15** (D) **$10,052.48**
(E) **Chelsea** (F) **452-6010**

Letter 2
Mrs. Rachel F. Stein
1605 Cheney Place
Lowell, MA 01851-9501
(A) **one-year** (B) **5057124**
(C) **November 20**
(D) **$11,562.37** (E) **Lowell**
(F) **565-4910**

Letter 3
Mr. Sean F. Reilly
10 Tremont Street
Boston, MA 02108-6107
(A) **30-month** (B) **6948239**
(C) **November 17** (D) **$6,157.44**
(E) **Boston** (F) **563-7000**

Form Letters

The letter below is an example of a form letter (also known as boilerplate). These letters are used when the same information is sent to many individuals. The letter can be "personalized" or "customized" by inserting the appropriate information in the blank spaces. The blanks are identified by letter or number so that the operator can quickly identify the information to be inserted.

On an electronic typewriter with memory, a form letter can be stored, retrieved when needed, and programmed to stop at the appropriate places so that the operator can insert the personalized data.

When prepared on a word processor or computer, the form letter can be stored on one disk and the personalized data on a separate disk. The word processor or computer can then be programmed to merge the text and the personalized information automatically. This procedure is known as document assembly or text merging.

	words
	opening lines 19

Our records indicate that your Franklin (A) certificate #(B) is due to mature   37
on (C). As you consider your reinvestment options, there are many ways   53
Franklin can help you to make the most of your money.   64

You can reinvest your funds totalling (D) in principal and accrued interest in   81
another certificate at the rate in effect on the day your present certificate   96
matures. Franklin offers a wide range of certificates with terms from   111
30 days to 10 years at attractive rates compounded daily.   122

If you wish to learn more about the many savings and investment opportuni-   137
ties we can offer you or if you have any questions concerning your account,   152
please call our (E) office at (F).   161

Don't delay. Prompt action on your part will insure that your funds will con-   177
tinue to earn high interest rates in the months and years ahead.   190

closing lines 201/**212**

UNIT 65   LESSONS 272 – 275
Evaluate Keyboarding/Language/Document Processing Skills

Performance Evaluated

1. To measure straight-copy speed and accuracy.

2. To evaluate language skills.

3. To measure production skills on correspondence, reports, and tables and forms.

Format Guides

1. Paper guide at *0* (for typewriters).

2. LL: 70 spaces for drills, paragraphs, and Language Skills activity; as required for documents.

3. LS: DS for Language Skills activity and paragraphs; as required for documents.

| Lessons 272-275 | Evaluate Keyboarding/Language/Document Processing Skills |

272a-275a ▶ 5 (daily)
Conditioning
Practice

each line twice SS
(slowly, then faster);
if time permits take
1′ writings on line 4

alphabet	1	Wilbur realized expert judges may check the value of the unique books.
figures	2	Published in 1987, this text has 546 pages, 130 pictures, and 27 maps.
fig/sym	3	I earned a commission of $3,149 (6%) on the sale of Lot #758 on May 2.
speed	4	If we wish them to do so, both of them may go with us to the sorority.

| 1 | 2 | 3 | 4 | 5 | 6 | 7 | 8 | 9 | 10 | 11 | 12 | 13 | 14 |

272b ▶ 30 Evaluate
Language Skills

1. In each sentence at the right, items have been underlined. The underlines indicate that there *may* be an error in spelling, punctuation, capitalization, grammar, or in the use of words or figures.

2. Study each sentence carefully. Key each line with the number and period. If an underlined item is incorrect, correct it as you key the sentence. In addition, correct any typographical errors you may make as you work.

3. When you have completed the sentences, and *before* you remove the copy, study each sentence carefully and correct any errors you may have missed.

1. She said: "they must insure complience with the electrical code."
2. Keep in mind: installation of the permanant wiring must be done now.
3. Do you beleive that ten 5-gallon cans will be suficient?
4. We must have acess to Conference Room Six for our meeting.
5. The profesional mens' banquet was held at Gibbs' country estate.
6. More than twenty-six foriegn managers will receive benifits.
7. Mary went to the librery, Ralph visited the planning comission.
8. According to "The New York Times," the firm's President will resign.
9. Approximately 10% of the participents voted "yes."
10. He questioned the expendeture on Line 27 in Report 206-A.
11. Ed Boyle the company Treasurer will implement the fiscle plan.
12. My question is this--What was the maximum morgage rate last year?
13. The custumer shipped the material in a large, wooden crate.
14. Each of the comittee members are expected to initial the report.
15. Its almost certain the committee will issue their report imediately.
16. Whose facilaties were used in monitoring the quality of the items?
17. Lopez's frequent absences was the subject of the correspondence.
18. The climate here is similer to that in southern California.
19. Don't she work on the avenue of the Americas in New York city?
20. The analyss was included on Page 39 of Fiscal study #14.

186a ▶ 5
Conditioning Practice

each line twice SS (slowly, then faster); DS between 2-line groups; if time permits, take 1' writings on line 1

alphabet 1 We have begun a check of quarterly expenses itemized in their journal.

figures 2 Check all of the memos filed under 215.39, 480.76, 583.19, and 679.20.

fig/sym 3 Acme computers (Model 286327) are listed at $945, less a 10% discount.

speed 4 Andy may work with a neighbor and me to dismantle and fix the bicycle.

| 1 | 2 | 3 | 4 | 5 | 6 | 7 | 8 | 9 | 10 | 11 | 12 | 13 | 14 |

186b ▶ 45
Sustained Production: Messages with Special Features

LP pp. 101-105 or plain full sheets

Time Schedule
Plan and prepare .... 5'
Timed production ....30'
Proofread; compute *n-pram* .....10'

1. Make a list of messages to be processed:
p. 319, 183b, Letter 2
p. 321, 184b, Message 1
p. 322, 185b: Send letter to
Miss Suzie F. Lee
62 Exeter Street
Boston, MA 02116-4120
using the following information.

(A) **six-month**
(B) **643910**
(C) **November 21**
(D) **$2,104.96**
(E) **Boston**
(F) **563-7000**

2. Arrange letterheads and plain paper for efficient handling. Address envelopes.

3. Work for 30' when directed to begin. Proofread each letter carefully before removing it from the machine. Correct errors neatly. If you finish before time is called, begin with Letter 1 and rekey on plain sheets as much as possible in the time remaining.

4. Compute *n-pram*; turn in messages arranged in the order given in Step 1.

187a ▶ 5
Conditioning Practice

each line twice SS (slowly, then faster); DS between 2-line groups; if time permits, take 1' writings on line 4

alphabet 1 He examined previous job analyses to standardize sequences of working.

figures 2 Line item 14 on page 27 indicates we produced 590,386 units in August.

fig/sym 3 Send 80 5″ × 3″ (12.7 × 7.6 cm) and 90 6″ × 4″ (15.2 × 10.1 cm) cards.

speed 4 The proficient handiwork of both girls may entitle them to the profit.

| 1 | 2 | 3 | 4 | 5 | 6 | 7 | 8 | 9 | 10 | 11 | 12 | 13 | 14 |

187b ▶ 45 *Measure Production Skills: Messages with Special Features*

LP pp. 107-111 or plain full sheets

Time Schedule
Plan and prepare .... 5'
Timed production ....30'
Proofread; compute *n-pram* .....10'

Documents 2, 3, and 4 are on p. 324.

1. Make a list of the variables as listed below for Document 1 addressed to
Mr. Ralph J. Devins
16 Franklin Lane
Duxbury, MA 02332-6075
Variables: (A) **one-year**
(B) **754029**
(C) **November 15**
(D) **$5,781.19**
(E) **Duxbury**
(F) **876-8830**

2. Arrange letterheads and plain sheets for efficient handling.
3. Key for 30' the documents given here and on p. 324. Proofread and correct each document carefully *before* you remove it from the machine or screen.
4. After the timed production, proofread and circle any errors you may have missed.
5. Compute *n-pram*.

Document 1
Form Letter
LP p. 107; LL: 1½″ margins; PB: line 14
Date: November 1, 19--

1. Using the list of variables you made in Step 1 at the left, key the form letter given on p. 322 in modified block format with indented paragraphs.
2. Use open punctuation.
3. Supply an appropriate salutation and complimentary close.
4. Correct errors made as you key.

~~dollars~~ in annual retail sales, direct mail ~~gets~~ garners almost 20 percent

of the total--a considerable increase over the 14 percent

~~gained~~ earned in the 1970's. The increase in sales through direct

mail ~~have~~ has led, a number ~~more and more~~ of the Fortune 500 companies to

begin direct mail sales, ~~as well as~~ as have such famous department

stores as Neiman-Marcus and Tiffany & Co.

There are many advantages ~~of~~ to using direct mail ad-

vertising. One of the major advantages is that, thanks to

the computerized mailing list, mail can be sent directly to

individuals who ~~may be~~ are probably interested in ~~a specific company's~~ purchasing a given

product or produc~~es~~ts. A new sc~~i~~ence, "individual

demographics," can pinpoint with amazing accuracy the buying

preferences of individuals through a computerized analysis

of ZIP Codes, automobile registration~~,~~s birth and marriage

certificates, ~~credit ratings,~~ and other personal information

frequently gained through questionnaires.

~~It is currently posible for any~~ a company ~~to~~ may rent a mailing

list tailored to meet its specific needs. Recently, Boutiques In-

ternational, Ltd. conducted a sample survey in ~~two~~ three large,

lc Metropolitan *lc* Areas to determine the type of people interested

in a new product line we ~~are~~ planning ~~to put on the~~ market.

From an analysis of that survey, we can ~~now~~ order a ~~a~~ national mailing

list of people with specific characteristics--people who are

most apt to buy our new product~~.~~s.

187b (continued)

Document 2
Electronic Message

plain paper
PB: line 7; LL: 60

Key *only* the data that would be entered by the sender and would appear on the screen. If you make an error, backspace and strike the correct key.

Total words: 118

```
login:  WTaylor
password:  CEO
Mon Apr 20 09:35:26 EST 1992
mail
To:  FJenkins
Subject:  Net Sales in the Omaha Region

A review of the quarterly reports from our branch offices
indicates that there may be some difficulties in the Omaha
regional office.  Net sales in that region are down almost
19 percent when compared with sales during the same period
last year.

Will you please study the quarterly report from Omaha and,
if necessary, contact Thomas Kelly, the regional chief, to
determine why there has been such a drastic drop in sales.

Please give me a report on this matter no later than 1600
hours on Friday of this week.

end-of-file
What next?  send
logout
```

Document 3
Letter with Special Features

LP p. 109
SM: 1″; PB: line 12

1. Key the letter in block format, open punctuation, for the signature of **Martin M. Stern, Trust Officer.**

2. Send the letter by **REGISTERED MAIL.** Provide an appropriate salutation and complimentary close. Correct errors.

3. Center the list of note numbers. Use the company name in the closing lines: **FRANKLIN NATIONAL BANK.** List the enclosures and indicate that a copy of the letter has been sent to **D. Elaine Hawkins.**

Document 4
Letter with Special Features

LP p. 111
SM: 1″; PB: line 12

1. Key the letter in Document 3 to

Adams Legal Associates
33 St. James Avenue
Boston, MA 02116-5348

to the attention of **Jessica T. Parsons.** In ¶ 2, change the name of the executor to **Ms. Parsons.**

2. Add a subject line: **ESTATE OF MURRAY T. MILES;** do *not* include the company name in the closing lines and do *not* send a copy of the letter to **D. Elaine Hawkins.**

	words
November 10, 19-- Mrs. Melissa F. Rowland 628 Cambridge Street Boston,	17
MA 02134-7490	24

At the direction of D. Elaine Hawkins, attorney-at-law, I am releasing to you   40
the following U.S. Treasury Notes which are enclosed.   Each note has a face   55
value of $10,000.   59

7456901	60
7935462	62
8054095	63

These notes are a part of the estate of Murray T. Miles and have been held in   79
trust by us. As executor of the estate, Mrs. Rowland, it will be your respon-   94
sibility to have the notes registered with the U.S. Treasury Department in   109
the names of the beneficiaries.   116

Under Probate Court Order No. 56230 of October 30, you are now authorized   131
to control the accounts, both savings and checking, on deposit with us in the   146
name of the decedent. Will you please complete and sign the enclosed signa-   161
ture cards prior to making any demands on these accounts.   173

closing lines 200/217

Document 12
Partial Text of Speech

Mrs. Scott: Please key in the form of a leftbound report this partial text of a speech Ms. Perez plans to present at the national meeting of FBLA.

Document 13
Partial Text of Speech

Mrs. Scott: Please key the partial text of speech on 5″ × 8″ cards with top and side margins of ½″ and bottom margins of ¼″ to ½″. Omit the title, and number each card at the left margin on the second line from the top edge. DS the text.

MILLIONS OF DOLLARS WORTH OF JUNK

"Junk" is a *word* ~~term that~~ we apply to something worthless, such as trash, *or garbage*. Many *people* ~~individuals~~ call advertisements they recieve through the postal service "junk mail." And yet, this *so-called* "junk" generates millions and millions of dollars in sales ~~each year~~ *annually*. In marketing parlance *STET* "junk mail" is *known as* direct mail--and important and ~~rewarding~~ *valuable* means of advertising.

The most popular media for advertising on a national and local basis are news papers and magazines; telivision ranks second; and direct mail, third. An interesting trend in the *percentage* ~~amount~~ of funds *expended* ~~spent~~ for advertising was first ~~noticed~~ *noted* in the 1970's. The per cent of expenditures on newspapers and magazine advertising began to ~~go down~~ *decrease* whereas the percent for direct mail began to increase. At first, it was believed, *this trend* ~~that it was~~ only a temporary aberration, but the trend has ~~been~~ continued. In the 1980's, money spent on newspaper and magazine advertising dropped more than 4%; *sp* the percent for direct mail increased by just about 3 percent. This *amount* may not seem to be ~~such a big number~~ *significant figure*, but it assumes some importance when *we* ~~you~~ remember that, nationwide, more than $100 billion is spent each year on advertising. Some experts have foecast *r* that advertising expenditures for direct mail will double in the 1990's.

Despite ~~In spite of~~ the grumbling about "junk mail," sales generated through this media *um* have continued to ~~grow~~ *increase*. The most recent figures reveal that of the more than $1.5 trillion

Learn to Format Memorandums and News Releases

Learning Goals

1. To learn/review how to format a formal memorandum.

2. To learn/review how to format a simplified memorandum.

3. To learn how to format a news release.

4. To build production skill on memorandums and news releases.

Format Guides

1. Paper guide at *0* (for typewriters).

2. LL: 70 spaces for drill copy; as directed or required for documents.

3. LS: SS drill lines with DS between 2-line groups; space documents as directed or required.

4. PI: 5 spaces, when a document format requires indention.

FORMATTING GUIDES: MEMORANDUMS/ NEWS RELEASES

Interoffice Memorandums

Interoffice memorandums are used to convey information among people *within* a firm. The address, personal titles (Mr., Mrs., Miss, Ms.), salutation, and complimentary close are omitted. Memorandums may be prepared in a formal or a simplified format.

Formal format. Formal memorandums are prepared on full- or half-sheet forms with preprinted headings (see model memo on p. 327). They are keyed in block format with 1″ side margins. The headings TO:, FROM:, DATE:, and SUBJECT: are printed in the left margin. The data to be inserted begins two spaces to the right of the headings, which should be at the margin stop set for a 1″ left margin.

The headings are double-spaced (DS), and a DS separates the last heading line from the message. The body is single-spaced (SS) with a DS between paragraphs. The operator's initials are placed at the left margin a DS below the message. If there are any attachments to the memo, the notation "Attachments" is placed a DS below the operator's initials.

Simplified format. Simplified memorandums are prepared on plain paper or on company letterhead (see model memo on p. 329). These memorandums do not include preprinted headings. Simplified memos are prepared in block format with 1″ side margins and are formatted as follows.

Date: plain paper, line 10; letterhead, a DS below the letterhead.

Addressee's name: on the 4th line space (QS) below the date. The name may be followed on the same line by a job title or department name.

Subject: in ALL CAPS a DS below the addressee's name.

Body: a DS below the subject line; single-spaced (SS) with a DS between paragraphs.

Writer's name: on the 4th line space (QS) below the last line of the body of the memo.

Operator's initials: a DS below the writer's name.

Attachments (if any): a DS below the operator's initials. Some firms prefer the use of the word "Enclosures," which is handled in the same way.

News Releases

News releases announce items of special interest to newspapers and other news media. The release is usually prepared on letterhead with the words "News Release" printed at the left and the words "For Release:" and "Contact:" at the right (see model release on p. 331).

Side margins of 1″ are used. Paragraphs are double-spaced (DS) and indented five spaces. The time of release is placed two spaces to the right of "For Release:" and the name and telephone number of the person to contact for additional information is keyed two spaces to the right of "Contact."

The body of the release (which always begins with the city, state, and date) begins a quadruple space (QS) below the heading information. The symbols ### are centered a double space (DS) below the last line to indicate the end of the release.

Document 7
Advertising Budget

Mrs. Scott: Key this budget beginning on line 12. Center the material horizontally. Compute the new total for each location.

BOUTIQUES INTERNATIONAL, LTD.

DS

Advertising Budget for Fiscal Year Beginning September 1, 19--

Eastern Division

Media	New York	Washington D.C.	Atlanta	Miami
Newspapers	$ ~~432,000~~ 480,000	$ ~~360,000~~ 400,000	$~~288,000~~ 320,000	$ ~~360,000~~ 400,000
Magazines	~~135,000~~ 150,000	~~112,500~~ 125,000	~~90,000~~ 100,000	~~112,500~~ 125,000
Television	~~243,000~~ 270,000	~~202,500~~ 225,000	~~162,000~~ 180,000	~~202,500~~ 225,000
Radio	~~189,000~~ 210,000	~~157,500~~ 175,000	~~126,000~~ 140,000	~~157,500~~ 175,000
Direct Mail	~~351,000~~ 390,000	~~292,500~~ 325,000	~~234,000~~ 260,000	~~292,500~~ 325,000
				DS
Total	$1,350,000	$1,125,000	$900,000	$1,125,000

Documents 8-11
Simplified Memorandums with Table

Mrs. Scott: Prepare memorandums for Miss Perez dated **June 12** to each of the boutique managers on the list below. Also, prepare mailing envelopes for the memorandums.

Using the information from the advertising budget table you already keyed, center the budget figures in table form with two headings in ALL CAPS: **MEDIA** and **AMOUNT**. DS above and below the headings, but SS the entries.

New York manager:
Mr. Byron T. St. George
Boutiques International, Ltd.
769 Fifth Avenue
New York, NY 10022-3969

Washington, D.C. manager:
Ms. Leona M. Jones
Boutiques International, Ltd.
2652 Virginia Avenue, NW
Washington, DC 20037-5697

Atlanta manager:
Mrs. Margaret J. Fulton
Boutiques International, Ltd.
260 Peachtree Street, NW
Atlanta, GA 30303-6568

Miami manager:
Ms. Juanita R. Sanchez
Boutiques International, Ltd.
2927 Florida Avenue
Miami, FL 33133-5281

The figures below represent the projected advertising ~~funds~~ budget for your office for the fiscal year beginning September 1, 19-- . The figures have been increased 10% over this year's budget to compensate for anticipated increases in costs ~~prices~~ caused by inflationary ~~pressures~~.

(Insert figures for specific office)

This budget ~~allocates~~ allots funds for local advertising only. As in the past, all national advertising ~~campaigns~~ will be conducted by this office in ~~cooperation~~ coordination with you and the managers of ~~all of the~~ our other boutiques.

Please let me have your ~~ideas~~ comments on this projected budget and any ~~other~~ recommended changes by June ~~19~~ 26. Keep in mind that once the budget has been ~~set~~ approved, no changes may be made without the ~~advanced~~ prior approval of this office.

188a ▶ 5
Conditioning Practice

each line twice SS
(slowly, then faster);
if time permits, take
1′ writings on line 4

alphabet 1 Mickey will award six prizes for jet travel at the gala banquet today.

figures 2 Stocks rose 48.1 points on June 29 but dropped 57.6 points on June 30.

fig/sym 3 They made payments of $349.25, $412.73, $507.80, $614.06, and $789.25.

speed 4 The auditor may suspend the fight for the title to the ancient chapel.

| 1 | 2 | 3 | 4 | 5 | 6 | 7 | 8 | 9 | 10 | 11 | 12 | 13 | 14 |

188b ▶ 45 Format Formal Memorandums

Memo 1
Formal Memo
LP p. 113

1. Study the information about formal memos on p. 325.

2. Note the format of the model memo on p. 327.

3. Prepare a copy of the model memo on p. 327.

Memo 2
Formal Memo
LP p. 115

Key the memo shown at the right.

Memo 3
Formal Memo
LP p. 117

Key the memo at the right again, but each time the name "Omnibus" appears, change it to "Omicron."

Note: The global search and replace feature on a word processor permits the operator to instruct the machine to change a word automatically wherever it appears in a document.

Note: If you do not have Lab Pac (LP) pages to use for the formal memo, follow these guidelines.

1. Set side margins at 1″.

2. Beginning on line 10, key each heading flush with the left margin.

3. Space twice after the colon and key the information following each heading.

words

TO: ~~Mrs.~~ Sharon C. Gross, Manager, Information Systems   FROM: 9
Brandon L. London, Communications Chief   DATE: September 14,   20
19--   SUBJECT: Word Processing Systems   26

As you ~~directed~~ *requested* in your (memo) of September 2, my staff   38

and I have been ~~looking into~~ *investigating* word processing systems for use   50

in our secretarail pool. Within the price guides *lines* you estab-   63

lished, we examined and tested six systems. After careful   75

~~thought~~ *Consideration*, we concluded that the Omnibus System *will best meet our needs.* ~~is best.~~   91

The Omnibus has dual disk drives *with 526K expandable memory*. Automatic features of   108

the Omnibus include automating centering, underlining, ~~and~~   118

decimal tabulation, *and carrier return.*   127

Among the desirable ~~aspects~~ *features* of the Omnibus are a 60,000-   138

word dictionary which automatically checks the spelling of   150

words and a "save" ~~feature~~ *mechanism* which prevents the loss of *stored* data   163

in the event of a power failure. Best of all, the Omnibus   175

is truly "user friendly." There are no ~~arduous~~ *difficult* commands to   188

learn since all instructions ~~used~~ are given in *simple* words.   199

We strongly recommend that ~~consideration~~ *approval* be given for   209

the purchase of six Omnibus Systems for installation at the   221

~~soonest~~ *earliest possible date.*   225

xx   226/**237**

Document 6
Questionnaire

Mrs. Scott: Key the questionnaire using these format guides.

- side margins, 1″
- column width, 3″
- space between columns, ½″

Key the questions so that the columns are *approximately* the same length.

Line 6 { QUESTIONNAIRE FOR SPECIAL PEOPLE

GETTING TO KNOW YOU . . . . so that we may ~~treat~~ *serve* you as a person and not just as another customer, will you please complete the following short questionnaire and return it in the enclosed envelope. For your cooperation, you may deduct 10% on your next purchase of $50 or less. Just use the certificate enclosed.

1. Are you married?
____Yes ____No

2. What is your age group?
____18-24 *5* ____35-45 ____65+ *56-*
____25-34 ____50-64 *66+*
5 *6* *5* *46-55*

3. How many children under the age of 18 do you have?
____None __1 __2 __3 *or more*
6

4. Which magazines do you read on a regular basis?
____Reader's Digest
____People
____Time
____Better Homes and gardens
____Fortune
____Sports Illustrated
____National Geographic
____Cosmopolitan

5. ~~Do you have a~~
____~~Microwave oven~~
____~~VCR~~
____~~CD player~~
____~~Stereo~~

6. What is your annual income? *7*
____$15,000 to $29,999
____$30,000 to $44,999
____$45,000 to $59,999
____$60,000 to $74,999
____$75,000 to $89,999
____$90,000+

8. What is your educational level? *4*
____High school
____Junior college
____Four-year college
____Master's degree
____Advanced degree

8. Which *three* of the ~~following~~ activities do you enjoy most?
____Watching TV
____Reading
____Traveling
____Playing sports
____Attending concerts
____Gardening
____Fishing or hunting
____Attending the theater
____~~Playing cards~~
Handicrafts

9 Recently, you purchased an item by Molyneaux. Was this item for yourself or a gift?
9. ____Myself ____Gift

10. If this item was for yourself, how would you rate it? *11 STET*
____Excellent
____Good
____Satisfactory
____Disappointing

11. What attracted you to this product? *12 STET*
____Attractive package
____Pleasing scent
____Handsome container

12. Would you purchase this item again? *13 STET*
____Yes
____No
____Undecided

13. In your opinion, is the price of this item *14 STET*
____About right ____Too high

3. What is your ZIP Code?

____ ____ ____ ____ ____

EAGLE & SONS

2299 Seward Highway ▪ Anchorage, Alaska ▪ 99503-4100   INTEROFFICE MEMORANDUM

TO: Warren E. Latouch, Director of Administration   9

FROM: Carla M. Boniface, Chief of Personnel   17

DATE: May 2, 19--   19

SUBJECT: Employee Evaluation Program _{DS}   25

As the company continues to expand, it is desirable that we estab-   38
lish an effective program for evaluating the performance of all   51
our employees. A sound evaluation program offers many advantages   64
to both the company and our employees, including the following: _{DS}   77

1. Assists employees in judging their own value and accomplish-   89
ments. Ratings should include strong points as well as short-   102
comings, with suggestions for improvement. _{DS}   110

2. Provides managers with information which they may use to de-   123
termine promotions or lateral reassignments in order to make the   136
most effective use of each employee's abilities. _{DS}   146

3. Provides a basis for determining increases in compensation or   159
for bonus payments to reward the most efficient employees. _{DS}   171

4. Requires supervisors to analyze the work done by their subor-   184
dinates and to recognize the contribution they make in the accom-   197
plishment of their mutual objectives. _{DS}   205

5. Promotes an atmosphere of mutual respect and teamwork among   217
supervisors and employees. _{DS}   223

6. Provides an evaluation of the effectiveness of other personnel   236
programs such as recruitment, selection, orientation, and training. _{DS}   250

It is essential that clear-cut policies be established for this   263
new evaluation program. To insure success, the objectives of the   276
program must be clearly established, thoroughly understood, and   289
fully accepted by all concerned. A recommended plan of action to   302
accomplish these objectives is attached. _{DS}   311

As a matter of priority, I recommend that the establishment of a   324
program to evaluate employee performance be placed on the agenda   337
of the executive committee for consideration at the earliest pos-   349
sible date. _{DS}   352

xx _{DS}   353

Attachment   355

Formal Memorandum

Document 2
Table

Mrs. Scott: Center the table vertically and horizontally.

Common Metric Measures
(With Approximate U.S. Equivalents)

Unit	Symbol	Equivalent
kilometer	km	0.62 mile
meter	m	37.37 inches
centimeter	cm	0.39 inch
millimeter	mm	0.039 inch
liter	l* or L*	1.057 quarts
milliliter	ml	0.27 fluidram
kilogram	kg	2.2046 pounds
gram	g	0.035 ounce

*May also be spelled in full & (liter).

Documents 3, 4, and 5
Letters

LP p. 117-121

Mrs. Scott: Please key this letter for Mr. Novak, dated **June 10**, in the block format, open punctuation, to the addressees below. Place appropriate columnar headings over the tabular items.

Mr. Byron T. St. George, Manager
Boutiques International, Ltd.
769 Fifth Avenue
New York, NY 10022-3969

Ms. Marcy L. LaCruz, Manager
Boutiques International, Ltd.
102 Rodeo Drive
Los Angeles, CA 90035-4729

Mr. Thomas C. Harding, Manager
Boutiques International, Ltd.
2600 January Avenue
St. Louis, MO 63139-2233

Boutiques International, Ltd., has entered into an exclusive agreement with Molyneaux Parfums, Ltd., of Paris, to market a new line of perfumes and toiletries.

Before marketing these items nationally, we have decided to market test a sample of the items in three Metropolitan Areas: New York, Los Angelos, and St. Louis. The test will determine (1) the relative effectiveness of two copy ads and (2) the types of people interested in these products. Via Airfreight, you will recieve 500 each of the following items to be retailed at the prices indicated.

Molyneaux Parfum No. 12, 7.5 ml	$62.95
Nouveau Eau De Toilette, 100 ml	72.99
LeOrleans Skin Creanm, 75 ml	29.00
Bule De Bain 2 L	48.50

A complete record of the name and address of each purchaser will be kept. Two weeks after purchase, a copy of the inclosed questionnaire will be mailed to the purchaser. Completed questionnaires will be returned to this office.

Three ad campaigns will be conducted. One will begin July 1 and continue for two weeks; one will begin August 1 and continue for two weeks; one will begin September 1 and continue for two weeks. Print copy for the ads will be faxed on June 15.

Please call me if you have any questions about this market test.

189a ▶ 5
Conditioning Practice

each line twice SS (slowly, then faster); DS between 2-line groups; if time permits, take 1′ writings on line 3

alphabet 1 Pam made the objective of the exercises clear by giving a weekly quiz.

figures 2 The population of the town rose from 75,204 in 1980 to 83,564 in 1990.

fig/sym 3 On 8/16/90, we sold 1,320 shares of Gee & Gee stock at $47.50 a share.

speed 4 Their firm goal is to visit the city and to fight the rigid amendment.

| 1 | 2 | 3 | 4 | 5 | 6 | 7 | 8 | 9 | 10 | 11 | 12 | 13 | 14 |

189b ▶ 45 *Format Simplified Memorandums*

plain full sheets

Memo 1

1. Study the information on formatting a simplified memo on p. 325.

2. Note the format of the model memo on p. 329.

3. Prepare a copy of the model memo on p. 329.

Memo 2

1. Format and key the rough-draft copy as a simplified memo dated **May 9, 19--**, to **All Division Chiefs** with the subject **COMPUTER ORIENTATION SESSIONS** for the signature of **Sarah T. Burton, Chief of Administration**.

2. Key the schedule as a table (DS) with the headings **Department** and **Time and Date**.

3. Make changes as marked.

Memo 3

Format and key the copy as a simplified memo; check the figures carefully.

words

opening lines 12

During the installation of the Omega VI *and peripherals* main frame computer, a series of orientations *sessions* for employees will be ~~led~~ *conducted* by the training section, *by department,* in accordance with the following schedule. 28 / 42 / 57

Administration, 9:30 a.m.-11:30 a.m., May 16; Purchasing, 1:30 p.m.-3:30 p.m., May 16; Marketing, 9:30 a.m.-11:30 a.m., May 18; Research and Engineering, 1:30 p.m.-3:30 p.m., May 18; Production, 9:30 a.m.-11:30 a.m., May 19. 78 / 90 / 102 / 110

All meetings will be held in room 102 of the Administration *Building* ~~Office~~. Please ask all employees to be prompt. *Paper and pencils for taking notes will be provided.* 122 / 135 / 143

closing lines 152

May 20, 19-- Paul A. Williams, President PRELIMINARY FINANCIAL FIGURES 14

Preliminary figures for the fiscal year ended April 30 indicate that net sales for the year reached $67,160,000--an increase of 12% over the previous year. Net income for this year totaled $1,679,000 or $.80 per common share. Total assets at year's end are estimated to exceed $48,600,000. 30 / 46 / 61 / 73

Shares of common stock outstanding at the end of the fiscal year numbered exactly 2,098,750 with 970,451 shareholders of record. Shares of the Cumulative Preferred $5 stock totaled 845,000 with 1,746 shareholders of record. 88 / 103 / 118

Based on these preliminary figures, it is recommended that we declare a cash dividend of $.32 per share of common stock. This will reflect our growth during this fiscal year and will represent an increase of $.10 over the previous year's dividend. 133 / 147 / 163 / 168

Elizabeth D. McNamara, Treasurer xx 175

UNIT 64 LESSONS 267 – 271
Advertising Department

Learning Goals

1. To increase your skills in planning and organizing a variety of production jobs.
2. To produce a variety of business documents of high quality within a reasonable time and with a minimum of assistance.
3. To become familiar with the functions performed and the documents produced in an Advertising Department.

Documents Processed

1. Formal Memorandum
2. Tables
3. Letters
4. Simplified Memorandums
5. Questionnaire
6. Manuscript of Speech
7. Speech Cards

267a-271a ▶ 5 (daily)
Conditioning Practice

each line twice SS (slowly, then faster); if time permits, take 1' writings on line 1

alphabet	1	After key tax cuts, we bought major equipment that vitalized our work.
figures	2	Change line item 25 on page 109 from 3,876 to 3,576 units we produced.
fig/sym	3	Does Model #37215-A printer (Serial #40689) sell for $1,647 or $2,398?
speed	4	Is the sign to the ancient chapel in the big field visible to the eye?

| 1 | 2 | 3 | 4 | 5 | 6 | 7 | 8 | 9 | 10 | 11 | 12 | 13 | 14 |

267b-271b ▶ 45 (daily)
Document Processing

1. You have been assigned to work as a word processing operator in the Advertising Department under the direction of Mrs. Joanna P. Scott, the office manager. Miss Rita L. Perez is the director of advertising; Mr. Robert T. Novak is the assistant director.

2. In this job, you will be required to prepare a variety of documents. Follow the directions given for each document. If no directions are given, use your best judgment.

3. Unless otherwise directed, complete each document in final form. Correct all marked and unmarked errors and those you may make.

4. Before beginning, review the material about the Advertising Department on page 427 as well as the major duties and special instructions.

Document 1
Formal Memorandum
LP p. 115

Mrs. Scott: Please key this memo to **All Copywriters** for Mr. Novak. Date it **June 9.** Use the subject **Metric Copy.**

A 1988 act of Congress provides that agencies of the govern- *business* ment XXXX must use the metric system of measurement in XXX activities. Since that time, a number of industries with whom we deal have begun converting to metric system. It is XikaXxXimpooxtanXx therefore, that all copywriters should be familier with the metric system.

Attached is a table of the most commonly used metric XXXXX measures. In preparing copy using metric measures, follow these guide lines. DS

1. Key metric units as abbreviations: 23 g (23 grams). Do not pluralize abbreviations and do not use a period after an abbreviation except at the end of a sentence.
2. Key metric unit letter abbreviations in lower case unless the unit name was derived from a propr name, such as "C" for Celsius. An uppercase L may be used as an abbreviation for liter to avoid confusing the lowercase l with the figure 1.
3. Space between a figure and the unit abbreviation that follows: 3 g (3 grams).

4. Express temprature in this manner: 24 C.
5. When the measure is a decimal, place a zero XX XXXXX XX before the decimal: 0.54 cm (0.54 centimeter).
6. Groups of three digits should be separated by a space rather than by comas: 0.142 035 g (0.142 035 gram).

DS between enumerated items.

KRĀEBIN INDUSTRIES

3875 SUGAR RIDGE DRIVE   ROANOKE, VA 24018-2419

May 5, 19-- _{QS}

All Department Chiefs _{DS}

INSTALLATION OF COMPUTER AND PERIPHERALS _{DS}

In accordance with the terms of our contract with Allied Business
Machines, installation of the Omega VI mainframe computer will
begin on June 1 and will be completed no later than June 16. A
systems check will begin immediately after installation; it is
scheduled to be completed by June 23. _{DS}

Concurrent with the installation of the Omega VI, peripheral equipment in the form of terminals and fax machines will be installed
in major departments of the company as shown below. _{DS}

Department	Peripherals
Administration	6 terminals
	1 fax machine
Purchasing	1 fax machine
Marketing	2 terminals
	1 fax machine
Research and Engineering	2 terminals
	1 fax machine
Production	1 terminal _{DS}

Please inform all of your employees of these plans so that they
will understand exactly what is taking place. A series of orientation sessions for all employees regarding the purpose and use
of the computer and peripheral equipment will be conducted by the
Training Section. Schedules of these sessions will be published
by the Administration Department in the very near future. _{QS}

A. Maynard Kelton, Executive Vice President _{DS}

xx

Simplified Memorandum

262b-266b (continued)

Document 12
Grievance Procedures
plain paper

Mrs. Schwartz: Key the grievance procedures as an unbound manuscript. Correct all marked and unmarked errors.

Document 13
Grievance Procedures
plain paper

Mrs. Schwartz: Key the grievance procedures as a leftbound manuscript for inclusion in the company's Standard Operating Procedures. After the first paragraph, single-space the steps that follow, but double-space between them.

BOUTIQUES INTERNATIONAL, LTD.

Grievance Procedures for Unionized Employees* *DS*

All actions taken by the company that effect em- *QS*

ployees will be based on the principals of fair ness and

individual merit. All employees have the right to fair

and equitable treatment. If *at any time* an employee beleives that

this basic right has been violated, she or he may take

the following steps.

Step 1. The employee will discuss the problem with *her or*

his ~~superior~~ *supervisor*. The ~~superior~~ *supervisor* will determine the *exact* nature of

the problem and ~~provide~~ *offer* a solution.

Step 2. In the event the employee is not satisfied

with the solution offered by ~~his~~ *the* supervisor, the employee

will then ~~state his~~ *submit the* problem in writing using Form 201,

"Grievance Statement" ~~which will be sent to the superior~~

~~of the employees' supervisor.~~ *to the supervisor's superior,* The superior will study

the problem, talk with both parties *if necessary,* ~~and provide~~ *and render* a written

decision.

Step 3. If the employee is not satisfied with the

written decision, she or he will *refer* ~~send~~ the problem to the

union representative, who will *take up* ~~discuss~~ the matter with

the union committee and, if necessary, the appeals com-

mittee.

Step 4. If the problem is not *resolved* ~~solved~~ during any of

the *previous* ~~other~~ steps, the matter will *be referred* ~~given~~ to an arbitrator,

who will determine an equitable settlement, *which will be binding on all parties.*

_____

*Source: Master Labor Agreement, Provision 692.1.

190a ▶ 5
Conditioning Practice

each line twice SS (slowly, then faster); DS between 2-line groups; if time permits, take 1' writings on line 3

alphabet	1	Have Jo fix the bad wiring and synchronize the company clocks quickly.
figures	2	Paragraphs 39.1, 47.2, 50.8, and 60.1 of the bylaws were added June 8.
fig/sym	3	Taxes rose 5.4% in 1983, 7.6% in 1985, 10.1% in 1987, and 12% in 1991.
speed	4	When the men turn the dials, they may fix the problem with the signal.

| 1 | 2 | 3 | 4 | 5 | 6 | 7 | 8 | 9 | 10 | 11 | 12 | 13 | 14 |

190b ▶ 45 Format News Releases

LP pp. 119-123

News Release 1

1. Study the information on formatting a news release on p. 325.

2. Note the format of the model news release on p. 331.

3. Prepare a copy of the model news release on p. 331.

News Release 2

Key copy given at the right as a news release for release **Immediately** with **David C. Taylor 401-896-3286** as the contact; make the changes as marked.

News Release 3

Key copy given at the right as a news release for release on **July 16, 19--** with **Lisa T. Cole 401-896-3289** as the contact.

words

opening lines 8

	words
OMAHA, NE, June 30, 19--. Harvey E. Jamison, president	19
and chief executive officer of the Forum Group, announced	31
today the merger of the firms company's import-export sub-	41
sidiary, Intercon, Inc., with the Boston-located based Atlan-	52
tis Group. In exchange for Intercon, Inc., the Forum Group	63
will attain receive 50% of the ownership equity in the ex-	71
panded Atlantis Group.	77
"With the merger, the Atlantis Group will rank in among	87
the top three import-export outfits companies in the United	98
States," said Jamison. "More importantly," he said added,	108
"this merger provides a unique opportunity for the Forum	120
Group to enlarge expand its international potential opera-	128
tions and capabilities."	133
T. Harlan Mayer, the present current president of the	142
Atlantis Group, will retire on September 1 of this year.	154
His job position will be assumed by Marian C. Bodner, who	164
is currently presently the executive vice president of Martin	175
Industries Inc., another part subsidiary of the Forum Group.	186
The replacement for Bodner will be divulged announced at a	196
later date. ###	199

opening lines 8

	words
(¶ 1) OMAHA, NE, July 14, 19--. A historic agreement has been made with	21
the Republic of China by the Forum Group, according to Harvey E. Jamison,	36
president and chief executive officer of Forum. Under the agreement, Forum	51
will open a branch office in Tianjin as the initial step in establishing a series	68
of centers to serve business interests throughout China.	79
(¶ 2) Charles C. Goldsmith, currently the assistant director of Forum's Inter-	94
national Trade Division, will head the Forum office in Tianjin. His immediate	109
assistant will be Paul Yi Chung. Born in China, Mr. Chung became a citizen	125
of the United States in 1962. He is a graduate of Williams Academy and the	140
Wharton School of Business, University of Pennsylvania. Mr. Chung has held	155
numerous high-level managerial positions during the past ten years and most	170
recently served as president of America-Pacifico, Ltd., a firm which special-	185
izes in trade with Far and Middle Eastern countries.	196
(¶ 3) Until appropriate office facilities can be established in Tianjin, the	210
Forum Group will be located in Hong Kong at 80 Moody Road, Kowloon City	225
Centre. It is anticipated that the Tianjin office will open in December of	240
this year. ###	243

Document 10
Statement of Policy

plain paper

Mrs. Schwartz: Please key this statement of policy as an unbound manuscript. DS the enumerated items. Correct the marked errors and any unmarked errors.

STATEMENT OF POLICY

Fair and Equitable Treatment of Employees

The basic policy of Boutiques International, Ltd.,

is to select the *individual* ~~person~~ best qualified to fill each posi-

tion regardless of race, color, creed, sex, ~~or~~ age *or national origin*. All

individuals ~~employees~~ in positions of autherity have the responsibil-

ity to ensure that all employees are treated fairly and

equitably *in all personel actions*.

To ~~i~~nsure that this policy is known *and understood* by all concerned,

the following ~~steps~~ *actions* will be taken.

1. A *statement* ~~state~~ of the policy will be *sent* ~~given~~ to all of

those who are in positions of authority including *but not restricted to,*

supervisors, administrators, and the heads of all

organizational elements.

2. Seminars will be held on a *periodic* ~~recurring~~ basis for

supervisory personel to review and update this

policy.

3. All advertisements for personnel will include the

statement *that* we are an "equal opportunity employer."

4. During their oreintation *program* ~~period~~, new employees

will be given a statement of the *company's* ~~firm's~~ fair and *equitable* ~~equal~~

treatment policy, together with a copy of the *procedures* ~~steps~~

to be followed in the event *any* an employee feels that he

or she has been the subject of discrimination.

Document 11
Simplified Memorandum

plain paper

Mrs. Schwartz: Please compose and key a simplified memorandum, dated **April 16,** for **Mr. O'Brian** to **Lucille K. Phillips, Vice President for Administration,** submitting the revised statement of policy on "Fair and Equitable Treatment of Employees" for her approval.

Tell Ms. Phillips that the policy has been revised to reflect the latest U.S. Supreme Court rulings on the implementation of the Equal Opportunity Act of 1972 as reflected in the amendments to the "Uniform Guidelines on Employee Selection Procedures," published

by the Equal Employment Opportunity Commission.

Ask Ms. Phillips to expedite her approval, since the next seminar for supervisors on fair and equitable treatment of employees is scheduled for **April 25.**

FORUM GROUP

Suite 82, Forum Building
5800 Dodge Center
Omaha, Nebraska 68132-6459

401-896-3000

words

News Release

For Release: Upon receipt 3
Contact: Christine M. O'Ryan 7
401-896-3175 QS 9

OMAHA, NE, March 21, 19--. The Forum Group, the holding com- DS 21
pany for the Forum Insurance Companies of North America with $1.8 34
billion in assets, has filed today a registration statement with 47
the Securities and Exchange Commission for the proposed sale of 60
$10 million of cumulative convertible preferred stock. 71

This offering will consist of 500,000 shares of preferred 83
stock with a liquidation value of $20 per share, which will be 95
convertible into the Forum Group's common stock. The company will 109
not be empowered to redeem the shares for the first three years 122
with funds raised at a lower cost than that of the new preferred. 135
The shares will otherwise be redeemable from the time of issuance 148
at a premium initially equivalent to the dividend rate and declin- 161
ing to redemption at $20 per share after eight years. The divi- 174
dend rate, offering price, and conversion ratio on the preferred 187
stock will be determined at the time of offering. 197

The brokerage firm of Houseman & Fields, Inc., will manage 209
the offering which is expected the latter part of April. DS 220

221

Model News Release

262b-266b (continued)

Documents 6-9
Form Letters

LP pp. 107-113

Mrs. Schwartz: Please key these letters dated **April 9** to the following applicants, using the form letters indicated. The letters will be signed by Mr. O'Brian.

Applicant 1

Mrs. Velma T. Monroe
Rural Route 5
Baton Rouge, LA 70807-2323
Position: **job analyst**
Letter 26

Applicant 2

Mr. Jun Hori
2030 North Magnolia Street
Hammond, LA 70401-9824
Position: **legal advisor**
Letter 27

Applicant 3

Miss Jennifer P. Jackson
1228 Broadway Street
New Orleans, LA 70118-7127
Position: **executive secretary**
Letter 28

Applicant 4

Mr. Mark C. Johnson
2309 Florida Street
Kenner, LA 70062-7216
Position: **records manager**
Letter 27

Form Letter 26

Thank you for your recent letter in which you applied for a position as a/an (insert title of position). We appreciate your interest in Boutiques International, Ltd.

Will you please complete the enclosed application form and return it to us promptly. After we have had an opportunity to review your background, we shall be able to determine if you have the necessary qualifications to fill the position.

Within two weeks after we receive your application form, we shall let you know if we have a vacant position for which you are qualified.

Form Letter 27

We acknowledge, with thanks, your application for a position as a/an (insert title of position). We may have a position for which you are qualified.

Will you please call our office at 504-3000, Ext. 280, and arrange for a personal interview so that we can discuss the position with you.

We are looking forward to meeting you as a prospective employee of Boutiques International, Ltd.

Form Letter 28

Recently, you were interviewed by a member of our staff for the position of (insert title of position) in the office of Boutiques International, Ltd. The competition for this job was very keen, and it was quite difficult to select the person to fill the position.

We regret that you were not selected for the position. We shall keep your application on file for six months and will call you if another vacancy occurs for which you may be qualified.

Again, we thank you for your interest in becoming an employee in our company.

191a ▶ 5
Conditioning Practice

each line twice SS (slowly, then faster); DS between 2-line groups; if time permits, take 1' writings on line 3

alphabet	1	Philip may serve freshly squeezed orange juice at breakfast next week.
figures	2	The show can be seen at 2:30 p.m. and 6:45 p.m. on May 17, 18 and 19.
fig/sym	3	Is the Model #5436 Printer (Serial #48391) listed at $1,325 or $2,790?
speed	4	She may go with us to the civic hall downtown for a world title fight.

| 1 | 2 | 3 | 4 | 5 | 6 | 7 | 8 | 9 | 10 | 11 | 12 | 13 | 14 |

191b ▶ 45
Sustained Production: Memos/News Releases

LP pp. 125-127
plain full sheets

Refer to Time Schedule in 192b.

1. Make a list of documents to be processed, including any special instructions.

p. 326, 188b, Memo 2, *except* change the name "Omnibus" to "Jupiter" each time it appears.

p. 328, 189b, Memo 2, *except* key the table SS.
p. 328, 189b, Memo 3
p. 330, 190b, News Release 2

2. Arrange letterheads and plain paper for efficient handling.

3. Work for 30' when directed to begin. Correct errors as you key. Proofread each document before removing it from the machine.

4. Compute *n-pram;* turn in documents in the order given in Step 1.

192a ▶ 5
Conditioning Practice

each line twice SS (slowly, then faster); DS between 2-line groups; if time permits, take 1' writings on line 1

alphabet	1	Vicky and Jay requested boxes of many sizes filled with writing paper.
figures	2	Please correct the errors on pages 3, 6, 8, 9, 21, 46, 50, 73, and 82.
symbols	3	The ratings are: Superior (****); Good (***); Fair (**); or Poor (*).
speed	4	An amendment to the audit may entitle the girls to the rich endowment.

| 1 | 2 | 3 | 4 | 5 | 6 | 7 | 8 | 9 | 10 | 11 | 12 | 13 | 14 |

192b ▶ 45 Measure Production Skills: Memos/News Releases

LP pp. 129-133
plain full sheets

1. Arrange letterheads and plain full sheets for efficient handling.
2. Key for 30' the documents below and on p. 333. Correct

errors neatly; proofread each document before you remove it from the machine.

3. After timed production, proofread and circle any errors you may have missed.
4. Compute *n-pram.*

Time Schedule

Plan and prepare .... 5'
Timed production .... 30'
Proofread; compute *n-pram* .. 10'

Document 1
Simplified Memorandum
Key the copy given at the right as a simplified memo.

	words
June 16, 19-- Paul A. Williams, President PLANNING CONFERENCE AGENDA	14

As you requested, the agenda for the Planning Conference to be held on June 25 has been changed. The report SEASONAL CHANGES which was scheduled for 10:15 a.m. has been eliminated as well as the MANAGERIAL EFFICIENCY report scheduled for 1:30 p.m. Instead, a report entitled THE ENVIRONMENTAL IMPACT OF PROJECT 209A will be presented by John R. Day, the project engineer, at 10:15 a.m. At 1:30 p.m., Marjorie K. Lamont, director of human relations, will discuss EXECUTIVE STRESS. — 28, 41, 55, 70, 83, 98, 111

Your closing remarks at the conference are now scheduled for 3:15 p.m., to be followed by general comments from participants who will suggest areas for future discussion. A revised copy of the agenda for this conference is attached. — 126, 140, 155, 158

Robert E. Pitts, Administrative Assistant xx Attachment — 169

Documents 2, 3, and 4 are on p. 333.

Document 3
Formal Memorandum

LP p. 105

Mrs. Schwartz: Since the Records Section is very busy, Ms. Morris has asked us to help her. Please key this memorandum for her to **Mr. O'Brian,** dated **April 7,** with the subject **Transfer of Documents.**

As requested in your memo (sp) of March 26 (28), we have begun transferring the paper files in our office to electronic media. I do not anticipate any difficulty in meeting the target dates.

Attached is a new revised job description for the Director of Human Resources. The revision represents includes a few minor/major editorial changes and two major changes.

1. Since training is now a responsibility of the Education and Training Department, which was set up established on February 1, this duty has been eliminated from the job description.

3. The responsibility for planning for human resources in the future, has been added to the revised job description.

Document 4
Table

plain paper

Mrs. Schwartz: Key this table; center it vertically and horizontally.

Document 5
Table

plain paper

Mrs. Schwartz: Key the table on employee benefits again, making these changes:

1. Change the secondary heading to read **(Not Including Administrative Personnel).**

2. Key the benefits in alphabetical order.

3. Add this source note preceding the footnote.
Source: In-House Survey Conducted March, 19--.

BENEFITS DESIRED BY A MAJORITY OF EMPLOYEES[*]

(In-House Survey Conducted March, 19--)

Benefit	Percent
Paid Vacations	100%
Paid Holidays	99
Life Insurance	95
Health Insurance	94 (96)
Parking Facilities	92
Jury Duty Leave	90
Funeral Leave	90
Rest Time	82
Pension Plan	74
Paid Sick Leave	70
Educational Assistance	68
Employee Discounts	56

*Not including benefits required by law such as Social Security and workers' compensation.

**Document 2
Formal Memo**

1. Key the copy given at the right as a formal memo to **All Word Processing Operators,** from **Kelly T. Rice, Chief of Document Processing.** Date the memo **July 8, 19--** with the subject **Care of Floppy Disks.**

2. List the enumerated items.

Note: The memos will be sent in reusable interoffice envelopes that do not require keyed addresses.

Reusable Company Mail Envelope

**Document 3
News Release**

Key the copy given at the right as a news release for release **Immediately** with **Elizabeth P. McNeil 401-896-3275** as the contact.

**Document 4
News Release**

Key the news release in Document 3 again with the following changes.

1. Eliminate the final sentence of ¶ 2.

2. In place of the final sentence of ¶ 2, substitute the copy in ¶ 4.

3. As the final ¶, key the material at the right.

words

opening lines 22

A few unfortunate accidents have occurred during the past several weeks   36
which have caused the loss of important documents stored on 5 1/4″ floppy   51
disks. These accidents were caused primarily by improper handling of the   66
disks. When using floppy disks, follow these basic rules.   78

1. Except when in use, keep the disks in their protective covers and store   93
them in the plastic boxes provided. Never cover disks with heavy objects.   108
2. When using the disks, do not touch the surface. Hold the disks gently by   124
the edges and insert them into the disk drives carefully. Under no circum-   138
stances attempt to force the disks into the drive. 3. Keep disks away from   154
metal or magnetized items. This includes paper clips and scissors. 4. Use   169
only felt markers to write on the label of a disk. If you use a ballpoint pen   185
or attempt to erase a label, you can ruin the disk. 5. Food of any kind, if   201
spilled on a disk, may ruin the disk. It is for this reason that eating in the   217
document processing room is forbidden.   225

Please keep these simple precautions in mind. Remember, pages of informa-   239
tion are stored on one floppy disk--information which can be lost in a second   255
by improper handling.   260

opening lines 9

(¶ 1) OMAHA, NE, September 16, 19--. At the annual meeting of the Forum   22
Group stockholders on September 15, Harvey E. Jamison, president and   36
chief executive officer, announced that ground-breaking ceremonies for a   51
new multipurpose corporate complex will be held October 1 on a site adja-   65
cent to Carter Lake in East Omaha.   72

(¶ 2) The corporate complex will include a ten-story office building and a ten-   87
story building with 240 condominium units. Connecting the two buildings   102
will be an enclosed mall with three department stores, 60 smaller shops, and   117
a recreational center with a complete health spa. Estimated cost of the com-   132
plex is $1.5 billion.   137

(¶ 3) The construction of this new multipurpose complex reflects a strong   150
corporate position in international commerce and increased growth. In this   166
fiscal year, the Forum Group expects a growth rate of 40% which it hopes to   181
sustain into the next decade.   187

(¶ 4) "Forum Park will be open within two years," Mr. Jamison announced,   200
"and will be the first complex in the United States to provide combined fa-   215
cilities for working, living, and recreation." ###   225

Document 4 word count 215

(¶ 5) The plans for the construction of the complex were greeted with great   229
enthusiasm by the stockholders, who gave Mr. Jamison a standing ovation   244
upon the completion of his announcement.   253

Mrs. Schwartz: Please key this corrected job description making the changes that are marked.

JOB DESCRIPTION

JOB TITLE _Director of Human Resources_ UNIT _Human Resources Dept._

REPORTS TO _Vice President for Administration_

SUBORDINATE STAFF _~~Eleven~~ Ten Section Chiefs_

DATE _~~July 9,~~ April 6 19--_ D.O.T. _166.117-018_

GENERAL STATEMENT OF THE JOB

Under the general direction of the Vice President for Administration, establishes the objectives, policies, and procedures for the efficient and effective use of human resources so that the overall objectives of the company will be achieved successfully.

SPECIFIC DUTIES OF THE JOB

1. Analyzes and evaluates jobs to determine the tasks performed and the qualifications required to complete the tasks, as a basis for recruiting, placing, and compensating employees.

~~7~~ 2. Provides employees with a variety of benefits that best suits their needs.

~~2~~ 3. Provides human resources required by all organizational elements by recruiting and selecting qualified employees.

~~4. Improves the value of human resources through training and, at the same time, aids employees to reach their full potential.~~

~~3~~ 5. Improves relations with employees through collective bargaining with unions and by implementing effective procedures for redressing grievances.

~~4~~ 6. Ensures that employees enjoy a safe working environment through safety campaigns, inspections, and education; investigates and corrects causes of all accidents.

~~6~~ 7. Maintains and safeguards all employee records.

8. Assures, through equal opportunity programs, that all employees are treated equitably, regardless of race, color, ~~religion~~ creed, age, and sex.

9. Establishes affirmative action programs to ensure and improve the recruitment and hiring of minorities.

~~5~~ 10. Provides for the physical ~~medical~~ well-being of employees through in-house medical facilities and a comprehensive health insurance plan.

10. Forecasts, through careful planning, the scope and conduct of an effective human resources program in the future.

Improve Keyboarding/Language Skills

Learning Goals

1. To improve your basic keyboarding skills with emphasis on figures and symbols.

2. To increase your keystroking speed and to improve your accuracy on straight copy.

3. To improve your communications skills.

Format Guides

1. Paper guide at *0* (for typewriters).

2. LL: 70 spaces.

3. LS: SS sentence drills with a DS between sets; DS paragraph writings; DS language skill sentences.

4. PI: 5 spaces when appropriate.

Lesson 193   *Keyboarding/Language Skills*

193a ▶ 5
Conditioning Practice
each line twice SS (slowly, then faster); if time permits, take 1′ writings on line 3

alphabet	1	Julio Vasquez asked for views on bylaws that experts are recommending.
figures	2	Her book, published in 1990, has 658 pages, 230 pictures, and 74 maps.
fig/sym	3	Ship 1,850 computer chips (Catalog #738924) to Black & Co. on July 16.
speed	4	Their neighbor did the field audit for them and it may make them rich.

| 1 | 2 | 3 | 4 | 5 | 6 | 7 | 8 | 9 | 10 | 11 | 12 | 13 | 14 |

193b ▶ 20 Improve Language Skills: Commonly Confused Words

1. Study the spelling and definitions of the words.

2. Key the line number (with period); space twice, then key the **Learn** sentence, noting the correct use of the words.

3. Key the line number (with period); space twice, then key the **Apply** sentences DS, selecting the word in parentheses that makes each sentence correct.

way (n) a course or route
weigh (vb) to determine heaviness

conscious (adj) aware; felt or perceived
conscience (n) sense of moral goodness

heard (vb) perceived by the ear
herd (n) a group of animals of one kind

accede (vb) to express approval or consent
exceed (vb) to extend beyond or surpass

discreet (adj) careful or prudent
discrete (adj) separate or distinct

minor (adj) lesser, smaller, or secondary
miner (n) one who digs or excavates

Learn 1. On our way to the depot, we can weigh the package.
Apply 2. He lost his (way, weigh) on his trip to the city.
Apply 3. How much did the football player (way, weigh)?

Learn 4. I was conscious of the fact that he had a guilty conscience.
Apply 5. In good (conscience, conscious), I cannot agree to the changes.
Apply 6. Is she (conscience, conscious) of the bad feeling between them?

Learn 7. We heard the herd of deer in the forest.
Apply 8. The tour group saw a (heard, herd) of elephants in Kenya.
Apply 9. We (heard, herd) the noise of the zoo animals.

Learn 10. Did they accede to our request to exceed the budget?
Apply 11. If you agree to the proposal, I will (accede, exceed) the point.
Apply 12. He will (accede, exceed) his authority if he fires my assistant.

Learn 13. As a unique, discrete unit, we should be discreet when we speak.
Apply 14. We use a set of (discreet, discrete) symbols for this computer program.
Apply 15. He was not very (discreet, discrete) when he gave us the confidential data.

Learn 16. The miner made a minor adjustment to his headlamp.
Apply 17. Did the (minor, miner) locate a vein of coal?
Apply 18. We made only (minor, miner) changes in the report.

Human Resources Department

Learning Goals

1. To become familiar with some of the major functions performed in a Human Resources Department.
2. To increase your knowledge of typical documents processed and tasks performed in a Human Resources Department.
3. To improve your skill in formatting special documents.

Documents Processed

1. Formal Memorandum
2. Job Description
3. Table
4. Form Letters
5. Statement of Policy
6. Simplified Memorandum
7. Grievance Procedures

262a-266a ▶ 5 (daily)
Conditioning Practice

each line twice SS (slowly, then faster); if time permits, take 1′ writings on line 4

alphabet	1	Suzi quickly indexed jokes for the performance she will give publicly.
figures	2	Based on 5,349,700 shares sold, the new stock rose 6 points to 83 1/2.
fig/sym	3	The balance ($829.35) was paid by Bell & Erby on May 6 by Check #7410.
speed	4	It may be a big problem if both of the men bid for the city dock work.

| 1 | 2 | 3 | 4 | 5 | 6 | 7 | 8 | 9 | 10 | 11 | 12 | 13 | 14 |

262b-266b ▶ 45 (daily)
Document Processing

1. You will now work as a keyboard technician in the Human Resources Department under the direction of Mrs. Rachel Schwartz, who is the administrative assistant to Henry K. O'Brian, Director of Human Resources.

2. In this job, you will be required to prepare a number of documents for members of the Human Resources Department. Before beginning, review the material about the department on page 427 as well as the major duties and special instructions.

3. Follow directions given for each document. If no format is specified, use your best judgment.

4. Unless directed to prepare a draft copy, key all documents in final form. Correct all marked and unmarked errors.

Document 1
Formal Memorandum
LP p. 101

Please key this memorandum for Mr. O'Brian, dated March 28, to Diane F. Morris, Chief of Records. Use the subject "Transfer of Documents."

SS Lucille K. Phillips, vice president for administration, *to the extent possible,* has notified me that all documents will be transfered from

paper files to electronic files by means of an optical ~~scanner~~ *character* recognition (OCR) *scanner*. Listed below is the schedule for converting records in your files.

Access Code	Documents	Target Date
8 18 3010	Individual Personel Records	April 30
8 18 3020	Correspondence	May 15
8 18 3030	Job Descriptions	June 1

SS Prior to converting the job descriptions, you should review and revise *where necessary,* all job description that are ~~two~~ *three* or more years old. When you do so please send me a copy of the job description for ~~this~~ *my* position.

193c ▶ 15 *Improve Basic Keyboarding Skills*

Take two 5' writings on the ¶s. Record *gwam* and errors.

all letters used | A | 1.5 si | 5.7 awl | 80% hfw

gwam 1' | 5'

A procedure is simply a series of steps which are followed in a regular or definite order to achieve a desired goal. In an office, standardized procedures are set up to insure that work is done in an orderly and efficient manner. Procedures are of special help to the employee on the job since, once the procedure is learned, the work can be done quickly with less effort. A procedure for processing written documents is an important element in the success of any office.

13 | 3 | 60
26 | 5 | 63
40 | 8 | 66
54 | 11 | 68
68 | 14 | 71
82 | 16 | 74
95 | 19 | 77

Although the procedure for the processing of documents differs from office to office, there are several major steps. The first step is the creation of the author's original material, which is known as input. Input may be in written, rough draft, or dictated form. The next step is to key the material which, when printed, is known as output. In many offices, the first time a document is keyed it is done as a rough draft since, without question, changes will be made.

13 | 21 | 79
27 | 24 | 82
40 | 27 | 85
54 | 30 | 87
68 | 33 | 90
83 | 35 | 93
95 | 38 | 95

After the author has made the final corrections and changes in the document, it is then produced in final form. It is at this point that the advantages of a word processor are most evident. Instead of keying the entire document again, the operator merely recalls the material from computer memory, keys the necessary changes and then simply gives the instructions to the printer to make a hard copy on paper. The final step is to transmit the document to the person for whom it is intended.

13 | 41 | 98
28 | 43 | 101
42 | 46 | 104
56 | 49 | 107
70 | 52 | 109
84 | 55 | 112
99 | 58 | 115

gwam 1' | 1 | 2 | 3 | 4 | 5 | 6 | 7 | 8 | 9 | 10 | 11 | 12 | 13 | 14 |
5' | 1 | 2 | 3 |

193d ▶ 10 *Improve Keystroking Skills: Figures*

Key each sentence twice *by touch.* If time permits, repeat sentences in which you made errors in figures.

1 Line items 2, 7, 9, 10, 28, 34, 59, and 63 must be ordered by July 15.

2 Please check paragraphs 4.1, 6.8, 7.3, 10.5, and 19.2 of the contract.

3 There are 246 seats in Room 201, 319 in Room 415, and 170 in Room 582.

4 Floppy disks 2506, 3718, 4923, 5701, and 6849 were not filed properly.

5 Prescription 16590 was renewed on June 3; 28374 was renewed on June 5.

6 Certificates 6390-167, 7428-936, and 8541-020 will mature on March 17.

7 On August 1 my office phone will be 389-6452; my home phone, 876-2103.

8 Her checking account number is 6418293045; savings account, 590376128.

| 1 | 2 | 3 | 4 | 5 | 6 | 7 | 8 | 9 | 10 | 11 | 12 | 13 | 14 |

261c ▶ 20 Improve Language Skills: Proofread/Correct

1. The paragraphs at the right include errors in spelling, punctuation, capitalization, and keystroking.

2. Key the paragraphs as an unbound report, correcting errors as you work. Title: **MATHEMATICS AND YOUR FUTURE.**

3. When you have completed the report, proofread it carefully and correct any errors you may have missed.

When asked to name there favorite sujbect in school, very few peopel list | 20
mathematics. This is probably true because solving problems with numbers | 35
require thought concentration and extra effort. When we study math; how- | 50
ever; we develope skills in solving problems; we learn to think thru a prob- | 66
lem logicaly, and we increase our ability to make good decisions. Farther--we | 82
enhance our ability to analyse situations and come to valid conclusoins. in | 97
many instances, their are no substitutes for applying mathematics in solving | 112
are problems. | 115

In to day's complex world, it is allmost impossible to exist without useing | 130
math. We use math everytime we buy an item, keep a cheking acount, verify | 146
the deductions made from our pay checks, and prepare our Income Taxes. | 160
In a sense math governs our personel lives since we must plan our spending | 175
and savnigs to avoid going to deeply into debt. A budget can help us to use | 191
our money wisely so that we can injoy life with out magor money problems. | 205

Mathematics is becoming more and more important in the busness world. | 220
Those with good back grounds in math qualify for a wider variety of jobs. | 235
One who can do only simpel arithmetic for example cannot hope to be pro- | 249
moted to a job wich require the worker to analyse and interpret financiel | 264
statements. Workers often find that they lose job oportunities to others who | 280
has higher levels of math skills. Math is a skill of such importence that it is | 297
worth puting extra effort in to it. | 304

261d ▶ 10 Improve Keystroking Skills: Figures and Symbols

1. Key each sentence. Do not correct errors.

2. Proofread the sentences carefully and correct errors in pencil.

3. Rekey the sentences from your corrected copy. Correct all errors.

1 The vote on Amendment 901-A was 518 "ayes" (58%) and 376 "nays" (42%).

2 The interest on Note #512846 is $356.25 ($7,500 for 6 months at 9.5%).

3 On May 9, I ordered 50 reams of 20# 8 1/2″ × 11″ paper (Stock #36472).

4 The Ajax Copier (Model #43895-B) lists for $2,687 less a 10% discount.

5 My statement of 1/8/90 (Account #93462) showed a balance of $4,593.76.

6 Sales (as of June 30) were $21,540,871--an increase of 29.6% over May.

7 The report stated, "Taxes for 1990 were $378,640--an increase of 25%."

8 The desks (Catalog #502648-P) ordered from C&L will cost $371.90 each.

194a ▶ 5
Conditioning
Practice

each line twice SS
(slowly, then faster);
if time permits, take
1' writings on line 3

alphabet 1 Anna may be required to organize the complex work of the vast project.

figures 2 The test scores were: 19, 24, 32, 46, 50, 57, 68, 70, 83, 91, and 96.

fig/sym 3 Sue's note read, "Profits of Erb & Lee Co. rose 8.3% to $627,195,420."

speed 4 The girl did sign both of the proxy forms for the auditor of the firm.

| 1 | 2 | 3 | 4 | 5 | 6 | 7 | 8 | 9 | 10 | 11 | 12 | 13 | 14 |

194b ▶ 20 Improve
Language Skills:
Proofread/Correct

1. In each sentence, items have been underlined. The underlines indicate that there *may* be an error in spelling, punctuation, capitalization, grammar, or in the use of words or figures.

2. Study each sentence carefully. Key the sentence (with number and period). If an underlined item is incorrect, correct it as you key the sentence. Also, correct any keyboarding errors you may make.

3. Check your work with your teacher; then rekey any sentences in which you made errors.

1. He said, "it is apparant that you did not read the lable."
2. "It is my beleief," he said, "That we must make a total commitment."
3. My neice visited these foreign countries, England, Spain, and Italy.
4. Keep in mind: guesswork is no substitute for good jugement.
5. A new version of The Taming of the Shrew is all ready in rehearsal.
6. Jane is an assistent to president Marks, not his Secretary.
7. The town counsel will meet in room 302 at 4 o'clock.
8. We must analize the questionaire on womens' rights very carefully.
9. Does the new rules on insurence supercede the old ones?
10. Have the committee filed it's report on the personel office?
11. Each of the men have benefitted from their experience.
12. There were thirty five occurrences of vandalism this month.
13. The restarant is located on 5th avenue near the labratory.
14. In March the morgage rate rose to 11 percent.
15. Bess's report card showed she achieved all most all As.

194c ▶ 10 Improve
Keystroking Skills:
Figures and Symbols

1. Take four 1' writings on each ¶5.

2. Strive for accuracy, especially when keying the figures and symbols.

gwam 1'

Borrowing money can be very expensive. If, for example, you bor- 13
row $2,000 at 8% interest and agree to pay it back in 15 monthly in- 27
stallments, you will pay $147 per month or a total of $2,205 (including 41
$205 in interest). The annual percentage rate, though, is actually 55
15%. An interest rate of "only" 1 1/2% per month equals an annual rate 69
of 18%. 70

The mortgage interest on a house may be greater than the original 13
cost of the house. A 20-year, 10% mortgage on $75,000 will require a 27
monthly payment of $727.50 or a total of $174,600 ($727.50 × 12 × 20). 42
A 30-year mortgage under the same terms would cost $660 a month or a 55
total of $237,600--$63,000 more than the 20-year mortgage. 67

194d ▶ 15
Improve Basic
Keyboarding Skills

1. Take two 1' writings on each ¶ of 193c, p. 335.

2. Take one 5' writing on the three ¶s combined.

Goal: Improved speed and accuracy.

260c ▶ 15 Improve Straight-Copy Skill

Take two 5' writings on the ¶s at the right. Record *gwam* and errors on the better writing.

all letters used | A | 1.5 si | 5.7 awl | 80% hfw

gwam 1' | 5'

Today we live in an age of information brought about by the amazing   14 | 3 | 61
growth in data and word processing by the computer. Success in business   28 | 6 | 64
demands information upon which vital decisions can be made. A computer   43 | 9 | 67
can produce volumes of data in the form of words and figures in a very   57 | 11 | 70
short time. Data, however, is simply the raw facts which must be re-   71 | 14 | 73
fined into useful information. Though a number of techniques may be   84 | 17 | 75
used to submit pertinent information, a formal report is often used.   98 | 20 | 78

As an employee in an office, you may be asked to assist in the   13 | 22 | 81
preparation of reports--to collect the essential data, outline the im-   27 | 25 | 84
portant concepts to be emphasized, and perhaps to prepare a first draft.   41 | 28 | 86
When the originator of the report has completed it, your job will be to   56 | 31 | 89
prepare it in an appropriate format. When doing so, it might also be   70 | 34 | 92
your responsibility to recheck the report for clarity and conciseness   84 | 36 | 95
and to verify that all facts and figures used are correct.   95 | 39 | 97

The operator who keys a report can do a great deal to assure that   13 | 41 | 100
the report is favorably received by arranging it so that it is attrac-   27 | 44 | 103
tive and neat. An untidy, poorly prepared report is certain to give a   41 | 47 | 106
bad impression. Extra attention must be given to the format of a re-   55 | 50 | 108
port; especially the margins and spacing. The report should be free   69 | 52 | 111
of errors in spelling, grammar, punctuation, and in the use of words   83 | 55 | 114
or figures. Each page should be proofread carefully to recheck all of   97 | 58 | 117
these points.   100 | 59 | 117

gwam 1' | 1 | 2 | 3 | 4 | 5 | 6 | 7 | 8 | 9 | 10 | 11 | 12 | 13 | 14
5' | 1   2   3

Lesson 261   Improve Basic Skills

261a ▶ 5 Conditioning Practice

each line twice SS (slowly, then faster); if time permits, take 1' writings on lines 1 and 4

alphabet 1 Pete found gold jewelry and necklaces in the excavation in Mozambique.
figures 2 Make a copy of the material on pages 12, 39, 56, 74, 83, 106, and 109.
fig/sym 3 They paid a local tax of 2% ($327.76) and a sales tax of 5% ($819.40).
speed 4 If the men work with proficiency, the big coalfield may make a profit.

| 1 | 2 | 3 | 4 | 5 | 6 | 7 | 8 | 9 | 10 | 11 | 12 | 13 | 14 |

261b ▶ 15 Improve Straight-Copy Skill

1. Take two 5' writings on the ¶s in 260c.

2. Strive to increase speed by 2 *gwam* with fewer errors.

3. Record *gwam* and errors on the better writing.

Five Star Corporation (A Simulation)

Learning Goals

1. To become familiar with the procedures followed in a typical document processing center.

2. To improve your ability to process documents from unarranged, rough-draft, and script copy.

3. To improve your ability to read and follow directions and to detect and correct unmarked errors.

Documents Processed

1. Formal Memorandum
2. Simplified Memorandum
3. Letters from Boilerplate
4. Tables
5. Report

FIVE STAR CORPORATION: A DOCUMENT PROCESSING CENTER SIMULATION

Work Assignment

You have been hired as a keyboard operator in the headquarters of the Five Star Corporation, operators of motels and hotels throughout the continental United States and Europe. The headquarters is located at 200 West Washington Street, South Bend, Indiana 46601-7230.

You will work in the Document Processing Center under the direction of Mrs. Diane C. Dunn, supervisor of the center, who reports to Ms. Margaret L. Maguire, chief of administration.

You will prepare a variety of documents prepared in handwritten or rough-draft form by executives or word originators. You will also key form letters from boilerplate (standardized paragraphs or letters). Documents dictated by executives are transcribed by word processing specialists in the center.

Five Star has established standard formatting procedures that specify the formats for letters, memos, reports, and tables. Excerpts from these procedures follow. As part of your orientation, Mrs. Dunn asks you to study these procedures carefully.

Standard Formatting Procedures

Documents are prepared in the following formats unless the originator indicates otherwise. Correct any errors you make as you prepare a document in final form. Correct any unmarked errors made by the originator in spelling, punctuation, grammar, etc.

Letters. Letters are keyed in the simplified block style, using a standard 6″ line with the date on line 12, regardless of the length of the letter. Except for rough drafts, key letters on letterhead stationery. Use current date if one is not specified and use your initials as reference.

Simplified memos. Simplified memos are keyed on plain paper in block format, using a standard 6″ line with the date on line 10. QS below the date and the last paragraph of the body. DS below other parts of the memo and between paragraphs. Use current date if one is not specified and use your initials as reference.

Formal memos. Formal memos are keyed on forms with printed headings in block format, using a standard 6″ line with the heading information at the same point as the left margin. DS below the heading information, between paragraphs, between the last line and your initials, and between your initials and any notation, such as "Attachment."

Reports. Reports are always prepared in unbound format, using a standard 6″ line, with the PB (page beginning) on line 10 (pica, 10-pitch) or line 12 (elite, 12-pitch). QS below titles; DS other parts, including the spacing above and below a divider line between the report and a reference notation, if one is used.

Tables. Tables are centered on the page vertically and horizontally. All headings are centered, including columnar headings. Use DS throughout the table, except when the tabular items are SS. DS below the last line of the table; key the divider line; DS below the divider line; key the source note. (SS a source note that consists of two or more lines.)

Improve Basic Skills

Learning Goals

1. To improve your basic keyboarding skills with emphasis on figures and symbols.
2. To increase your keystroking speed and to improve your accuracy on straight copy.
3. To improve your communications skills.

Format Guides

1. Paper guide at *0* (for typewriters).
2. LL: 70 spaces for drills, timed writings and language skills.
3. LS: SS sentence drills with a DS between groups; DS paragraph writings and language skill sentences.
4. PI: 5 spaces.

Lesson 260	Improve Basic Skills

**260a ▶ 5
Conditioning
Practice**

each line twice SS
(slowly, then faster);
if time permits, take
1′ writings on lines 2
and 3

alphabet 1 Equalizing my daily work load was the objective of the office experts.

figures 2 On July 15, my telephone number was changed from 634-5817 to 932-8026.

fig/sym 3 The sales tax on Invoice #14397-610 will be $329.62 (4% of $8,240.50).

speed 4 When he is at the dock, my neighbor may fix the rotor of the big auto.

| 1 | 2 | 3 | 4 | 5 | 6 | 7 | 8 | 9 | 10 | 11 | 12 | 13 | 14 |

**260b ▶ 30 Improve
Language Skills:
Proofread/Correct**

1. In each sentence at the right, items have been underlined. The underlines indicate that there *may* be an error in spelling, punctuation, capitalization, grammar, or in the use of words or figures.
2. Study each sentence carefully. Key the line number. If an underlined item is incorrect, correct it as you key the sentence. In addition, correct any keyboarding errors you may make as you work.
3. When you have completed the sentences and *before* you remove the copy, study each sentence carefully and correct any errors you may have missed.

1. In doctor Millers' opinion, the patiant can be released.

2. Did the custumer order 6 or 8 banners for the festival?

3. She said its a posibility we will meet in the world trade center.

4. Mary our President will preside at the instalation of officers.

5. Ron's and Betty's joint report was about our foriegn policy.

6. This is the point, will they receive their benifits?

7. If she don't apply now, she can not obtain a masximum morgage.

8. The firm of Martin & Hayes have been hired to raise the wharehouse.

9. Wanda choose a large, red book to record her expendatures.

10. According to table 3789 42% of the funds have all ready been spent.

11. The facultie will meet in room 1,082 at 3:00 PM.

12. In edition we flue to these cities, Oslo, Cairo, Paris, and Rome.

13. Each man drove their own car to the sight of the Shopping Center.

14. Jill said, 'the theater was pact for the commissions' report.'

15. Did he autherize us to buy 12 copies of the book "Fiscul Planning"?

16. In the passed, 6 absences was grounds for disciplinary action.

17. Whose responsible for implementing the plan; Don or Leslie?

18. This year Ross's comissions rose from the $60s to the mid $80s.

19. The superviser, who just arrived, will establish new scedules.

20. In my judgement only 1/4 of the man were at the confrence.

195a-198a ▶ (daily)
Conditioning Practice

each line twice SS
(slowly, then faster);
if time permits, take
1' writings on line 1

alphabet 1 Jerry criticized queries we have been making on the six final reports.

figures 2 Please ship Orders 1271, 3965, 6238, and 0845 by parcel post tomorrow.

fig/sym 3 Ship us 60 reams of 20# 8 1/2″ × 11″ paper (Stock #943) at $2.75 each.

speed 4 If the men work with proficiency, the big coalfield may make a profit.

| 1 | 2 | 3 | 4 | 5 | 6 | 7 | 8 | 9 | 10 | 11 | 12 | 13 | 14 |

195b-198b ▶ 45 (daily)
Document Processing

Document 1
Formal Memorandum

LP p. 137

Mrs. Dunn: Please key this material as a formal memorandum for my signature. Address it to **all keyboard operators.** Date the memo **April 16** and use the subject **DOCUMENT PROCESSING LOG.** Log the document in your Document Processing Log on LP p. 135, or your supervisor will provide your Document Processing Log sheet.

Log #101

Effective May

Beginning ~~June~~ 1, 19--, all operators will ~~keep~~ maintain a weekly ~~Word~~ Document

Procesing Log Sheet. The ~~information given~~ data below will be en-

tered on the Log sheet for each document ~~you~~ process ed.

Document code. The suprevisor will log in each document by placing

a Code Number ~~which will be placed~~ in the upper right-hand

corner. In correspondance, the ~~log~~ code number will be keyed follow ing the op-

erator's initials; in all other documents, it will be placed

a (DS) below the last line.

Originator. The word originator of the document will be iden-

tified by name and (dept), ~~i.e.,~~ e.g., "Carter/Sales."

Document. The document will be identified by ~~sort:~~ type letter,

memo, report, table, form, etc.

Input. The form in which the document was recieved will be in-

dicated as RD (rough draft), S (handwritten), B (boilerplate), or

STAT (statistical).

Time in. ~~Indicate~~ Enter time work on document was ~~received~~ begun.

Time out. ~~Indicate~~ Enter time document was ~~finished~~ completed. If work on a

document is ~~delayed~~ interrupted for more than ten minutes, complete the in-

formation for the document on the log sheet and re-enter it when work is ~~begun~~ continued.

(continued, p. 339)

Document 14
Table
plain full sheet

Mr. Devereau: Please key this updated report of the company's participation in the United Community Fund Campaign.

BOUTIQUES INTERNATIONAL, LTD.

[United Community Fund Campaign

Report of Progress as of October ~~1~~ 15, 19--

Organizational Unit	Percent of Participation	Amount
Administration Division	~~42~~% 64%	$ ~~882~~ 1,344
Advertising Department	~~51~~ 72	~~1,020~~ 1,440
Customer Service Center	~~58~~ 81	~~1,160~~ 1,620
Finance Division	~~48~~ 67	~~709~~ 989
General Services Department	~~60~~ 84	~~902~~ 1,263
Human Resources Department	~~55~~ 74	~~1,154~~ 1,553
Information Processing Center	~~67~~ 86	~~737~~ 946
Industrial Relations Department	~~45~~ 68	~~682~~ 1,031
Legal Department	~~70~~ 84	~~1,750~~ 2,100
Maintenance Department	~~40~~ 52	~~255~~ 332
Marketing Division	~~63~~ 85	~~756~~ 1,020
Planning and Research Department	~~72~~ 89	~~1,083~~ 1,339
Public Relations Office	~~80~~ 92	~~1,679~~ 1,931
Purchasing Division	~~53~~ 71	~~799~~ 1,071

Document 15
Formal Memorandum
LP p. 99

Mr. Devereau: Key this memorandum from **Miss Jackson** to **Henry K. O'Brian, Director of Human Resources.** Date the memo **May 20.** Use as a subject line: **TOYS-FOR-TOTS CAMPAIGN.**

¶ Will you please include the following notice in the next edition of the "Employees' Newsletter":

¶ Again this year we will participate in the annual "Toys-for-Tots" campaign conducted by the local Army Reserve Units.

¶ Please help us by volunteering to participate ~~in this worthwhile campaign~~ as a coordinator in your area. Call Dan Devereau (Extension 592) who will act as the overall coordinator for the campaign.

We are getting an early start this year in gathering volunteers for this worthwhile campaign.

Time. Enter the _∧*exact* time, in minutes, that was required to complete the document.

~~Total~~ lines. Indicate the total lines in the document. Count each line regardless of length (including any titles or subtitles). Count three lines for the opening lines of a letter*s* and *and memos* three lines for the closing lines. Count four lines for *all letter* envelopes and one line for *all* COMPANY MAIL envelopes.

Document 2
Simplified Memorandum
plain full sheet
Mrs. Dunn puts on your desk the note shown at the right.

4/17/--   Log #108

Please key the following as a simplified memorandum for my signature to Michael C. Beauvais, Supervisor, Data Processing, with a subject, "*Document* ~~Word~~ Processing Log Sheets."

As agreed during our meeting with Ms. Maguire on March 30, we will begin the work measurement program in the Document Processing Center on May 1. The weekly *Document* ~~Word~~ Processing Log Sheets, separated by operator, will be forwarded to the Data Processing Center on the Monday following the week in which the work was performed. As we agreed, you will provide me with a weekly and monthly report, by operator, which will show the total time, the total weighted lines keyed, and the average (mean) weighted lines per hour. Copy will be weighted as indicated below.

Copy	Weight
Boilerplate (B)	1.0
Handwritten (S)	1.3
Rough Draft (RD)	1.6
Statistical (STAT)	2.0

SS {

255b-259b (continued)

Document 12
Simplified Memorandum
plain full sheet

Mr. Devereau: Key this message as a simplified memorandum from **Ms. Quan** in reply to **Miss Jackson**'s memo of May 3. Date the memo **May 16.** Subject line: **SCHEDULE FOR OPEN HOUSE.**

As you requested in your memo [sp] of May 3, attached is a copy of the /proposed schedule for the open house to be ~~conducted~~ held on July 15.

The tours will begin at 30-minute intervals ~~beginning~~ from 9 a.m. until 4 p.m. with a (1)[sp]hour break for lunch ~~beginning~~ at noon. Upon arrival, the guests will be directed to the Meeting room, which will accomodate 30 people. There ~~guests~~ they will receive a breif [sp] greeting and then view the company film which was /recently updated.

Inasmuch as Warehouse B is on the route from the Shipping Complex to the Shipping Dept. [sp], I have added a "walk-through" tour of the /Warehouse [lc].

A schedule of the ~~individuals~~ people who will be responsible for each ~~part~~ segment of the tour will be prepared ~~within a very short time~~ published no later than June 1.

Document 13
Schedule
plain full sheet

Mr. Devereau: Key the open house schedule which will be attached to the memo to Miss Jackson. Quadruple-space after the heading information and between the activities.

BOUTIQUES INTERNATIONAL, LTD.

Open House

July 1~~2~~15, 19--

Time	Activity	Location
9:00 a.m.	Greetings Film: "Boutiques International-- at Home and Abroad"	Meeting Room
9:20 a.m.	Tour of Mail Room	Mail Room
9:30 a.m.	Explanation of Order Processing	Computer Room Complex
9:45 a.m.	Tour of Shipping Department (Through Warehouse B en route)	Shipping ~~Room~~ Employees'
10:00 a.m.	Refreshments	~~Executive Conference Room~~ Lounge

195b-198b (continued)

Documents 3 and 4
Letters from Boilerplate
LP pp. 139-141

Mrs. Dunn: Mark F. Schwartz, national coordinator for group facilities, requests that we prepare Form Letter 12, dated **April 18,** for the addressees below. Insert the appropriate information as shown.

Letter 1
Mrs. Rita C. Smith
President
Flower Clubs of America
P.O. Box 3870
Little Rock, AR 72203-1440
(A) **Mrs. Smith** (B) **December of this year** (C) **Dallas Central Five Star** (D) **March of next year**
(Log #124)

Letter 2
Mr. Louis F. DiAngelo
Executive Director
National Greentree Association
401 Sixth Avenue
Des Moines, IA 50309-5901
(A) **Mr. DiAngelo** (B) **January of next year** (C) **Boston Five Star Plaza** (D) **April of next year**
(Log #125)

Document 5
Table
plain full sheet

Mrs. Dunn: Denise T. Brach, an assistant marketing manager, requests that we key the table at the right, making the changes marked.
(Log #136)

Document 6
Table
plain full sheet

Mrs. Dunn: Ms. Brach requests that we prepare a table showing occupancy rates for both February and March. Head the second column **February** and the third column **March.**
(Log #148)

FORM LETTER 12

RESERVATIONS FOR GROUP FACILITIES

Thank you, (A), for your inquiry regarding the availability of group facilities in (B) at the (C).

We are very sorry indeed that the facilities you desire are completely booked through (D). Reservations for conventions, banquets, meetings, and other large events are usually made at least a year in advance. Planning for these events takes considerable time and coordination to ensure that they are successful.

Enclosed is a pamphlet showing the group facilities that are available at the (C). May we arrange to serve your organization at a later date? If you wish to discuss your special event, simply call 1-800-219-4600 and one of our service representatives will be happy to assist you.

MARK F. SCHWARTZ, NATIONAL COORDINATOR FOR GROUP FACILITIES

OCCUPANCY RATE FOR THE MONTH OF ~~FEBRUARY~~ MARCH

Northeastern Division

Location	Rate
Albany Five Star Motel	72% ~~71%~~
Atlantic City Five Star Casino Plaza	83% ~~79%~~
Baltimore Harbor Five Star Hotel	71% ~~68%~~
Boston Five Star Plaza	85% ~~79%~~
Buffalo Five Star Motel	81% ~~83%~~
New Bedford Five Star Ocean Motel	61% ~~64%~~ *
New York Central Five Star Hotel	84% ~~81%~~
New York Downtown Five Star Hotel	75% ~~72%~~
Philadelphia Five Star Hotel	73% ~~70%~~
Pittsburgh Five Star Hotel	71% ~~66%~~
Portland (Maine) Five Star Motel	71% ~~63%~~

*Rate affected by major road construction.

Document 9
Simplified Memorandum
plain full sheet

Mr. Devereau: Key this message as a simplified memorandum, dated **May 3,** from **Miss Jackson** to **Nancy P. Quan,** a **Public Relations Specialist.** Subject line: ANNUAL BOUTIQUES INTERNATIONAL OPEN HOUSE.

¶ Will you please assume responsibility for planning and ~~organizing~~ supervising the annual Boutiques International open house for the public, which has been scheduled for July 15.

¶ Last year's open house proved ~~quite~~ very successful and can be used as a basis for planning this year's event. You will find copies of last year's schedule in the files. This year, however, I would like to eliminate the visit to the executive conference room and substitute in its place a ~~trip~~ visit to the employees' lounge where refreshments ~~may~~ can be served.

¶ Please let me have your ~~suggestions~~ recommendations for a schedule of events for the open house by May ~~15~~ 18.

Document 10
Letter
LP p. 97

Mr. Devereau: Key this letter in block format for **Miss Jackson**'s signature to **Dr. Helen N. Tanner, President of the Allied Service Clubs, 926 Canal Street, New Orleans, LA 70112-4579.** Date the letter **May 5** and send a copy to **Christine C. Mays.**

Thank you for inviting ~~us~~ Boutiques International to participate in the annual banquet of the Allied Service Clubs of New Orleans to be held at the Park plaza hotel on June 20 at 7 p.m.

Ms. Christine C. Mays, our director of sales, will represent us at this important meeting. Ms. Mays has been a member of the New Orleans Chamber of Commerce for ~~a number of~~ the past nine years and was recently elected vice president of that group.

As you requested, Ms. Mays will be prepared to speek for a period of not more than (10) minutes at the conclusion of the banquet. She will send you a transcript of her remarks within ~~a~~ the next few weeks.

Boutiques International appreciates and welcomes the opportunity to participate in this major public affair.

Document 11
Simplified Memorandum
plain full sheet

1. Compose and key a simplified memorandum to **Ms. Mays** from **Miss Jackson** dated **May 5** to which you will attach a copy of the letter to Dr. Tanner (Document 10). Supply an appropriate subject line.

2. Call Ms. Mays' attention to the fact that Miss Jackson has promised that she will send a transcript of her remarks within the next few weeks.

3. Request Ms. Mays to send a copy of her remarks to the Public Relations Office before she sends them to Dr. Tanner.

Document 7
Unbound Report
plain full sheets

Mrs. Dunn: Josef Tuberski, an administrative assistant in the guest facilities branch, is helping to prepare a brochure about the corporation. He has requested that we key his first draft as an unbound manuscript.

Follow the instructions he has given on the bottom of his draft and be on the lookout for un-marked errors.

Log #157

FIVE STAR CORPORATION--A ~~STUDY IN~~ MODEL OF SUCCESS

For more than (40) *sp* years, the Five Star Corporation has set the s̶t̶a̶n̶d̶a̶r̶d̶s̶ pace for the hospitality/travel industry through a program of expansoin and improvement to meet the d̶e̶m̶a̶n̶d̶s̶ needs of our guests world wide. The corporation is dedicated to f̶u̶r̶t̶h̶e̶r̶ growth and improvement to ensure that it remains in the forfront of the industry.

The Five Star ʌh̶a̶s̶ *Corporation* consists of the following four major components, which are distinct and serve diverse needs.

The Five Star hotels serve large metropolitan areas with accommodations for individuals and groups. There is̲ t̶o̶d̶a̶y̶ now at least one Five Star Hotel in every city in the (U.S.) with a population of 300,000 or more *sp*

The Five Star logo is famous throughout the United States and Europe and represents first class acommodations at reasonable rates. At the end of t̶h̶e̶ p̶r̶e̶v̶i̶o̶u̶s̶ last year, there were 806 Five Star Inns, for a total of more than 150,000 rooms. Since the beginning of this year, 16 new inns have b̶e̶e̶n̶ b̶u̶i̶l̶t̶ opened in the (U. S.) alone. *sp*

A few hotels in the Five Star family have been n̶a̶m̶e̶d̶ designated as plazas. These are deluxe facilities with spacious meeting rooms. Future plazas are planned in coordinination with h̶u̶g̶e̶ large shopping malls in metropolitan a̶r̶e̶a̶s̶ centers. Construction on Five Star Plazas is currently under way in New Orleans and Seatle.

Located in p̶r̶o̶m̶i̶n̶e̶n̶t̶ popular tourist areas, suites meet our guests' needs for extended visits. The suites feature eficiency units with complete kitchens, lounge areas, and sleeping acommodations for as many as eight p̶e̶r̶s̶o̶n̶s̶ people. The suites have been very populer with families on vacation and profesional people on l̶o̶n̶g̶ extended stays.

Please move ¶4 ahead of ¶3 and add these side headings:

¶3 Five Star Inns

¶4 Five Star Hotels

¶5 Five Star Plazas

¶6 Five Star Suites

Document 4
Letter
LP p. 87

Mr. Devereau: Key this letter to **Mr. Christopher P. Chase, President of the New Orleans United Community Fund, 920 Common Street, New Orleans, LA 70112-4786** for **Miss Jackson**'s signature. Date the letter **April 26** and prepare it in modified block format with indented ¶s. Be sure to correct all marked and unmarked errors.

It is with pleasure *and pride* that I accept your invitation to ~~conduct~~ *chair* the annual campaign of the New Orleans United Community Fund which will ~~kick off~~ *begin* in (Sept.) *sp* of this year.

As you ~~recommended~~ *suggested,* I am inviting four ~~individuals~~ *leaders* in the community to join me, as a steering comittee, to plan, organize, and direct the campaign. These people are

Mrs. Lorraine T. Feliciana, Special Assistant
Office of the Mayor

The Reverend Father John P. Delacroix, Vice ~~Chairman~~ *Chancellor*
Xavier Theological Seminary

Ms. Alica B. Currant, Director
Citizens Action Group

Mr. Ralph C. Baronne, Vice President
New Orleans Business Association

Through regular reports, I will keep you informed of the activities *and progress* of the steering comittee.

Documents 5-8
Letters on Executive-Size Stationery
LP pp. 89-95

Mr. Devereau: Key this letter to the individuals listed in Document 4 for **Miss Jackson**'s signature. Date the letter **April 28** and prepare it in modified block format. Be sure to correct all marked and unmarked errors. The address for each individual is given below.

Mrs. Feliciana:
1300 Perdido Street
New Orleans, LA 70112-4001

Father Delacroix:
7300 Palmetto Street
New Orleans, LA 70125-4321

Ms. Currant:
202 Loyola Avenue
New Orleans, LA 70112-5094

Mr. Baronne:
820 Gravier Street
New Orleans, LA 70112-5183

Mr. Christopher T. Chase, president of the New Orleans United Community Fund, has ~~asked~~ *invited* me to ~~conduct~~ *chair* the annual campaign of the Community fund which will ~~start~~ *begin* in September of this year.

I am ~~quite~~ *very* pleased that you agreed in our tele phone conversation today to join ~~me~~ in this worth while effort by becoming a member of the steering committee. The first meeting of the committee will be held in the conferance room of Boutiques International on May ~~14~~ *15* at ~~9~~ *10* a.m.

This campaing should ~~prove to~~ be an interesting and exciting ~~one,~~ *challenge* and I am looking forward to working ~~together~~ *with you* to acheive our campaign ~~objectives~~ *goals.*

Measure Basic Language/Production Skills

Measurement Goals

1. To measure your speed and accuracy on straight-copy material.

2. To measure your communication skills.

3. To measure your ability to produce documents neatly and correctly.

Machine Adjustments

1. Paper guide at *0* (for typewriters).

2. LL: 70 spaces for drills, paragraphs, and Language Skills activity; as directed or necessary for documents.

3. LS: DS sentences and timed writings; space problems as directed or as necessary.

Lessons 199-200	Language/Production Skills

199a-200a ▶ 5 (daily)
Conditioning Practice

each line twice SS (slowly, then faster); if time permits, take 1′ writings on line 1

alphabet	1	Duke may vote for any major law liberalizing changes in export quotas.
figures	2	Ken bowled 197, 209, and 237, but May's scores were 198, 235, and 246.
fig/sym	3	The tax was 3% in 1974, 5.2% in 1983, 5.6% in 1987, and 10.2% in 1991.
speed	4	She did fix the dual signals to make the big sign to downtown visible.

| 1 | 2 | 3 | 4 | 5 | 6 | 7 | 8 | 9 | 10 | 11 | 12 | 13 | 14 |

199b ▶ 30 Evaluate Language Skills

1. In each sentence at the right, items have been underlined. The underlines indicate that there *may* be an error in spelling, punctuation, capitalization, grammar, or word/figure usage.

2. Study each sentence carefully. Key the line, with the number and period. If an underlined item is incorrect, correct it as you key the sentence. Also, correct any keyboarding errors you may make.

1. "After you finish," he said, "Take the form to the Personel office."
2. Keep in mind: the committee will explore the matter farther.
3. Their's a new shop on 6th Avenue that sells VCR cassettes.
4. Almost 60% of the men in the neighborhood voted "yes."
5. Neither Diane nor Mary are planning to go to the movie.
6. Maria our supervisor will attend the meeting, too.
7. We will schedule you're program over the next two year period.
8. Its my opinion that we will not receive our benifits this week.
9. Angela's and Lisa's report was very well done.
10. The panel reccomended that we accept the lowest bid.
11. The time past quickly as we entered the systom into the computer.
12. The comission on teen problems will make it's findings public.
13. The corparate officers will meet in the executive dining room.
14. Whose responsible for the maintanance of the facsimile machine?
15. Chris did better than me with 5 Bs on her report card.
16. Paul and Jess left for the new boy's club imediately after lunch.
17. In 1991 472 employees enrolled for health care under policy 645820.
18. The magazine, "Computer Monthly," offers many intresting articles.
19. We're planning too leave on Friday for the spring festival.
20. Tina Jones' test scores make her elligible for a scholarship.

Document 2
Leftbound Report
plain full sheets

Mr. Devereau: Prepare the information contained in Document 1 as a leftbound report which will be included in the company's organizational manual.

Use as a heading:
OFFICE OF PUBLIC RELATIONS.

5̶4̶. Arrange for and conduct public contact programs to promote goodwill for the company.

7̶5̶. Provide corporate ~~and~~ leadership in community improvements and participate in welfare and social-betterment programs.

4̶6̶. Prepare fact sheets, *audio* news releases, scripts, photographs, motion picture, tape, or vidio recordings to distribute to media representatives and others who may be interested in publicizing company activities.

6̶7̶. Prepare, edit, or clear all speeches to be given by company executives at public ~~affairs~~ *functions.*

Document 3
News Release
LP p. 85

Mr. Devereau: Key this news release for immediate release with **Miles T. Nicolas 504-565-6452** as the contact.

¶ NEW ORLEANS, LA, April 16, 19--. Ground-breaking ceremonies for the Prentiss Memorial Recreation Center will be held May 3 at 10 a.m., according to an announcement by Ramon C. Delachaise, president of Boutiques International, Ltd. The recreation center will be located along the Mississippi River adjacent to Bridge City. "The Prentiss Recreation Center will serve as *an enduring* ~~a living~~ memorial to Gregory T. Prentiss, the founder of Boutiques International," said Mr. Delachaise. "It has been designed to serve the citizens of New Orleans, all of whom have contributed to our success."

¶ The new recreation center will include a gymnasium with complete locker facilities, an arts and crafts center, and an auditorium for meetings, *theatrical productions,* and concerts. Future plans call for the addition of an indoor swimming pool.

¶ The entire cost of the center will be funded by the Prentiss Foundation. When completed, the center will be operated by the New Orleans Department of Parks and Recreation with funds augmented by the Prentiss Foundation.

# # #

199c ▶ 15 Measure Basic Keyboarding Skills

Take two 5' writings on the ¶s at the right. Record *gwam* and errors on the better writing.

all letters used | A | 1.5 si | 5.7 awl | 80% hfw

gwam 1' | 5'

	gwam 1'	5'
Policies and procedures are set up by the managers of a business	13	3
to promote efficiency. A policy is considered to be a decision that	27	5
is made in advance, since it provides a guide or rule of action that	41	8
can be used to solve problems that arise frequently. To be effective,	55	11
a policy must be written in a clear, concise manner and, of the utmost	69	14
importance, be understood by all. Procedures are more specific and	83	17
set forth the exact steps to be taken in implementing policies.	95	19
Policies are used by managers as aids in making decisions at all	108	22
levels of a business. Policies promote efficiency since they save a	122	24
great deal of time, provide ready solutions to many day-to-day prob-	136	27
lems, and allow managers to do their jobs with more freedom of action.	150	30
Care must be taken to insure that policies are fair and accord equi-	164	33
table treatment to all employees. Further, all policies must be re-	177	35
viewed on a regular basis and revised when needed to meet all new or	191	38
changing conditions.	195	39
Many of the tasks performed by people in a business setting are	208	42
standard or routine in nature. To save time and to promote efficiency,	222	44
an organization may specify a set of step-by-step procedures for per-	236	47
forming these routine tasks. These procedures are almost always writ-	250	50
ten and are included in a manual for training and reference purposes.	264	53
If, on the job, you learn these procedures quickly and employ them in	278	56
order to produce work of high quality, you will be well on your way	292	58
to success.	294	59

gwam 1' | 1 | 2 | 3 | 4 | 5 | 6 | 7 | 8 | 9 | 10 | 11 | 12 | 13 | 14 |
5' | 1 | 2 | 3 |

200b ▶ 45 Measure Document Production Skills

Key the documents on this page and pages 344 and 345 for 30 minutes. Correct all errors.

Time Schedule

Plan and prepare .... 5'
Timed production ....30'
Proofread; compute *n-pram* .....10'

Document 1
Letter on Executive-Size Stationery

LP p. 143, block format; open punctuation

words

July 11, 19-- Mr. Carlos T. Bolivar 1100 Ponce De Leon Avenue San Juan, 14
PR 00907-3385 Dear Mr. Bolivar 21

It is a pleasure for me to welcome you formally to the executive group of 36
Alpha Electronics, Inc. You were selected from a group of five highly quali- 51
fied individuals to be the regional distributor in our Island Division, which 66
includes Puerto Rico and the U.S. Virgin Islands. 77

As a regional distributor, you will work under the direct supervision of 91
Jessica C. Madison, director of marketing, in accordance with the policies 106
and standard operating procedures established by our executive group. 120

We have scheduled a two-week orientation program for you in New Haven 134
beginning on Monday, August 1. A copy of your itinerary is enclosed. 149

(continued, p. 344)

Learning Goals

1. To acquaint you with some of the major functions of a public relations office.

2. To increase your proficiency in producing typical documents processed in public relations operations.

3. To improve your ability to process special documents using your best judgment.

Documents Processed

1. Formal Memorandums
2. Leftbound Report
3. News Release
4. Letters
5. Simplified Memorandums
6. Schedule
7. Table

Lessons 255-259 | Public Relations Office

255a-259a ▶ 5 (daily)
Conditioning Practice

each line twice SS (slowly, then faster); DS between 2-line groups; if time permits, take 1' writings on line 4

alphabet	1	Black may join in requesting to have six of the township lots rezoned.
figures	2	The company hired 357 employees in 1989, 401 in 1990, and 624 in 1992.
fig/sym	3	Panel 74296A will measure exactly 50.80 cm by 68.58 cm (1′8″ by 2′3″).
speed	4	If the firm's audit is right, half of the men did sign a formal proxy.

| 1 | 2 | 3 | 4 | 5 | 6 | 7 | 8 | 9 | 10 | 11 | 12 | 13 | 14 |

255b-259b ▶ 45 (daily)
Document Production

1. Your next job as a keyboard technician will be in the Office of Public Relations. You will work under the direction of F. Daniel Devereau, who is the administrative assistant to Michelle C. Jackson, Director of Public Relations.

2. In this job you will be required to prepare a variety of documents originated by members of the Public Relations staff.

3. Follow directions given for each document. If no format is specified, use your best judgment.

4. Unless directed to prepare a draft copy, key all documents in final form. Correct all marked and unmarked errors.

Document 1
Formal Memorandum
LP p. 83

Mr. Devereau: Prepare a formal memorandum from **Miss Jackson** to **ALL EXECUTIVES, ADMINISTRATORS, AND SUPERVISORS,** dated **April 15,** with the subject: **Public Relations Office.**

We at Boutiques International have always sought to be exemplary corporate citizens and have reconized our responsibility to contribute to and improve the communitys in which we operate. In reality, it is the ~~task~~ job of every member of Boutiques International to be an "embassador of goodwill" by mantaining friendly and cooperative relations with the citizens of our communitys.

To insure that we "put our best foot forward," the Public Relations section of the Marketing Division has been active for many years. Public relations has become increasingly important and, in recognition of that fact, the Executive Board has established the Office of Public Relations, effective April ~~12~~ 15, ~~which~~ will become a ~~member~~ part of the special staff reporting directly to the executive vice president, Seymore T. Brown.

This office The duties of the Public Relations Office will be to

1. Establish and conduct a public relations program designed to create and maintain a favorable corporate image with the public.

3 2. Inform the public of those ways in which the firm serves the interests of society.

2 3. Communicate to the public information regading the companys' programs, activities, achievements, and point of view.

(continued, p. 435)

200b (continued)

Reservations have been made for you during your stay in New Haven at the   163
Peachtree Plaza Hotel effective July 31. If you have any questions prior to   179
the orientation program, please call Mrs. Madison.   189

We are looking forward to your joining us in a long and mutually beneficial   204
association as the regional director of the Island Division.   217

Sincerely yours Keith T. Kona, President xx Enclosure   227/**241**

Document 2
Simplified Block Letter
LP p. 145
List the enumerated items
in ¶ 1.

July 14, 19-- MS LINDSAY M SAXE CHAIRPERSON ELECTRONICS TRADE   12
SHOW SAXE RESEARCH ASSOCIATES INC 351 FIFTH AVENUE NEW YORK   24
NY 10118-7820 EVALUATION OF PANEL DISCUSSION   34

Thank you, Lindsay, for sending me the evaluation sheets completed by those   49
ic Office--Today and To-   63
inistrative assistant has   78
e following conclusions.   93
age rating of 8.2. Most   108
vorable, although a few   122
ding her. This may have   137
tion system. 2. Dr. Ira   152
6.1. Many people noted   167
follow. 3. Mrs. Lila T.   182
enthusiastic comments   196
rmation processing sys-   211
  216

ysical arrangements ex-   230
lained that they were un-   245
room. In future shows,   261
of the conference rooms,   276
  286

[Handwritten note: Document 2 is not Executive style even tho lab pac p. shows it is. Use whole sheet.]

It was a pleasure working with you on this trade show. I hope these evalua-   301
tions will be helpful in planning for next year's show.   312

KEITH T. KONA, PRESIDENT xx   317/**324**

Document 3
Simplified Memo
plain full sheet

DATE: July 15, 19-- TO: Keith T. Kona, President SUBJECT: ORIENTATION   11
FOR CARLOS T. BOLIVAR   15

Carlos T. Bolivar, who was recently selected to be the regional distributor of   31
our Island Division, has informed me that because of a previous commitment,   46
he will not be able to travel to New Haven for the two-week orientation pro-   61
gram we have scheduled for him beginning on August 1.   72

At Mr. Bolivar's request, I have rescheduled his orientation program to be-   87
gin on August 15. Attached is a revised itinerary for Mr. Bolivar, which has   102
also been provided to all personnel involved in his orientation program. The   118
Peachtree Plaza has been notified that Mr. Bolivar will not arrive until   133
August 14, and the hotel has made the change in his reservations.   146

Jessica C. Madison, Director of Marketing xx Attachment   157

Documents 4 and 5
are on p. 345.

Document 16
Announcement
full sheet
Miss Morales: Please prepare the announcement attractively on the page.

BOUTIQUES INTERNATIONAL, LTD.

Chinaware Replacement Service

Did some one break a plate of your ~~best~~ *favorite* chinaware ser-

vice? Are some of your ~~plates~~ *cups* chipped? We are ~~happy~~ *pleased* to an-

nounce another personal service to ~~assist~~ *help* you ~~in replacing~~ *replace*

certain
any ~~peice~~ *pieces* of chinaware which may be chipped, cracked, or

broken. This special service applies to all sets of china *included*

in our *current* catalog.

The ~~price~~ *cost* for replacement service is qui~~et~~ nominal. An

example for our best-selling chinaware is ~~given~~ *shown* below.

DS

Royal Worcester, Mayfair Pattern

STOCK NUMBER	PIECE	COST* ~~PRICE~~
FC473021	Bread and Butter plate	$ 8.75
FC473022	Cereal bowl	18.00
FC473023	Coffee pot	51.00
FC473024	Cup (tea)	17.50
FC473025	~~Large~~ Dinner plate	18.25
FC473026	Pepper shaker	16.00
FC473027	Salad plate	15.90
FC473028	Salt shaker	16.00
FC473029	Saucer	19.00
FC473030	Souffle	31.00

For ~~further~~ information, *regarding your pattern,* please call 1-800-504-3022.

* Shipping not included.

200b (continued)
Document 4
News Release

LP p. 147

Key the document given at the right as a news release for release immediately. The contact will be **Megan Ryan, (401) 896-3175.**

OMAHA, NE, September 20, 19--. Sweeping changes in the executive staff of   23
the Forum Group have been announced by Harvey E. Jamison, president and   37
chief executive officer. "These changes," according to Jamison, "are par-   52
tially the result of a reorganization designed to invigorate and stimulate the   68
activities and growth of the Group."   75

Alyce T. Higgins, formerly president of Continental Business Enterprises,   91
has been named executive vice president for marketing, replacing Matthew   105
W. Columbo, who retired on September 1. Higgins, a graduate of the Wharton   120
School of Business, will also serve as a member of the executive committee.   135

J. Robert Schmitt has been appointed a senior vice president and general   150
counsel. A former director of the Alliance Foundation, Schmitt has prac-   164
ticed law for more than 20 years and is the senior partner in the firm of   179
Schmitt, Solomon, and DeVito.   185

Katherine P. Quinn, currently a senior vice president, has been promoted to   200
the position of executive vice president for operations. In this position, she   216
will direct the overall operations of the Group worldwide. Quinn has held   231
several administrative and executive positions in the Forum Group over the   246
past 18 years. ###   250

Document 5
Formal Memorandum

LP p. 149

Key the document shown at the right as a formal memorandum. List the enumerated items in ¶ 3.

TO: **All Managerial Employees** FROM: Michael T. Robinson, Executive   11
Vice President DATE: July 19, 19-- SUBJECT: TRAVEL POLICIES   20

Eagle & Sons recognizes that the costs related to travel are a necessary part   36
of doing business. At the same time, travel costs are a major expenditure   51
and must be effectively controlled.   58

Prior to making travel plans, alternatives must be considered. These include   74
correspondence (including overnight mail), exchange of information by   88
facsimile transmission, and telephone calls (including teleconferencing). If   103
these alternatives are inadequate, travel plans should be made.   116

Requests for travel will be submitted to the director of administration and   132
will include the following: 1. Purpose of the travel, including a justification   144
for not using alternative means. 2. Specific destination, with preference   159
for mode of transportation and hotel or motel accommodations. 3. Dates   174
and desired times of departure and return.   183

Upon approval, all travel arrangements will be made by the travel coordina-   197
tor in the administration office. The most efficient mode of travel that meets   213
the needs of the individual will be selected. Hotel/motel reservations will be   229
made at a convenient location.   235

Care should be taken to incur the lowest possible costs. Meal costs are lim-   250
ited to the actual cost plus tip. Entertainment costs are limited to meals un-   266
less approval for more lavish entertainment has been approved in advance.   281

Upon return, a request for reimbursement for any costs incurred should be   296
submitted to the finance office. Receipts must be provided for each item   311
except for minor costs such as tips and local telephone calls. The adminis-   326
tration office is responsible for the supervision of these policies to insure   341
compliance by all employees. xx   348/355

Miss Morales:

Prepare the letter to the managers of our branches in London, Paris, Rome, and Hong Kong. You will find their names and addresses and the names of the customer service managers in the files.

Key the letter, dated **October 16,** in modified block format with indented ¶s and open punctuation.

Provide an appropriate salutation and subject line. The letter will be signed by **Mr. Peterson.**

INFORMATION FROM THE FILES:

London Branch:

**Mr. Anthony P. Middleton, Manager, Boutiques International, Ltd., 10 Berkeley Street, London, England W1X 6NE
Mr. Thomas Browne**

Paris Branch:

**Ms. Lilli S. Carpentier, Manager, Boutiques International, Ltd., 8 Place de la Republique, Paris, France 75011
Mr. Francois P. Casini**

Rome Branch:

**Mrs. Maria DiAngelo, Manager, Boutiques International, Ltd., Via Aurelia Antica 411, Rome, Italy 00165
Mrs. Concetta P. Firpo**

Hong Kong Branch:

**Mr. Kunio T. Lee, Manager, Boutiques International, Ltd., 48 Nathan Road, Kowloon City Centre, Hong Kong
Ms. Tiem Kim**

There will be a meeting of all customer service managers, will be held on November 15 at the Pierre Hotel in New Orleans. A tentative list of items topics to be discussed follows.

1. Implementing plans procedures for establishing providing wedding consultants for customers.

2. Planning Developing new personalized services.

3. Revising current policies about regarding return of merchandise.

4. Analyzing major customers complaints, received from customers.

5. Beginning Implementing the SELL USA Campaign.

6. Discussing Reviewing special problems in customer relations encountered by each branch office.

Will you please arrange for your customer service manager, (name), to come fly to New Orleans arriving on November 14. A reservation was has been made for (him, her) at the Pierre Hotel.

If you have any more additional topics you would like to add to the agenda for this conference meeting, please send them to my assistant, Miss Carla T. Morales, before November 1. as soon as you possibly can.

EXTEND STATISTICAL DOCUMENT PROCESSING SKILLS

Keyboard operators in most offices must be able to prepare statistical documents with a high level of proficiency. This phase is designed to help you develop this important job qualification. After intensive practice in formatting and processing tables and forms, you will apply those skills in an office job simulation which imitates the work of a real office.

Specifically, Phase 9 (Lessons 201-225) will help you:

1. Develop your ability to work with minimum directions and to use your decision-making skills.

2. Increase your table processing skills.

3. Improve your skill in processing purchase requisitions, purchase orders, and invoices.

4. Apply your skills in a simulated office position where you will process a variety of documents typical of those used in modern offices.

5. Improve your language and composition skills.

251b-254b (continued)

Document 9
Table

full sheet

Miss Morales: Center this table vertically and horizontally.

FINE CHINA DEPARTMENT

Best␣Selling Dinnerware Sets During the Month of ∧August ~~September~~

Stock Number	Dinnerware	Sets Sold
FC47302	Royal Worcester, Mayfair Pattern	~~672~~ 685
FC58491	Wedgwood, Eaton Pattern	~~613~~ 593
FC47302	Aynsley, Spring Flower Pattern	~~589~~ 591
FC69524	Noritake, Fugi Pattern	~~542~~ 563
FC70635	Royal Doulton, Floral Pattern	~~497~~ 508
FC89524	Coalport, Golden Wheat Pattern	~~403~~ 423
FC34000	Golden Tara, Irish Summer Pattern	~~371~~ 385
FC56222	Spode, Rose Garden Pattern	~~295~~ 271
FC67404	Wedgwood, Avon Pattern	~~228~~ 253
FC47305	Royal Doulton, Gold Leaf Pattern	246
~~FC43090~~	~~Delft, Blue Onion Pattern~~	~~196~~

Document 10
Formal Memorandum

LP p. 73

Miss Morales: Please key this memo, dated **October 9**, from **Mr. Peterson** to **Richard C. Murray** who is the **Director of Marketing**. Subject: **THE PERSONAL TOUCH.**

Document 11
Table

full sheet

Miss Morales: Please rekey the table in Document 9 to show the figures for both months. Make all necessary changes.

The heading for Column 3 will be **August** and the heading for Column 4 will be **September**.

To fu*r*ther customize our ~~contacts~~ relations with our customers, I
recommend
~~suggest~~ that we have ~~each~~ the packer place the following message

in each order.

Dear ~~Boutiques International~~ Customer

Thank you for patronizing Boutiques International.

My name is _____. I hope you
will be pleased by the care I have taken to package
your order. If you have any questions about ∧your order, please call 1-800-504-3220.

Have a good day.

I bel*ie*ve that this ∧message will add another "personal touch" to our

contacts with our customers and, at the same time, give packers
satisfaction and
a greater feeling of ∧pride. To save time in packing, a rubber
on it
stamp with his or her name ∧can be provided each packer.

UNIT 48 LESSONS 201 – 206
Format/Process Tables

Learning Goals

1. To improve keyboarding skill on straight copy.
2. To improve statistical keyboarding skill.
3. To improve skill in formatting/processing tables.

Format Guides

1. Paper guide at *0* (for typewriters).
2. LL: 70 spaces.
3. LS: SS sentence drills; DS ¶s; as directed for problems.
4. Tab sets: 5 spaces for ¶s; as needed for problems.

Lesson 201	Tables with Totals and Source Notes

201a ▶ 5
Conditioning Practice

each line twice SS (slowly, then faster); DS between 2-line groups; if time permits, take 1′ writings on line 2

alphabet 1 Jeb asked him a very zany question before each good example was given.

figures 2 My daughter will arrive on Flight 906 at Gate 35 on 12/18 at 4:37 p.m.

fig/sym 3 Ray sold 56 new advertisements ($13,780) between 12/14/91 and 1/30/92.

speed 4 Eight busy men may fix the penalty box when they visit the city field.

| 1 | 2 | 3 | 4 | 5 | 6 | 7 | 8 | 9 | 10 | 11 | 12 | 13 | 14 |

201b ▶ 12 Improve/Check Keyboarding Skill: Statistical Copy

1. Two 1′ writings on each ¶; find *gwam*, circle errors.
2. One 3′ writing on ¶s 1-3 combined; find *gwam*, circle errors.

all letters used | A | 1.5 si | 5.7 awl | 80% hfw

gwam 1′ │ 3′

The two professors who are taking 35 students to study in foreign countries met with the parents of the students on the night of February 19 in Room 612. The major purpose of the meeting was to give information to the parents of the students who were to study from March 15 to May 15 in Florence, Italy, and Vico Morote, Switzerland.

13 | 4
27 | 9
41 | 14
55 | 18
68 | 23

Every parent was informed that the group would be required to leave O'Hare Airport (Chicago) on All World Flight #908 on the evening of March 15. Flight #908 will go directly to Milan, Italy, where the group will stay the first evening. After the trip to Milan, the students will be taken to Florence where they will study until April 30.

14 | 27
27 | 32
42 | 36
56 | 41
68 | 45

On May 1 every student and teacher will take an express train to Vico Morote, Switzerland, where they will remain until May 15. When class is over on May 15, every student will take an overnight express train to Frankfurt, Germany, for return on All World Flight #47. Flight #47 is to land at O'Hare early in the evening on May 16.

13 | 50
27 | 54
41 | 59
55 | 64
67 | 68

gwam 1′ | 1 | 2 | 3 | 4 | 5 | 6 | 7 | 8 | 9 | 10 | 11 | 12 | 13 | 14 |
　　　3′ | 　1　 | 　　2　　 | 　　3　　 | 　　4　　 | 　　5　　 |

Document 7
Announcement

full sheet

Miss Morales: Use your best judgment in centering this announcement attractively on the page. Use as a heading: **EXCLUSIVELY FOR BOUTIQUES INTERNATIONAL CUSTOMERS.** Change the ALL-CAPS paragraph headings to ALL-CAPS side headings.

Document 8
Announcement

full sheet

Miss Morales: Marketing has decided to delay the special wedding arrangements for approximately six months. Rekey Document 7, omitting the paragraph on wedding arrangements. Also, move paragraph 1 to the end of the document and move the final paragraph to the beginning of the document.

SPECIAL TOLL-FREE NUMBERS FOR OUR CUSTOMERS. ¶For Orders. Call 1-800-504-3210 24 hours a day, 7 days a week to order items on approved accounts or credit cards. ¶For Information. Call 1-800-504-3220 for any questions on orders previously placed. ¶For Account Information. Call 1-800-504-3230 for any questions regarding your account. Be sure to have your account number available.

GIFT SERVICE. What shall I give Uncle Dwight for his birthday? Is there something special I can give my wife (or husband) on our anniversary? For help with gift shopping for a gift, simply call a member of our staff at 1-800-504-3240. Our trained experts can help you to select a gift for any occasion. Your gift will be placed packaged in a handsome gift box with an appropriate card.

NEED QUICK DELIVERY? All orders are filled the day following receipt. Please allow more time for items marked with asterisks {**}. If you need an item earlier quickly, we can offer one- or two-day service by either PRIORITY MAIL or FEDERAL EXPRESS. SERVICE.

WEDDING ARRANGEMENTS. Is there a wedding in your future? Our special consultants can aid you in all phases aspects of planning the wedding, including etiquette, attire of wedding party, and selection of trousseau. They We can also provide advice on the selection of silverware style and patterns for china and glassware. They We will even tape the wedding ceremony and reception for your enjoyment in years to come. through the years. Call TOLL FREE 1-800-504-3250 for complete details.

COMPLETE CUSTOMER SATISFACTION IS OUR GOAL. Our policy aim is to provide you superior products excellent items at reasonable good prices. If you are not completely satisfied with your purchase, simply return the item within 30 days for a full refund. The only exception to this policy is personalized items which may be returned only if we have made an error.

201c ▶ 25 Recall
Basic Table Format

full sheets; correct errors
References: p. 288, RG 11

Table 1
3-Column Table
with Totals
DS body; CS: 6 spaces

PROPERTY VALUES			words
			3
Property	This Year	Last Year	14
Scrubbs Ranch	$ 1,355,750	$ 1,308,457	23
State Street	754,900	749,500	29
Westlake Mall	5,387,000	5,401,750	36
Airport Complex	7,980,250	6,906,900	43
Center City	2,450,500	2,250,750	54
Total	$17,928,400	$16,617,357	60

Table 2
3-Column Table
with Source Note
SS body; decide spaces
between columns

Table 3
Reformat Table 2; DS body;
decide a different number of
spaces between columns

SOME ENDANGERED MAMMALS			words
			5
Mammal	Scientific Name	Historic Range	19
Bobcat	Felis rufus escuinapae	Central Mexico	28
Cheetah	Acinonyx jubatus	Africa to India	37
Gorilla	Gorilla gorilla	Central & West Africa	46
Giant panda	Ailuropoda melanoleuca	China	54
Gray whale	Eschrichtius robustus	North Pacific Ocean	65
Leopard	Panthera pardus	Africa & Asia	72
Tiger	Panthera tigris	Asia	78
			81

Source: U.S. Fish and Wildlife Service, U.S. Interior Department.   95

201d ▶ 8
Language Skills:
Word Choice

1. Study the spelling and definition of each pair of words.

2. Key the **Learn** line, with the number and period, noting the proper use of the often confused words.

3. Key the **Apply** lines, with the number and period, using the word that completes each sentence correctly.

berth (n) a built-in bed on a ship or vehicle	**bold** (adj) fearless; courageous
birth (n) the act or condition or being born	**bowled** (vb) knocked over with something rolled

Learn 1. The cat's birth unexpectedly took place in the ship's upper berth.
Apply 2. The farmer is planning for the (birth/berth) of a foal next month.
Apply 3. The cost of the cruise includes a cabin with two (births/berths).

Learn 4. The bold little boy bowled a strike to win the game.
Apply 5. I am seeking a (bold/bowled) hiker to climb the mountain with me.
Apply 6. We (bold/bowled) three games before going to the movies on our last date.

Lesson 202   Tables with Leaders and Totals

202a ▶ 5
Conditioning
Practice

each line twice SS
(slowly, then faster);
DS between 2-line
groups; if time permits,
take 1' writings on line 3

alphabet 1 Jake will buy a very good quality zinc from the experts at the stores.
figures 2 The license plate numbers for her cars are 247951, 836067, and 443086.
fig/sym 3 Leah just renewed Policies #23-4598-623 (auto) and #35-9107-44 (home).
speed 4 My field hand saw the small dirigible signal the men in the cornfield.

| 1 | 2 | 3 | 4 | 5 | 6 | 7 | 8 | 9 | 10 | 11 | 12 | 13 | 14 |

251b-254b (continued)

Documents 2-6
Form Letters from Boilerplate

LP pp. 63-71

Miss Morales: We use boiler-plate files to create many documents used in responding to customer orders. A boilerplate file, such as this one, contains standardized paragraphs which can be combined to create documents.

Prepare letters dated **October 6, 19--**, to the addressees below for **Mr. Peterson's** signature using the paragraphs indicated and inserting the appropriate information. Use block format, open punctuation, with these letters of average length.

Document 2
Mr. Jeremy R. Polk
16301 Thomas Street
Biloxi, MS 39532-6785
1-1 **a lead crystal bud vase**
2-3 **Ireland; three weeks**
3-2

Document 3
Mr. Kevin T. Miles
4210 Ash Lane
Dallas, TX 75223-9569
1-2 **a solid brass desk clock**
2-1 **$78.75**
3-4

Document 4
Mrs. Rose L. Moss
250 Florida Boulevard
Baton Rouge, LA 70801-4042
1-4 **a Limoges jewelry box**
2-3 **France; two weeks**
3-2

Document 5
Ms. Alyse C. Brown
9601 Kanis Road
Little Rock, AR 72205-6930
1-3 **October 1; lead crystal swan**
2-4 **September 27**
3-4

Document 6
Dr. C. Elinor Crane
1410 Coleman Avenue
Macon, GA 31207-5286
1-1 **a silver vanity set**
2-2 **ten days**
3-1

Paragraphs for Form Letters

Paragraph 1 Options

1-1 **Thank you,** (name of customer), **for your recent order for** (name of item).

1-2 **Thank you,** (name of customer), **for your inquiry regarding your order for** (name of item).

1-3 **Your letter of** (date of letter) **indicates that you have not yet received the** (item) **you ordered.**

1-4 **This letter will confirm our telephone conversation today regarding your order for** (item).

Paragraph 2 Options

2-1 **Unfortunately, our stock of this item has been completely depleted and we are unable to obtain additional quantities. By separate mail, we are sending a refund check in the amount of $**(amount).

2-2 **This item is not currently in stock; however, we expect a shipment within the next** (number of days) **and will ship it at that time. We regret the delay.**

2-3 **As you know, this item is a special order from a firm in** (location); **and we have not received the item from them. We do expect, however, to ship the item to you within the next** (time period).

2-4 **Your order was shipped on** (date) **and should have arrived by now. If you have not received it, please let me know immediately so that I can check it for you.**

Paragraph 3 Options

3-1 **Thank you for shopping with Boutiques International. We look forward to serving you in the future.**

3-2 **Please call me (800-504-3200) between 9 a.m. and 5 p.m. Central Time if you have any additional questions.**

3-3 **For your special shopping needs, keep in mind that Boutiques International is eager to serve you.**

3-4 **Enclosed is a copy of our latest catalog. Be sure to look for the many new, unique items now available.**

202b ▶ 10 Learn to Format Tables with Leaders

full sheet; DS body; decide spaces between columns; insert leaders as shown

To align leaders

Key the first line of the first column; space once; note the position of the printing point indicator or cursor (on an odd or even number); key a period, then space alternately across the line stopping 2 or 3 spaces before the next column. On lines that follow, align the periods with those in line 1. Leave at least one blank space before keying the first period in the leader on a line.

```
             RADIO STATION FORMATS

Classical music . . . . . . .  .   WKTC-AM
Country music . . . . . . .  .  .   WYRM-FM
News and weather  . . . . . .  .   WNWZ-AM
Rock music  . . . . . . .  .  .  .   WZZR-FM
Talk show . . . . . . . . .  .   WXRE-AM
```

202c ▶ 35 Format/Process Tables with Leaders and Column Headings

full sheets unless otherwise directed; correct errors

Table 1
2-Column Table with Leaders

DS body; decide spaces between columns; insert leaders

words

```
            CELTIC REDS EXECUTIVE BOARD                    6

          Office                        Incumbent         12

President . . . . . . . . . . . . . . . . .  Huerta Perez  22
President-elect . . . . . . . . . . . . .  Frank Linberg  33
First Vice President  . . . . . . . .  Josephine Luiz     44
Second Vice President . . . . . . . .  Karen Appelt       54
Corresponding Secretary . . . . . . .  Rodney Luther      65
Recording Secretary . . . . . . . . .  Barbara Miller     76
Historian . . . . . . . . . . . . . .  John Tomczak       86
Past President . . . . . . . . . . .  Robert O'Hare       97
```

Table 2
3-Column Table with Leaders and Totals

DS body; CS: 16 spaces between columns 1 & 2; 6 spaces between columns 2 & 3; insert leaders between columns 1 & 2

Note: Do not key leaders in the *Total* line.

Table 3

Reformat Table 1 on a half sheet, long edge at top; DS body; decide spaces between columns. Change the name of the Second Vice President from **Karen Appelt** to **Elizabeth Austin.**

```
            SCHOLARSHIP FUND DRIVE                          5
                                First
      (Status report--End of fourth Quarter)              12

      Donor                 Pledge      Paid              19
Scott Twinskey . . . . . . .  $250      $105             29
Mary Rob-Yates . . . . . .  .  360       200             36
Sam bukitsch . . . . . . . .  170        75              43
Jeanne Batz  . . . . . .  .   380       240              51
Juan Salazar . . . . . . .  .  240        90             58
richard Simms  . . . . . .   190        60              66
Alberti Alvarez . . . . .  .  300       180             73
chun Wau Wacker . . . . .  .  250        75             80
T. G. Bailey . . . . . .  .   400       160             91
      Total                 $2,450    $1,185            96
```

Learning Goals

1. To increase your skill in planning, organizing, and formatting a variety of documents.

2. To key in acceptable formats a series of typical documents processed in a Customer Service Center.

3. To increase your production skill.

Documents Processed

1. Unbound Report
2. Letters
3. Sales Announcement
4. Table
5. Simplified Memorandum

Lessons 251-254

251a-254a ▶ 5 (daily)
Conditioning Practice

each line twice SS (slowly, then faster); if time permits, take 1′ writings on line 4

alphabet	1	Jan Zweibel quickly solved the problem by using very complex formulas.
figures	2	They purchased four calculators: Nos. 40741, 51902, 63254, and 68037.
fig/sym	3	Kern & Werner offered a discount of $437 (10% and 2%) on Order 864591.
speed	4	She may sue the panel of men if they entitle the six girls to the pay.

| 1 | 2 | 3 | 4 | 5 | 6 | 7 | 8 | 9 | 10 | 11 | 12 | 13 | 14 |

251b-254b ▶ 45 (daily)
Document Processing

Your first experience as a keyboard technician will be in the Customer Service Center under the supervision of Miss Carla T. Morales, administrative assistant to Harold J. Peterson, who is the director of the center. Before you begin work, Miss Morales asks you to review the functions of the Customer Service Center on p. 427 as well as your major duties and the special instructions.

Document 1
Statement of Policy

full sheet

Miss Morales: Prepare this Statement of Policy in final form as an unbound report. Watch for and correct any unmarked errors. Use **CUSTOMER RELATIONS** as a main heading; use **Statement of Policy** as a secondary heading.

The success and continued growth of Boutiques International depends upon satisfied customers. To ensure continued progress, we must strive to increase and retain the number of customers who de sire the goods and servides we provide. our customers.

Satisfing our customers demands that we determine there specefic requirements, desires, and preferances. Each customer must be made to feel that we are totaly comitted to serving him or her in an affective manner.

Courtesy and attention are key concepts in customer relations. All customer contacts, specificaly complaints, must be treated in a manner that will convince the customer that we have his or her best interests at heart. All questions and compleints will be resolved quickly in a prompt and curteous manner.

To provide add the "personal touch," all contacts with customers who have major problems or questions will be made in person whenever possible. In matters of vital importance, a representative from the nearest local branch will visit the customers; in other cases, the customer will be contacted by telephone. Each personal contact will be followed by a letter of confirmation. Minor or routine questions and problems will be resolved by correspondence.

Boutiques International has earned a reputation for providing goods of the highest qualety at reasonabel prices. We are also noted for the personal specialised services we provide all customers. We must continually strive to up hold our reputation so that we will merit customer confidance and satisfaction.

203a ▶ 5
Conditioning Practice

each line twice SS (slowly, then faster); then a 1′ writing on line 4

alphabet 1 Mindy requires size six or seven jackets for both perky girls to wear.

figures 2 My order for 1,475 boxes and 3,690 bags was shipped by truck on 12/28.

fig/sym 3 He took the monitor (#3246-B), CPU (#784-9B), and keyboard (#05-61-B).

speed 4 My antique dish in the hall in the downtown chapel is authentic ivory.

| 1 | 2 | 3 | 4 | 5 | 6 | 7 | 8 | 9 | 10 | 11 | 12 | 13 | 14 |

203b ▶ 7 Improve Language Skills: Word Choice

1. Study the spelling and definition of each pair of words.

2. Key the **Learn** line, with the number and period, noting the proper use of the often confused words.

3. Key the **Apply** lines, with the number and period, using the word that completes each sentence correctly.

bridal (adj) of or pertaining to a bride or a wedding

bridle (n) a harness fitted about a horse's head, used to restrain or guide

cooperation (n) working together toward a common end

corporation (n) a business enterprise chartered by the state with its own rights, privileges, and liabilities

Learn 1. The riding instructor gave a bridle as a bridal gift to Sue and Tom.
Apply 2. The photographer took three pictures of the (bridal/bridle) party.
Apply 3. The trainer had a difficult time putting the (bridal/bridle) on the colt.
Learn 4. The cooperation of the workers made the corporation successful.
Apply 5. Most businesses depend on (cooperation/corporation) to get things done.
Apply 6. The (cooperation/corporation) has an elected board of directors.

203c ▶ 8
Recall Procedures for Centering Column Headings

CS: 8 spaces
Key the drills as directed below.
Drill 1: Center by column entries.
Drill 2: Center by column headings.
Drill 3: Center by longest item in each column, whether a heading or an entry.

	Director	Gross	Net
Drill 1	Saundra Murphy	$1,482.95	$1,284.25

	Automobile	Body Style	Engine Size
Drill 2	Apollo	Sedan	4.2 L

	Business Name	City	Employees
Drill 3	Hoppe, Inc.	Baltimore	201

203d ▶ 30
Format/Process Tables with Column Headings of Variable Lengths

full sheets; correct errors
References: p. 288, RG 11

Table 1
Table Centered by Longest Item in Column (Whether Entry or Column Heading)
DS body; CS: 8 spaces

QUALITY TEAM LEADERS			words
			4
Leader	Department	Extension	15
Thomas Broggi	Planning	8475	20
Elizabeth Pyncheski	Personnel	8299	27
Gerri Holmes-Ray	Accounting	8344	34
Karen Stoverton	Marketing	8070	40
Juan Hernandez	Transportation	8765	47
Vera Senti	CIS	8432	51
Randi Welesko	Advertising	8279	57
Pat Zimwalt	Purchasing	8645	63

BOUTIQUES INTERNATIONAL, LTD.

As part of your orientation program, Miss Angela E. Benson, a personnel administrator in the Human Resources Department, asks you to study these excerpts from the COMPANY INFORMATIONAL HANDBOOK.

Functions of Special Offices
  Customer Service Center
  Public Relations Office
  Human Resources Department
  Advertising Department
Formatting Documents
Job Competencies
Major Duties
Special Instructions

Excerpts from COMPANY INFORMATIONAL HANDBOOK
Functions of Special Offices

Customer Service Center

1. Promotes customer satisfaction.
2. Studies customer needs and preferences.
3. Solves customer problems in an expeditious manner.
4. Resolves any customer complaints promptly and equitably.
5. Provides personal, specialized customer services.

Public Relations Office

1. Strives to create and maintain public goodwill.
2. Prepares informational materials, including booklets and speeches.
3. Cooperates with public and private organizations in community projects.
4. Serves as a clearinghouse for all official contacts with the public.
5. Plans and conducts special activities to enhance public goodwill.

Human Resources Department

1. Provides required human resources.
2. Develops programs to help employees reach their maximum potential under safe and healthful working conditions.
3. Establishes a fair and equitable schedule of compensation, including desirable employee benefits.
4. Evaluates performance of employees.
5. Monitors equal opportunity policies.

Advertising Department

1. Stimulates and promotes the sale of goods.
2. Selects appropriate media for promoting sales.
3. Prepares sales promotional material.
4. Plans and conducts special advertising campaigns.
5. Upholds ethical standards in sales promotion.

Formatting Documents

Each major office of the company is free to adopt any document format it chooses. Follow directions given by the document originator. If no format is specified, use your best judgment in placing the material neatly on the page.

Job Competencies

To be successful as a keyboard technician you must possess these qualifications.
1. Excellent keyboarding skills.
2. A thorough knowledge of grammar, punctuation, spelling, and formatting.
3. The ability to use reference materials such as dictionaries, directories, and manuals.
4. Good proofreading skills.
5. The ability to listen, understand, and follow directions.
6. The ability to plan, organize, and complete your work with a minimum of assistance.
7. The ability to get along well with others.

Major Duties

Under the direction of a specified supervisor, you will do the following:
1. Compile information as the basis for preparing business documents.
2. Key documents such as correspondence, reports, forms, and tables.
3. Prepare business documents from handwritten or rough-draft copy and from source materials.
4. Compose short documents based on data and instructions provided.
5. Compute amounts in pencil or by using a calculator.

Special Instructions

As a keyboard technician, you will be expected to
1. Use the proper format for a document.
2. Provide date for correspondence (use the current date if a date is not given).
3. Provide an appropriate salutation, complimentary close, keyed signature and title of the originator of correspondence, and your initials.
4. Include the proper notation if the content of the document indicates there are enclosures or attachments.
5. Correct errors you make as you prepare a document in final form.
6. Correct any unmarked errors made by the originator of the document in spelling, punctuation, grammar, and word usage.
7. Proofread all documents and correct any errors you may have missed *before* you remove a document from the machine.
8. Produce neat, error-free, usable business documents.

Table 2
3-Column Table with Multiple-Line Column Headings
DS body; CS: 8 spaces

Table 3
Reformat Table 2; decide spaces between columns; convert the multiple-line headings into single-line headings as follows:
Column 2: **Birth Date**
Column 3: **Birth Place**

words

NOTABLE ENTERTAINERS			4
	BIRTH *lc*	BIRTH *lc*	7
ENTERTAINER *lc*	DATE *lc*	PLACE *lc*	15
Steve Allen	12/26/21	New York, NY	22
Chevy Chase	10/8/43	New York, NY	29
Bill Cosby	7/12/37	Philadelphia, PA	36
Jose Feliciano	9/10/45	Lares, Puerto Rico	45
Michael Jackson	8/29/58	Gary, IN	51
Paul Newman	1/26/25	Cleveland, OH	58
Tom Selleck	1/29/45	Detroit, MI	64

Lesson 204 | Tables with Horizontal/Vertical Rules

204a ▶ 5
Conditioning Practice

each line twice SS (slowly, then faster); DS between 2-line groups; if time permits, take 1' writings on line 2

alphabet 1 Chad thought Pamela's long joke about the next quiz wasn't very funny.
figures 2 Bill is to read pages 271-305 for history and pages 69-84 for English.
fig/sym 3 Mary bought 30 (15%), David bought 78 (39%), and Lynn bought 92 (46%).
speed 4 The busy maid is to rush the cocoa to the eight men on the dorm panel.

| 1 | 2 | 3 | 4 | 5 | 6 | 7 | 8 | 9 | 10 | 11 | 12 | 13 | 14 |

204b ▶ 10 *Learn to Format Tables with Horizontal and Vertical Rules*

Study the illustration at the right, observing the spacing between the keyed copy and the rules. Then key the table on a full sheet; DS body; CS: 8 spaces. Use the vertical spacing format guides to key the horizontal rules. Begin each rule at the beginning of the first column and end each aligned with the final stroke in the last column. Remove the page and, using a pen (preferably black ink), draw vertical rules at the midpoint between columns.

Note: When formatting tables with horizontal rules, the most error-free method of vertical spacing is to set the machine for single spacing and return twice for double-spaced entries.

THIRD QUARTER SUBSIDIARY PERFORMANCE
DS
(In Millions of Dollars)
SS

Subsidiary	Total Assets	Net Income
Emerald Isle	129.754	1.477
Century Savings & Loan	217.748	2.006
TGP Transportation	304.127	3.032
Reeves Manufacturing	93.373	1.233
Total	745.002	7.748

PHASE 11

BOUTIQUES INTERNATIONAL, LTD.
SPECIAL OFFICE SIMULATIONS

You have been hired as a keyboard technician by **Boutiques International, Ltd.**, a mail order firm that sells fine wares from all over the world. The company's headquarters are located at **801 Canal Street, New Orleans, LA 70112-3500.** The company has branch offices in London, Paris, Rome, and Hong Kong, and shops in major cities throughout the United States.

Initially, you will work at the company's headquarters as a replacement for employees who are ill or on vacation. This will give you an opportunity to work in some of the special offices of the company.

Your goals at Boutiques International are to

1. Increase your knowledge of typical office procedures.

2. Learn how to plan and organize your work.

3. Produce acceptable documents quickly and efficiently.

4. Improve your basic keyboarding and communications skills.

5. Become familiar with the functions of some of the special offices of a large corporation--Customer Service Center, Public Relations Office, Human Resources Department, and Advertising Department.

204c ▶ 35
Format/Process Tables with Horizontal and Vertical Rules

full sheets; correct errors

Table 1
Table with Horizontal Rules
DS body; decide spaces between columns

Subentries are indented 3 spaces.

BOYCE UNIVERSITY ENROLLMENT REPORT			
College	Last Year	This Year	
Arts and Sciences			40
Commuting students	3,658	3,767	46
Resident students	5,220	5,324	52
Business			54
Commuting students	4,791	5,030	60
Resident students	5,768	5,998	66
Education			68
Commuting students	1,236	1,310	75
Resident students	987	1,056	81

Table 2
Table with Horizontal and Vertical Rules
SS body; decide spaces between columns; box the table by inserting vertical lines between columns

Table 3
Reformat Table 1; SS body within each college group; DS between the college groups. Using the two totals given below, add a total line to the table.

Last year's total: **21,660**
This year's total: **22,485**

Total words: 108

NOTABLE BUSINESS EQUIPMENT INVENTIONS			
(From 1642 to 1899)			
Invention	Date	Inventor	Nationality
Adding machine	1642	Pascal	French
Calculating machine	1833	Babbage	English
Typewriter	1867	Sholes	U.S.
Stock ticker	1870	Edison	U.S.
Telephone	1876	Bell	U.S.-Scottish
Cash register	1879	Ritty	U.S.
Fountain pen	1884	Waterman	U.S.
Ballpoint pen	1888	Loud	U.S.
Tape recorder	1899	Poulsen	Danish

Source: The World Almanac.

Lesson 205   Review: Table Processing

205a ▶ 5
Conditioning Practice

each line twice SS (slowly, then faster); DS between 2-line groups; if time permits, take 1' writings on line 3

alphabet 1 That expensive black racquet is just the wrong size for many children.
figures 2 Linda has 72 blue, 68 yellow, 49 red, 30 green, and 15 orange marbles.
fig/sym 3 Norman was born 7/10/42, Mary was born 9/3/46, and I was born 5/15/48.
speed 4 The ensign works with the official to right the problem with the dock.

| 1 | 2 | 3 | 4 | 5 | 6 | 7 | 8 | 9 | 10 | 11 | 12 | 13 | 14 |

Resume

```
                    DIANNA E. WARRENS
                    3559 Longfellow Drive
                    Portland, ME  04107-7486
                      (207) 256-8673

EDUCATION

   High School:          Memorial High School (received diploma
                         in May, 1990)

   Business Courses:     Keyboarding for Information Processing
                         Document Processing Applications
                         Office Procedures/Machine Transcription
                         Business Computer Applications

   Current Skill Level:  Keyboarding straight-copy rate:  70 words
                         a minute.
                         Machine transcription rate:  35 words a
                         minute.

SCHOOL ACTIVITIES

   Business Professionals of America, Community Service Chairperson
   during junior and senior years (responsible for organizing and
   conducting various community service projects for organizations
   in the Portland area.)

   Member of National Honor Society, junior and senior years.

   Senior Class Secretary (responsible for preparing agenda and
   recording minutes of meetings.)

WORK EXPERIENCE

   Administrative Assistant, Karsten Insurance Company, Portland,
   ME, January 1990 to present.  Work 20 hours a week performing
   tasks assigned by the office manager; key correspondence, pro-
   cess insurance applications and claims, answer telephone, greet
   clients, and file correspondence.

   Camp Counselor, Parks and Recreation Department, Portland, ME,
   summers 1988 and 1989.  Organized, directed, and supervised ac-
   tivities for camp participants.

REFERENCES

   Ms. Audra Westbrook, Office Manager, Karsten Insurance Company,
   3619 Quebec Street, Portland, ME  04101-7475, (207) 249-8324.

   Mr. Jason Thrasher, Director, Parks and Recreation Department,
   2990 Ridgeway Road, Portland, ME  04104-1830 (207) 836-2990.

   Ms. Mary St. James, Business Instructor, Memorial High School,
   688 Cleveland Street, Portland, ME  04103-2701 (207) 836-3800.
```

Application Form

APPLICATION FOR EMPLOYMENT

AN EQUAL OPPORTUNITY EMPLOYER

PLEASE PRINT WITH BLACK INK OR USE TYPEWRITER

NAME (LAST, FIRST, MIDDLE INITIAL): Warrens, Dianna E.
SOCIAL SECURITY NUMBER: 701-325-4899
CURRENT DATE: June 4, 19--

ADDRESS (NUMBER, STREET, CITY, STATE, ZIP CODE): 3559 Longfellow Drive, Portland, ME 04107-7486
HOME PHONE NO. (207) 256-8673

REACH PHONE NO.
U.S. CITIZEN? YES X NO
DATE YOU CAN START June 15, 19--

ARE YOU EMPLOYED NOW? Yes
IF SO, MAY WE INQUIRE OF YOUR PRESENT EMPLOYER? Yes

TYPE OF WORK DESIRED: Office
REFERRED BY: Jasper Employment Agency
SALARY DESIRED: * Open

IF RELATED TO ANYONE IN OUR EMPLOY, STATE AND NAME AND POSITION: No

DO YOU HAVE ANY PHYSICAL CONDITION THAT MAY PREVENT YOU FROM PERFORMING CERTAIN KINDS OF WORK? YES NO X IF YES, EXPLAIN

HAVE YOU EVER BEEN CONVICTED OF A FELONY? YES NO X IF YES, EXPLAIN

EDUCATIONAL INSTITUTION	LOCATION (CITY, STATE)	DATES ATTENDED FROM MO. YR.	TO MO. YR.	DIPLOMA, DEGREE, OR CREDITS EARNED	CLASS STANDING (CHK QUARTER) 1 2 3 4	MAJOR SUBJECTS STUDIED
COLLEGE						
HIGH SCHOOL Memorial High School	Portland, Maine	8 86	5 90	Diploma	X	Business
GRADE SCHOOL						
OTHER						

LIST BELOW THE POSITIONS THAT YOU HAVE HELD (LAST POSITION FIRST)

1. NAME AND ADDRESS OF FIRM
Karsten Insurance Company
3619 Quebec Street
Portland, ME 04101-7475
NAME OF SUPERVISOR Ms. Audra Westbrook
EMPLOYED (MO-YR) FROM 1/90 TO present
DESCRIBE POSITION RESPONSIBILITIES Keyed correspondence, processed routine insurance claims, answered telephone, greeted clients, and filed documents.
REASON FOR LEAVING

2. NAME AND ADDRESS OF FIRM
Parks and Recreation Department
2990 Ridgeway Road
Portland, ME 04104-1830
NAME OF SUPERVISOR Mr. Jason Thrasher
EMPLOYED (MO-YR) FROM Summers TO 1988 and 1989
DESCRIBE POSITION RESPONSIBILITIES Organized, directed, and supervised activities for six-year-old camp participants.
REASON FOR LEAVING It was a summer job only.

3. NAME AND ADDRESS OF FIRM
NAME OF SUPERVISOR
EMPLOYED (MO-YR) FROM TO
DESCRIBE POSITION RESPONSIBILITIES
REASON FOR LEAVING

I UNDERSTAND THAT I SHALL NOT BECOME AN EMPLOYEE UNTIL I HAVE SIGNED AN EMPLOYMENT AGREEMENT WITH THE FINAL APPROVAL OF THE EMPLOYER AND THAT SUCH EMPLOYMENT WILL BE SUBJECT TO VERIFICATION OF PREVIOUS EMPLOYMENT. DATA PROVIDED IN THIS APPLICATION, ANY RELATED DOCUMENTS, OR RESUME, I KNOW THAT A REPORT MAY BE MADE THAT WILL INCLUDE INFORMATION

CONCERNING ANY FACTOR THE EMPLOYER MIGHT FIND RELEVANT TO THE POSITION FOR WHICH I AM APPLYING, AND THAT I CAN MAKE A WRITTEN REQUEST FOR ADDITIONAL INFORMATION AS TO THE NATURE AND SCOPE OF THE REPORT IF ONE IS MADE.

Dianna E. Warrens
SIGNATURE OF APPLICANT

Letter of Application

```
3559 Longfellow Drive
Portland, ME  04107-7486
June 1, 19--

Ms. Lydia Kent
Personnel Director
Norton Industries
333 Highland Street
Portland, ME  04103-8488

Dear Ms. Kent:

Mr. Keith Riles, director of the Jasper Employment Agency, in-
formed me of the employment opportunity in your document process-
ing department with Norton Industries.  Mr. Riles shared the job
description and outlined the requirements for the position.  I
believe I possess the necessary qualifications and would like to
be considered for the position.

Last week I graduated from Memorial High School.  While attending
Memorial, all of my elective credits were used to take courses from
the business department.  From these courses I acquired skills in
the areas of document processing, office procedures, computer ap-
plications, and transcription techniques.

My part-time job with Karsten Insurance Company allowed me to apply
and refine the skills I gained from the course work.  The job also
required me to deal with the public, work under pressure to meet
deadlines, work as part of a team, and learn how to operate new of-
fice equipment.

A career in today's technology-oriented office is very exciting
to me.  Since I am eager to begin that career on a full-time basis,
I shall call your office next week after you have had an opportu-
nity to review the resume which is enclosed.  I look forward to
discussing the document processing position with you.

Sincerely,


Dianna E. Warrens

Enclosure
```

Follow-Up Letter

```
3559 Longfellow Drive
Portland, ME  04107-7486
June 8, 19--

Ms. Lydia Kent
Personnel Director
Norton Industries
333 Highland Street
Portland, ME  04103-8488

Dear Ms. Kent:

Thank you for allowing me to meet with you to discuss
the position in your document processing department.
Being able to observe the department in action and meet
with Mr. Conrad as well as several other employees gave
me a much better understanding of the requirements of the
job as well as the opportunities available with Norton
Industries.

The company tuition reimbursement program is particu-
larly appealing to me.  It was a very difficult deci-
sion for me to forego further schooling in order to start
a career immediately.  Your program would allow me to
do both.

If there is additional information that I can provide
to assist you in making your decision, I would be happy
to do so.  I am looking forward to hearing from you.

Sincerely,


Dianna E. Warrens
```

205b ▶ 45
Sustained Production: Tables with Leaders and Horizontal and Vertical Rules

Time Schedule
Plan and prepare .... 5′
Timed production .... 30′
Proofread/circle errors .... 7′
Compute *n-pram* .... 3′

1. Make a list of tables to be processed:
page 348, 201c, Table 2
page 349, 202c, Table 1
page 351, 203d, Table 3
page 352, 204c, Table 3

2. Arrange supplies: full sheets, correction materials, list, etc.

3. When directed to begin, key for 30′ the listed tables. Correct errors neatly. Proofread each table carefully before removing it from the machine. If you finish before time is called, key as much of the

two tables identified below as you can in the time remaining.
page 348, 201c, Table 1
page 349, 202c, Table 2

4. Compute *n-pram* and then turn in the tables arranged in the order given in Step 1.

Lesson 206 — Evaluation: Table Processing

206a ▶ 5
Conditioning Practice

each line twice SS (slowly, then faster); DS between 2-line groups; if time permits, take 1′ writings on line 3

alphabet	1	Maja was to have five pens and extra clips in a kit for your big quiz.
figures	2	Sandy was 25 years old when she moved to 4360 Rosegarden Road in 1987.
fig/sym	3	She arrived at 12:47 a.m. on Flight #860 (Gate 38) with 59 classmates.
speed	4	Pam kept the big emblem in a fir box by the enamel bowls on the shelf.

| 1 | 2 | 3 | 4 | 5 | 6 | 7 | 8 | 9 | 10 | 11 | 12 | 13 | 14 |

206b ▶ 45
Measure Production: Tables

Time Schedule
Plan and prepare .... 5′
Timed production .... 30′
Proofread/circle errors .... 7′
Compute *n-pram* .... 3′

Supplies: full sheets and correction materials

Procedures: Key the tables on this and the next page for 30′. Proofread each table carefully before removing it from the machine. Correct errors neatly.

Table 1
Table with Leaders
DS body; CS: 20 spaces between columns 1 & 2 and 4 spaces between columns 2 & 3

Tables 2-6 are on p. 354.

			words
SWIFT CONSTRUCTION			4
(New Building Plans for 19-- Catalog)			11
Building Plan	Code	Price	21
Traditional Log Home	SCP025	$25.00	33
Stackwood Barn	SCP015	15.00	45
Earth-Sheltered Home	SCP020	17.50	57
Little Red Barn	SCP031	12.50	68
Family-Sized Storm Shelter	SCP033	17.50	80
Backyard Multi-Rec Set	SCP038	5.00	92
Multipurpose Greenhouse	SCP022	10.00	104
Multi-Use Workbench	SCP039	5.00	116
Special Dollhouse	SCP040	7.50	127
Solar Greenhouse	SCP010	15.00	139
Heavy-Duty Garden Cart	SCP035	10.00	151

Application Form

Many companies require that their standard application form be completed even though a resume and application letter have been sent. In some cases the applicant must complete the form in longhand at the company location. In other cases the applicant may take the form and return it later, in which case it should be keyed. In either case, particular attention should be given to neatness and accuracy. In addition, directions should be followed carefully.

One way to help ensure neatness is to make a photocopy of the form to complete as a rough-draft copy. Then the final form can be completed more easily.

Follow-Up Letter

The follow-up letter is an important part of the job search. It is a thank you for the time given and courtesies extended to you during the interview. If you can honestly do so, discuss the positive impressions you have of the company and indicate your continued interest in the job.

Lessons 248-250 — Apply for Employment

248a-250a ▶ 5 (daily)
Conditioning Practice

Each day check to see that equipment is in good working order by keying the lines at the right at least twice.

alphabet	1	Mr. Gomez was quite favorably pleased with the six market projections.
figures	2	Only 1,985 of the 12,476 voting delegates had registered by 10:30 p.m.
fig/sym	3	I sent Check #714 for $4,368.90 to C. L. Walker & Sons on November 25.
speed	4	If they pay me to do so, I may make their formal gowns for the social.

| 1 | 2 | 3 | 4 | 5 | 6 | 7 | 8 | 9 | 10 | 11 | 12 | 13 | 14 |

248b-250b ▶ 45 (daily)
Prepare Employment Documents

Documents 1-4
LP p. 47 and
7 plain full sheets

Your teacher encourages you to apply for the job with **Boutiques International, Ltd.,** which is described in the job announcement shown at the right. Using the illustrations on page 425 as guides, prepare the following employment documents.

1. Resume. Using your personal data, compose at the keyboard a resume. Revise and key a final copy.

2. Letter of Application. Compose at the keyboard your application letter to **Mr. Henry K. O'Brian.** Revise and key a final copy.

3. Application Form (LP p. 47). On a plain sheet, key the information that you will include on the application form used by Boutiques International, Ltd. for all potential employees. Key the application form, using the personal data that you keyed on the plain sheet.

4. Follow-Up Letter. Compose at the keyboard a follow-up letter similar to the one on the next page. Revise and key a final copy.

KEYBOARDING TECHNICIAN

Large international mail order firm hiring keyboarding technicians. Firm looking for applicants who have

- excellent keyboarding skills.
- a good knowledge of formatting, grammar, spelling, and punctuation.
- the ability to listen to, understand, and follow directions.
- the ability to plan, organize, and complete work with a minimum of assistance.
- the ability to work well with others.

Send letter of application and resume to

Mr. Henry K. O'Brian
Director of Human Resources
Boutiques International, Ltd.
801 Canal Street
New Orleans, LA 70112-3500

An Equal Opportunity Employer

206b (continued)

Table 2
3-Column Table with Multiple-Line Column Headings and Source Note
DS body; CS: 6 spaces

LAND VEHICULAR TUNNELS IN U.S.
(Over 5,000 Feet in Length)

Name	Location	Length in Feet
E. Johnson Memorial	Colorado	8,959
Eisenhower Memorial	Colorado	8,941
Allegheny	Pennsylvania	6,070
Liberty Tubes	Pennsylvania	5,920
Zion National Park	Utah	5,766
East River Mountain	West Virginia & Virginia	5,412
Tuscarora	Pennsylvania	5,326

Source: The World Almanac.

(word counts: 6, 12, 13, 21, 28, 35, 41, 48, 54, 64, 70, 74, 82)

Table 3
4-Column Table from Revised Copy
DS body; decide spaces between columns

BUSINESS EXPENSE SUMMARY
(Renato Huarte)   DS

Quarter	Travel	Meals	Lodging
First	$325.65	$175.69	$300.50
Second	294.58	225.43	124.47
Third	437.95	175.48	256.45
Fourth	371.57	202.87	76.77
Total	$1,429.75	$960.71	$677.22

(word counts: 5, 8, 19, 26, 32, 37, 49, 56)

Table 4
Table with Horizontal and Vertical Rules
DS body; decide spaces between columns; insert horizontal and vertical rules

Table 5
Reformat Table 3; DS body; CS: 10 spaces; add horizontal rules

Table 6
Reformat Table 2; DS body; decide spaces between columns; add horizontal rules

INVENTORY REPORT OF DISCONTINUED APPLIANCES
(Number of Units Remaining)

Appliance	Last Month	This Month
Microwave oven--M-010-B	135	101
Dishwasher--D-320-A	25	20
Videocassette recorder--C-005-A	142	123
Refrigerator--R-279-C	47	29
Portable television--T-863-A	107	83
Electric hair dryer--D-539-C	127	101
Total	583	457

(word counts: 9, 14, 27, 34, 47, 53, 59, 67, 73, 80, 88, 101, 104, 116)

Apply for Employment

Learning Goals

1. To learn the appropriate content and format for employment documents.

2. To prepare your personal employment documents for a specified job.

Documents Prepared

1. Resume
2. Application Letter
3. Application Form
4. Follow-Up Letter

APPLY FOR EMPLOYMENT

Now that you have completed your cooperative work experience, you are ready to apply for a job. Guidelines for preparing employment documents are provided at the right; examples are illustrated on page 425. Review these guidelines and examples carefully.

Employment Document Guidelines

Employment documents provide applicants an opportunity to present their best qualities to prospective employers. These qualities are represented by the specific content of the documents as well as by the format, neatness, and accuracy of the documents. The care with which these documents are prepared is a strong indication to a company of the highest level of performance they can expect of the applicant; therefore, special attention should be given to their preparation.

The most common types of employment documents are the resume (or personal data sheet), application letter, application form, and the follow-up letter.

Resume

The resume should be a factual presentation of your skills, abilities and traits that would be of value to the prospective employer. It is usually one page and contains the following major categories of information: personal, education, school activities, work experience, and references. The order in which the major categories are listed may vary, with the most significant qualifications for the particular job listed first. However, personal information is usually listed first and references are usually listed last.

Personal information typically includes name, address, and telephone number. Other personal information should only be included if it relates directly to the job qualifications.

The education section is a listing of the high schools you have attended. If you have attended more than one high school, you should list the schools attended in reverse chronological order (most recent school listed first). In this section you may also list courses completed that are specifically related to the job, skill levels achieved if appropriate (such as keyboarding speed), and grades earned. Grade point average, if B or above, may be listed.

In the school activities section, list organization memberships, offices held, scholarships, awards, and honors. In particular, list activities that will demonstrate leadership abilities.

List work experience in reverse chronological order with a brief description of duties. If experience is limited, jobs not related to the business office, such as babysitting or lawn mowing, should be listed because such jobs demonstrate responsibility and initiative.

Include a variety of references, such as teachers and former employers. Always request permission from the people you plan to list as references before using their names.

Application Letter

The letter of application should include three sections. The first section (paragraph) may state something positive about the company, how the applicant learned of the opening, and the specific position the applicant is seeking.

The second section may contain two or three paragraphs which provide evidence that the applicant is qualified for the position. Avoid merely repeating the information on the resume. This is the time to interpret that information and to show how those qualifications can be beneficial to the company. The applicant should focus on what he/she can do for the company-- not what the job will do for him/her.

The last section (paragraph) should request an interview. Some authorities suggest that the applicant should be proactive rather than reactive, meaning that the applicant should suggest a time to call the company to request an interview rather than ask the company to call or write to set up the interview. The logic of this recommendation is that company representatives may become so busy that they neglect to respond to the letter; whereas, they may respond positively to a telephone request for the interview. This action is appropriate only after allowing adequate time for the company representative to inspect the application letter and resume.

UNIT 49   LESSONS 207 – 212
Format/Process Business Forms

Learning Goals
1. To develop skill in formatting purchase requisitions, purchase orders, and invoices.
2. To improve tabulating skills.
3. To improve language skills.

Format Guides
1. Paper guide at *0* (for typewriters).
2. LL: 70 spaces.
3. LS: SS sentence drills; DS ¶s; as needed for problems.
4. Tab sets: 5 spaces for ¶ indention; as needed for problems.

FORMATTING GUIDES: BUSINESS FORMS

Purchase Requisition
A form used by an employee to request the purchasing department to order items such as supplies, equipment, or services.

Purchase Order
A form used by the purchasing department of one company to order merchandise or services from another company.

Invoice
A form used by one company to bill a person or another company for services or merchandise purchased from the company that sends the invoice.

Guides for Formatting Business Forms

1. Set left margin and tab stops for the items to be keyed in the columns so the items (except the items keyed under the description head) are approximately centered under the form's column headings. The description column items should begin 1 or 2 spaces to the right of the vertical line.

2. When appropriate, use these margin and/or tab stops to begin lines to be keyed in the heading portion of the business form. For example, the address lines on many forms can begin at the tab stop set for the description column.

3. SS the items to be keyed in the column beginning a double space below the horizontal rule under the column headings.

4. When amounts in a column are totalled, underline the amount for the last item; then DS and key the total. Business forms can have totals keyed with or without commas separating thousands and hundreds.

5. Forms are often mailed in window envelopes (see RG 7). Caution must, therefore, be taken to ensure that the address is formatted and keyed so it will be seen in the envelope's "window."

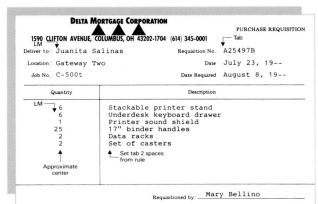

Formatted Purchase Requisition

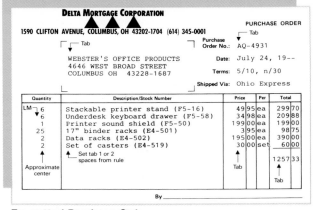

Formatted Purchase Order

Lesson 207   *Keyboarding Skills/Purchase Requisitions*

207a ▶ 5
Conditioning Practice

each line twice SS
(slowly, then faster);
DS between 2-line
groups; if time permits,
take 1′ writings on line 2

alphabet	1	Peggy and Kami will enjoy a quiet, lazy bath after very hard exercise.
figures	2	Dave has 9,687 names and 12,534 addresses stored on one 80-track disk.
fig/sym	3	My electric bill was $135.98 (up 6%); my gas bill was $92.47 (up 10%).
speed	4	The auditor for a sorority cut by half the big goal for the endowment.

| 1 | 2 | 3 | 4 | 5 | 6 | 7 | 8 | 9 | 10 | 11 | 12 | 13 | 14 |

words

Document 2
Reference Page

Using the information given below, prepare a reference page for the report.

Kleinschrod, Walter A. "A Multi-sensory Approach to PC Training." Today's Office. May 1989, 66.

Tedesco, Eleanor Hollis, and Robert B. Mitchell. Administrative Office Systems Management. New York: John Wiley & Sons, 1987.

Document 3
Unbound Report with Footnotes

Rekey Document 1 as an unbound report with footnotes. Use the information below when keying footnotes.

¹Walter A. Kleinschrod, "A Multisensory Approach to PC Training," Today's Office, May 1989, p. 66.

²Eleanor Hollis Tedesco and Robert B. Mitchell, Administrative Office Systems Management (New York: John Wiley & Sons, 1987), p. 183.

	words
Formalized classes taught by company employees	380
(trainers) are also offered by many larger organizations.	392
In addition to teaching classes, the trainers are available	404
readily to assist employees with questions about software	417
features.	420

The User's Manual — *specific* — 427

another resource — *is the user's manual*

~~Users' manuals are also~~ used for training purposes.	440
The user's manual provides descriptions, examples, and in-	451
structions regarding the use of the particular software prod-	463
uct. For the real computer novice, the user's manual is	475
usually the least effective training resource. However, after	487
developing some skill with the ~~the~~ software, employees can ex-	499
pand their expertise with the software by referring to the	511
user's manual as a base source.	517

No single method for computer training ~~employees~~ can be	526
recommended. Most organizations use a combination of ~~the~~	537
methods ~~listed above~~ to keep human resources functioning at a	547
competitive level.	551

references 609

ENRICHMENT ACTIVITY: Timed Writings

IMPROVE KEYBOARDING: SPEED AND CONTROL

Use the paragraphs to increase your skills. Follow the procedure below.

1. Take two 1' speed writings on each of the three paragraphs; find *gwam* and determine errors on each writing.

2. Take two 1' control writings on each of the three paragraphs. Strive for no more than 2 errors on each 1' writing.

3. Take a 5' writing on the three paragraphs combined; find *gwam;* determine errors.

all letters used | D | 1.8 si | 6.3 awl | 70% hfw

	gwam 1'	5'
With today's automated equipment, more documents are created in	13	3	61
the office than ever before. Most office managers are concerned about	27	5	64
managing the enormous number of documents that flow in and out of their	41	8	67
firms. Many of these documents are essential for a firm's daily opera-	56	11	70
tions. Executives use these important documents to arrive at decisions	70	14	73
that affect the direction of their firm. These decisions are more often	85	17	76
the right ones when they are based on documented information rather than	99	20	79
on intuition.	102	20	79
Because of the usefulness of the documents to executives, many	13	23	82
firms now control documents via a records management program. A few of	27	26	84
the functions of such a program include document retrieval, retention,	41	29	87
protection, and disposition. Each of these functions is essential for	55	31	90
the efficient handling of a firm's documents. How adequately the docu-	70	34	93
ments are managed in a firm is directly related to the quality of the	84	37	96
staff employed in the records management program.	93	39	98
Larger firms will utilize a records management department or cen-	13	42	100
ter to operate the records program. A variety of jobs are available in	27	45	103
such centers for individuals interested in working with records. The	41	47	106
required qualifications will vary by the type of position. A high school	56	50	109
graduate with some training in filing and office procedures may qualify	71	53	112
for a job as a records manager. Duties such as sorting, indexing, fil-	85	56	115
ing, and retrieving documents are performed by the records manager.	98	59	117

gwam 1' | 1 | 2 | 3 | 4 | 5 | 6 | 7 | 8 | 9 | 10 | 11 | 12 | 13 | 14
5' | 1 | | 2 | | 3

1. Three 1' writings on ¶ 1; find *gwam;* circle errors.
2. Practice ¶ 2 in the same way.
3. Two 3' writings on ¶s 1-2 combined; find *gwam;* circle errors.

all letters used | A | 1.5 si | 5.7 awl | 80% hfw

gwam 1' | 3'

Simply stated, self-esteem is the feeling you have about yourself. | 14 | 5
If you feel good about yourself, you are likely to have a high degree of | 28 | 9
self-esteem. If you feel bad about yourself, you are said to have a low | 43 | 14
degree of self-esteem or self-respect. It is important that you have | 57 | 19
the highest possible level of self-esteem because it influences the per- | 71 | 24
sonality you exhibit and the quality of life you will likely experience. | 86 | 29
It is equally important that you realize that you can increase your de- | 100 | 33
gree of self-esteem by knowing more about yourself and your values. | 114 | 38

If you place a high level of importance on achieving a particular | 13 | 42
objective and are unable to attain that objective, you could have a | 27 | 47
problem with self-esteem. One way to keep a high level of self-esteem | 41 | 52
is to think about successful experiences that make you feel good about | 55 | 56
yourself rather than just failures that have a tendency to lower self- | 69 | 61
esteem. Even though you are likely to experience failure at times, it | 83 | 66
is important for your self-esteem that you learn from rather than dwell | 98 | 71
on the negative aspects of your failures. | 106 | 73

gwam 1' | 1 | 2 | 3 | 4 | 5 | 6 | 7 | 8 | 9 | 10 | 11 | 12 | 13 | 14
3' | 1 | | 2 | | 3 | | 4 | | 5

207c ▶ 30
Format/Process Purchase Requisitions

LP pp. 171-173

Document 1
Purchase Requisition
Prepare the purchase requisition shown at the right. Follow placement/spacing guides shown in color. Proofread and circle errors.

Documents 2 and 3 are on page 357.

words

DELTA MORTGAGE CORPORATION

PURCHASE REQUISITION

1590 CLIFTON AVENUE, COLUMBUS, OH 43202-1704 (614) 345-0001

┌─ Tab

LM

Deliver to: Juanita Salinas   Requisition No. A25497B | 5

Location: Gateway Two   Date July 23, 19-- | 10

Job No. C-500t   Date Required August 8, 19-- | 14

Quantity	Description	
LM 6	Stackable printer stand	20
6	Underdesk keyboard drawer	26
1	Printer sound shield	30
25	17" binder handles	35
2	Data racks	38
2	Set of casters	41

Approximate center

▲ Set tab 2 spaces from rule

Requisitioned by: Mary Bellino | 44

247a ▶ 5
Conditioning Practice

Key each line twice. Then take two 30″ writings for speed on line 4 and two 30″ writings for control on line 1.

alphabet	1	Many of the duck plaques were just the right size for David's exhibit.
figures	2	Checks 63, 79, 85, 104, and 122 were not included with this statement.
fig/sym	3	They paid $5,896 in taxes ($2,740) and interest ($3,156) on the house.
speed	4	It may be the duty of the island officials to handle the tax problems.

| 1 | 2 | 3 | 4 | 5 | 6 | 7 | 8 | 9 | 10 | 11 | 12 | 13 | 14 |

247b ▶ 45 *Evaluate Formatting Skills: Reports*

Time Schedule
Plan and prepare .... 5′
Timed production .... 30′
Proofread; compute *n-pram* .. 10′

1. Format and key Documents 1, 2, and 3 for 30 minutes. Proofread and correct errors before removing documents from the machine.
2. After time is called (30′), proofread again and circle any uncorrected errors. Compute *n-pram*.

Document 1
Leftbound Report with Internal Citations
Prepare the report given at the right as a leftbound report.

INSERT A
1. Employees work at their own pace.
2. Instruction is individualized. Training can be scheduled when trainees need it rather than when class enrollment is large enough.
3. Employees receive instruction at their desk terminals, making the instruction cost-effective. There is no need to send either employees or instructors to training sites. Travel costs and employee/instructor travel time are eliminated (Tedesco and Mitchell, 1987, 183).

words

TRAINING RESOURCES   4

According to a 1989 projection, American firms will buy   15

more than 29 million copies of software and purchase 5 million   28

additional personal computers togo along with the 40 million   40

that are used in American business offices, Instruction of   60

some type is essential for training office personnel to oper-   72

ate this hardware and software that is being purchased.   86

The instruction is bieng provided in a variety of ways.   99

Tutorials (computer-based training) instructor-directed   111

training, and users' manuals are (frequently) being used to   123

train office personnel to become proficient users of the   136

technology that is a vital part of today's offices.   147

    150

Many software packages come with tutorials. The   160

tutorials provide instruction that allows the learner to   172

master the basics of the software package. Tutorials use   183

prompts that ask questions or give instructions to guide the   195

learner through the material. Some of the advantages of this   208

type of training are listed below.   215

INSERT A   317

Many companies use a variety of instructor-directed ap-   324

proaches to training personnel on hardware and software.   341

These include classroom instruction offered by educational   356

institions and classroom instruction offered by vendors.   371

(continued, p. 422)

Document 2
Purchase Requisition
Prepare the purchase requisition shown at the right. Proofread; circle errors.

Document 3
Purchase Requisition
Repeat the purchase requisition of Document 2, making the following changes. Increase the order for **Glue stick** by 5. Add to the requisition **10 rolls** of **Transparent tape.**

words

DELTA MORTGAGE CORPORATION

▲ ▲ ▲

PURCHASE REQUISITION

1590 CLIFTON AVENUE, COLUMBUS, OH 43202-1704 (614) 345-0001

Deliver to: *Barbara Merkitz*   Requisition No. *R-4975*   5

Location: *Building 5, Room 315*   Date *March 1, 19--*   12

Job No. *9854-BM*   Date Required *March 21, 19--*   16

Quantity	Description	
1	*Secretarial handbook*	21
1	*ZIP Code directory*	25
5	*Glue stick*	28
2	*Flowchart template*	32

Requisitioned by: *Samuel Gillespie*   35

Lesson 208   Language Skills/Purchase Orders

208a ▶ 5
Conditioning Practice

each line twice SS (slowly, then faster); DS between 2-line groups; if time permits, take 1' writings on line 3

alphabet   1   Becky Gazeto is not exempt from equal justice if she violated the law.
figures   2   Eastern College has 5,789 boys and 6,431 girls in 20 different majors.
fig/sym   3   My new house (267-A Westbury Drive) was appraised at $153,400 in 1989.
speed   4   Eight was the divisor for half of the problems Al did on the city bus.

| 1 | 2 | 3 | 4 | 5 | 6 | 7 | 8 | 9 | 10 | 11 | 12 | 13 | 14 |

208b ▶ 10
Language Skills: Word Choice

1. Study the spelling and definitions of each pair of words.
2. Key the **Learn** line, with the number and period, noting the proper use of the often confused words.
3. Key the **Apply** lines, with the number and period, using the word that completes each sentence correctly.

decree (n) an authoritative order; edict

degree (n) a unit division of a temperature scale

deference (n) courteous respect

difference (n) the fact, condition, or degree of being different

Learn   1.   When it is over 80 degrees, we give a decree for air conditioning.
Apply   2.   The principal gave the (decree/degree) to stop running in the corridors.
Apply   3.   My guess is that today's temperature is six (decrees/degrees) higher.

Learn   4.   Joe and Si's age difference may explain the deference Joe gets.
Apply   5.   The (deference/difference) between Jim and Harry is like day and night.
Apply   6.   It was out of (deference/difference) that I opened the door for my guests.

246b (continued)

words

Document 2
Table

Format and key the table at the right on a full sheet. Center column headings; CS: 8.

SPECIAL RESORT ACTIVITIES

May–September

Activity	Date(s)	Coordinator	
Festival of the Stars	May 15–17	J. Dennis Phelps	19 / 29
Mesa Ski Exhibit	May 29	Scott Snell	36
Hot Air Balloon Day	June 15	Marsha Schneider	45
American Jazz Festival	June 28	Carlos Santiago	55
Wildlife Art Exhibit	July 15	Rhea Bosworth	63
Mesa Bicycle Classic	July 29	Sydna Mincher	72
Little Big-Top Circus	August 8	Cha Xang	80
Hang Gliding Contest	August 20	Scott Snell	89
Mesa Golf Classic	September 3–4	Carmen Pascual	98

Document 3
Purchase Order

LP p. 43

Key the purchase order shown at the right with the changes that have been marked.

Document 4
Purchase Order

LP p. 43

Key the purchase order again, making the following changes:

Order only **1 1″** **Changeable Letter Set**. Include 1 **2″** **Changeable Letter Set (B5915)** with the order. The 2″ set sells for **$37.50 each.**

MESA MOUNTAIN RESORT
727 Apache Road
Boulder, CO 80537-5565
(303) 234-5989

PURCHASE ORDER

Purchase Order No.: B3617 — 1

MONTOYA OFFICE SUPPLY
5889 WILLOUGHBY AVENUE
LOS ANGELES CA   90038-6222

Date: March 18, 19-- — 9 / 13

Terms: 2/10, n/30 — 21

Shipped Via: Bel Aire Freight — 24

Quantity	Description/Stock Number	Price		Per	Total		
1	Diskette Tray Cabinet (Q2813) *(Q3604)*	~~279~~ 239	98 46	ea	~~279~~ 239	98 46	34
1	Desktop Organizer (P3709)	86	95	ea	86	95	43
2	Changeable Letter Board (B5613)	79	49	ea	158	98	53
2	1" Changeable Letter Set (B4321)	18	50	ea	37	00	64
					~~562~~ 522	~~91~~ 39	65

By _____

**Document 1
Purchase Order**
Prepare the purchase order shown at the right. Follow placement/spacing guides shown in color. Proofread; circle errors.

DELTA MORTGAGE CORPORATION

1590 CLIFTON AVENUE, COLUMBUS, OH 43202-1704 (614) 345-0001

PURCHASE ORDER

words

┌ Tab

WEBSTER'S OFFICE PRODUCTS
4646 WEST BROAD STREET
COLUMBUS OH   43228-1687

Purchase Order No.: AQ-4931 — 2

Date: July 24, 19-- — 10

Terms: 5/10, n/30 — 14 / 21

Shipped Via: Ohio Express — 24

Quantity	Description/Stock Number	Price		Per	Total		
LM 6	Stackable printer stand (F5-16)	49	95	ea	299	70	34
6	Underdesk keyboard drawer (F5-58)	34	98	ea	209	88	44
1	Printer sound shield (F5-50)	199	00	ea	199	00	54
25	17" binder racks (E4-501)	3	95	ea	98	75	63
2	Data racks (E4-502)	195	00	ea	390	00	71
2	Set of casters (E4-519)	30	00	set	60	00	81
	Set tab 1 or 2 spaces from rule				1257	33	83

Approximate center

Tab

Tab

By _____

**Document 2
Purchase Order**
Prepare the purchase order as you did in Document 1. Add the figures in the total column and enter the total under the column.

**Document 3
Purchase Order**
Rekey the purchase order of Document 2, making the following changes.

Increase the order for **Glue stick** by 5 (use the same unit price but calculate a new total). Add to the order **10 rolls** of **Transparent tape** (Stock no. **A8-176**) at **$1.47 per roll.** Compute new totals as needed.

DELTA MORTGAGE CORPORATION

1590 CLIFTON AVENUE, COLUMBUS, OH 43202-1704 (614) 345-0001

PURCHASE ORDER

SCHRIBNER'S OFFICE SUPPLIES
281 HAMILTON STREET
HARTFORD CT 06106-2989

Purchase Order No.: AB-1076 — 2

Date: March 2, 19-- — 10

Terms: 2/10, n/30 — 14 / 21

Shipped Via: Air Express — 23

Quantity	Description/Stock Number	Price		Per	Total		
1	Secretarial handbook (B5-46)	10	95	ea	10	95	33
1	ZIP Code directory (B5-478)	5	95	ea	5	95	41
5	Glue stick (C1-175)		89	ea	4	45	48
2	Flowchart template (D2-548)	4	50	ctn	9	00	60

By _____

245b (continued)

Document 3
Simplified Memorandum
plain paper

Key the memorandum shown at the right in simplified format. Date the memo **March 16, 19--**, and send it to **Conrad G. Nelson, Manager.** Use **EQUIPMENT PURCHASE UPDATE** as the subject line. The memo is from **K. Renae Stevens, Purchasing Director.**

Document 4
Simplified Memorandum
plain paper

Rekey Document 3. Add the following as the final paragraph of the memo.

If you are hesitant about postponing a final decision or would like to discuss the situation further, please let me know.

Last week I met with Ms. Karla Sather, Fenton Office Ma- 24

and Mr. Jerome Reynolds, JB Office Products,

chines, to discuss our equipment needs. I also spent part of 46

equipment

last week in Los Angles visiting several vendors to make sure 60

is

that I havent overlooked anything that currently available. 73

The capabilities of some of the equipment are realy un- 84

believable. However, I ~~truly~~ beleive that we should postpone 95

making any final decisions for a few months. Several of the 108

vendor mentioned that they are expecting major break throughs 120

Ms. Sather

to be announced very shortly. ~~Karla~~ also mentioned that she 133

expects a signficant descreased in the cost of the equipment 145

that I am currently considering. 152

Lesson 246 — Evaluate Forms and Table Skills

246a ▶ 5
Conditioning Practice

Key each line twice. Then take two 30″ writings for speed on line 4 and two 30″ writings for control on line 1.

alphabet	1	Quin may reject my idea of leaving two dozen oak trees by the complex.
figures	2	As of July 30, 12,465 copies of the 1987 edition were still available.
fig/sym	3	We received their order (#152-67) amounting to $3,498 on September 20.
speed	4	The eight city officials may sign the forms when they see the auditor.

| 1 | 2 | 3 | 4 | 5 | 6 | 7 | 8 | 9 | 10 | 11 | 12 | 13 | 14 |

246b ▶ 45 Evaluate Formatting Skills: Forms and Tables

Time Schedule
Plan and prepare .... 5′
Timed production .... 30′
Proofread; compute *n-pram* .. 10′

1. Arrange materials for ease of handling (LP p. 43).

2. Format and key Documents 1-4 for 30′. Proofread and correct errors before removing documents from machine.

3. After time is called (30′), proofread again and circle any uncorrected errors. Compute *n-pram*.

Document 1
Table

Format and key the table at the right on a full sheet. Center column headings; leave 6 spaces between columns 1 and 2; leave 4 spaces between columns 2 and 3.

LODGING RATES 3

April 1, 19-- through March 31, 19-- 10

Dates	Traditional	Garden Terrace	
			23
			29
			42
April 1 - May 20	$60.75	$75.75	49
May 21 - September 10	75.75	90.75	55
September 11 - December 10	55.00	70.00	63
December 11 - January 5	68.00	83.00	70
January 6 - February 1	53.50	68.50	77
February 2 - March 31	68.50	93.00	84
			96

Documents 2-4 are on p. 420.

209a ▶ 5
Conditioning Practice

each line twice SS
(slowly, then faster);
DS between 2-line
groups; if time permits,
take 1' writings on line 2

alphabet	1	Biggi excluded a very quick jaunt to the new zoo from my travel plans.
figures	2	You can find answers to the 150-point test on pages 8, 32, 46, and 79.
fig/sym	3	Runner #3019 was first (49 min.) and runner #687 was second (52 min.).
speed	4	The rifleman saw my hand signal to go right at the fork by the shanty.

| 1 | 2 | 3 | 4 | 5 | 6 | 7 | 8 | 9 | 10 | 11 | 12 | 13 | 14 |

209b ▶ 15 Improve
Tabulating Technique

LL: 70 spaces

1. Clear tab stops.

2. Starting at the left margin, set 4 tab stops 11 spaces apart.

3. Key the copy once, tabulating from column to column.

4. Take as many 2' writings as time permits to improve tabulating skills.

gwam 2'

$102.93	84%	#7560	(100)	$22.77	3	28
$609.87	79%	#8096	(806)	$76.80	6	31
$534.12	43%	#5124	(341)	$42.51	9	34
$394.01	38%	#9183	(471)	$72.03	12	37
$389.21	76%	#1602	(278)	$40.51	16	40
$354.12	24%	#3476	(208)	$96.87	19	43
$268.40	19%	#7351	(862)	$53.79	22	47
$145.67	29%	#6708	(541)	$27.03	25	50

209c ▶ 30
Format/Process Invoices

LP pp. 177-179

Document 1
Invoice
Prepare the invoice shown at the right. Follow placement/spacing guides shown in color. Proofread; circle errors.

words

PARK'S BUSINESS PRODUCTS
5704 Hollis Street Oakland, CA 94608-2514 (415) 227-9009

INVOICE

Tab ➞ CENTURY PRODUCTIONS INC
1661 EAST 32D STREET
LONG BEACH CA 90807-5291

Date: October 21, 19--   8
Customer
Order No.: AP-1659-T   13
                               20

Terms	Shipped Via	Our Order No.	Date Shipped	
6/10, n/30	Safeway Shipping, Inc.	2-44-7A	10/20/--	30

Quantity	Description/Stock No.	Unit Price	Amount	
1	Electronic Postal Scale {PS2PR}	299 95	299 95	40
2	Electric Sharpener {KP33-BG}	49 95	99 90	49
5	Double Desk Set {N1-5201}	57 00	285 00	57
24	Drafting Pencil {N5-5007}	61	14 64	66
500	Envelopes 9" x 12" {P2-S28}	07	35 00	76
			DS	
			734 49	77
	Sales Tax {6%}	Tab	44 07	83
			DS	
			778 56	84

— Set tab 1 or 2 spaces from rule
Approximate center
— Indent 3 spaces
Tab

Documents 2 and 3 are on page 360.

245a ▶ 5
Conditioning Practice

Key each line twice. Then take two 30″ writings for speed on line 4 and two 30″ writings for control on line 1.

alphabet	1	Greg fixed the four new pairs of jumper cables very quickly for Shizu.
figures	2	There were 28 computer graphs and 17 tables between pages 309 and 456.
fig/sym	3	The next two flights (#308 & #796) leave Chicago at 1:45 and 2:00 p.m.
speed	4	The city may pay Eva and me to work on the problem of the title forms.

| 1 | 2 | 3 | 4 | 5 | 6 | 7 | 8 | 9 | 10 | 11 | 12 | 13 | 14 |

245b ▶ 45
Evaluate Formatting Skills: Letters and Memorandums

Time Schedule

Plan and prepare .... 5′
Timed production .... 30′
Proofread; compute *n-pram* .. 10′

1. Arrange materials for ease of handling (LP pp. 39-41).

2. Format and key Documents 1-4 for 30′. Proofread and correct errors before removing documents from machine.

3. After time is called (30′), proofread again and circle any uncorrected errors. Compute *n-pram*.

Note: To find *n-pram* (net production rate per minute), deduct 15 words for each uncorrected error; divide remainder by 30 (time).

Document 1
Letter
LP p. 39

Format in block style with mixed punctuation the letter shown at the right.

Document 2
Letter
LP p. 41

Format in block style with open punctuation the letter shown at the right.

Address letter to
Ms. Kathleen C. Travis
729 Manhattan Drive
Huntington Beach, CA 92647-4248
Date the letter **March 16, 19--**

Closing lines:
Sincerely

Jonathan W. Sutter
Customer Relations

Documents 3 and 4 are on p. 419.

words

March 15, 19-- Mr. Ross A. Medina 5410 Peppermint Drive San Jose, CA   14
95148-3167 Dear Mr. Medina: 19

We are pleased to provide you with more information about Mesa Mountain   34
Resort. Mesa Mountain is a great place to spend time relaxing and enjoying   49
the great outdoors at affordable prices.   57

Guests at our resort can choose from a variety of activities. Sailing, hiking,   73
fishing, golfing, and rafting are just a few of the many activities that are   89
available for guest participation on a daily basis. The mountain water slide,   105
hot air balloon rides, nature trails, and an abundance of outdoor beauty bring   120
our guests back year after year.   127

Two special resort activities are planned for each month of the summer.   142
These activities range from the jazz festival to the hang gliding contest. A   157
complete listing along with the dates of the activities is enclosed.   171

We are confident that if you come to Mesa Mountain Resort, you will make it a   187
part of your yearly vacation plans. To make reservations, call 1-800-234-6891.   203

Sincerely, Ms. Michelle C. Slattery Director of Sales and Marketing xx   217
Enclosures   219/**232**

---

opening lines 21

    Thank you for bringing to our attention the problems you   33
encountered *when checking out on march 5*. The situation has *been* reviewed with the desk clerk,   52
and we are *confident* ~~sure~~ that he will use more tact *in dealing with our guests* in the future.   70

    The error with your bill was ours. Your reservation was   81
for our "Traditional" room; we *accomodated* ~~gave~~ you *with* our "Garden Terrace" room.   98
Unfortunately, we also charged you for the "Garden Terrace" *room*   111
check is enclosed that reflects the difference in cost *between the two rooms*.   127

    We appreciate your providing us with this information.   138
Only through customer feedback ~~that~~ we can improve the *quality of* ser-   151
vice we offer our guests.   157

closing lines 169/**183**

209c (continued)

Document 2
Invoice
Prepare the invoice shown at the right. Proofread; circle errors.

Document 3
Invoice
Reformat the invoice of Document 2, making these changes.

Change the quantity of **Color Film ASA 1000** from 24 to **18**, **Color Film ASA 400** from 12 to **24**, and drop the Black and White Film from the invoice. Compute new extensions, totals, and taxes as needed.

		words
PARK'S BUSINESS PRODUCTS	INVOICE	
5704 Hollis Street Oakland, CA 94608-2514 (415) 227-9009		

| MARY WELLS STUDIO
20497 TILLMAN AVENUE
LONG BEACH CA 90746-3515 | Date: November 5, 19-- | 7 |
| | Customer Order No.: MW-101-N | 11 / 18 |

Terms	Shipped Via	Our Order No.	Date Shipped	
10/10, n/30	Overland Transit	2-66-1A	11/5/--	27

Quantity	Description/Stock No.	Unit Price	Amount	
2	Prefix Dater {R1-16P}	14 95	29 90	35
1	Numbering Machine {RL-RN57}	44 95	44 95	44
12	Black and White Film {MS-159}	3 14	37 68	52
24	Color Film ASA 1000 {MS-156}	6 11	146 64	61
12	Color Film ASA 400 {MS-155}	5 37	64 44	71
			323 61	73
	Sales Tax {6%}		19 42	79
			343 03	80

Lesson 210   Review: Forms Processing

210a ▶ 5
Conditioning Practice

each line twice SS (slowly, then faster); DS between 2-line groups; if time permits, take 1′ writings on line 3

alphabet	1	Vicki expects to question dozens of boys and girls for the major show.
figures	2	Al's agent needs to sell 43 tables, 59 beds, 187 chairs, and 206 rugs.
fig/sym	3	The stopwatch (#34-908) and pedometer (#21-756) are on sale this week.
speed	4	My neighbor and the girl are to visit an ancient chapel on the island.

| 1 | 2 | 3 | 4 | 5 | 6 | 7 | 8 | 9 | 10 | 11 | 12 | 13 | 14 |

210b ▶ 45 Build Sustained Document Processing Skill: Forms

Time Schedule

Plan and prepare	5′
Timed production	30′
Proofread; circle errors	7′
Compute n-pram	3′

1. Make a list of documents to be formatted/processed:

page 357, 207c, Document 2
page 358, 208c, Document 2
page 360, 209c, Document 2
page 360, 209c, Document 3

2. Arrange supplies and LP pp. 179-183.

3. When directed to begin, key for 30′ from the list of documents, correcting all errors neatly. Proof-

read before removing the documents from the machine.

4. Compute n-pram for the 30′ period.

5. Turn in documents in the order listed in Step 1.

243c ▶ 30 *Prepare For Evaluation: Letters, Memos, and Tables*

Prepare a list of the problems at the right.

Prepare for the production measurement of letters, memos, and tables by keying the problems from your list. Use plain sheets for all documents.

Letter: p. 302, 172c, Document 1
Memo: p. 302, 172c, Document 3
Table: p. 352, 204c, Table 1
Table: p. 350, 203d, Table 1

Lesson 244	Prepare for Evaluation: Forms and Reports

244a ▶ 5 *Conditioning Practice*

Key each line twice; then take two 30" writings for *speed* on line 4 and two 30" writings for *control* on line 1.

alphabet 1 Maria Jackson will have the best grade for the six philosophy quizzes.

figures 2 Is the Little Rock, AR, ZIP Code I requested 72205-3674 or 72205-1698?

fig/sym 3 The loan (#270-38) was made on 12/14/89 for $68,000 at a rate of 9.5%.

speed 4 Both of them may go with me to the lake to do the work on the chapels.

| 1 | 2 | 3 | 4 | 5 | 6 | 7 | 8 | 9 | 10 | 11 | 12 | 13 | 14 |

244b ▶ 15 *Evaluate Language Skills Application*

1. Key each sentence, with the number and period, making the needed corrections. DS between sentences.

2. After keying all sentences, proofread each one. Mark any correction that still needs to be made.

1. Their home that is located at Ten Silver Lake Road are for sail.

2. The number of applicants recieving financial aid have increased.

3. The finance committee members is working on that recomendation

4. Everyone in the class are making arrangments to attend the play.

5. The balence do on their account is three hundred dollars.

6. Christina was born on January ten 1970 in brooklyn New York.

7. Do you no if she has scheduled a concert for anaheim california?

8. Is Dr. Van Burens' ph.d in chemistry from harvard or columbia?

9. Mr. and mrs. j. b. West live at 1 devney drive near 5th Avenue.

10. The center on our team is six ft. two in. tall and weighs 200 lbs.

11. They took the cold wet dog to the washington humane association.

12. Can you accomodate sixteen people for dinner on Thursday, May 22nd?

13. The plain from Los Angeles will arrive at approximately eleven p.m.

14. There corperate loan with First national bank of Miami was approved.

15. The Friday activitys were arranged too celebrate independence day.

16. Its our commitment to establish a Monument at 23 Lexington Avenue.

17. If you right to senator Swindell be sure to include your resume.

18. Each year at regestration the coach said "This mite be the year."

19. Rebecca has all ready past the exam on chapter 8, pages 316-359.

20. The mens' supervisers will meet inside if the whether is still bad.

244c ▶ 30 *Prepare for Evaluation: Forms and Reports*

Prepare a list of the problems at the right.

Prepare for the production measurement of forms and reports by keying the problems from your list.

Forms: p. 358, 208c, Document 1, LP p. 37
Report: p. 283, 159c, Document 3, plain paper
Report: p. 284, 160b, Document 1, plain paper

211a ▶ 5
Conditioning Practice

each line twice SS (slowly, then faster); DS between 2-line groups; if time permits, take 1' writings on line 2

alphabet	1	Fog is a major hazard for the very swift bird Kal acquired in Phoenix.
figures	2	She wrote checks 398-429 in May, 430-457 in June, and 458-461 in July.
fig/sym	3	The next junior/senior prom can be at 7:35-10:50 p.m. on 4/29 or 6/18.
speed	4	The man got six bowls, eight forks, and a few big pans for the social.

| 1 | 2 | 3 | 4 | 5 | 6 | 7 | 8 | 9 | 10 | 11 | 12 | 13 | 14 |

211b ▶ 45 *Measure Document Production Skill: Forms*

Time Schedule
Plan and prepare .... 5'
Timed production .... 30'
Proofread; circle errors .... 7'
Compute *n-pram* .... 3'

1. Arrange supplies and LP pp. 183-187.

2. When directed to begin, key for 30' from the following documents, correcting all errors neatly. Proofread before removing the documents from the machine.

3. Compute *n-pram* for the 30' writing.

4. Turn in all documents completed in the order shown.

Document 1
Purchase Requisition

words

DELTA MORTGAGE CORPORATION

PURCHASE REQUISITION

1590 CLIFTON AVENUE, COLUMBUS, OH 43202-1704 (614) 345-0001

Deliver to: *Janet McClellan* — 5

Location: *Suite 355* — 10

Job No. *A-636* — 14

Requisition No. *A-1547-J*

Date *March 2, 19--*

Date Required *March 25, 19--*

Quantity	Description	
1	Executive Pedestal Desk	19
1	Walnut Credenza	23
1	Executive Swivel Tilt Chair	29
3	Guest Conference Chair	34
2	25" Deep File Cabinet	39

Requisitioned by: *Heather Bowles* — 41

Documents 2-4 are on page 362.

14:36

Evaluation

Evaluation Goals

1. To evaluate straight-copy speed and accuracy.
2. To improve skill in formatting and keying letters, memos, tables, reports, and purchase orders.
3. To evaluate skill in formatting and keying letters, memos, tables, reports, and purchase orders.
4. To evaluate language skills.

Format Guides

1. Paper guide at *0* (for typewriters).
2. LL: 70 spaces for drills and language skills activities; as required by document formats.
3. LS: SS for drills and language skills activities unless otherwise instructed; as required by document formats.
4. PI: 5 spaces, when appropriate.

Lesson 243	Prepare for Evaluation: Letters, Memorandums, and Tables

243a ▶ 5
Conditioning Practice

Key each line twice. Then take two 30″ writings for speed on line 4 and two 30″ writings for control on line 1.

alphabet	1	Maxine was amazed frequently by the project check arriving so quickly.
figures	2	The combined population of the same 23 towns in 1989 was only 146,750.
double letters	3	The litter of kittens with the funny feet put the boys in a good mood.
speed	4	With their profit they may pay for an emblem of the shantytown chapel.

| 1 | 2 | 3 | 4 | 5 | 6 | 7 | 8 | 9 | 10 | 11 | 12 | 13 | 14 |

243b ▶ 15 Evaluate Straight-Copy Skill

Take two 5′ writings; record *gwam* and errors on the better writing.

all letters used | A | 1.5 si | 5.7 awl | 80% hfw

	gwam 3′	5′
Information shown in a graphic form has always been a vital part of	5	3	60
the communication process--whether or not the message presented is in an	9	6	62
oral or written form. Most of the graphics used in the past were created	14	9	65
by a media or art center. Today, because of the computer, however, more	19	12	68
data than ever is being shown with the use of graphics. Computers using	24	14	71
various software programs make it quite easy to prepare graphic data to	29	17	74
enhance the process of communicating.	31	19	76
Graphics are used for a variety of reasons. One of the major reasons	36	21	78
sons is that graphics can help the writer or speaker send a clear and a	41	24	81
complete message using as few words as possible. Some have said that	45	27	84
a picture is worth a thousand words. Graphics also allow the sender to	50	30	87
emphasize specific parts of the message as well as to add more interest	55	33	90
to the message. Recent progress in computer technology has greatly en-	59	36	93
hanced the graphic-producing abilities of many business firms.	64	38	95
Many different types of graphics can be used to help present data.	68	41	98
A few common types of graphics that computers are now able to generate	73	44	101
include maps, bar graphs, and pie charts. The capabilities of desktop	78	47	103
publishing further enhance the visuals that can be used to present all	82	49	106
kinds of information. In the future, as graphics become an expected	87	52	109
part of information, they will be sure to play an even greater role in	92	55	112
the exchange of ideas in the business world.	95	57	114

gwam 3′ | 1 | 2 | 3 | 4 | 5
5′ | 1 | 2 | 3

**Document 2
Purchase Order**

							words

DELTA MORTGAGE CORPORATION

▲ ▲ ▲

1590 CLIFTON AVENUE, COLUMBUS, OH 43202-1704 (614) 345-0001

PURCHASE ORDER

SIMMON'S OFFICE FURNITURE
43 CORTLAND STREET
DETROIT MI 48203-3598

Purchase Order No.: *T-4587-2* — 2
Date: *March 5, 19--* — 10, 14
Terms: *10/30, n/90* — 21
Shipped Via: *Wilson Shipping* — 24

Quantity	Description/Stock Number	Price	Per	Total	words
1	Executive Pedestal Desk (E4-1230)	390 00	ea	390 00	34
1	Walnut Credenza (E4-1230-1)	375 00	ea	375 00	44
1	Executive Swivel Tilt Chair (E4-1330)	430 00	ea	430 00	55
3	Guest Conference Chair (E4-1420)	286 00	ea	858 00	66
2	25" Deep File Cabinet (F1-2125)	151 00	ea	302 00	77
				2355 00	79

By _____

**Document 3
Invoice**

PARK'S BUSINESS PRODUCTS
5704 Hollis Street   Oakland, CA 94608-2514   (415) 227-9009

INVOICE

WESTERLY MANUFACTURING
7301 FULTON STREET
HOUSTON TX 77022-4498

Date: August 3, 19-- — 8
Customer Order No.: O-6538-T — 11, 18

Terms	Shipped Via	Our Order No.	Date Shipped	words
5/30, n/60	Reliable Transit	LT-5009-Z	8/1/--	27

Quantity	Description/Stock No.	Unit Price	Amount	words
15	Card File {X8-5363}	6 29	94 35	34
1	Literature Rack {T5-LRF56}	184 00	184 00	43
1	Time Card Rack {T5-RRF95}	55 25	55 25	51
10	Multi-Pack File Labels {F1-437}	3 89	38 90	61
50	Interior Folders {F1-384}	13	6 50	70
			379 00	71
	Sales Tax {6%}		22 74	78
			401 74	79

Document 4
Reformat the invoice in Document 3, making these changes.

Change our order number to **LT-5011-Y**. Change the order for **Item F1-437** from 10 to **20** at **$3.59 each**. Make all necessary changes to extensions and totals.

239b-242b (continued)

Documents 13-14
Ruled Forms
LP p. 35

LP p. 35

SANDRA MORENO
Administrative Assistant

I have written in the information on photocopies of the registration forms for the symposium Ms. Jones will be attending. Please key this information on the original forms. *Sm*

Symposium Registration Form
(July 24-26)

Jones — Ann
Last Name — First Name

Midwestern Office Products
Firm/Affiliation

3871 Bridge Avenue
Address

Davenport — IA — 52807-7002
City — State — Zip

(319) 887-2424 — (319) 887-5767
Office Telephone — Home Telephone

Payment Method:

X_ Credit Card ___ Check

Secure Card 6815 0716 10106 — 1/95
Card Name and Number — Expiration Date

_____
Signature

Mail to: International Technology Symposium
510 Gettysburg Court
Washington, DC 20335-2111

Hotel Reservation Form

Jones — Ann
Last Name — First Name

Midwestern Office Products
Firm/Affiliation

3871 Bridge Avenue (319) 887-2424
Address — Phone

Davenport — IA — 52807-7002
City — State — Zip

July 23 — July 26
Arrival Date — Departure Date

Payment Method:
(First night's deposit required to confirm reservation.)

X_ Credit Card ___ Check (to McKinley Inn for $105)

Secure Card 6815 0716 10106 — 1/95
Card Name and Number — Expiration Date

_____
Signature

Mail to: McKinley Inn
5568 Georgia Avenue
Washington, DC 20335-2464

Document 15
Income Statement

SANDRA MORENO
Administrative Assistant

Ms. Koontz needs an income statement for the first quarter for a meeting tomorrow. I called the Accounting Department to get the figures that are marked on the First-Quarter Budgeted Income Statement. Some formatting guides are marked on the copy to assist you as you key the document. *Sm*

1½"

MIDWESTERN OFFICE PRODUCTS
~~Budgeted~~ Income Statement
For Quarter Ending March 31, 19--

QS   2sp   1" RM

1" LM

	$1,125,000	1,234,680
Expected sales revenue		
Deduct ~~expected~~ cost of goods sold	675,000	740,808
Estimated gross margin	$ 450,000	493,872

Deduct ~~estimated~~ expenses controllable
(by department managers):

Sales	$205,000	224,790	
Information Processing	58,000	56,500	
Accounting	47,000	48,550	
Personnel	29,000	339,000	358,190
	28,350		
Margin for non controllable expenses	$ 111,000	135,682

Deduct expenses noncontrollable
(by departments):

Administration	$ 45,000	
Occupancy	25,000	70,000
~~Estimated~~ net income before taxes	$ 41,000	65,682

212a ▶ 5
Conditioning Practice
each line twice SS (slowly, then faster); DS between 2-line groups; if time permits, take 1' writings on line 4

alphabet 1 Cody will acquire six blue jackets to give as door prizes to freshmen.

figures 2 I will fly 3,670 miles in May, 2,980 miles in June, and 1,450 in July.

fig/sym 3 Cookbook prices increased 14% from 7/1/89 to 6/30/90 in 25 bookstores.

speed 4 Claudia, the girl with the rifle, saw six turkeys by the lake at dusk.

| 1 | 2 | 3 | 4 | 5 | 6 | 7 | 8 | 9 | 10 | 11 | 12 | 13 | 14 |

212b ▶ 10 *Improve Keyboarding Skill*

1. Key a 1' timed writing on each ¶.

2. Key a 5' timed writing on ¶s 1-2 combined; find *gwam*; circle errors.

all letters used A 1.5 si 5.7 awl 80% hfw

	gwam 1'	5'
Efficiency is one word that you probably have heard repeatedly.	13	3	46
At home your parents have probably told you to use your time in an effi-	27	5	49
cient manner so you can study, do your household chores, and still have	42	8	52
time to play or relax. Most of your teachers have probably encouraged	56	11	55
you to arrange your work area in an orderly manner so you can utilize	70	14	58
your study time efficiently. If you have a part-time job, your super-	84	17	60
visor has likely stressed the importance of being efficient when com-	98	20	63
pleting the tasks assigned to you.	105	21	65

Efficiency is one word that you probably have heard repeatedly. At home your parents have probably told you to use your time in an efficient manner so you can study, do your household chores, and still have time to play or relax. Most of your teachers have probably encouraged you to arrange your work area in an orderly manner so you can utilize your study time efficiently. If you have a part-time job, your supervisor has likely stressed the importance of being efficient when completing the tasks assigned to you.

Efficiency is a quality that you can improve. You can improve it by doing required tasks with a minimum waste of time and effort. Most people improve efficiency by keeping their work area in order so supplies can be easily retrieved when needed. Another way to improve it is to try to be accurate. By being accurate, you will not need to repeat work because of undetected errors. Also, you will be more efficient if you don't think endlessly before making a decision. Rather, get the facts you need, consider all the possibilities, and then make a decision.

	gwam 1' / 5'
Efficiency is a quality that you can improve. You can improve it	13 24 67
by doing required tasks with a minimum waste of time and effort. Most	27 26 70
people improve efficiency by keeping their work area in order so sup-	41 29 73
plies can be easily retrieved when needed. Another way to improve it is	56 32 76
to try to be accurate. By being accurate, you will not need to repeat	70 35 79
work because of undetected errors. Also, you will be more efficient if	84 38 81
you don't think endlessly before making a decision. Rather, get the	98 41 84
facts you need, consider all the possibilities, and then make a decision.	113 44 87

gwam 1' | 1 | 2 | 3 | 4 | 5 | 6 | 7 | 8 | 9 | 10 | 11 | 12 | 13 | 14 |
5' | 1 | 2 | 3 |

212c ▶ 35
Prepare for a Simulation

In the simulation in Unit 50, you will process a variety of documents similar to those you have done during the school term.

1. List the page numbers below and review the Formatting Guides for

Letters: pp. 275 and 318
Memos & News Releases: p. 325
Reports: p. 281
Tables: p. 288

2. Prepare a list of the documents at the right. From this list,

choose and practice selected documents before you start Unit 50.

List of Documents
Letter (plain paper)
  p. 276, 155b, Letter 2
Memo (plain paper)
  p. 332, 192b, Document 1

News Release (plain paper)
  p. 330, 190b, News Release 1
Report (plain paper)
  p. 284, 160b, Document 1
Tables (plain paper)
  p. 292, 165c, Table 4
  p. 349, 202c, Table 2

Document 12 Report

SANDRA MORENO
Administrative
Assistant

Here is a rough-draft document with the highlights of the speech Ms. Koontz has prepared for the July 15 annual meeting of the sales representatives. She would like it keyed as a topbound manuscript with footnotes for distribution after the presentation. Use **REMARKS BY PRESIDENT SARA KOONTZ** for the main heading and **19-- Annual Sales Representatives Meeting** for the secondary heading.

Sm

Insert A

1. In every sale, even at the individual consumer level, more decision makers are involved.
2. The time needed to close a sale has increased dramatically.
3. Where before customers used to accept "generic" solutions and products, now they are demanding specific, "custom-made" solutions.
4. Customers are now looking for a different, higher-level, longer-term relationship with the salespeople and the companies with which they deal.[1]

Insert B

1. Recruiting top salespeople.
2. Ability to keep top salespeople.
3. Quality of training.
4. Opening accounts.
5. Holding new accounts.
6. Product/technical knowledge.
7. Reputation among customers.[2]

Footnote Information

[1]Larry Wilson, Changing the Game: The New Way to Sell (New York: Simon and Schuster, Inc., 1987), pp. 21-22.

[2]"America's Best Sales Forces," Sales & Marketing Management, June 1989, p. 34.

[3]Ibid., pp. 39-45.

I have two objectives ~~that I have~~ for this year's ~~annual~~ sales meeting. First, I would like to recieve recommendations from you on changes that need to be made to increase sales and how management can assist with the proposed changes. Second, I would like your assistance in developing a sales philosophy for Midwestern Office Products.

Major Changes in Selling

There are major shifts taking place in the field of sales. According to Wilson, these changes included the following.

Insert A

During your afternoon meetings consider these changes and the implications they have for Midwestern Office Products sales strategies. If your discussion brings out areas where changes are needed make recommendations along with justification ~~reasons~~ for the changes. Management ~~We~~ will consider these recommendations as plans are made to enhance the sales efforts.

Sales Philosophy

<u>Sales & Marketing Management</u> recently conducted a survey with participants from various industries. The participants were asked to rate the top 10 companies within their own industries according to the companies' efectiveness in these 7 sales functions ~~areas~~.

Insert B

Each of the companies that ranked number one in its area of specialization had a strong sales philosophy as the basis for its success. Slogans that capsulize the sales philosophies of a few of these succesful companies are listed below to help generate discussion on an appropriate sales philosophy for Midwestern ~~Office products~~.

<u>Caterpillar</u>. "Give the customer something that he will be able to make money with."
<u>International Business Machines</u>. "Providing information systems technology--hardware, software, and services--to enable our customers to be successful in whatever business they are in."
<u>Xerox Corporation</u>. "To develop a sales force that uses quality tools, understands customer requirements, and can provide total solutions to all customer requirements."[3]

Clearview Manor
(A Document Processing Simulation)

Learning Goals

1. To apply previously learned keyboarding, formatting, and language knowledge and skills at levels expected of a document processor in an entry-level position.

2. To produce in usable form a variety of business documents within a reasonable time when given minimal directions and supervision.

Documents Processed

1. Modified Block Letters
2. Simplified Memo
3. Tables
4. Leftbound and Unbound Reports
5. Business Forms
6. News Release

CLEARVIEW MANOR: A DOCUMENT PROCESSING SIMULATION

Before you begin processing the documents in this simulation, read carefully the information at the right.

Make notes of any formatting guides that you think will save time during the completion of the documents.

Daily Work Plan
Conditioning practice .... 5'
Document processing .... 45'

Work Assignment

You have just been employed as a Document Processor I in the Conference Center of Clearview Manor. Located in the Pocono Mountains in Pennsylvania, Clearview Manor is a well-known resort/conference center with outstanding meeting, exhibit, and recreational facilities.

The primary functions of the Conference Center staff are to

1. Promote the conference center as a place where businesses and professional associations can hold conferences, seminars, etc.
2. Assist clients in designing event activities to take full advantage of the facilities.
3. Work closely with clients during the event to ensure that their needs are met.

The Conference Center director, Ms. Helen T. Caldwell, is ultimately responsible for all functions of the center. The following people report to her. The marketing manager, Mr. Thomas R. Quinnones, is responsible for securing clients for the conference center. The operations manager, Ms. Anne Wells-Baker, works with clients during events. The catering manager, Mr. Bill Timbly, is responsible for all food and beverages served during events.

Your supervisor is Mr. Quinnones, the marketing manager. Most of the work he gives you will be in handwritten or draft form. Information about each document you process should be recorded on the Document Processing Log on LP p. 191, or the one provided by your supervisor.

Follow these procedures in completing the Document Processing Log sheet. In the **Code** column, record the textbook page number, followed by a period and the document number--for example, **p365.1**. In the **Originator** column, enter the name of the person who originated the document and his or her department--for example, **Quinnones/Marketing**. Indicate the type of document in the **Document** column: form, letter, memo, etc. Use the codes listed on the log sheet to indicate the type of source copy in the **Input** column.

In the **Time In** column, record the exact starting time; when the document is complete or when work is interrupted for more than 10', record the exact ending time in the **Time Out** column. (Incomplete documents that are "logged out" must be "logged in" again when processing resumes.) Determine the time required (in minutes) to process each document (**Time** column). Count each line regardless of length; enter the number in the **Lines** column.

The following excerpts from the Document Processing Manual should be helpful to you in formatting and processing documents. You may also rely on other desk resources such as *Century 21 Keyboarding, Formatting, and Document Processing,* Fifth Edition.

Excerpts from CLEARVIEW MANOR DOCUMENT PROCESSING MANUAL

Interoffice correspondence is processed in simplified memorandum format on plain paper. Final copies of letters are prepared on Clearview Manor letterhead; draft copies are done on plain paper. The preferred letter format is modified block with blocked paragraphs and open punctuation. All correspondence is keyed on a 6½" line (SM: 1"); use the current date. You are to supply your reference initials and notations for any copies, attachments, or enclosures.

Tables are keyed DS and centered vertically and horizontally on plain full sheets. CS: an even number of spaces.

Reports are prepared on plain paper. Use leftbound format unless otherwise specified. Footnotes are used for references and explanatory notes.

News releases are prepared on letterhead and are formatted as shown in Unit 44, *Century 21 Keyboarding, Formatting, and Document Processing,* Fifth Edition.

Proofread and correct each document carefully before you begin a new one. Check keyed numbers with the numbers in the source document. Include proofreading and correction time as part of the time you spend completing a document before you record the ending time on your log sheet.

Document 6
Agenda

SANDRA MORENO
Administrative
Assistant

Prepare the attached
agenda for the August
Board of Directors
meeting. *Sm*

Documents 7-8
Address Cards LP p. 35

SANDRA MORENO
Administrative
Assistant

Ms. Koontz would like ad-
dress cards prepared
from the attached busi-
ness cards. *Sm*

Documents 9-11
Simplified Memorandums

SANDRA MORENO
Administrative
Assistant

Three members of the
sales staff exceeded last
year's first-quarter hardware sales by more than
five percent. **Ms. Koontz**
would like the attached
memorandum sent to

Eva Lewis (17.4%)
Kerry Munson (7.5%)
Dave Bromberg (7.3%)

Date the memo **June 12**;
use **FIRST-QUARTER
SALES** for the subject
line; use the figures in
parentheses to complete
the memorandum; correct
any unmarked errors you
may find and any keying
errors you may make.
Sm

DS {
AGENDA
Board of Directors Meeting
August 1, 19--

1.   Opening Remarks . . . .   Sara C. Koontz, President

2.   ∧Proposed Facilities Expansion . . . . .   Ann M. Jones, Vice∧President #

3.   Compensation Program . . . . .   Ann M. Jones

4.   Report on Sales Rep Meeting . .   Sydna T.∧Espinoza, Sales #

5.   Second∧Quarter Earnings . . . .   Sara C. Koontz

6.   Adjournment

3   Learning Center Justification . .   T.∧M. Chaney, Sales Manager #

FIRST NATIONAL BANK

Miss Jennifer S. Alexander
Executive Vice President

3526 East 15th Street
Davenport, IA 52803-5522
(319) 632-4477

Fenton & Collinsworth Architects
200 Iowa Street
Davenport, IA 52801-7317

Mr. Richard A. Collinsworth, AIA

(319) 721-7710

Congratulations∧ (first name)! I just recieved the

first-quarter sales repot∧ r ∧from Thomas Channey. Your 19--

sales for that quarter have increased by (percentage)

over sales∧s for the same quarter (fo) last year.

∧Your efforts have helped us surpass the goal we set

for∧ hardware company sales for last quarter. Overall, there

was∧a 5.5% increase during that period. When the

sales∧ figures for made by the new sale∧s representative are in-

cluded with the figures, the company h∧sows a 13.5%

increase. If sales continue at this rate we will

easily accede the 11% projected growth rate⊙

for the year∧

213a-217a ▶ 5 *(daily)*

Conditioning Practice

Key the lines as many times as you can in 5' at the beginning of each work session during the simulation.

alphabet	1	I will need a pretty gift box for the quartz clock I have to send Jim.
figures	2	A school received 8,032 applications for 4,675 freshmen spots in 1989.
fig/sym	3	Jan said, "Buy Model #3746 or #1098 at a 25% discount at Frey & Sons."
speed	4	Diane and my busy neighbor may dismantle the shanty on the big island.

| 1 | 2 | 3 | 4 | 5 | 6 | 7 | 8 | 9 | 10 | 11 | 12 | 13 | 14 |

213b-217b ▶ 45 *(daily)*

A Document Processing Simulation

Work Assignment: As you complete each document in this simulation, record the information required on the Document Processing Log on LP p. 191 (or use one that your supervisor has provided).

Document 1
Letter

Mr. Quinnones: Here is a draft of a letter we can send to people who request information about our facilities. Prepare a formatted copy on plain paper so I can review it again. Use today's date, the name and business address given below, an appropriate salutation and complimentary close, and my name and title.

Mrs. Susan L. Kellog
M. S. Kuga Company
620 Harvey Avenue
Pontiac, MI 48053-2913

Document 2
Memo

Mr. Quinnones: Process this memo from me to **Ms. Caldwell.** Use her full name and title and supply all other parts of the memo.

Thank you for inquiring about holding a conference at Clearview Manor. Enclosed is a packet of information which describes the meeting, exhibit hall, resort, and recreational facilities.

Clearview Manor Conference Center is well equipped with state-of-the-art audiovisual and videotaping technology, complete computer compatibility, excellent food service, and a professional staff to provide needed assistance and service.

Please review the packet. If you need additional information about the facilities or want to discuss available dates, please call or write me.

During the past few months, it has become apparent to me and to others who have contact with prospective clients that the brochure we use to describe the Conference Center must be revised. This need is evident because we are getting numerous questions about the center's capability to handle groups planning to do extensive videotaping or use computers in a classroom setting.

I would like to have your approval to revise the brochure to include information about these and other features missing from the present brochure and then seek prices to print the revised brochure in four colors.

We will not need to pay a professional typesetter because we will be able to format the copy using the new desktop publishing software that will be installed in the very near future.

365

Letter File for Employees Quitting or Retiring

Letter 4:

Mrs. Janet A. Garrison
1701 Kruse Avenue
Davenport, IA 52804-3553

Paragraphs: B2, M, E2
Years: **15**
Department: **Information Processing Center**

Sm

B1 I am sorry to hear that you will be leaving Midwestern Office Products. We sincerely appreciate your efforts on behalf of the company during the past (number) **years**.

B2 It seems impossible that you are retiring. The years do have a way of quickly passing. If one considers the status of Midwestern Office Products (number) **years** ago and where it is today, it is easy to recognize that time has passed swiftly.

M You have made significant contributions to the (name of department) **and** to the overall success of Midwestern. Because of talented people like you, our firm has become one of the leaders in serving the technology needs of organizations in this area. Your effort in helping us attain this leadership status is genuinely appreciated.

E1 Best wishes in your future professional endeavors.

E2 Best wishes in your future personal endeavors.

Document 5
Itinerary

SANDRA MORENO
Administrative
Assistant

Prepare the itinerary in final form for Ms. Jones.

Sm

```
                        ITINERARY
                      Ann M. Jones
            International Technology Symposium
                          QS
July 23

3:15 p.m.          Depart Davenport on Atlantic Airlines--Flight
                   #618 for Washington D.C.

6:05 p.m.          Arrive Washington D. C.   Accomodations at
                   McKinley Inn, 4568 Georgia Avenue.

July 24
7:00 a.m.          Breakfast with Martin Johnson at hotel.
8:00 a.m.          International technology symposium, meetings
                   until 4:00 p.m.

5:30 p.m.          Dinner with Chi Xang at Capitol Hilton.

July 25

8:00 a.m.          International Technology Symposium, meetings
                   until 2:00 p.m.

3:00 p.m.          Meeting with Marshall Sneed.

7:30 p.m.          John F. Kennedy Center for the Performing Arts
July 26            performance of the Washington Opera.

8:30 a.m.          Depart Washington D.C. on Atlantic Air Lines--
              SS   Flight #482 for Davenport.

10:25 a.m.         Arrive Davenport.
```

Document 3
Table

Mr. Quinnones: Key this table of room sizes. We will use the information in this format until the new brochure is printed, if it is approved.

CLEARVIEW MANOR
CONFERENCE CENTER ROOM SIZES
(Ceiling Height is 10')

Areas	Dimensions L X W	Banquet Seating	Theatre Seating	Classroom Seating*
Left Suite	31' x 20'	50	72	48
Center Suite	56' x 54'	250	376	244
Right Suite	31' x 18'	40	60	36
Entrance Suite	28' x 40'	90	130	84
Board Room	26' x 16'	N/A	N/A	18
Exhibit Area	146' x 110'	(Space for 300 exhibitors.) 100		

* Tables: 2' wide, 6' long; upholstered chairs: 22" wide.

Document 4
Letters

LP pp. 193-197

Mr. Quinnones: Send this letter to each of the three people whose business cards are given at the right. The information you need is supplied on each card.

Note: Use these Code numbers: p366.4a, p366.4b, p366.4c.

Wednesday, June 6, 19—

Helen T. Wilde, Ph.D.
Executive Director
(914) 753-2285

Eastern Economic Association
98 Highview Avenue
New Rochelle, NY 10801-5316

Thursday, May 3, 19--

Mrs. Emma T. Zappalo

LANDMARK DEVELOPERS
103 Vine Street
Shamokin, PA 17872-5533

Telephone:
(717) 362-9462

Telecopier:
(717) 391-5555

Monday, May 21, 19--

SCIENTIFIC RESEARCH, INC.

David F. Moore
Sales Manager
(301) 654-9278

500 Gorusch Ave.
Baltimore, MD
21218-3549

Thank you for selecting Clearview Manor for your function scheduled for (day, month, year).

Enclosed are two copies of the contract. After reviewing the contract, sign one copy and return it to me. Keep the other copy for your records. You must return the signed contract within ten days to guarantee the dates and facilities.

As indicated in the contract, you can choose to revise your food service guarantees up to 48 hours prior to the event. If the Catering Department does not receive a revised guarantee from you, the information in the contract will be used.

If I can be of further assistance to you, please call me. Clearview Manor's Operating Manager will call you about three weeks before your function to finalize all the arrangements.

239a-242a ▶ 5 *(daily)*
Conditioning Practice

Each day check to see that the equipment is in good working order by keying the lines at the right at least twice.

alphabet	1	Joaquin and Kay were puzzled over the exact amount of my storage bill.
figures	2	Nevada sent 187 of the 936 entries, Idaho sent 450, and Utah sent 299.
fig/sym	3	Invoice #687 for $2,958.40 was sent to J&K Supply Company on March 13.
speed	4	If I go to the city to see the man with the maps, I may visit the spa.

| 1 | 2 | 3 | 4 | 5 | 6 | 7 | 8 | 9 | 10 | 11 | 12 | 13 | 14 |

239b-242b ▶ 45 *(daily)*
Document Production: Executive Office

Documents 1-4
Modified Block Letters
LP pp. 27-33

SANDRA MORENO
Administrative
Assistant

Ms. Koontz would like letters dated **June 10, 19--**, prepared from the attached boilerplate for the following individuals who have accepted positions or who have terminated employment.

Letter 1:

Mr. Joshua T. Heintz
424 Bluff Drive
Davenport, IA 52802-6112

Paragraphs: **B, M2, E1**

Department: **Information Processing Center**

Letter 2:

Ms. Lea S. Fong
725 East Street
Davenport, IA 52803-2141

Paragraphs: **B, M3, E3**

Department: **Accounting Department**

Letter 3:

Mr. Dennis M. Dupree
858 Glen Place
Davenport, IA 52804-7834

Paragraphs: **B, M1, E1**

Department: **Sales Department**

Letter File for New Employees

B Welcome to Midwestern Office Products! We are pleased that you have chosen to become part of our organization, and we are looking forward to your assistance in helping us achieve our goals and objectives in the years ahead.

M1 You will enjoy working with Thomas Chaney. He has been with the company for 12 years and is highly regarded by his colleagues. Since he was promoted to sales manager five years ago, company sales have grown tremendously. The new sales strategies that he implemented have been very successful.

M2 If you enjoy working with the latest technology, I am certain that you will enjoy being part of Olivia Reinhold's staff. Our Information Processing Center was recently featured in a national office technology magazine and is the envy of many organizations, due to the efforts of Ms. Reinhold and her talented staff.

M3 You will enjoy working with Rhonda Little; she is outstanding. She is one of those rare individuals who possesses people skills as well as technical expertise. She has completely computerized the Accounting Department since being appointed accounting supervisor.

E1 I am confident that your association with us will be rewarding. I am looking forward to visiting with you in person at the next meeting of the (name of the department).

E2 Your association with us will be rewarding. I am looking forward to meeting you the next time I visit the (name of the department).

E3 I am confident that your work in the (name of the department) will be rewarding. I am looking forward to meeting you soon.

Document 4 is on p. 412.

Document 5
Table

Mr. Quinnones: The catering manager has given me these three menu cards. Format all three of them on one full sheet. Use **CLEARVIEW MANOR MENUS** as the main heading and **(Proposed for May through October, 19--)** as the secondary heading. **Breakfast** is to be the 1st column heading; **Luncheon** the 2d; **Dinner** the 3d. Key the numbers after the meals because they will be used to prepare a price list.

Keep the composite menu until I give you the price list to key. When both are completed, fasten them together with the menu on top of the price list.

Breakfast

Scrambled Eggs served with choice of Bacon, Ham, or Sausage -- 1

French Toast served with choice of Bacon, Ham, or Sausage -- 2

Breakfast Steak with Scrambled Eggs -- 3

Corned Beef Hash with Scrambled Eggs -- 4

Eggs Benedict -- 5

Banana
~~Blueberry~~ Pancakes -- 6

Luncheon

Baked Stuffed Chicken Breast with Sauce Poulette -- 1

Marinated London Broil with Deluxe Mushroom Sauce -- 2

Broiled Fillet of Lemon Sole ~~with Lemon Butter~~ -- 3

Open-Faced Prime Rib of Beef Sandwich -- 4

Braised Swiss Steak -- 5

Steak Sandwich -- 6

Dinner

Broiled Breast of Chicken a la Kiev with Sauce Supreme -- 1

Baked Stuffed Center-Cut Pork Chop with ~~Deluxe~~ Mushroom Sauce -- 2

Broiled Fillet of Boston Scrod -- 3

Broiled ~~Jumbo~~ Shrimp Stuffed with Crabmeat -- 4

Prime Rib of Beef -- 5

Veal Marsala -- 6

Document 6
Report

Mr. Quinnones: Here is a copy of a report that Dr. Richard Simms, a speaker at tomorrow's math teacher conference, faxed to us. He needs us to process a final copy and print 150 copies of it. Dr. Simms has asked that the enumerations be keyed in the hang-indent style. With this exception, use the usual report format. Be sure to record your time on the log so we can bill him for your time.

Note: Dr. Simms does not want us to prepare a reference page for this report.

A NEED TO KNOW METRICS

~~There is a need~~ today, ~~for~~ students need to learn two systems of measurements--the metric system which is used throughout the world and the English or Customary system which is the most often-used system in the United States. /1/ *make this superscript without diagonals if possible.*

Rationale for the Instruction

Instruction relating to the basic components of the metric system must be included in the curriculum of our nation's schools because *all* people must have an understanding of the metric system to function in today's society. Metrics are everywhere! Automobile engines, soft drink containers, ~~medicine,~~ nutrition information listed on food packages, jean *and* sizes, film, and most of the nuts, ~~and~~ bolts, *and screws* ~~which are~~ used to assemble products imported to the United States are examples of common items which are measured in metric units.

(continued, p. 368)

Executive Office

Production Goals

1. To improve your ability to plan and organize work.
2. To improve your ability to make decisions or acceptable judgments.
3. To apply your language skills.
4. To assess the quality of work processed.
5. To integrate knowledge and skills previously acquired.

Documents Processed

1. Letters
2. Itinerary
3. Agenda
4. Address Cards
5. Simplified Memorandums
6. Topbound Report with Footnotes
7. Ruled Forms
8. Income Statement (Table)

MIDWESTERN OFFICE PRODUCTS: EXECUTIVE OFFICE

Before beginning the documents on pages 411-415, read the copy at the right. When planning the assigned documents, refer to the formatting guides given here to refresh your memory about proper formatting and spacing of documents.

Work Assignment

Because a full-time employee has been hired in the Sales Department, you have been reassigned to work in the Executive Office of Midwestern Office Products. Your work will be assigned by Ms. Sandra Moreno, who is the administrative assistant in the Executive Office.

The documents you process during this assignment will be for Ms. Sara C. Koontz, the company president, or for Ms. Ann M. Jones, the administrative vice president. Ms. Moreno will attach written instructions for each of the documents you are to process.

Excerpts from Midwestern's "Guide to Document Formats" that are applicable to the Executive Office are included here. Refer to the Guide as needed when processing the various documents. Use your textbook as a reference when Ms. Moreno's directions and the Guide are not sufficiently detailed.

When necessary, supply missing parts for documents. Use your judgment when specific formatting directions are not given. Correct errors in punctuation, spelling, capitalization, etc. Proofread each document carefully (even if your equipment includes a spell-check program) to produce correctly formatted, error-free documents.

Boilerplate Document

A boilerplate document is a letter or memo created by combining selected paragraphs that previously have been composed and filed (stored). Midwestern uses boilerplate paragraphs for documents created on a recurring basis. Paragraphs are labeled as beginning (B), middle (M), and ending (E) to ensure that the boilerplate documents will "flow" smoothly. Each boilerplate letter consists of a beginning and ending paragraph and, of course, one or more middle paragraphs. The different software packages utilized by the departments have various names for the function used to merge the files of the stored paragraphs. If you are keying on this kind of electronic equip-

ment, consult your user's manual for the software package your department uses to determine the name and operation of this function.

Guide to Document Formats

Use the following guides as a quick reference to document formats.

Memorandums--Simplified
Stationery: **plain sheets.**
SM: **1".**
Memo parts: **all begin at LM.**
LS: **QS below date and last line of body; DS below other parts; SS paragraphs.**
PB: **line 10.**

Letters--Modified Block, Mixed Punctuation
Stationery: **letterheads (executive size).**
SM: **1".**
LS: **SS with DS between paragraphs.**
PB: **line 12.**

Reports--Topbound
Stationery: **plain sheets.**
References: **footnotes.**
SM: **1".**
PB (first page): **line 12, 10-pitch; line 14, 12-pitch.**
PB (second and succeeding pages): **line 10.**
BM: **at least 1".**
LS: **DS text.**
Enumerations: **SS with SS between items; key in hang-indent format.**

Address Card

| NAME | Alexander, Jennifer S. (Miss) |
| TITLE | Executive Vice President |

ADDRESS	First National Bank
	3526 East 15th Street
	Davenport, IA 52803-5522

TELEPHONE NO. (319) 632-4477

213b-217b (continued)

Additional excerpt from CLEARVIEW MANOR DOCUMENT PROCESSING MANUAL:

To hang-indent: For each enumerated item, key the number and period and space twice. Set a tab stop at the point where the first letter of the first word will be keyed. For lines that follow, tab over so that each line begins flush under the first letter of the first word in the line above.

<u>Goals of the Instruction</u>

Students must ~~be required to~~ complete a series of learning activities which will enable them to

1. Understand, read, write, *and* pronounce the basic metric measures for length, weight, and capacity.
2. Add, subtract, multiply, and divide *metric* measurements.
3. Convert from one metric unit to another.
4. Solve problems that use metric measurements.
5. ~~To~~ convert commonly used metric measures to English measures and vice versa.

DS between items

<u>Instructional Strategies</u>

aids To accomplish the learning goals, a variety of learning ~~activities~~ such as charts, oral and written exercises, and word problems can and should be used extensively in the learning process. The chart is an excellent learning resource which can be used to accomplish many of the objectives.

<u>Charts</u>. The chart below is an example of how ~~the~~ basic metric units of length can be presented in visual form. A similar chart for weight and capacity could be developed.

METRIC UNITS OF LENGTH

Unit	Abbreviation	Equivalent in Meters	Common English Equivalents
Millimeter	mm	0.001 m	-----
Centimeter	cm	0.01 m	1 foot = 30 cm
Decimeter	dm	0.1 m	-----
Meter	m	1 m	1 yard = .9 m
Dekameter	dam	10 m	-----
Hectometer	hm	100 m	-----
Kilometer	km	1000 m	1 mile = 1.6 km

<u>Using the Chart</u> *lc*. The chart above can be used in numerous ways to accomplish the instructional objectives.

1. The first column of the chart can be used for an oral exercise in which students are asked to pronounce each ~~of~~ unit of measurement.

2. The second column of the chart can be used to show students the metric abbreviations ~~and that they are written in lowercase letters.~~ *for metric units, which are always shown in lowercase letters.*

(continued, p. 369)

238a ▶ 5
Conditioning Practice

each line twice SS (slowly, then faster); if time permits rekey selected lines

alphabet	1	Quin, zip your fox jacket and get your gloves to brave the March wind.
fig/sym	2	Fred Jones & Company's telephone number was changed to (381) 509-2647.
left shift	3	Lisa appointed Jack, Paul, Ingrid, Helen, and Mae to make decorations.
speed	4	Turn down the lane by the foggy lake to see the hay and the cornfield.

| 1 | 2 | 3 | 4 | 5 | 6 | 7 | 8 | 9 | 10 | 11 | 12 | 13 | 14 |

238b ▶ 18 Improve Straight-Copy Speed and Accuracy

1. Three 1' writings on ¶ 1 for speed. **Goal:** Increase speed by 2-4 *wam*.

2. Follow Step 1 for ¶ 2.

3. Three 1' writings on ¶ 1 for accuracy. **Goal:** No more than 1 error a minute.

4. Follow Step 3 for ¶ 2.

5. A 3' writing on all ¶s.

6. Determine *gwam*/errors.

all letters used | A | 1.5 si | 5.7 awl | 80% hfw

	gwam 3'
To realize maximum benefit from the many time-management techniques	5 · 62
that can be used, one should make a major effort at self-management.	9 · 66
One step in this process involves making a list of the less enjoyable	14 · 71
tasks performed. Then a scheme to associate some pleasure with these	19 · 76
tasks, such as doing them with a friend or following them with a reward,	23 · 81
should be implemented to help reduce the drudgery of the tasks.	28 · 85
Another self-management exercise is to analyze a task that never	32 · 89
gets done by questioning why one doesn't really want to complete that	37 · 94
unfinished job. Psychologists tell us that actions reflect our desired	41 · 99
behavior and that sometimes when we say that we would like to do some-	46 · 103
thing but do not have the time, we probably just do not want to do it.	51 · 108
Understanding this point can help one to learn to apply the pleasure	55 · 113
technique to tedious tasks.	57 · 115

gwam 3' | 1 | 2 | 3 | 4 | 5 |

238c ▶ 12 Check Language Skills

Key the paragraph at the right correcting errors in subject/verb agreement and pronoun/antecedent agreement. Correct keyboarding errors.

238d ▶ 15 Improve Keyboarding Skill

Repeat 237d, p. 408, as directed.

Since neither of the other committee members were prepared for the meeting, each of them were asked to submit a written report by next week. After that time, the committee can meet again to compile their final recommendation to the president. Before making the decision, however, all members will cast its votes concerning the recommendation. The president hopes that the chairperson as well as committee members are happy with the final recommendation.

3. The chart's third column can be used to explain that the meter is the basic unit used to measure length and that other units are ~~either~~ parts ~~of a meter~~ or multiples of a meter. The chart ~~orders~~ *lists* the units of measurement from the smallest to the largest.

4. The third column can also be used to show students how they can convert from one metric unit to another by moving the decimal point in the meter measurement to the left to convert to smaller units or to the right to convert to larger units.

5. The last column of the chart can be used to establish the relationship between ~~various~~ metric and English ~~units of~~ *selected* measurements ~~&~~ *units.*

Summary

The metric system of measurement must be taught along with the English system. It is a system that can be presented in an understandable manner if the teacher establishes goals and uses good examples, illustrations, and applications to present the content. The chart is an example of an illustration that can ~~be easily~~ be used easily to enhance learning.

make superscript. (If not possible, make it "1.##")

[1] Roswell E. Fairbank, Robert A. Schultheis, and Raymond M. Kaczmarski, <u>Applied Business Mathematics</u>, ~~Thirteenth Edition~~ (Cincinnati: South-Western Publishing Co., 1990), p. 167. *13th ed.*

Document 7
Table

Mr. Quinnones: Format and key the price list to accompany the composite menu you completed. Use **(Proposed Prices, May through October, 19--)** as the secondary heading.

CLEARVIEW MANOR PRICE LIST*

Meal no.	Breakfast	Luncheon	Dinner
1	$ 6.95	$ 8.95	$ 14.25
2	6.25	9.25	15.50
3	10.95	8.95	15.95
4	6.95	10.50	17.75
5	8.25	7.95	19.50
6	6.35	9.50	18.95

* Prices do not include 6% tax and 15% gratuity.

The comittee decided to except the advice of the consultant concerning the installation of electrical outlets. The principal reason for doing so was their knowledge of the consultant's prior succesful projects. The comittee members knew that they had to have acess to more outlets if they were to move foreword with plans to expand, and they were confidant that the consultant had studied their needs and their facilaties carefully. They believed that such a profesional person would weigh the alternatives and make a reccomendation that would be in their best intrest.

237d ▶ 15
Improve Keyboarding Skill

all letters used | A | 1.5 si | 5.7 awl | 80% hfw

1. A 1' writing on ¶ 1; find *gwam*.

2. Add 4-8 *gwam* to the rate attained in Step 1, and note quarter-minute checkpoints from table below.

3. Take two 1' guided writings on ¶ 1 to increase speed.

4. Practice ¶s 2 and 3 in the same way.

5. A 5' writing on ¶s 1-3 combined; find *gwam* and determine errors.

Quarter-Minute Checkpoints

gwam	¼'	½'	¾'	1'
40	10	20	30	40
44	11	22	33	44
48	12	24	36	48
52	13	26	39	52
56	14	28	42	56
60	15	30	45	60
64	16	32	48	64
68	17	34	51	68
72	18	36	54	72

gwam 1' | 5'

Speaking before a group of people can cause a great deal of anxiety for an individual. This anxiety is so extensive that it was ranked as the greatest fear among adults in a recent survey. Such fear suggests that many people would rather perish than go before the public to give a talk. Much of this fear actually comes from a lack of experience and training in giving public speeches. People who excel in the area of public speaking have developed this unique skill through hard work.

Planning is a key part to giving a good talk. The talk should be organized into three basic parts. These parts are the introduction, the body, and the conclusion. The introduction is used to get the attention of the audience, to introduce the topic of the talk, and to establish the credibility of the speaker. The body of the speech is an organized presentation of the material the speaker is conveying. The conclusion is used to summarize the main points of the talk.

Several things can be done to lower the level of anxiety during a talk. Learning as much as possible about the audience prior to the talk can reduce uncertainty. Advanced planning and preparing are essential; the lack of either is a major cause of anxiety. Having the main points written on note cards to refer to when needed is also helpful. Using visual aids can also lessen the exposure a person feels. These are but a few ideas that may be used to develop better speaking skills.

	14	3	61
	28	6	64
	42	8	67
	56	11	69
	71	14	72
	84	17	75
	98	20	78
	13	22	80
	28	25	83
	42	28	86
	56	31	89
	71	34	92
	85	37	95
	95	39	97
	13	41	99
	27	44	102
	41	48	105
	56	50	108
	70	52	111
	84	55	113
	98	58	116

gwam 1' | 1 | 2 | 3 | 4 | 5 | 6 | 7 | 8 | 9 | 10 | 11 | 12 | 13 | 14
5' | 1 | 2 | 3

213b-217b (continued)

Document 8
Invoice
LP p. 199

Mr. Quinnones: Here is a handwritten copy of the invoice we will send to the mathematics conference speaker who had us key and print a handout for his session. Everything you need is on the form except the cost of your time. You will have to multiply your time by $14.00 per hour to get the processing cost. Round your time to the nearest quarter hour to compute the cost. Once you have the cost, complete the extensions as needed.

CLEARVIEW MANOR	P.O. Box A, Pocono Manor, PA 18349-2010 (717) 225-9988		INVOICE

DR RICHARD K SIMMS
BECKLEY COLLEGE
WASHINGTON PA 15301-4211

Date: *Current*
Customer Order No.: *via phone*

Terms	Delivery	Our Order No.	Event Date
30 days	client pick up at manor	1101	current

Quantity	Service/Product	Unit Price	Amount
	Per hour report processing fee (3 pages)	14 00	
450	Per page duplicating fee	04	18 00
	Total		

Document 9
News Release
LP p. 201

Mr. Quinnones: I made this draft on my typewriter at home. Please format it as a news release. State that it is for immediate release and name me as the contact person.

POCONO MANOR, PA, (current month, day, year). Clearview Manor, one of the oldest resort hotels and conference centers in the Pocono Mountains, is expanding its conference center facilities. Construction ~~isxscheduledxtoxwillxtoxbeginxwithxaxmonthxonxa~~ of this new addition will provide ~~modernxupxtoxdate~~ flexible space for meetings, banquets, and exhibits.

The addition will be made at the north end of the ~~present~~ existing conference center ~~and~~ near the present executive dining room area. ~~MxxxThomasxRxxQuinnones~~ Ms. Helen T. Caldwell, conference center director, said that the ~~addition~~ facility will provide Clearview Manor with an additional 3,000 square feet of space. She stated, "The architects have designed the facility in such a manner that we can convert ~~fromxanxopen~~ within a matter of minutes from a completely open space to six fully-equipped individual meeting rooms."

Mulaney ~~and~~ Associates, Inc., ~~are~~ is serving as the architectural firm and Baumann Brothers is the general contractor. ~~Itxisxestimatedxexpectedxthat~~ The facility will be ready for use within five months. Mr. Thomas R. Quinnones, the marketing manager, is ~~nowxaccepting~~ already scheduling groups into the new space. He said, "We are finding that this additional space is in high demand by the many groups who use the resort and conference center facilities at Clearview Manor."

#

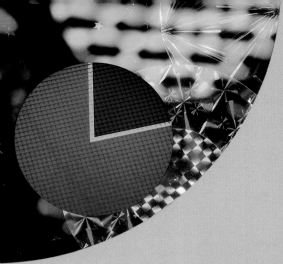

Improve Keyboarding/Language Skills

Learning Goals

1. To improve keyboarding speed and accuracy on straight copy.
2. To assess straight-copy speed and accuracy.
3. To check language skills.

Format Guides

1. Paper guide at *0* (for typewriters).
2. LL: 70 spaces.
3. LS: SS sentence drills with DS between groups; DS paragraph writings.
4. PI: 5 spaces.

| Lesson 237 | Improve Keyboarding/Language Skills |

237a ▶ 5
Conditioning Practice

each line twice SS
(slowly, then faster);
if time permits, rekey
selected lines

alphabet	1	I drove the jazz quartet up to the front walk in my big luxurious car.
figures	2	Mid-State's office ordered Models #30271 and #46958 at $1,269.41 each.
right shift	3	Did Eric, Betty, and Todd make the debate team along with Ann and Wes?
speed	4	Both of the haughty men risk a big penalty if they dismantle the auto.

| 1 | 2 | 3 | 4 | 5 | 6 | 7 | 8 | 9 | 10 | 11 | 12 | 13 | 14 |

237b ▶ 18 Improve Straight-Copy Speed and Accuracy

1. Three 1' writings on ¶ 1 for speed. **Goal:** Increase speed by 2-4 *wam* on each writing.
2. Follow Step 1 for ¶ 2.
3. Three 1' writings on ¶ 1 for accuracy. **Goal:** No more than 1 error a minute.
4. Follow Step 3 for ¶ 2.
5. A 3' writing on ¶s 1 and 2 combined.
6. Determine *gwam*/errors.

all letters used | A | 1.5 si | 5.7 awl | 80% hfw

                                                                    gwam 3'

All people have exactly the same number of hours a day for the   4 | 61

tasks that are required, for the tasks that are elective, and for ac-   9 | 66

tivities that are just for pleasure. Some people, though, organize   13 | 71

their schedules in such a way as to accomplish noticeably more of the   18 | 75

tasks and activities than do others. Do such individuals have a deep   23 | 80

secret, or do they just have superior time-management skills?   27 | 84

If the answer is that these are people who excel in applying good   31 | 88

time-management techniques, then they are apt to recognize the necessity 36 | 93

of establishing priorities. To establish priorities means that they   41 | 98

must judge which tasks or activities are the most essential and place   45 | 103

those items high on their priority list. Then they must schedule their 50 | 107

day to work steadily to complete with few deviations the items in the   55 | 112

order in which they appear on the list.   57 | 115

gwam 3' | 1 | 2 | 3 | 4 | 5 |

Document 10
Unbound Report
Mr. Quinnones: I have made some revisions to the first-draft brochure copy you formatted for me. Prepare another draft in unbound report form. I have added some information at the end to be included in this draft.

tr
CONFERENCE CENTER
CLEARVIEW MANOR

QS

Situated
~~Located~~ 2,000 feet high on 2,700 acres of beautiful Pocono
lc
Mountainside, ~~the~~ Clearview Manor is a unique ~~learning,~~ meeting,

training, and resort facility for business and professional

groups. Located two miles west of Mt. Pocono on Route 314,

Clearview Manor provides an opportunity for groups to combine
t
excellent conference facilities with outs^anding resort facil^ities
i
and activities.

The Conference Center
is known for its outstanding
lc
The Center ~~has~~ large and small meeting rooms with up-to-date

computer and communication capabilities, spacious exhibit area,

and elegant dining areas which provide the necessary flexible
s
space to meet the needs of ~~every~~ group^ from five to five hundred.

Meeting rooms. With nearly 6,000 square feet of meeting

room space, the Conference Center is a perfect choice for meet-
space
ings. The ~~meeting rooms~~ can be divided into eight separate, com-
rooms   *in size*
pletely soundproof meeting ~~areas~~ for groups ranging^ from 18 to
rooms
75. If larger ~~areas~~ are required, the space can be divided to

handle two large groups--one at 376 and another at 262.
m
Exhibit area. The Conference Center can accomo^date approxi-
o
mately 100 exhibitors in an unobstructed area of 15,00^ square
has   to
feet. Each exhibitor ~~can~~ access^ alternating current, three-phase
s
60-cycle, 120/208-volt^ or 120-volt, single-phase current for

both light and power cir^cuits. Telephone, computer, radio,

~~braodcast cable~~ and closed circuit television connections can
Exhibitors can make convenient
be made.^ ~~D~~elivery ~~can be made~~ through a roll-up door 10 feet

high by 11 feet wide from a straight and level delivery drive.

(continued, p. 372)

Document 12
Modified Block Letter
LP p. 25

LINDA HENRY
Office Supervisor

Perry A. McDaniel, one of our Sales Representatives, would like the attached form letter sent to

Mrs. Julia C. Ward
Word Processing Supervisor
James and Associates
2100 Claude Road
Hunstville, AL 35806-8000

Variable 1:
electronic typewriters

Variable 2:
(319) 887-4404

Date letter May 11
L H

Here is the information you requested regarding guarantee, service, and training programs for our <variable 1>.

Equipment Guarantee. All equipment is guaranteed for three months from the date of delivery. During the warranty period, equipment will be repaired or replaced at no charge. After the warranty has expired, you can continue to have us service the equipment at an hourly rate charge plus parts.

Service. A response time of eight hours or less is guaranteed for all service calls. If the equipment requires longer than eight hours to service, a loaner will be provided free of charge until the equipment is repaired. Our service, we have been told, is among the best customer service provided in the industry.

Training Programs. Our Educational Division provides seminars to assure that our customers are utilizing the many capabilities of the equipment. The seminars are provided free of charge during the first six months after the purchase of the equipment. Technicians are available during every workday to respond to any questions a customer has about the equipment.

I enjoyed meeting with you and demonstrating our <variable 1>. If you have additional questions about our products or customer service policies, just call me at <variable 2>.

Sincerely

Document 13
Sales Figures

LINDA HENRY
Office Supervisor

Prepare a table comparing the January-March Hardware and Software sales figures for last year with this year's. Use the sales figures in Document 4 for this year's figures.
L H

JANUARY-MARCH SALES COMPARISON
Past Two Years

Sales Representative	Hardware Last Year	This Year	Software Last Year	This Year
Sam Johnson	$144,846	$ xxx,xxx	$ 2,617	$ x,xxx
Bob Black	--		--	
Eva Lewis	138,558		5,032	
Kerry Munson	113,654		3,624	
Mary Ramirez	149,695		3,780	
Lydia Mendez	131,860		3,159	
Perry McDaniel	151,985		6,870	
Dave Bromberg	162,598		5,254	
Totals	$993,196	$x,xxx,xxx	$30,336	$xx,xxx

Dining facilities. The Center is prepared to provide an elegant cuisine of fine dining, informal buffets, nutritious snacks, and diet menus for a few to thousands. The Center's master chef can provide many choices from the standard breakfast, lunch, dinner, and reception menus, or will be happy to discuss special menus upon request.

General Information. The Conference Center staff can provide special requests for such things as entertainment, unusual decorations, and theme parties or meetings. Courier service can be provided for pickup or delivery of materials shipped via the rapid delivery services. Personnel for collecting tickets or staffing registration and information tables can also be provided. The state sales tax is 6 percent and will be added to all accounts. In addition, a gratuity of 15 percent will be charged on all food and beverage service.

Mr. Quinnones: Add these paragraphs to the end of the report in the order they are numbered. I have taken them from existing brochures.

Travel Information ⑤
Clearview Manor is easily accessible by automobile or plane. If you are driving, you should use Exit 44 on Interstate 80 and follow the directional signs to Clearview Manor. If you are flying, use the Wilkes-Barre/Scranton Airport. Airport limousine, taxi, or automobile rental services are conveniently available.

② Lodging.
Every room at Clearview Manor is spacious and professionally furnished with two double beds, a sofa, a table, and two chairs. Each room is equipped with a direct-dial telephone system, a safe, a refrigerator, color TV featuring cable and movie stations, and AM & FM radio with built-in alarm clock.

The Resort ①
Clearview Manor's resort facilities provide everything necessary to make your stay pleasant and memorable. The resort offers top-quality accommodations, exceptional dining experiences, and a wide variety of entertainment and activities to choose from.

④ Recreational facilities.
There's always something to do at Clearview Manor. Golf is available at the Manor's 18-hole golf course, and tennis can be played on the two indoor or five outdoor courts. Squash and racquetball can be played on air-conditioned indoor courts. In addition, resort guests can swim indoors or outdoors, and walk, jog, or hike for miles on well-marked trails. During the winter, guests can ski cross country on well-patrolled trails, ride for miles on a snowmobile, or skate on the indoor or outdoor rinks.

③ Dining and entertainment.
Clearview Manor's popular Top-of-the-Mountain restaurant is known for its continental cuisine and quality service. The Top of the Mountain is open 7 days a week for breakfast, lunch, and dinner. The adjoining Manor Lounge is perfect for a relaxing conversation after a busy day. Later in the evening it's just the place to enjoy the greatest names in entertainment, which Clearview Manor provides each night of the week.

Document 9
Simplified Block Letter
LP p. 21

LINDA HENRY
Office Supervisor

Format the attached information as a simplified block letter for **Thomas M. Chaney** to use in the exhibit area of the Regional Office Automation Convention. Use the following for the letter address.

Convention Participants
Hotel Tuscany
3400 Fillmore Street
Davenport, IA 52806-4721

Date letter
May 25   *LH*

Welcome to the 19-- Regional Office Automation Convention. I'm sure you are enjoying learning about the lastest developments in the fast-paced world of office technology.

One piece of equipment that is being demonstrated is the Elec II 40-character display, electronic typewriter. The typewriter has 32 K of basic memory, text merging in memory capability, and a print speed of 17 # characters per second. The list price for the typewriter is $1,285. A word processor upgrade and a sheet feeder are additional features that can be added to enhance the electronic typewriter capabilities.

If you have any questions regarding the equipment Elec II, please ask the person demonstrating the equipment or one of our sales representatives at the exhibit area.

Documents 10-11
Formal Memorandums
LP p. 23

LINDA HENRY
Office Supervisor

Key two copies of the attached information as formal memorandums on half sheets for Mr. Chaney. One copy goes to **Lori Chin** and other copy to **Malcolm Deters**. (Both work in the Information Processing Center.) Date the memos **May 10** and supply a subject line.

LH

Thank you for agreeing to assist our sales representatives at the 19-- Regional Office Automation Convention on May 25. An informational meeting to will be held on May 15 will to give you the opportunity to to help you prepare for the convention. At this time Then you can meet our convention sales force and discuss with them the types of documents information processing applications you will demonstrate during the convention.

Any questions you have about regarding this assignment will be answered during this meeting. I am looking forward to working with you.

LP p. 203

Document 11
Reservation Form

Mr. Quinnones: Here is a reservation form that needs to be keyed before I sign and distribute it.

CLEARVIEW MANOR

CLEARVIEW MANOR CONFERENCE CENTER
ROOM/FACILITY RESERVATION FORM

COMPLETE THIS FORM in full and give it to the marketing manager at least two weeks prior to the event date(s).

Direct all inquiries to the marketing manager, (717) 226-5435.

1) Name of Group: *Quadcore Computer Systems, Inc.*

2) Group Contact: *Miss Andrea L. Norman*   3) Phone number (717) *543-6060*

4) Number of People Expected: *28*   Date of Event *May 17-20, 19--*

5) Description of Event: *Seminar: Maintenance Management with Microcomputer LANs*

6) Special Preparations:

☒ Maintenance (specify): *classroom-style setup for 28*

☒ Resort Lodging: *block reserve 28 rooms (evenings of 5/17 - 5/19)*

☒ Food service: *lunch to be served each day*

☒ Audio-Visual: *overhead projector/screen; flip chart; VCR/monitor*

☒ Security: *open seminar room at 8:30 a.m.; lock at 5:30 p.m.*

☒ Other: *4 tables at front of room for microcomputers*

7) Room/Facility

Room/Facility	Date	Time
Right Suite - seminar	*May 17-20*	*8:30 a.m.* to *5:30 p.m.*
Left Suite - lunch	*May 17-20*	*12 noon* to *1 p.m.*
Entrance Suite - reception	*May 17*	*8 p.m.* to *10:30 p.m.*
		to
		to

8) Reservation Requested By (signature): _____

9) Department: *Marketing*   Date: *March 3, 19--*

NOTE: Please report any changes to the operations manager.

Date Received: _____ Operations Manager: _____

APPROVED: ☐   DENIED: ☐

COMMENTS: _____

Document 8
Price List

> **LINDA HENRY**
> **Office Supervisor**
>
> Attached is a price list that has been marked with price increases and new products. Prepare a new price list for distribution to sales representatives reflecting those changes. These changes will be effective as of June 1. A few formatting marks have been included to assist you in preparing the copy. *LH*

List the groups of equipment in alphabetical order.

PRICE LIST
DS
Effective May 1, 19--

Blocked Headings *QS*

Printers *DS*	Price	Order Number
Star I	$ 249	100-PSI
Star II	329	200-PSII
~~Super Star~~	489	300-PSS
Quality I	~~399~~ 419	150-PQI
Quality II	~~459~~ 479	250-PQII

QS

Typewriters	Price	Order Number
Star 6000	$ ~~799~~ 829	6000-ETS
Star 6086	~~899~~ 939	6086-ETS
Elec I	1,085	349-ETEI
Elec II	1,285	350-ETEII
EIT 521	849	521-ETEIT
EIT 621	1,089	621-ETEIT

Copiers	Price	Order Number
Quality Copier I	$6,939	305-CQCI
Quality Copier II	9,729	310-CQCII
Pro Copier 380	4,349	380-CPC
Pro Copier 690	6,799	690-CPC

Computers	Price	Order Number
McGregger 600	$1,299	600-COM-MG
McGregger 6000	1,999	6000-COM-MG
Werner I	~~1,549~~ 1,599	300-COM-WI
Werner II	2,349	400-COM-WII
PC-50 Dixon	2,459	50-COM-DIX
PC-95 Dixon	2,949	95-COM-DIX

Extend and Measure
Keyboarding/Language Skills

Learning Goals

1. To improve basic skills in keyboarding, word choice, and document production.
2. To prepare for measurement of skills in language usage; in keying straight copy; and in preparing letters, memos, reports, tables, invoices, and purchase orders.

Format Guides

1. Paper guide at *0* (for typewriters).
2. LL: 70 spaces for drill copy; as needed for documents.
3. LS: SS drill lines; DS ¶s; or as directed within an activity.
4. PI: 5 spaces, unless otherwise directed.

Lesson 218   *Keyboarding/Prepare for Measurement*

218a ▶ 5
Conditioning Practice

each line twice SS (slowly, then faster); then a 1′ writing on line 4

alphabet	1	Drew thought a jinx had kept them from solving the big puzzle quickly.
figures	2	The association had 7,863 members in 62 chapters in 45 states in 1990.
shift keys	3	Ms. Eppots asked to see Mary, Rob, Janis, Zoe, and Naomi before class.
speed	4	Lana sat by the aisle with them for the sorority ritual at the chapel.

| 1 | 2 | 3 | 4 | 5 | 6 | 7 | 8 | 9 | 10 | 11 | 12 | 13 | 14 |

218b ▶ 20
Improve Keyboarding Skill: Guided Writing

1. A 3′ writing on ¶s 1-2 combined; calculate *gwam.*
2. A 1′ writing on ¶ 1; calculate *gwam* to establish your base rate.
3. Add 2-6 words to Step 2 *gwam;* use this as your goal rate.
4. Take three 1′ speed writings on ¶ 1, trying to reach your quarter-minute checkpoints as the guides (¼, ½, ¾, time) are called.
5. Follow Steps 2-4 for ¶ 2.
6. Repeat Step 1. Compare *gwam* on the two 3′ writings.
7. Record on LP p. 3 your better 3′ *gwam.*

all letters used | A | 1.5 si | 5.7 awl | 80% hfw

	gwam 3′	5′
Have you ever paused to consider how you can improve your ability	4	3 | 37
to take quizzes, tests, and examinations? You should realize that you	9	5 | 39
can improve your performance by improving your test-taking ability.	14	8 | 42
One thing you can do is to understand that good performance does not	18	11 | 45
mean that you must receive the highest score in your group. Rather, it	23	14 | 48
means that you should score at the highest level you can.	27	16 | 50
Test results generally can be improved if you become concerned,	31	19 | 53
positive, and realistic about major tests and follow improvement strate-	36	22 | 56
gies. If you are concerned about your results, you are likely to be	41	24 | 58
motivated to do your best. If you have a positive attitude, you are	45	27 | 61
likely to learn from the strengths and weaknesses that test scores can	50	30 | 64
reveal. If you are realistic, you are likely to set proper goals and	55	33 | 67
be able to achieve them.	56	34 | 68

gwam 3′ | 1 | 2 | 3 | 4 | 5
     5′ | 1 | 2 | 3

Document 6
Purchase Order
LP p. 17

LINDA HENRY
Office Supervisor

Prepare a purchase order for the computer accessories that Mr. Mundy has requisitioned. I have written the stock numbers and price information on the requisition. Order the items from this company.

Ellis Computer Products
425 East Ivy Avenue
St. Paul, MN 55101-2444

Use the following information to complete the purchase order.

Purchase Order No.:
QZ 1039
Date: **May 8, 19—**
Terms: **2/10, n/30**
Shipped Via: **Watson Freight**

LH

Document 7
Formal Memorandum
LP p. 19

LINDA HENRY
Office Supervisor

Mr. Chaney would like the attached information formatted as a formal memo and sent to **Ms. Olivia Reinhold, IPC Supervisor**. Date the memo **May 8, 19--** and supply an appropriate subject line.

LH

MIDWESTERN OFFICE PRODUCTS

3871 BRIDGE AVENUE, DAVENPORT, IA 52807-7002 (319) 887-1462

PURCHASE REQUISITION

Deliver to: **Marvin Mundy**
Location: **400E**
Job No. **698-Drake**

Requisition No. **38569**
Date **May 6, 19--**
Date Required **May 20, 19--**

Quantity	Description	Price	Total
20	Computer Locks (9461-C)	27.95 ea	559.00
10	Surge Protectors (7648-C)	36.15 ea	361.50
5	Five-way Switchboxes (5230-G)	109.00 ea	545.00
10	Keyboard Extension Cables (7609-B)	16.45 ea	164.50
1	Standby Power System (1568-G)	279.95 ea	279.95
			1,909.95

Requisitioned by: **Marvin Mundy**

The 19-- Regional Office Automation Convention will be held at the Hotel Tuscany here in Davenport on May 25. We are planning to give demonstrations of the Elec II electronic typewriter, the Pro Copier 690, and the McGregor 6000 computer. President Koontz suggested that personnel from the Information Processing Center give the demonstrations. Would it be possible for you to assist us by providing IPC personnel?

If so, we would like the individuals you select to be specialists with the equipment who can present the professional image that is critical to advance our sales efforts. I'll phone you within a few days to give you specific details about the convention.

218c ▶ 25
Prepare for Measurement
2 plain full sheets; LP p. 205; correct errors.

Letter 1
Modified Block Format
Key the letter at the right in modified block format, indented ¶s, and mixed punctuation. If necessary, see p. 136.

Letter 2
Simplified Block Format
Rekey Letter 1 in simplified block format. If necessary, see p. 308.

Letter 3
Block Format
LP p. 205
or executive-size stationery
Rekey Letter 1 in block format, open punctuation. Omit the subject line and company name. If necessary, see p. 308.

	words
Current date Mrs. Sheila T. Rapowski Beta Safe & Lock 3684 Berger	14
Avenue St. Louis, MO 63109-1101 Dear Mrs. Rapowski Subject YOUR	26
HELP IS NEEDED	29

(¶ 1) For over fifty years, Scientific Products has manufactured many prod-   42
ucts designed to satisfy special needs of customers.   53

(¶ 2) On the enclosed survey are several short questions that will allow you   67
to tell us your feelings about products we are currently considering. The   82
survey requires only a few minutes to complete and can be returned to us in   97
the enclosed postage-paid envelope.   105

(¶ 3) Please respond so that we will have your input when we determine the   119
future products to manufacture to meet your special needs. Your response   133
will be kept confidential, and we will not place your name on mailing lists we   149
share with other firms.   154

Sincerely SCIENTIFIC PRODUCTS Ms. Linda L. Kugas, President xx   167
Enclosure postscript The enclosed coin is a token of our appreciation. We   180
hope it will brighten the day of a small child you know.   191

Lesson 219	Keyboarding/Prepare for Measurement

219a ▶ 5
Conditioning Practice
each line twice SS (slowly, then faster); then a 1' writing on line 4

alphabet 1 A jazz player acquired six or seven big weekend dates from his agents.
figures 2 Jan's 67 stores in 19 states gave discounts of 20, 35, and 48 percent.
shift keys 3 I may visit Perry, Columbus, Langley, Wooster, and South high schools.
speed 4 Six girls may visit the city to see the giant robot make an auto body.

| 1 | 2 | 3 | 4 | 5 | 6 | 7 | 8 | 9 | 10 | 11 | 12 | 13 | 14 |

219b ▶ 10
Language Skills: Word Choice
1. Study the spelling and definition of the words.
2. Key the line number (with period); space twice, then key the **Learn** sentence, noting the correct use of the words.
3. Key the line number (with period); space twice, then key the **Apply** sentences DS, selecting the word in parentheses that makes each sentence correct.

divers (adj) various; several; sundry

diverse (adj) distinct in kind; disparate; unlike

everyday (adj) suitable for ordinary days or routine occasions

every day (adj & n) each and all days without exception

Learn 1. The twins had diverse opinions about divers items of clothing.
Apply 2. The yearbook should include (divers/diverse) pictures of the soccer team.
Apply 3. The (divers/diverse) positions of the two boys led to the debate.
Learn 4. See if Marilyn can wear everyday clothing to the office every day.
Apply 5. He is to practice keying straight copy (everyday/every day).
Apply 6. I think I have established an (everyday/every day) routine.

232b-236b (continued)

Document 4
Sales Report

> **LINDA HENRY**
> **Office Supervisor**
>
> Prepare the attached Quarterly Sales Report in final form for Mr. Chaney. *LH*

Note: Be sure to keep a copy of this document since you will need information from this table to complete Document 13.

QUARTERLY SALES REPORT

January-March 19--

(alphabetize)

Representative	Hardware	Softwaare	*Printware*
Mary Ramirez	$ 153,132	*$* 5,520	*$ 1,183*
Sam Johnson	144,690	2,579	*1,567*
Lydia Mendez	133,409	4,407	*249*
Bob Black	*79,234*	*2,135*	*498*
Perry McDaniel	157,095	8,195	*489*
Kerry Munson	122,167	3,397 *8*	*918*
Dave Bromburg *e*	174,459	3,096	*2,821*
Eva Lewis	162,598	7,240	*2,040*
Totals	*$ 1,126,703*	*$ 36,570*	*$ 9,765*

Document 5
Invoice
LP p. 17

> **LINDA HENRY**
> **Office Supervisor**
>
> Grovesdale Business College requested us to delay their order until they met with department members. They have now decided to purchase the PC-95 Dixon rather than the PC-50.
> Key an invoice with the information and changes marked on their purchase order. Our Order No. is **C63-896**; use **May 8** for the date. *LH*

GROVESDALE BUSINESS COLLEGE

4225 WILSON AVENUE, DES MOINES, IA 50317-6700
515-245-7171

PURCHASE ORDER

MIDWESTERN OFFICE PRODUCTS
3871 BRIDGE AVENUE
DAVENPORT IA 52807-7002

Purchase Order No.: 108-493Z
Date: May 4, 19--
Terms: 3/10, n/30
Shipped Via: Dalton Transit

Quantity	Description/Stock Number	Price	Per	Total
2	Elec II Typewriters (350-ETEII)	1,285 00	ea	2,570 00
2	Quality II Printers (250-PQII)	479 00	ea	958 00
2	PC-~~50~~ *95* Dixon Computers (~~50~~ *95*-COM-DIX)	~~2,459 00~~ *2,949 00*	ea	~~4,918 00~~ *5,898.00*
				~~8,446 00~~
	Sales Tax			~~422 30~~
				~~8,868 30~~
				9,426 00
				471 30
				9,897 30

By ______________________________

219c ▶ 35
Prepare for Measurement
plain full sheets; correct errors

Document 1
Unbound Report
Key the copy at the right as a 2-page unbound report. Use **FINDLEY HIGH SCHOOL BUSINESS CLUB ACTIVITIES** as the title.

Document 2
Simplified Memo
Use the material at the right to key a 2-page memo in simplified format to **Evelyn W. Lane, Principal.** The memo is from **Hazel W. Woodley, Business Club Advisor.** Use the title of the report as the subject; use today's date. Eliminate the side headings but retain the paragraph headings. Add this copy as the last paragraph.

May I have your written authorization that the Business Club can conduct these projects. I would like to have your response within ten days so I will have an answer before the club's next meeting.

```
Evelyn Lane
Page 2
Current date
```

Second-Page Heading (begin on line 6)

Document 3
Leftbound Report
Begin rekeying Document 1 as a 2-page leftbound report. Prepare a title page showing that the report was prepared by the **Findley High School Business Club.**

The members of the Findley High School Business Club met last week and decided to conduct the projects listed below. Please consider this document as the club's request for permission to organize and conduct these projects during this school year. The proposed projects will publicize the business education program to students, parents, and other members of the community that Findley High School serves. In addition, they will bring recognition to current business education students.

Fall Semester Projects

The following projects have been suggested for the fall semester. These projects will help to draw students' attention to the business education program early in the school year.

Poster contest. The club will sponsor a poster contest in late September to recruit new members into the Business Club. The posters will be displayed throughout the high school building and the winner will receive a coupon good for two dinners at George's Family Restaurant.

Open house. Club members will participate in the Business Education Department's Fourth Annual Open House. The members will 1. Greet the guests at the main entrance. 2. Escort the guests to the Business Education Department where the program will be held. 3. Demonstrate the computer hardware and software that is used in the business classes. 4. Serve refreshments in the hall outside the accounting classroom.

Spring Semester Projects

During the spring semester, Business Club members will conduct activities designed to advertise the business education program to the community outside the school. The following projects have been proposed.

Mall exhibit. Senior and alumni club members will staff an exhibit booth at Findley Shopping Mall during the two weeks preceding course selection at the high school. The exhibit will focus on what is learned in business classes and opportunities for business education graduates.

Radio talk show. The Business Club officers will appear on "High School Perspectives," a weekly talk show on WDCF. The show will focus on the business education curriculum, the cooperative education program, and the activities of the Business Club at Findley High School.

Career day. Club members will assist the faculty with the career day program for junior high students. A member will "shadow" each junior high student who tours the Business Education Department to explain the advantages of business courses and the activities of the department.

	words
	22
	38
	52
	67
	82
	97
	107
	116
	131
	146
	152
	170
	184
	199
	211
	227
	241
	256
	271
	286
	297
	307
	321
	336
	349
	366
	381
	396
	408
	425
	440
	454
	466
	482
	497
	511
	524

Lesson 220	*Keyboarding/Prepare for Measurement*

220a ▶ 5
Conditioning Practice
each line twice SS (slowly, then faster); then a 1' writing on line 4

alphabet 1 Buzz likely will be the paid judge for the exclusive quarter-mile run.
figures 2 Harry can call Darlana at 375-4901 on Monday or 268-9103 on Wednesday.
shift lock 3 She will learn COBOL and BASIC in C1201 and PASCAL and MUMPS in C1301.
speed 4 The men may focus on their work if they are apt to make a tidy profit.

| 1 | 2 | 3 | 4 | 5 | 6 | 7 | 8 | 9 | 10 | 11 | 12 | 13 | 14 |

the workplace, the <u>current</u> problem of educating/training company

personal with today's hardware and software is going to grow.   In

a recent study, one out of every there businesses surveyed

reported trouble with getting the proper training.   Midwestern *(Stoltenberg, 1988, 63)*

customers are not, ~~one of the three having~~ trouble because of the *among those reporting*

training available through the (LC). *Sp*

Benefits of Support Services

DS   Customer surveys have shown that the level of customer
satisfaction has increased since the implementation of training programs through the (LC). *Sp* The indirect advertising done
by satisfied customers has resulted in increased revenues.
This fact is not surprising since positive **word-of-mouth advertis-**
ing is one of the most powerful information sources for
attracting potential customers, while negative word-of-mouth
advertising can be one of the most destructive sources
(Berkowitz, Kerin, and Rudelius, 1989, 104).
      This word-of-mouth advertising is working for Midwestern.
During the last 12 months, Sales Representatives has reported
a much higher referral rate as well as in increased number of
new contacts initiated through the customer.   A large number
of these contacts mention training as being an important factor in their decisions regarding equipment purchases.   The (LC) *Sp*
is essential to making these sales.

Document 3
Agenda

LINDA HENRY
Office Supervisor

Format the attached
agenda for the sales rep-
resentatives meeting in
July.   *LH*

Leaders: Key leaders by alternating periods and spaces, noting
whether the first period is on an
odd or even space. End leaders
2 or 3 spaces to the left of the
beginning of the second column.

AGENDA

Business Meeting for Sales Representatives

8:0̸0 a.m., July 15
   ³

DS

1.   Greetings . . . . *Sara C. Koontz, President*

2.   Proposed District Realignment . . *Ann M. Jones, Vice President*

3.   New Product Presentations . . . . .

         SuperStar Printer . . . . *Lori A. Chin*
         Werner II Computer . . . . *Malcolm J. Deters*

4.   ᶜComputerized Expense Reporting . . *Rhonda C. Little*

5.   Convention assignments . . . . . . *Thomas M. Chaney*
   ⁷
6̸.   Adjournment

6.   *Incentive Program Changes . . . Ann M. Jones*

APPENDICES

Document 2
Report

LINDA HENRY
Office Supervisor

Mr. Chaney would like the attached material prepared as a leftbound report. Correct any unmarked errors that you find as you key the document. The table insert and information for the reference page are shown below. *L H*

Table Insert

LINDA HENRY
Office Supervisor

Year	% Increase
1	2%
2	6%
3	12%
4	22%
5	33%

L H

References

LINDA HENRY
Office Supervisor

Berkowitz, Eric N., Roger A. Kerin, and William Rudelius. <u>Marketing</u>. 2d ed. Boston: Richard D. Irwin, Inc., 1989.

Romei, Lura K. "Pick a key—any key...." <u>Modern Office Technology</u>, March 1989, 12.

Stoltenberg, John. "Turning Problems Into Profits." <u>Working Woman</u>, May 1988, 63.

L H

LEARNING CENTER JUSTIFICATION

Justifying the existence of the company Learning Center (LC) is a relatively simple task. The growth rate of revenues for the 5-year period prior to the existence of the LC was 10% (2% per year). Since the LC was implemented 5 years ago, company revenues have increased significantly, as illustrated below.

(Insert Table)

Without the LC, this growth would not have been possible. More important, however, is the fact that the LC has been utilized extensively during the past year and is an integral part of the projected growth. Without the support provided by the LC, the projected growth will not happen. Several recent articles document the need for providing quality training for personnel working with today's technology.

Need for Support Services

For most business organizations to be successful in the information age, it is critical that sophisticated technology (hardware and software) be operated by personnel who have been educated/trained to utilize the capabilities of the technology. Romei (1989, 12) believes that corporations need to recognize that putting computers on desks is only part of solving the technology puzzle. The other part is investing money to train personnel so they may become productive users of the investment in hardware and software. Through user training, the LC assures our clients a high return on their technology investments.

More businesses than ever are eager to tap into the productivity-boosting and cost-saving potential of new software and hardware. As more technology is introduced into

APPENDIX A
Numeric Keypad Operation

Learning Goals

1. To learn key locations and keyboarding technique on the numeric keypad of a microcomputer.

2. To learn to enter figures rapidly and accurately by touch (without looking).

Practice Procedure

Follow directions given on an instructional diskette for learning key locations and for initial practice. Then return to this book for additional drill and practice.

Use of these activities on word processing software is not recommended.

Activity 1	4/5/6/0

1a ▶ Get Acquainted with Your Data-Entry Equipment

Figure keys 1-9 are in standard locations on numeric keypads of microcomputers (as well as on 10-key calculators).

The zero (0 or Ø) key location may vary slightly from one keyboard to another.

The illustrations at the right show the location of the figure keys on popular makes of microcomputers.

Consult your operator's manual to learn how to correct an error you detect as you enter figures.

Apple IIe numeric keypad

IBM PC

Tandy 1000

1b ▶ Take Correct Operating Position

1. Position yourself in front of the computer just as you do for entering alphabetic copy--body erect, both feet on floor for balance.

2. Place this textbook at the right of the keyboard.

3. Curve the fingers of the right hand and place them on the numeric keypad:
   first (index) finger on 4
   second finger on 5
   third finger on 6
   thumb on 0

232a-236a ▶ 5 *(daily)*
Conditioning Practice
Check each day to see that the equipment is in good working order by keying the lines at the right at least twice.

alphabet 1 To what extent was Kazumori involved with my projects before quitting?

figures 2 Please ship Order 1750 for 36 word processors, 49 desks, and 28 lamps.

fig/sym 3 Sales discounts (5%) in 1990 amount to $14,682, an increase of $1,735.

speed 4 If they go to the social with us, they may also visit their six girls.

| 1 | 2 | 3 | 4 | 5 | 6 | 7 | 8 | 9 | 10 | 11 | 12 | 13 | 14 |

232b-236b ▶ 45 *(daily)*
Document Production: Sales Department

Document 1
Simplified Block Letter
LP p. 15

LINDA HENRY
Office Supervisor

Here is a rough draft of a letter Mr. Chaney would like keyed in simplified block letter format. Since the letter will be sent to all sales representatives, we will do a mail merge using our sales rep address file. Key the letter address exactly as it appears on the rough draft. Mr. Chaney would like the following postscript included with the letter. **"Please notify me immediately if there are other items you would like included on the agenda for the business meeting."** *L H*

Note: Key the letter address as shown with the variables keyed inside the < >'s. If your machine does not have the < > keys, use the ( )'s.

May 6, 19--

\<Sales Representative\>
\<Address\>
\<City, State, and ZIP\>

ANNUAL MEETING FOR SALES REPRESENTATIVES

The annual meeting for company sales representatives is scheduled for July 15. Please arrange your schedules so that you will be able to spend the *entire* day with us at corporate headquarters.

The business meeting for sales reps is scheduled for 8:30 *a.m.* in the conference room. District realignment, new expense reporting procedures, and incentive program changes will be discussed. Since these items have a major impact on all sales reps, you will want to be present. The afternoon ~~will~~ sessions are still being planned. You will receive a *complete* program within the next ② weeks. *Sp*

I am looking forward to seeing you again on the 15th.

~~Sincerely your,~~

Thomas M. Chaney, *SALES MANAGER*

xx

Enclosure

c Ann M. Jones

1c ▶ Enter Data Using Home Keys: 4, 5, 6, 0

1. Turn equipment "on".

2. Curve the fingers of your right hand and place them upright on home keys:
   first (index) finger on 4
   second finger on 5
   third finger on 6
   fourth finger on + bar
   thumb on 0 or Ø (zero)

3. Using the special ENTER key to the right of the keypad, enter data in Drill 1a as follows:
   4 ENTER
   4 ENTER
   4 ENTER
   Strike ENTER

Note: Ignore any decimal (.) or comma (,) that may appear in an entry or total figure.

4. Check TOTAL figure on display screen. It should show 12 on the computer display.

5. If you do not get 12 as the total, reenter the data.

6. Enter and check columns b, c, d, e, and f in the same way.

7. Using the special ENTER key to the right of the keypad, enter data in Drill 2a as follows:
   44 ENTER
   44 ENTER
   44 ENTER
   Strike ENTER

8. Check TOTAL figure and reenter data if necessary.

9. Continue Drill 2 and complete Drills 3-5 in a similar manner.

Note: In Drills 4 and 5, strike 0 (zero) with the *side* of your right thumb.

Technique cue
Strike each key with a quick, sharp stroke with the *tip* of the finger; release the key quickly. Keep the fingers curved and upright, the wrist low, relaxed, and steady.

Drill 1

a	b	c	d	e	f
4	5	6	4	5	6
4	5	6	4	5	6
4	5	6	4	5	6
12	15	18	12	15	18

Drill 2

a	b	c	d	e	f
44	55	66	44	55	66
44	55	66	44	55	66
44	55	66	44	55	66
132	165	198	132	165	198

Drill 3

a	b	c	d	e	f
44	45	54	44	55	66
55	56	46	45	54	65
66	64	65	46	56	64
165	165	165	135	165	195

Drill 4

a	b	c	d	e	f
40	50	60	400	500	600
40	50	60	400	500	600
40	50	60	400	500	600
120	150	180	1,200	1,500	1,800

Drill 5

a	b	c	d	e	f
40	400	404	406	450	650
50	500	505	506	540	560
60	600	606	606	405	605
150	1,500	1,515	1,518	1,395	1,815

Production Goals

1. To integrate knowledge and skills previously learned.

2. To improve the efficiency (speed and accuracy) with which you complete documents.

3. To improve ability to follow standard formatting guides.

4. To manage time wisely in the production process.

Documents Processed

1. Letters

2. Formal Memorandums

3. Tables

4. Leftbound Report with Internal Citations

5. Agenda

6. Invoice

7. Purchase Order

MIDWESTERN OFFICE PRODUCTS: SALES DEPARTMENT

Before beginning the documents on pages 399-406, read the copy at the right. When planning the assigned documents, refer to the formatting guides given here to refresh your memory about proper formatting and spacing of documents.

Work Assignment

One of the secretaries in the Sales Department quit yesterday without giving notice. Ms. Linda Henry, the office supervisor for the Sales Department, has requested the Information Processing Center (IPC) supervisor to provide a temporary replacement until a permanent replacement can be hired. Since your work in the IPC has been of such high quality, Ms. Reinhold has asked you to assist Ms. Henry.

The majority of the documents you process during this assignment will be for the sales manager, Mr. Thomas M. Chaney. Ms. Henry will attach written instructions for each of the documents you are to process.

You will be given the Sales Department's "Guide to Document Formats," which summarizes the formats used by Midwestern Office Products. Refer to this Guide as needed when processing the various documents. Personnel in the Sales Department use either the modified block letter style or the simplified block letter style. Ms. Henry will indicate the originator's preference with her written instructions. Since Midwestern Office Products has based its word processing manual on your textbook, you may also use the text as a reference when Ms. Henry's directions and the "Guide to Document Formats" are not sufficiently detailed.

When necessary, supply missing parts for documents. For some documents you will be required to use your judgment since specific formatting directions will not be given. Correct errors in punctuation, spelling, capitalization, etc. Proofread each document carefully (even if your equipment includes a spell-check program) to produce correctly formatted, error-free documents.

Guide to Document Formats

Use the following guides as a quick reference to document formats.

Memorandums--Formal

Stationery: forms with preprinted headings.
SM: 1".

LS: DS between major parts of memo and between paragraphs. SS paragraphs.

Letters--Simplified Block

Stationery: letterheads.
SM: Set for 6″ line.
LS: SS with a DS between paragraphs.
PB: line 12.

Letters--Modified Block

Stationery: letterheads.
SM: short, 2″; average, 1½″; long, 1″.
LS: SS with a DS between paragraphs.
PB: short, line 18; average, line 16; long, line 14.

Reports--Leftbound

Stationery: plain sheets.
References: internal citations.
SM: left, 1½″; right, 1″.
PB (first page): line 10, 10-pitch; line 12, 12-pitch.
PB (second page): line 6, page number; line 8, text.
BM: at least 1″.
LS: DS text; SS tables.

Agendas

Stationery: plain sheets.
SM: 1″.
LS: DS, unless otherwise indicated.
PB: line 10.

Tabulated Documents

Stationery: plain full sheets.
LS: DS or SS, as indicated.
CV (center vertically).
CH (center horizontally).
CS: Even number of intercolumn spaces. Use more space between 2-column groups (when 2 columns are grouped under one common heading) than between individual columns.
Column Headings: Centered over column unless otherwise indicated. If 2 columns are grouped together below one heading, center heading over both columns.

2a ▶ *Improve Home-Key Technique*

Enter and check the columns of data listed at the right as directed in Steps 1-9 on p. A-3.

	a	b	c	d	e	f
	4	44	400	404	440	450
	5	55	500	505	550	560
	6	66	600	606	660	456
	15	165	1,500	1,515	1,650	1,466

2b ▶ *Learn New Keys: 7, 8, 9*

Learn reach to 7

1. Locate 7 (above 4) on the numeric keypad.

2. Watch your index finger move up to 7 and back to 4 a few times *without striking keys.*

3. Practice striking 74 a few times as you watch the finger.

4. With eyes on copy, enter the data in Drills 1a and 1b; check the total figures; reenter data if necessary.

Learn reach to 8

1. Learn the second-finger reach to 8 (above 5) as directed in Steps 1-3 above.

2. With eyes on copy, enter the data in Drills 1c and 1d; check the total figures; reenter data if necessary.

Learn reach to 9

1. Learn the third-finger reach to 9 (above 6) as directed above.

2. With eyes on copy, enter the data in Drills 1e and 1f; check the total figures; reenter data if necessary.

Drills 2-4

Practice entering the columns of data in Drills 2-4 until you can do so accurately and quickly.

Drill 1

a	b	c	d	e	f
474	747	585	858	696	969
747	777	858	888	969	999
777	474	888	585	999	696
1,998	1,998	2,331	2,331	2,664	2,664

Drill 2

a	b	c	d	e	f
774	885	996	745	475	754
474	585	696	854	584	846
747	858	969	965	695	956
1,995	2,328	2,661	2,564	1,754	2,556

Drill 3

a	b	c	d	e	f
470	580	690	770	707	407
740	850	960	880	808	508
704	805	906	990	909	609
1,914	2,235	2,556	2,640	2,424	1,524

Drill 4

a	b	c	d	e	f
456	407	508	609	804	905
789	408	509	704	805	906
654	409	607	705	806	907
987	507	608	706	904	908
2,886	1,731	2,232	2,724	3,319	3,626

2c ▶ *Learn to Enter Data with Unequal Numbers of Digits*

Enter single, double, and triple digits in columns as shown, left to right. The computer will align the digits automatically.

a	b	c	d	e	f
4	90	79	4	740	860
56	87	64	56	64	70
78	68	97	78	960	900
90	54	64	60	89	67
4	6	5	98	8	80
232	305	309	296	1,861	1,977

231a ▶ 5
Conditioning Practice

each line twice SS (slowly, then faster); if time permits, rekey selected lines

alphabet 1 Avoid such fizzling fireworks because they just might explode quickly.

figures 2 Ava's three trips earned air mileage of 1,086, 1,923, and 1,475 miles.

fig/sym 3 The #5346 item will cost McNeil & Company $921.78 (less 10% for cash).

speed 4 Pamela may sign the form for the men to do the dock work for the city.

| 1 | 2 | 3 | 4 | 5 | 6 | 7 | 8 | 9 | 10 | 11 | 12 | 13 | 14 |

231b ▶ 18
Improve Straight-Copy Speed and Accuracy

1. Three 1' writings on ¶ 1 for speed. **Goal:** Increase speed by 2-4 wam.

2. Follow Step 1 for ¶ 2.

3. Three 1' writings on ¶ 1 for accuracy. **Goal:** No more than 1 error a minute.

4. Follow Step 3 for ¶ 2.

5. A 3' writing on all ¶s.

6. Find gwam; circle errors.

all letters used | A | 1.5 si | 5.7 awl | 80% hfw

gwam 3'

In today's automated office, integrated software can help not only   5 | 60
to save time but also to expand capabilities and improve the quality   9 | 64
of the final product. It enables an office worker to develop a spread-   14 | 69
sheet quickly, change that data into graph form, and then move the graph   19 | 74
into a report. In the report, text can then be used to analyze and give   24 | 79
additional meaning to the data shown in the graph.   27 | 82

This kind of integration can be realized in one of three ways: 31 | 86
with a single package, with a software series, or with an integrator   36 | 91
program. The single package is better than the other two because it   40 | 95
requires just a few steps to move data from one program to another.   45 | 100
The software series has separate programs, but they use common com-   49 | 105
mands for ease in moving the data. The integrator moves data between   54 | 109
unlike programs.   55 | 110

gwam 3' | 1 | 2 | 3 | 4 | 5 |

231c ▶ 12 Check Language Skills

Most of the sentences at the right contain errors in number usage, spelling, or word choice, as labeled. Key each sentence, with the number and period, correcting errors in the copy and any keyboarding errors you may make.

Number usage

1. 22 seniors, 12 juniors, and 8 sophomores left on May tenth.
2. My address was 428 East Sixtieth Street; now it is 1 Park Place.
3. We purchased 12 computers, 6 printers, and 18 tables.

Spelling

4. My recomendation is that you select your categories soon.
5. Arrangments have allready been made to purchase the stationary.
6. Base your decision on experiance and careful analasis of the data.

Word choice

7. Did you hear that your required to choose your class ring today?
8. Want you speak to the heir of the property about cleaning the flue?
9. The bases of the recent duel was a disagreement about a loan.

231d ▶ 15 Assess Keyboarding Skill

Repeat 230d, p. 396, as directed.

3a ▶ Reinforce Reach-Strokes Learned

Enter and check the columns of data listed at the right as directed in Steps 1-9 on p. A-3.

a	b	c	d	e	f	g
44	74	740	996	704	990	477
55	85	850	885	805	880	588
66	96	960	774	906	770	699
165	255	2,550	2,655	2,415	2,640	1,764

3b ▶ Learn New Keys: 1, 2, 3

Learn reach to 1

1. Locate 1 (below 4) on the numeric keypad.

2. Watch your first finger move down to 1 and back to 4 a few times *without striking keys.*

3. Practice striking 14 a few times as you watch the finger.

4. With eyes on copy, enter the data in Drills 1a and 1b; check the total figures; reenter data if necessary.

Learn reach to 2

1. Learn the second-finger reach to 2 (below 5) as directed in Steps 1-3 above.

2. With eyes on copy, enter the data on Drills 1c and 1d; check the total figures; reenter data if necessary.

Learn reach to 3

1. Learn the third-finger reach to 3 (below 6) as directed above.

2. With eyes on copy, enter the data in Drills 1e, 1f, and 1g; check the total figures; reenter data if necessary.

Drills 2-4

Practice entering the columns of data in Drills 2-4 until you can do so accurately and quickly.

Drill 1

a	b	c	d	e	f	g
414	141	525	252	636	363	174
141	111	252	222	363	333	285
111	414	222	525	333	636	396
666	666	999	999	1,332	1,332	855

Drill 2

a	b	c	d	e	f	g
114	225	336	175	415	184	174
411	522	633	284	524	276	258
141	252	363	395	635	359	369
666	999	1,332	854	1,574	819	801

Drill 3

a	b	c	d	e	f	g
417	528	639	110	171	471	714
147	280	369	220	282	582	850
174	285	396	330	393	693	936
738	1,093	1,404	660	846	1,746	2,500

Drill 4

a	b	c	d	e	f	g
77	71	401	107	417	147	174
88	82	502	208	528	258	825
99	93	603	309	639	369	396
264	246	1,506	624	1,584	774	1,395

3c ▶ Enter Data Containing Commas

Enter the data in Columns a-g; check totals; reenter data as necessary.

Note: Even though number data often include commas to separate hundreds from thousands, do not enter them.

a	b	c	d	e	f	g
14	25	36	17	28	39	174
174	285	396	197	228	339	285
1,014	2,025	3,036	9,074	1,785	9,096	1,736
1,740	2,850	3,960	4,714	8,259	6,976	3,982
7,414	8,250	9,636	1,417	2,528	3,639	2,803
753	951	321	283	173	357	196
1,474	2,585	3,696	4,974	5,285	6,398	1,974
2,785	3,896	4,914	8,795	6,836	7,100	8,200
15,368	20,867	25,995	29,471	25,122	33,944	19,350

Check Language Skills

The sentences at the right contain errors in punctuation, capitalization, and spelling, as labeled. Key each sentence, with the number and period, correcting errors in the copy as well as any keyboarding errors you may make.

Punctuation
1. Although Terry ran well he was beaten by Franklin, Julio and James.
2. Di, the chair of the committee collected reports from the members.
3. Efficient loyal employees are valued by most companies.

Capitalization
4. The President of the Latin Club called the meeting to order on time.
5. Will school be dismissed on president's day?
6. Here is my advice: exercise slowly at first and speed up gradually.

Spelling
7. The hotel was able to accommodate all of the corperate employes.
8. The bank was expecially pleased that the morgage was released.
9. The supervisor offerred technicle assistance on the project.

230d ► 15
Assess Keyboarding Skill

Two 5' writings. Record *gwam*/errors for the better of the two writings on LP p. 1.

| all letters used | A | 1.5 si | 5.7 awl | 80% hfw | | gwam 1' | | 5' |

	gwam 1'	5'
Stress qualifies as either good or bad depending on the circum-	13	3	59
stances and ability of people to cope. It is good when it has resulted	27	5	62
from a pleasant event, such as a promotion. In addition, it may in-	41	8	65
crease job performance if the pressure is not too great. On the other	55	11	67
hand, stress is bad when caused by an unpleasant event, such as being	69	14	70
passed over for a prized promotion. Furthermore, it may interfere with	83	17	73
the performance of a task when the pressure is excessive.	95	19	75
The major point to recognize is that stress is quite normal and	107	21	78
will be experienced at times by all. Avoiding stress is not an issue,	122	24	81
but learning to handle day-to-day stress in a proper manner is. A few	136	27	84
methods that work are taking the time for regular exercise, getting	149	30	86
enough sleep, and eating well-balanced meals. These specific methods	163	33	89
relate to personal habits. In addition, using some stress reducers	177	35	92
that more directly relate to the job will also be helpful.	189	38	94
A good way to reduce stress in the office is to use techniques	201	40	97
known to improve time management. These include analyzing the tasks	215	43	99
performed to see if all are necessary, judging which ones are most im-	229	46	102
portant so that priorities can be set, and using most of the time to	243	49	105
do the jobs that are most important. Office workers who do not use	256	51	108
these procedures may expend considerable energy in less valuable tasks	271	54	110
and feel stressed when more important ones go unfinished.	282	56	113

gwam 1' | 1 | 2 | 3 | 4 | 5 | 6 | 7 | 8 | 9 | 10 | 11 | 12 | 13 | 14 |
5' | 1 | 2 | 3 |

4a ▶ Review Key Locations

Enter and check the columns of data listed at the right as directed in Steps 1-9 on p. A-3.

a	b	c	d	e	f	g
44	55	66	714	414	525	636
14	25	36	825	474	585	696
74	85	96	936	400	500	600
132	165	198	2,475	1,288	1,610	1,932

4b ▶ Improve Keyboarding Facility

Enter the data listed in each column of Drills 1-3; check each total; reenter the data in each column for which you did not get the correct total.

Drill 1

a	b	c	d	e	f	g
14	19	173	1,236	1,714	4,174	4,074
25	37	291	4,596	2,825	5,285	5,085
36	18	382	7,896	3,936	6,396	6,096
74	29	794	5,474	7,414	1,400	9,336
85	38	326	2,975	8,525	2,500	8,225
96	27	184	8,535	9,636	3,600	7,114
330	168	2,150	30,712	34,050	23,355	39,930

Drill 2

a	b	c	d	e	f	g
1	3	40	123	114	1,004	8,274
14	36	50	789	225	2,005	9,386
174	396	70	321	336	3,006	7,494
2	906	740	456	774	7,004	1,484
25	306	360	174	885	8,005	2,595
285	20	850	285	996	9,006	3,686
805	50	960	396	500	5,005	6,006
1,306	1,717	3,070	2,544	3,830	35,035	38,925

Drill 3

a	b	c	d	e	f	g
126	104	107	707	4,400	3,006	1,714
786	205	208	808	5,000	2,005	2,825
324	306	309	909	6,600	1,004	3,936
984	704	407	1,700	7,000	9,006	7,144
876	805	508	2,800	8,800	8,005	8,255
216	906	609	3,900	9,000	7,004	9,366
3,312	3,030	2,148	10,824	40,800	30,030	33,240

4c ▶ Enter Data with Decimals

Enter the data in Columns a-f, placing the decimals as shown in the copy.

a	b	c	d	e	f
1.40	17.10	47.17	174.11	1,477.01	10,704.50
2.50	28.20	58.28	285.22	2,588.02	17,815.70
3.60	39.30	69.39	396.33	3,996.03	20,808.75
4.70	74.70	17.10	417.14	4,174.07	26,909.65
5.80	85.80	28.20	528.25	5,285.08	30,906.25
6.90	96.90	39.30	639.36	6,396.06	34,259.90
24.90	342.00	259.44	2,440.41	23,916.27	141,401.75

Improve Keyboarding/Language Skills

Learning Goals

1. To improve keyboarding speed and accuracy on straight copy.
2. To assess straight-copy speed and accuracy.
3. To check language-skills competency.

Format Guides

1. Paper guide at *0* (for typewriters).
2. LL: 70 spaces for drills and paragraphs.
3. LS: SS drill lines; DS paragraphs.
4. PI: 5 spaces for paragraphs.

| Lesson 230 | Improve Keyboarding/Language Skills |

230a ▶ 5
Conditioning Practice

each line twice SS
(slowly, then faster);
if time permits,
rekey selected lines

alphabet	1	Open your gift quickly, but avoid scuffing the floor Zelma just waxed.
figures	2	Flights leave for Denver at 6:48, 9:36, 10:27, and 11:56 each morning.
fig/sym	3	The coat costs $358.14 (with a 20% discount), and I have only $297.60.
speed	4	Did six or eight firms bid on the authentic map of the ancient island?

| 1 | 2 | 3 | 4 | 5 | 6 | 7 | 8 | 9 | 10 | 11 | 12 | 13 | 14 |

230b ▶ 18
Improve Straight-Copy Speed and Accuracy

1. Three 1' writings on ¶ 1 for speed. **Goal:** Increase speed by 2-4 *wam*.
2. Follow Step 1 for ¶ 2.
3. Three 1' writings on ¶ 1 for accuracy. **Goal:** No more than 1 error a minute.
4. Follow Step 3 for ¶ 2.
5. One 3' writing on both ¶s.
6. Find *gwam;* circle errors.

all letters used | A | 1.5 si | 5.7 awl | 80% hfw

gwam 3'   5'

Some people seem to have a greater level of job stress than others, — 5 | 3 | 35

and the reason for the differences may not be revealed by just a quick — 9 | 6 | 38

observation. Without taking time to analyze a situation, one may assume — 14 | 8 | 41

that the jobs of highly stressed people are much more demanding; but a — 19 | 11 | 43

close examination may point out that the real discrepancy is in the way — 24 | 14 | 46

people react to a potentially stressful situation. — 27 | 16 | 48

For example, some job-related problems, such as the quality of — 31 | 19 | 51

work performed by co-workers, cannot be resolved by the office worker. — 36 | 22 | 54

The reaction of one person may be to recognize and accept the situation — 41 | 25 | 57

whereas the reaction of another may be to worry about the dilemma. The — 46 | 27 | 59

person whose attitude is to make the best of such a plight will likely — 50 | 30 | 62

become less stressed than the one who worries. — 53 | 32 | 64

gwam 3' | 1 | 2 | 3 | 4 | 5 |
5' | 1 | 2 | 3 |

Improve Keyboarding/Language Skills

5a ▶ Review
Key Locations

Enter and check the columns of data listed at the right.

a	b	c	d	e	f	g
477	588	707	107	41.6	141.4	936.6
417	528	808	205	52.9	252.5	825.6
717	825	909	309	63.3	393.3	719.4
1,611	1,941	2,424	621	157.8	787.2	2,481.6

5b ▶ Improve
Keyboarding Facility

Enter the data listed in each column of Drills 1-4; check each total by entering the data a second time (from bottom to top).

If you get the same total twice, you can "assume" it is correct. If you get a different total the second time, reenter the data until you get two totals that match.

Drill 1

a	b	c	d	e	f	g
5	77	114	5,808	1,936	9,300	6,936
46	89	225	3,997	2,825	8,250	3,896
3	78	336	9,408	3,796	10,475	7,140
17	85	725	5,650	8,625	7,125	4,874
28	98	825	3,714	9,436	12,740	2,515
9	69	936	2,825	8,514	12,850	8,360
10	97	704	6,796	4,174	9,674	1,794

Drill 2

a	b	c	d	e	f	g
99	795	1,581	1,881	2,642	4,573	2,185
67	657	1,691	1,991	2,772	4,683	3,274
88	234	1,339	2,202	2,992	5,477	9,396
96	359	1,221	2,432	3,743	6,409	4,585
84	762	1,101	3,303	3,853	6,886	5,872
100	485	1,144	4,650	4,714	7,936	6,903

Drill 3

a	b	c	d	e	f
1,077	3,006	5,208	7,104	1,774	7,417
1,400	3,609	5,502	8,205	2,885	8,528
1,700	3,900	5,205	9,303	3,996	9,639
2,008	4,107	6,309	7,407	4,174	3,936
2,500	4,400	6,600	8,508	5,285	5,828
2,805	1,704	6,900	9,609	6,396	4,717

Drill 4

a	b	c	d	e	f
1.4	14.00	170.40	1,714.70	7,410.95	1,147.74
2.5	17.00	170.43	2,825.80	8,520.55	2,258.88
3.6	25.00	250.90	3,936.90	9,630.65	3,369.93
7.4	28.00	288.50	4,747.17	10,585.78	7,144.74
8.5	36.00	369.63	5,878.25	11,474.85	8,255.85
9.6	39.00	390.69	6,969.39	12,696.95	9,366.63

226b-229b (continued)

Documents 11 and 12
Tables

> **OLIVIA REINHOLD**
> **IPC Supervisor**
>
> From the information attached, please process two double-spaced tables, one comparing the Star 6087 and EIT 621 (columns 1, 2, and 3) and one comparing the Star 6087 and the Elec II (columns 1, 2, and 4). OR

ELECTRONIC TYPEWRITER FEATURES

Features	Star 6087	EIT 621	Elec II
Basic Memory	31K	32K	32K
Upgradeable Memory	no	to 6~~5~~4K	no
Display	24 characters	40 characters	40 characters
Print Speed	16 cps	17 cps	17 cps
Maximum Writing Line	13.2"	14"	13.5"
Characters on Printwheel	92	100	92
Search Capability	yes	yes	no
Automatic Bold	no	yes	yes
Sheet Feeder	no	no	optional
Text Merging in Memory	no	~~no~~ yes	yes
Word Processor Upgrade	optinoal	no	optional
Suggested List Price	$899	$1,089	$1,285

Source: Electronic Typewriter Guide, 1992.

Document 13
Simplified Memo
plain paper

> **OLIVIA REINHOLD**
> **IPC Supervisor**
>
> Please process this memo from **Carlos J. Menez, Director of Human Resources,** to **All Department Managers.** Date 1/20 OR

"Greater Graphics" is a half day seminar promoting the increased use of graphics with a desktop publishing system. This program is sponsored by Brooks Information Systems. It will be held on February 15, 19--, from 9:00am to 11:30am, at the Brooks Building, 450 Cedar Street, Room 618

The fee for this seminar is $50 and will be paid from the HRD budget for the first twelve people making a reservation through my office.

Please disbribute this information to the people in your department who you think should consider attending.

B   C   D

ST QUARTER SALES - REGION 1

   QUOTA   SALES   OVER/UNDER

$1,750,000 $2,362,500   35.00%

Page: 1   Line: 12   J_SMART.LTR

Dear John:

Congratulations! You not only met your sa
you exceeded it by 35% which is tops in th
This is just a quick note to tell you how much we
appreciate your work and that you have won a trip
the Bahamas all expenses paid for a week.

I'll see you next week at the sales meeting
will be my pleasure to present you with th
award certificate. Meanwhile, we have
quota 20% for the next quarter. Go

F2 LAYOUT
F3 SWITCHES

F4 PRINT BLK.
F5 PRINT DOC.

F6 HEADR FILE
F7 FOOTR FILE
F8 FMAT. FILE

F9 LINEFEED
F0 FORMFEED

APPENDIX B
Automatic Features/Editing Functions of Electronic Equipment

Learning Goals

1. To learn the basic functions of electronic equipment.

2. To learn the specific commands for your particular software package.

3. To apply these functions and commands to perform the activities.

Practice Procedure

Follow the directions for each activity. Practice the drills until you feel comfortable enough to move to the next activity.

Study the software documentation and note the command for each function.

KNOW WHAT'S HAPPENING...

"For the times they are a-changin" went the words of a popular tune some years ago. And my how they've changed! A quick look at the composition of the United States labor force illustrates only one component of change. In 1920, close to 80 percent of the work force consisted of agricultural and industrial workers. The dominant sector of today's labor force, close to 90 percent, consists of information and service workers. Today's information technologies--such as electronic typewriters, personal computers, FAX machines, scanners, intelligent copiers and printers, electronic mail, and telecommunication devices--are having a major impact on workplace roles. Due to the information explosion, many of the new career opportunities in today's marketplace are based on computer technology.

The tools we work with have changed and will continue to change. For example, look what's happened to the typewriter and the world of document preparation. The user of a manual typewriter purchased an eraser to correct errors. The user of an electric may have had the luxury of correct-o-type to fix blunders. The electronic typewriter user may be able to store a few phrases or pages before printing a document. A personal computer, also called a microcomputer, makes document creation, formatting, and editing even easier when word processing software is used.

As the tools we work with continue to change, we ourselves must adapt to remain successful workers and fulfilled individuals. This section has been designed to inform you of some of the features and functions you will encounter when using an electronic typewriter and/or personal computer with word processing software to prepare documents.

KNOW THE "IN BRIEF" SECTION...

"In Brief" is designed to give you a generic description of the most commonly used word processing features. Read each one carefully. Since directions for each feature differ from program to program and not all programs contain every feature, study your software user's manual to learn the specific step-by-step instructions for your particular program. The software commands given in "In Brief" are for WordPerfect Versions 4.2 and 5.0.

KNOW YOUR SOFTWARE...

Software is a program, a set of directions (instructions) that tells your computer to perform a specific task. Word processing software is a package that allows the user to create and format a document, save (store/file) it, retrieve and edit the text, and print the document. Some commonly used word processing features are insert and delete, center, move, copy, indent, columns and decimal alignment, page numbering, boldface, underline, and print. It is important to become familiar with your software package.

KNOW WHAT TO DO...

(1) Read the "In Brief" feature section. (2) Study the user's manual for your equipment. (3) Study your software documentation for the specific function. (4) Read the directions for the lesson, then key the drills accordingly.

KNOW YOUR EQUIPMENT...THE KEYBOARD...

For a quick review of the components of a personal computer, refer to pages viii and ix. Since many word processing functions require the user to strike a combination of keys, the keyboard arrangement of the three popular machines shown on these pages may help. Use the numbered items listed there to identify each key. If you are using a different computer, consult the instruction booklet that came with the equipment.

OLIVIA REINHOLD
IPC Supervisor

Please process the attached letter for **Miss Patricia S. Wilmer, Manager of Exhibits.** Send it to the addressee shown on the attached business card. Fill in the blanks as follows:

Paragraph 1, **Madison, Wisconsin**

Paragraph 2, **Tonya Swartz**

Date 1/20   OR

Thomas M. Imuta, President
Imuta and Barone Industries
414 Corydon Road
Eau Claire, WI 54701-6600

OLIVIA REINHOLD
IPC Supervisor

Miss Wilmer would like another copy of the letter you just processed. She cannot remember the name of the office manager to whom you should send the letter, so use the salutation **"Ladies and Gentlemen"** and address the letter as follows:

Attention Office Manager
Wetherby and Associates
726 Alliance Road
Rockford, IL 61103-3799

Fill in the blanks as follows:

Paragraph 1, **Kansas City, Missouri**

Paragraph 3, **Al Davidson**

Date 1/20   OR

Integrated program. Integrated packages permit the creation, editing, and integration of text, graphics, spread sheets, and data bases with less effort than would otherwise be required. In particular, the editing of text should be completed here where it can be done much more efficiently than in the DTP program. Then the document is moved to the DTP program for further manipulation.

DTP program.

Page layout and design are perfected in the DPT program. Metzner elaborates: Text can be flowed around the various graphic presentations, such as charts, tables, and drawings. Headings and head lines can be sized and styled. Borders can be added and cover pages can be designed to generate professional-quality output. (Metzner, 1988, 34)

Thank you for stopping by our exhibit during the recent Office Systems Conference in _____. We appreciate your interest in all of our new products.

Since you expressed interest in desktop publishing we are enclosing a desktop publishing report that may be helpful as you plan to implement desktop publishing in your company. In addition we would like to give you and your company's most likely users an on-site demonstration of our DTP 8000 system.

_____ our Office Systems Consultant for your area, will call you next week to arrange a convenient time.

(Send a copy to consultant—Tonya or Al.)

Activity 1
Backspace Erase Feature

1. Read the "In Brief" copy at right.
2. Study software documentation to learn to use the backspace erase feature.
3. Read sentences at right.
4. Key each line twice DS using the backspace erase feature when needed.

BACKSPACE ERASE

An electronic editing tool that allows you to backspace and delete a previously keyed character (or characters).

Every time you strike the backspace erase key, the character to the left of the cursor is automatically erased (deleted).

1 Work is not only a way to make a living: It's the way to make a life!

2 The majority of new jobs will come from small, independent businesses.

3 Planning a career today requires more thought than it ever did before.

Activity 2
Cursor (Arrow) Keys

1. Read the "In Brief" copy at right.
2. Study software documentation to learn to use cursor keys.
3. Read sentences at right.
4. Key the sentences DS.
5. Using arrow keys, move the cursor to:
x in **flexibility**, line 1
v in **effectively**, line 3
d in **attitudes**, line 1
p in **compete**, line 3
m in **motivation**, line 2

CURSOR

A blinking light on the screen that identifies the position where text (copy) will be entered or edited. Arrow keys (cursor keys) used to move the cursor around the screen may be located on your computer's numeric keypad or as a separate group of keys between the main keyboard and the keypad.

LEFT/RIGHT CURSOR (ARROW) KEYS

These keys move the cursor one space at a time in a left or a right direction.

UP/DOWN CURSOR (ARROW) KEYS

These keys move the cursor up or down one line at a time.

1 Today, job seekers must possess a flexibility of skills and attitudes.

2 Getting the job you want requires motivation, energy, and preparation.

3 To compete effectively for the most attractive jobs, be well informed.

Activity 3
Strikeover, Insert, and Delete Editing Features

1. Read the "In Brief" copy at right.
2. Study software documentation to learn to use strikeover, insert, and delete features.
3. Read sentences at right.
4. Key each sentence DS as shown.
5. Make these changes (use the arrow keys to move the cursor):
Line
1, insert " after **career (career")**
1, replace 2d e in **seperate** with an **a**
2, delete b in **jobb**
2, delete r in **carreer (career)**
2, delete space in **it self**
3, insert c in **piking (picking)**
3, insert e in **carer (career)**
3, insert l in **chalenge (challenge)**
4, delete **s** in **keys**
4, replace 2d **s** in **sequence** with **c**
4, insert c and s in **aces (access)**

STRIKEOVER/REPLACEMENT MODE

Editing feature that allows you to position the cursor and key over (strikeover) characters. Existing text is automatically erased and replaced by new text.

INSERT

Editing feature that allows you to add characters without rekeying the entire

document. New text is inserted and existing text is pushed to the right or down to make room for the addition.

DELETE

Editing feature that removes (erases) any character or characters, including blank spaces, identified (highlighted) by the cursor. Existing text to right moves over and text below moves up to close the space.

1 Today the two terms "career and "job" have totally seperate meanings.

2 Consider your jobb as a way to a carreer, not a career in and of it self.

3 No longer is piking a carer to get a job the chalenge workers face.

4 The keys is choosing the best sequense of jobs with aces to a career.

Document 7
Purchase Order LP p. 9

> **OLIVIA REINHOLD**
> **IPC Supervisor**
>
> Please process this purchase order. I suggest that you verify the $ amounts by calculating extensions and the total.
>
> *OR*

Document 8
Report

> **OLIVIA REINHOLD**
> **IPC Supervisor**
>
> Please prepare a final copy of this report. Insert the following items:
>
> Report Title:
> **DESKTOP PUBLISHING**
>
> Side Headings:
> Paragraph 3, **Hardware Requirements**
>
> Paragraph 4, **Software Requirements**
>
> Key **REFERENCES** a QS below the last line of body copy; begin list QS below head.
>
> "Desktop Publishing Drives a High-Tech Company." **Modern Office Technology**, May 1988, 80-88.
>
> Lloyd, Julian. "Desktop Publishing." **Office Guide**, July 1988, 62-63.
>
> Metzner, Kermit. "Desktop Publishing: Pretty as a Picture." **Office Systems 88**, March 1988, 33-38.
>
> *OR*

MIDWESTERN OFFICE PRODUCTS

3871 BRIDGE AVENUE, DAVENPORT, IA 52807-7002 (319) 887-1462

PURCHASE ORDER

TWINING OFFICE SUPPLY
700 BROWN STREET
DAVENPORT IA 52802-4566

Purchase Order No.: 416221~~e~~ 368
Date: ~~July 10~~, 19-- *January 20*
Terms: 2/10, n,30
Shipped Via: Wayne Express

Quantity	Description/Stock Number	Price		Per	Total	
15 ~~10~~ bx	File Folders--862-380-41	15 ~~14~~	10 ~~88~~	bx	226 ~~148~~	50 ~~80~~
12 dz	Pencils--862-T-860	1	39	dz	16	88
12 ~~10~~ dz	Razorpoint Pens--862-SW-BK	8	88	dz	88	80
2 dz	Markers--862-04467	7	49	dz	14	98
10 bx	*Staples*--862-467	106.56	71	bx	7	10
					~~269~~	~~26~~
					372	02

By _____

---

according to Metzner (1988, 34),

Desktop publishing (DTP) allows in-house production of high-quality output that almost looks typeset. ~~reported Metzner (1988, 34).~~ Some of the benefits of in-house production include faster turnaround time, lowered production costs, increased control over the publication process and improved layout and design (Modern Office Technology, 1988, 80).

Although most automated companies own some of the components required for DTP, some hardware and software additions and/or modifications are usually necessary.

According to Lloyd (1988, 62-63, the hardware requirements include a personal computer with at least 512K of random-access memory (RAM) and graphics capability. He further indicates that a mouse, although optional is helpful. A mouse is described by Metzner (1988, 34) as a hand held device attached to the computer; it is used by moving the device around on a hard surface to reposition images and arrows or other indicators as well as to activate commands.

The additional hardware required is a laser printer.

As a minimum, two kinds of software are needed for a DTP project. Ideally, an integrated program is used to create a document before it is transferred to the DTP program.

(continued, p. 393)

Activity 4
Margins, Tabs, and Vertical Spacing

1. Read the "In Brief" copy at right.

2. Study software documentation to learn to set a 60-space line, 5-space paragraph indent tab, and double spacing.

3. Read copy below right.

4. Key the paragraph.

RULER/FORMAT LINE

Line at the top or botom of the screen or accessible within a document used to set the document format consisting of left and right margins, tab stops, text alignment and line-spacing.

MARGINS

The blank space on the left and right sides and at the top and bottom of a page. Left and right margins can be adjusted according to the desired line space; top and bottom margins can also be adjusted.

TABS

Stops set in the ruler/format line that allow you to indent paragraphs and lists and to align columns in tables. When you strike the TAB key, the cursor moves to the desired tab stop. If you key more than one line, the following lines align with the left margin instead of the tab stop.

SPACING

The space between lines of text. Line-spacing may be set for SS (1) or DS (2). A quadruple space is keyed by striking the return an appropriate number of times.

The average person spends 9 percent of the time writing, 16 percent reading, 30 percent speaking, and 45 percent listening. The fact that an individual is given two ears and only one mouth indicates the proper proportion of listening to speaking. Therefore, take heed of the Korean proverb: "Fools chatter; wise men listen."

Activity 5
Word Wrap and Soft and Hard Returns

1. Read the "In Brief" copy at the right.

2. Study software documentation to learn to use the word wrap and soft and hard returns.

3. Read paragraphs at right.

4. Use your program's default settings (or set a 70-space line and a 5-space paragraph indent tab).

5. Key the paragraphs DS using hard returns only between paragraphs.

6. As you key, correct any mistakes using the backspace key.

7. Proofread; make any necessary corrections using the strikeover, insert, and delete functions.

8. With the arrow keys, move the cursor to the beginning of the first ¶. Change to a 50-space line, 5-space paragraph indent tab. Then strike the down arrow repeatedly. What happened?

9. With the arrow keys, move the cursor to the beginning of the first ¶. Change to a 60-space line, 5-space paragraph indent tab. Then strike the down arrow repeatedly. What happened?

WORD WRAP

An automatic feature that determines whether the word being keyed will extend beyond the right margin. If so, the program automatically "wraps the text around" to the beginning of the next line while the user continues keying. A carriage return is necessary only when mandatory, such as at the end of a paragraph or a line of statistical copy.

SOFT RETURN

Automatically entered by the program at the end of a line of copy when text is being "wrapped around" to the next line. When you adjust the margins or insert and/or delete copy, the program automatically changes the position of the soft return.

HARD RETURN

Entered by striking the return key. Hard returns can be removed only by deleting them with backspace erase or the delete feature.

How does your word processing program know where to set the margins when you don't key the numbers? Simple. The program sets them according to the default. A default is a setting entered into a program by the designer. Paper size (8½ × 11 inches), pitch (pica--10), left and right margins, and tab settings are example of preset defaults.

Let's say your program has a default setting of 10 for the left margin and 74 for the right. Should you desire a longer or shorter line of copy, simply change the default setting. Defaults are created to appeal to the majority of users most of the time. Designers try to assume exactly what settings users will want to work with.

OLIVIA REINHOLD
IPC Supervisor

Please prepare this document as a report to accompany the memo from Mr. Chaney. Insert the following items:

Report Title: LASER PRINTERS

Side Headings:
Paragraph 2, **Key Features of Laser Printers**

Paragraph 3, **Major Advantages of Laser Printers**

Key **REFERENCES** a QS below the last line of body copy; begin list a QS below head. *OR*

Key features and major advantages of *laser* printers should be given careful consideration when a new *printer* one is selected. *¶2* Some of the *key* features of laser printers are *identified* discussed by Hart (1988, 49, 51). They *include capacities* are the ability to print a wide range of fonts and type faces, to combine text and graphics, and to print "an entire page at a time, rather than character by charater or line by line" (Hart, 1988, 51). These capabilities offer *several* many printing advantages.

~~The~~ three major advantages of using laser printers are desktop-publishing capability, high-speed printing and high-quality printing. With desk top publishing, many companies have *substantially* reduced printing costs while maintaining high quality publications. And with an output speed of ten pages per minute, an acceptable office standard reported by Brindza (1988, 106), a large volume of work can be *processed* printed by one printer.

Brindza, Stephen. "Advancing Technology Hones in on Printing." Modern Office Technology, October 1988, 102-106.

Hart, Roger. "Computer Printers: How to Choose One." Office Systems 88, October 1988, 48-52.

Documents 5 and 6
Tables

OLIVIA REINHOLD
IPC Supervisor

This table was received from the Accounting Department with directions to prepare the table once with columns 1-4, including totals, and a second time with columns 1-3 and 5, omitting totals.

Main Heading: NET CHANGES IN INCOME

Secondary Heading:
FY 1990-FY 1991

Please DS each table on a full sheet. *OR*

Product Group	FY-1990	FY-1991	$ Change	%
Hardware	$3,636,482	$4,100,236	$463,754	12.8
Software	121,386 421	166,281	44,895 860	37.0 ~~36.9~~
Printware	56,223	41,862	(14,361)	-25.5
Instruction	89,248	104,286	15,038	16.8
Supplies	21,224	27,864	6,640	31.3
Consulting	47,863	66,291	18,428	38.5
Total	$3,972,426 461	$4,506,820	$534,394 359	

Activity 6
Review Setting Margins, Tabs, Vertical Spacing, Word Wrap, Insert, Delete, and Strikeover Features

1. Read the ¶ at the right.

2. LL: 60 spaces; LS: DS; ¶ indent tab: 5 spaces.

3. Key ¶s as is; do not correct errors; use a hard return only between ¶s.

4. Make these changes:

Paragraph 1
Line
1, replace **s** in **sertain** with **c**
2, replace 2d **e** in **seperate** with **a**
2, delete space in **up scale**
2, delete space in **down scale**
3, hyphenate **not so rich**
3, change **people** to **individuals**
4, replace **there** with **their**
4, change **area** to **field**
5, insert **entertainment** after **education**
6, change **you** to **yourself**
7, change **imagine** to **picture**

Paragraph 2
Line
8, delete **l** in **successfull**
9, change **they're** to **they are**
10, delete space in **any one**
10, delete space in **under stand**
11, change **&** to **and**
11, replace **T** in 2d **They** with **t**
12, delete space in **care fully**
12, delete **r** and insert **l** in **generraly (generally)**

1　　Research has shown that sertain personality traits

2　seperate the up scale from the down scale, the rich from

3　the not so rich. These traits bring people success

4　regardless of there chosen area--business, sports,

5　education, or politics. One of the necessary

6　traits is the ability to envision you succeeding. If you

7　can imagine it, you can achieve it.

8　　Another trait of successfull individuals is goal

9　setting. Usually they're not any more intelligent than

10　any one else. However, they set their goals, under stand

11　them, & make sure they are achieved. They don't rush; They

12　plan their actions care fully. Generraly they live by the

13　rule "plan your work, then work your plan."

Activity 7
Underline Text Automatically While Keying

1. Read the "In Brief" copy.

2. Study software documentation to learn to underline existing text and how to underline text automatically while keying.

3. LL: 70 spaces; LS: DS.

4. Read sentences at right.

5. Key sentences using automatic underscore where shown.

6. When finished, proofread your work, making any corrections using insert, delete, and strikeover features.

7. Underline these words in the existing text:

Line:
1, **listening**
2, **information, notes**
3, **listening**
4, **First**

UNDERLINE EXISTING TEXT

Position the cursor (or printwheel) at the beginning of the existing text. Hold down the left shift key and strike the hyphen key. You may have to identify the block of text by entering a specific command (*such as the Alternate and F4 keys*) and then enter the underline command (*such as the F8 key*).

UNDERLINE TEXT AS YOU KEY (AUTOMATIC)

Turn on automatic (continuous) underlining by striking a keystroke combination (*such as Code and u*), or strike the assigned function key (*such as F8*). As you key, the text will be underlined. When you're finished, turn automatic underlining off by striking the same key or combination.

1　The four steps to listening are: <u>sense</u>, <u>interpret</u>, <u>evaluate</u>, <u>respond</u>.

2　<u>Active</u> <u>listening</u> involves processing the information and taking notes.

3　A <u>conversation</u> requires both listening for main ideas and <u>interacting</u>.

4　First on the list of very <u>nonproductive</u> listening habits is <u>fidgeting</u>.

5　If you fidget, you may <u>tug</u> your <u>earlobe</u>, <u>shuffle</u> your <u>feet</u>, or <u>squirm</u>.

226a-229a ▶ 5 *(daily)*
Conditioning Practice
Key the lines at least twice a day to ensure that your equipment is working properly.

alphabet	1	Zack, be a good fellow and keep quiet as you relax to enjoy his movie.
figures	2	Of the 647 seniors and 893 juniors, 1,250 attended the prom last week.
fig/sym	3	List your expenses: taxi $59, air fare $260, mileage $37 (148 miles).
speed	4	Their visit may end the problems of the firm and make us a big profit.

| 1 | 2 | 3 | 4 | 5 | 6 | 7 | 8 | 9 | 10 | 11 | 12 | 13 | 14 |

226b-229b ▶ 45 *(daily)*
Document Processing
Documents 1 and 2
Letters LP pp. 5-7

OLIVIA REINHOLD
IPC Supervisor

Process these letters for **Ms. Diane A. Palmer, Learning Center Director.** Provide missing letter parts, including a subject line. Use the date of **January 16, 19—** and the information below.

Mr. Reginald R. Gates
Office Manager
Tucker and James Trucking
2000 Adams Street
Davenport, IA 52803-8115

(A) Document Maker
(B) February 10, 16, and 24

Mrs. Doris C. Johnson
Administrative Vice President
Miller Construction Co.
750 North Colfax Avenue
Minneapolis, MN 55405-1004

(A) Project Manager
(B) February 11, 17, and 25
OR

Document 3
Simplified Memo plain paper

OLIVIA REINHOLD
IPC Supervisor

Key this memo to **All Sales Representatives** from **Thomas Chaney, Sales Manager,** whose secretary is ill. Date it **January 16, 19—**. *OR*

Recently you expressed an interest in receiving information about our (A) Instructional Program for next month. We now have three sessions scheduled and hope that your new users of (A) will be able to participate in one of them.

The dates are (B) from 1:30 p.m. to 4:30 p.m. with an optional two-hour open lab following. All sessions will be held in our Learning Center at this location. All instructional materials will be provided; however, participants may wish to bring their (A) Operator's Manuals if they have already purchased the software.

The cost of this instructional program is $50 per person or $40 per person if three or more from your company register. The enclosed registration form should be completed and returned in time for us to receive it at least two days prior to the training session your users wish to attend. If you have questions, call me at (319) 887-1462.

The enclosed report about laser printers ~~should~~ *will* be helpful to you when working with clients who should be thinking about updating their printers. ~~Although~~ *Even though* clients may not have mentioned the need for a new printer, simply describing the *key* main features and major advantages of a laser may cause your clients to start thinking about one.

I suggest that you give *a copy of* this report to every client who does not already have a laser printer. ~~It's~~ *It is* a good introductory sales piece.

I am sending a supply of about 100 copies. ~~If~~ *When* you need more, let me know.

Activity 8
Bold Text

1. Read the "In Brief" copy.
2. Study software documentation to learn to bold text.
3. Set a 70-space line, DS.
4. Key the sentences using the bold feature where shown.
5. Proofread your work. Make any necessary corrections and print a copy.

BOLD TEXT

The bold feature emphasizes text by printing characters darker than others. This bold effect is created when the printer strikes each designated character twice. Turn on the bold command by striking the assigned key or keystroke combination (such as the F6 key or the Code and b keys). Key the text to be printed in bold, which may appear highlighted on the screen. Turn off the bold command by striking the same key or keystroke combination.

1 **Boom boxes** and various other background noises are **distractions** to us.

2 Your **emotions** and **personal ideas** influence your reaction to a speaker.

3 One huge roadblock we all face is an **overestimation** of our **importance**.

4 A **passive listener** simply nods in **agreement** throughout a **conversation**.

Activity 9 Center Text Horizontally

1. Read the "In Brief" copy.
2. Study software documentation to learn to center text.
3. Set a 50-space line, SS.
4. Read the drills below.
5. Key each line of each drill using automatic centering, if offered. If not, center each drill manually. Underline and bold the text as shown.

AUTOMATIC CENTERING

To center automatically, position the cursor (or printwheel) at the left margin. Hold down the designated key combination (such as Code and c); the cursor moves to the center of the line. As you key, the cursor backs up (but does not print). To print the centered copy, strike the return key. You may have to enter the center command (such as shift and F6 keys). The cursor moves to the center of the line. As you key, the letters back up once for every two characters. Strike the return key (hard return).

Drill 1

STAND UP AND DELIVER

Express Your Opinion Concisely
Be Confident
Beware--Your Body Language is also "Speaking"
Your Tone of Voice Says it All
Pay Attention to Your Listener
Observe Body Language of Others

Drill 2

A KEY TO EFFECTIVE COMMUNICATION: MATCHING STYLES WITH CONTENT

Small Talk--Chatty, Noncommittal
Control Talk--Take Charge
Search Talk--Analyze Problems; Possible Solutions
Straight Talk--Handle Conflicts Constructively

Drill 3

GAMESMANSHIP PROBLEMS AT WORK

Answer a Question with a Question
Discuss Others Rather than One's Self
Send Incomplete Messages
Provide Superficial Information About an Issue
Use We or They rather than I or You
Withhold Important Information

Information Processing Center

Production Goals

1. To follow carefully the standard formatting guides for processing documents.
2. To produce high-quality documents by proofreading and correcting all errors.
3. To work efficiently in completing the various documents assigned.

Documents Processed

1. Letters in Block Format with Open Punctuation
2. Simplified Memorandums
3. Unbound Report with Internal Citations
4. Tables with Blocked Column Headings
5. Purchase Order

MIDWESTERN OFFICE PRODUCTS: INFORMATION PROCESSING CENTER

Before beginning the documents on pages 390-394, read the copy at the right. When planning the assigned documents, refer to the formatting guides given here to refresh your memory about proper formatting and spacing of documents.

Work Assignment

Your first assignment with Midwestern Office Products is in the Information Processing Center (IPC) where you will work under the direction of Ms. Olivia M. Reinhold, the IPC supervisor. All documents that you process will be assigned by Ms. Reinhold and will be returned to her for approval before they are sent to the originator.

Along with specific document formatting guidelines, Ms. Reinhold gives you the following information and instructions.

The documents that you will process will be from handwritten and rough-draft copy, typewritten copy, and boilerplate. You may need to supply letter parts that have not been provided by the document originator, and you will have to correct language-skills errors that have not been marked for correction.

Unless otherwise instructed, use the formats described in the Guide to Document Formats.

Guide to Document Formats

Letters--Block Format, Open Punctuation

Stationery: letterheads.
SM (side margins): short, 2″; average, 1½″.
PB (page beginning): short, line 18; average, line 16.
Letter parts: all begin at LM (left margin).
LS (line spacing): QS below date and complimentary close; DS below other parts.
Attention line: first line of address.
Subject line: DS below salutation, ALL CAPS.
Enclosure notation: DS below reference initials.
Copy notation: DS below reference initials or below enclosure notation when used.

Envelope (Large #10)

Address placement: 5 spaces left of center.
Format: ALL CAPS, no punctuation.

Memorandums--Simplified

Stationery: plain sheets.
SM: 1″.
PB: line 10.
Memo parts: all begin at LM.
LS: QS below date and last line of body; DS below other parts.

Tables

LS: DS (body may be SS), including space above and below 1½″ divider line separating body and source note; underline last figure above totals.
CV (center vertically): calculate PB by subtracting lines used from lines available and dividing by 2; disregard fraction; if even number results, space down that number of lines; if odd number results, use next lower number and space down that number of lines.
CS (columnar spacing): 6 to 20 (even number).
CH (center horizontally): backspace from center once for every 2 strokes of longest line of each column and once for every 2 intercolumn spaces. Set LM (if the equipment you are using has an automatic centering feature, use it to determine the LM setting). From LM space forward once for each stroke in longest line of column plus once for each space in intercolumn. Set tab and continue spacing forward to set remaining tabs.
Column heads: blocked at LM and tabs.

Reports--Unbound

Stationery: plain sheets.
References: internal citations.
SM: 1″.
BM (bottom margin): 1″.
PB (first page): line 10, 10-pitch; line 12, 12-pitch.
PB (second and succeeding pages): line 6, page number. line 8, text.
LS: QS below main or secondary head; DS text.

Activity 10
Required Space Feature

1. Read the "In Brief" copy at right.
2. Study software documentation to learn to use the required space feature.
3. Set a 60-space line, DS.
4. Read sentences at right.
5. Key sentences using required space feature where needed.
6. Proofread; make any necessary corrections.
7. Print a final copy.

HARD (REQUIRED) SPACE

A feature that guards against breaking a line of printed text between title and surname (Mr. Magoo), initials (B. L. Smith), month and date (December 7, 1941), and parts of a formula (a + b + c), etc. Inserting hard (required) spaces between items of text causes the printer to regard the phrase as one word. When you strike a specific key (such as the Home key), along with the space bar, you enter a "hard space." (A special symbol or code may appear on the screen.) The printer will print the text containing the hard space on one line.

1 A cartoon personality that won the hearts of many was Mr. Magoo.

2 The movies have brought us many stars; for example, Zsa Zsa Gabor.

3 The Declaration of Independence was signed on Thursday, July 4, 1776.

Activity 11
Review Margins, Tabs, Spacing, Required Space, Automatic Center, Underline, and Bold Features

1. Read paragraphs at right.
2. Set a 70-space line, 5-space paragraph indent tab, DS.
3. Center headings; use underline and bold where shown.
4. Key the document.
5. Proofread your work. Make any necessary corrections and print a copy.

PERSONAL STYLE

HOW TO MAKE YOURSELF SPECIAL

The basis for style--one's distinctive manner of expression--comes from within. Style is not something we're born with but rather a combination of abilities that we learn as we mature, just as we learn to speak Russian, repair leaky faucets, or drive a car. Style is a very personal achievement; it's a quality that money cannot buy. As a matter of fact, style has nothing at all to do with money.

WHAT IT TAKES...

Personal style is a mixture of six main elements. (1) Knowing what to add and when to stop is a matter of **balance** and **restraint**. (2) Paying **attention to detail** allows you to think things through to create comfort and satisfaction. (3) **Consideration** means you are alert to other people's needs and sensitivities and respond to them. (4) **Poise, grace,** and **self-confidence** come from knowing one's self without being vain. (5) The ability to **make good choices** helps you make the right decision at the right time. (6) **Individuality** is the distinctive expression of your personal preferences. (7) **Identity** means you have a point of view that marks your place in the game plan of life.

PHASE 10

MIDWESTERN OFFICE PRODUCTS: COOPERATIVE WORK EXPERIENCE

You have been hired by Midwestern Office Products to work half days in a cooperative work experience program. Midwestern sells a wide range of automated office equipment, software, and printware. In addition, the company offers consulting services in selecting office systems and determining office layout. Midwestern also offers hands-on instruction in its Learning Center.

During the cooperative work experience, you will work first in the Information Processing Center (IPC) to become familiar with the kinds of documents processed by the company. Following that experience, you will work in the Sales Department

replacing an employee who quit. You will also be asked to work in the Executive Office when the work load there becomes excessive. In these assignments, you will produce letters, reports, tables, and forms that require editing and revising to correct errors.

Throughout this work experience, you will continue to receive in-school instruction and drills to improve document processing productivity and language-skill development. In addition, you will learn to prepare employment documents and will take tests to establish your employability as an office worker.

Activity 12
Learn to Use the Hyphenation Feature

1. Read the "In Brief" copy at right.

2. Study software documentation to learn to use the hyphenation feature.

3. Read paragraph at right; identify the required, soft, and/or hard hyphen character features.

4. Set a 70-space line and a 5-space paragraph tab, then key the paragraph DS using your program's hyphenation feature.

5. When finished, proofread your work making any corrections and/or changes.

6. Print a final copy.

HARD (REQUIRED) HYPHEN

Entered when the user strikes the hyphen key. Regardless of where the hyphen appears within the paragraph, the program prints it. Hard hyphens are used in telephone numbers, a numeric range, certain phrases that should not be broken (jack-o-lantern), and compound words (self-confident). A hard hyphen can be deleted by the user.

SOFT (GHOST OR NONREQUIRED) HYPHEN

An electronic feature that allows the user to decide whether a word should be hyphenated to avoid a very ragged right margin. When the hyphenation feature is "on," the cursor stops when a word will not fit on the line. Some programs automatically insert a soft hyphen; others allow the user to make the decision. Should the location of the hyphenated word change during reformatting, the soft hyphen is deleted automatically.

HYPHEN CHARACTER

A feature used for keying dates or minus signs in formulas. The hyphen character may require the user to strike a specific key *(such as the Home key)* before striking the hyphen key. The feature prevents a minus or a dash from being separated from related characters when it occurs at the end of a line.

> Most of us never realize the important role imagination plays in our lives. Imagination sets the goal "picture" upon which we act (or fail to act). Imagination is the way we are built--our automatic mechanism works on our "creative imagination." Depending on what a person imagines to be true about herself/himself and her/his environment, that individual will always act and feel and perform accordingly. Therefore, why not imagine yourself successful? If you picture yourself performing in a certain manner, it is almost the same as the actual performance. Mental practice helps to make perfect.

Activity 13
Learn About Pagination (Page Format) Features

1. Read the "In Brief" copy at right and on the next page.

2. Study software documentation to learn about pagination (page format) features.

3. Identify the features available on your software.

4. Create a checklist on "how to perform" each feature; use a step-by-step enumerated format.

5. Set a 60-space line and a 5-space indent tab for the enumerations.

6. Key each checklist, center the headings; indent each step (enumerations).

7. When finished, proofread your work making any corrections using any of the electronic features introduced thus far.

PAGE BREAK

The point (generally a given line count) at which a page ends. When the printer reaches the page break, it automatically advances a new sheet or allows the user to insert paper.

AUTOMATIC (SOFT/NONREQUIRED) PAGE BREAKS

A feature (sometimes called page format) that allows the user to select the number of lines allowed on the page (generally 54). When the program recognizes the given number of lines, it automatically inserts a soft page break. When repagination occurs (a paragraph is added or deleted, for example), all soft page breaks are deleted and new ones inserted automatically.

CONTROLLED (HARD/REQUIRED) PAGE BREAKS

A special command inserted by the user to ensure that a page remains intact during automatic pagination. When the program recognizes the special command, it breaks the page at that point. Usually hard page breaks must be deleted by the user.

HEADER/FOOTER

Text line (or lines) printed consistently in the top margin (header) or bottom margin (footer) of each page of a multiple-page document. A header/footer may include such information as the document title, page number, and date. Rarely does a single document contain both a header and a footer.

(continued, p. A-15)

words

Document 3
Invoice
LP p. 219
Prepare an invoice from the information at the right.

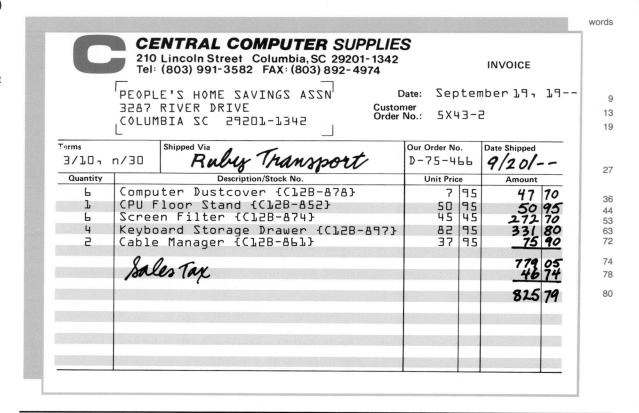

	CENTRAL COMPUTER SUPPLIES			
	210 Lincoln Street Columbia, SC 29201-1342			
	Tel: (803) 991-3582 FAX: (803) 892-4974		INVOICE	

PEOPLE'S HOME SAVINGS ASSN   Date: September 19, 19--   9
3287 RIVER DRIVE   13
COLUMBIA SC 29201-1342   Customer Order No.: 5X43-2   19

Terms	Shipped Via	Our Order No.	Date Shipped	
3/10, n/30	*Ruby Transport*	D-75-466	9/20/--	27

Quantity	Description/Stock No.	Unit Price	Amount	
6	Computer Dustcover {C12B-878}	7 95	47 70	36
1	CPU Floor Stand {C12B-852}	50 95	50 95	44
6	Screen Filter {C12B-874}	45 45	272 70	53
4	Keyboard Storage Drawer {C12B-897}	82 95	331 80	63
2	Cable Manager {C12B-861}	37 95	75 90	72
			779 05	74
	Sales Tax		46 74	78
			825 79	80

Document 4
Invoice
LP p. 219
Prepare an invoice from the information at the right.

Document 5
Invoice
LP p. 221
Use the information below and on the purchase order you prepared in Document 2 to process an invoice. Address it to
ADVERTISING SPECIALISTS
2065 ARTHUR AVENUE
TROY MI 48083-2502
Date it **July 25, 19--**.
Add 6% sales tax of **$9.98.** Use our order no. **936-81-A.** Use ship date of **7/23/--**.
Total words: 80
If you complete Documents 1-5 before time is called, start over. Use LP p. 221.

	DELRAY TIRE & AUTO CENTER			
	155 Erie Street Marquette, MI 49855-1317 (616) 342-9185		INVOICE	

EVERETT CONSTRUCTION CO   Date: October 1, 19--   8
1079 ALTAMONT STREET   12
MARQUETTE MI 49855-4945   Customer Order No.: A-54-92   19

Terms	Shipped Via	Our Order No.	Date Shipped	
5/10, n/30	Customer Pick Up	2245-12	9/25/--	28

Quantity	Description/Stock No.	Unit Price	Amount	
4	Treadloc Truck Tires {95-a65921t}	105 99	423 96	38
4	All-Terrain Tires {95-A58312C}	49 99	199 96	48
1	Ace Heavy-Duty Batery {28-A9609B}	59 99	59 99	59
			683 91	61
	Sales Tax		41 03	65
			724 94	66

WIDOW/ORPHAN

The widow/orphan feature prevents the printing of the last line of a paragraph at the top of a new page (widow) and the first line of a paragraph at the bottom of a page (orphan). The widow/orphan feature "protects" documents from containing these undesirable formatting features.

Before the widow/orphan feature is turned on, the cursor must be at the beginning of the text to be protected--usually at the beginning of the document. The feature may be turned on and off within a document. Use widow/orphan protection for proper page breaks in all documents of two or more pages.

Activity 14
Applying What You've Learned About Pagination

1. Read the copy at right.

2. Set a 60-space line and 5-space paragraph tab.

3. Center the title on line 10, pica; line 12 elite; QS between title and first line of body.

4. Key this document; DS all paragraphs.

5. If available, use the soft hyphen feature as you key.

6. Use the pagination feature allowing 54 lines per page; do <u>not</u> allow widows and orphans.

7. Create a header on line 6 of the second page; place the title **JOB HUNT** at the left margin and the page number flush right.

8. Proofread your work; make any necessary corrections.

9. Print a copy.

SHAKING THE BUSHES--THE JOB HUNT!

Finding a job can be faster and easier--and even more enjoyable--if you chart your course in the right direction.

First and foremost, know what you want to do. You should have some idea about "what you want to be when you grow up." Be active; don't let fate control your course! Take the initiative in your job hunt. Visit many prospects. The more you interview, the more comfortable you become. Another plus: Your enthusiasm about job hunting starts to soar.

Don't be too aggressive. Coming straight out and asking for a job is an approach considered to be too direct by many employers.

Be a Sherlock Holmes. Search for those individuals who are in the position to hire you. Try information interviewing. Talk to the people you will be working for (and with) as well as those to whom you will report directly. By asking questions such as How do you like your job? What do you do here? and What problems do you encounter? you gather information about a potential career.

The lyrics from a recent Broadway play said it well: **"Who am I anyway; am I my resume?"** <u>Absolutely</u>! Make sure your resume relates specifically to your objective. Focus on your skills, knowledge, experiences, and activities. Today's employer is looking for a well-rounded individual who can make a contribution to the company as well as to the community.

Sell yourself. Stress your fine points, such as your ability to communicate (oral and written skills), adaptability, flexibility, ability to learn, and your willingness to be retrained if need be. Smile! It's the enthusiasm in your eyes that clinches the interview.

Follow through. Send a thank-you note to the interviewer. Call to let the person know you're genuinely interested. Remember--persistence pays off.

225b ► 45 *Evaluate Production Skill: Business Forms*

LP pp. 217-221

Time Schedule

Plan and
prepare .... 5'
Timed
production........30'
Proofread; com-
pute *n-pram* .....10'

1. Arrange materials for ease of handling.

2. Format and key Documents 1-4 for 30'. Proofread and correct errors before removing each form from the machine.

3. After time is called (30'), proof-read again and circle any uncorrected errors. Compute *n-pram*.

**Document 1
Purchase Requisi-
tion**

LP p. 217

Prepare a purchase requisition from the in-formation at the right.

**Document 2
Purchase Order**

LP p. 217

Prepare a purchase order from the infor-mation at the right.

Documents 3-5 are on page 387.

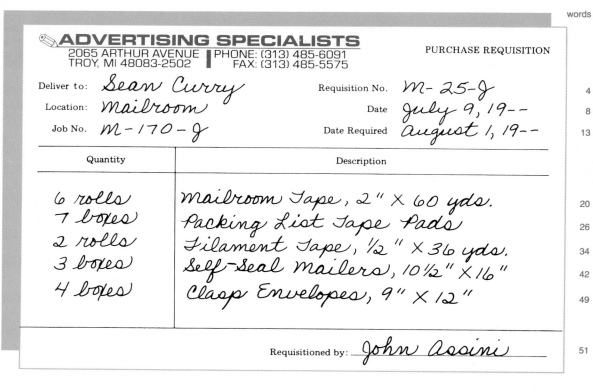

words

ADVERTISING SPECIALISTS
2065 ARTHUR AVENUE | PHONE: (313) 485-6091
TROY, MI 48083-2502 | FAX: (313) 485-5575
PURCHASE REQUISITION

Deliver to: *Sean Curry*   Requisition No. *M-25-J* — 4
Location: *Mailroom*   Date *July 9, 19--* — 8
Job No. *M-170-J*   Date Required *August 1, 19--* — 13

Quantity	Description	
6 rolls	Mailroom Tape, 2" X 60 yds.	20
7 boxes	Packing List Tape Pads	26
2 rolls	Filament Tape, ½" X 36 yds.	34
3 boxes	Self-Seal Mailers, 10½" X 16"	42
4 boxes	Clasp Envelopes, 9" X 12"	49

Requisitioned by: *John Assini* — 51

ADVERTISING SPECIALISTS
2065 ARTHUR AVENUE | PHONE: (313) 485-6091
TROY, MI 48083-2502 | FAX: (313) 485-5575
PURCHASE ORDER

Purchase Order No.: *B-4932-6* — 2

*D&F OFFICE SUPPLIES
46500 NEWTON STREET
WAYNE MI 48188-1630*

Date: *July 11, 19--* — 9
Terms: *5/10, n/30* — 15
Shipped Via: *Harper Express* — 22

Quantity	Description/Stock Number	Price		Per	Total	
6 rolls	Mailroom Tape (3750)	3	19	ea	19 14	31
7 boxes	Packing List Tape Pads (624-P)	6	09	bx	42 63	42
2 rolls	Filament Tape (898)	2	99	ea	5 98	50
3 boxes	Self-Seal Mailers (18-288)	21	25	bx	63 75	60
4 boxes	Clasp Envelopes (37790)	8	69	bx	34 76	71
					166 26	72

By _____

Activity 15
Learn to Search a Document for a Character String

1. Read the "In Brief" copy.

2. Study software documentation to learn to use the search feature.

3. Set 60-space line and 10-space paragraph tab.

4. Read paragraph at right, then key it DS as is.

5. Position cursor at beginning of text; search for character string **halo effect.** How many occurrences?

6. Return to beginning of document; search for the string **psychologists.** How many?

SEARCH

A *string* is a group of characters. A group of letters (hugs), numbers (394,823,315), symbols ("@&%!@#+*), or alphanumeric characters (A34C23Z9884TI) are all regarded as a string. A search feature allows you to search forward (and sometimes backward) through the document to locate a character string or a code (tab, hard return, etc.).

When you enter the proper command *(such as striking the F4 key)*, the program prompts (asks) you to enter the word to search for. When you strike the same key (or the return key), the program begins searching the document. Every time the designated string is found, the program highlights it or positions the cursor on it.

Research has shown that most employers make up their minds about job applicants in the first 30 seconds of an interview. These findings are based on what many psychologists refer to as the halo effect. The term halo effect refers to the first impression a person makes. A good first impression is called by psychologists a positive halo effect. A not-so-good first impression is called a negative halo effect. The point is that the first impression lingers--like a halo--causing it to become a lasting impression.

Activity 16
Learn to Use the Search and Replace Feature

1. Read the "In Brief" copy.

2. Study software documentation to learn to use the search and replace feature.

3. Set a 70-space line and a 10-space paragraph tab.

4. Read paragraph at right, then key it DS as is.

5. Move cursor to the beginning of text.

6. Search for every occurrence of **affect** and replace it with **effect.**

7. Move cursor to the beginning of document again.

8. Search for every occurrence of **hula** and replace it with **halo.**

SEARCH AND REPLACE

A feature that searches forward (or backward) through a document until it finds the designated character string or code and then replaces it with a new string that the user designates. Some programs also allow you to delete a string using the replace feature. A *discretionary replace* (sometimes called *selective search* or *search with confirmation*) allows you to replace character strings selectively. A

global replace will automatically replace every occurrence of the designated character string. By entering the proper command, the program prompts you with special directions such as "Search For:" and "Replace With:". When the command is executed, the program locates each occurrence of the character string and replaces it with the new string.

Regardless of whether the hula affect is negative or positive, it radiates in all directions from the first affect or impression. People with a positive hula affect project a positive self-image, have a firm handshake, maintain eye contact, and smile. Generally, individuals who do not paint a confident and competent image have a cold, clammy handshake, do not maintain eye contact, and, therefore, radiate a negative hula affect.

Table 3
4-Column Table

Key the table at the right;
DS body; CS: 6 between
Columns 1 & 2; 10 be-
tween Columns 2 & 3; 6
between Columns 3 & 4.

MARCH BIRTHDATES   3

(Includes Employees as of 2/15/--)   10

Employee	Birthdate	Employee	Birthdate	25
Eleanor Byer	3/2/42	Jordan Brown	3/15/51	33
Royce McKnight	3/2/35	Nydia Ros	3/17/64	41
Judith Zupi	3/4/55	Kasi Jamshidi	3/24/70	49
Michele Linmar	3/5/68	Paul Lang	3/25/57	57
Sandy Testa	3/7/32	Brett Medich	3/29/49	65
Anna Alams	3/9/45	Ryan Notaro	3/31/62	73

Table 4
**3-Column Table with
Source Note**

Key the table at the right;
DS body; CS: 10.

OLDEST U.S. COLLEGES AND UNIVERSITIES   8

Name	Location	Year	15
Harvard University	Cambridge, Mass.	1636	23
William and Mary College	Williamsburg, Va.	1693	32
Yale University	New Haven, Conn.	1701	40
Princeton University	Princeton, N.J.	1746	48
Columbia University	New York, N.Y.	1754	56
University of Pennsylvania	Philadelphia, Pa.	1756	66
Brown University	Providence, R.I.	1764	74
Rutgers University	New Brunswick, N.J.	1766	83
Dartmouth College	Hanover, N.H.	1769	90

94

Source: The World Book Encyclopedia.   106

Lesson 225   Evaluation: Business Forms

225a ▶ 5
*Conditioning
Practice*

each line twice SS
(slowly, then faster);
if time permits, take
1' writings on line 3

alphabet	1	Marji plans to study her new notes before taking the next civics quiz.
figures	2	I would like to have 875-4210 or 875-3690 for my new telephone number.
symbols	3	Practice the percent (%), asterisk (*), dollar ($), and ampersand (&).
speed	4	The busy fieldhand kept the fox in a pen to keep it cozy and in sight.

| 1 | 2 | 3 | 4 | 5 | 6 | 7 | 8 | 9 | 10 | 11 | 12 | 13 | 14 |

Activity 17
Learn to Copy a Block of Text

1. Read the "In Brief" copy.
2. Study software documentation to learn to copy a text block.
3. Set a 60-space line and 5-space paragraph tab.
4. Read paragraph at right, then key it DS. Center the title using the bold feature.
5. Since the paragraph does not flow very well, it is your asignment to edit it.
6. Instead of trying to rewrite the original paragraph, copy it below its present location.
7. Use all the editing features you have learned until the paragraph is exactly as you want it.
8. Delete the original paragraph.
9. Print a copy.

COPY

Editing feature that allows you to define a block of text (word, phrase, sentence, paragraph, page, or document) in one location of a document and copy (repeat) it in another location of the same document or in a different document. The original block remains intact. First you identify the copy command by striking a specific keystroke combination *(such as the shift and F4 keys)*. Next you identify the block to be copied (word, phrase, etc.). Then you position the cursor in the location where the copied text will appear. To complete the copy function, strike the return key or a special function key as directed in your documentation.

THE RIGHT STUFF

Are you "cut out" to be an entrepreneur? Do you have the "right stuff" to launch a successful business? Some say success depends on education. Others base it on business savvy. Many still call it luck--being in the right place at the right time! What about an individual's personality? Clearly there is no single set of experiences from which today's entrepreneur emerges. What are your goals? Do you have a burning desire to be your own boss? If not, perhaps your goal is to start a business that grows rapidly and helps you amass a fortune. Depending on your goal, personality may be the key in determining your success and happiness.

Activity 18
Learn to Move a Block of Text

1. Read the "In Brief" copy.
2. Study software documentation to learn to move a text block.
3. Set a 70-space line and a 5-space paragraph tab.
4. Read paragraphs at right, then key SS as shown.
5. Using the move feature, make the following changes:

Line
1, move **today** after **loosely**
3, move **simply** after **it**; switch **tear** and **wear**
4, move **people** after **often**
10, move **television** after **viewing**
13 and 14, switch position of lines

6. Use the move feature to move second paragraph to end of the document.
7. Print a copy.

MOVE

Editing feature commonly called "cut and paste" that allows you to remove (cut) a block of text from one location in a document and place (paste) it in a different location within the same document. The original block is removed. First you identify the move command by striking a specific keystroke combination. Next you identify the block to be moved (cut out). Then you position the cursor in the location where the moved text will be retrieved (pasted). Finally, strike the return key or a special function key.

1   Stress today is a term used very loosely. Even though stress is
2   something we are all aware of, we may find the term very difficult to
3   define. To simply put it, stress is the rate of tear and wear within
4   the body. People often report events as stressful when in reality
5   these events turn out to be only symptoms. Some of the more fre-
6   quently reported stressful events include the following:
7
8   Unfortunately, a common mistake we all make is to respond to
9   stressful situations by avoiding them! A pizza binge, a night of
10 television viewing for eight hours straight, or sleeping the weekend
11 away produces nothing but guilt.
12
13 * Disagreements and conflict with friends and family.
14 * Too heavy a workload with never-ending deadlines.
15 * Demands being made by everyone around you.
16 * Social activities that are much more pressure than fun.

224a ▶ 5
Conditioning Practice

each line twice SS
(slowly, then faster);
if time permits, take
1' writings on line 2

alphabet	1	Patrick will come back to judge the quality of the next seven waltzes.
figures	2	Tina surveyed 3,657 women, 2,980 men, and 1,940 children last January.
fig/sym	3	Buy 13 color #620-X monitors and 9 #478-A CPU's and get a 5% discount.
speed	4	Their city auditor may fish off the dock at the lake by the cornfield.

| 1 | 2 | 3 | 4 | 5 | 6 | 7 | 8 | 9 | 10 | 11 | 12 | 13 | 14 |

224b ▶ 45 *Evaluate Production Skill: Tables*

Time Schedule
Plan and prepare .... 5'
Timed production .... 30'
Proofread; compute *n-pram* .... 10'

1. Arrange 4 full sheets for ease of handling.

2. Format and key Documents 1-4 for 30'. Proofread and correct errors before removing each table from the machine.

3. After time is called (30'), proofread again and circle any uncorrected errors. Compute *n-pram*.

Table 1
3-Column Table with Total Line
Key the table at the right; DS; CS: 10.

words

TEN LARGEST AREA ADVERTISING AGENCIES			8
Ranked by Millions of Dollars in Billings			16

Name	Billings	Employees	
Carlson Advertising	$118.5	202	32
Robert Harn Agency	104	158	37
HARR Advertising	55.8	95	42
Rendar-Gazdacko	21.0	25	47
Crea, Peake, & Weisz Inc.	16.4	36	54
Sundy Group	13.5	35	58
Park/Vladnoski	13.3	24	62
DeMark Communications	12	42	68
Cavicchia Group	11.1	27	73
Abdel Kamal Agency	10	18	80
Total	$375.6	662	84

Table 2
4-Column Ruled Table
Key the table at the right; DS body; CS: 6.

PRINTING BIDS RECEIVED				5
For 19-- Sales Catalog				9
				22

Firm	Contact	Telephone	Bid	
				39
DataPrint	John Wolff	221-3300	$30,970	47
Beyer Printing	Sig Beyer	829-6143	29,450	56
Typeset Press	E. V. Henry	247-7000	29,250	64
Reed & Park	A. J. Reed	682-3633	28,540	72
Publisher's Choice	Bob Arch	241-8200	27,985	81
Copy Mate	Val Mejeas	243-8010	27,750	88
VIP Press	Peg Scott	362-6700	26,450	95
				107

Activity 19
Learn to Use the Indent Feature

1. Read the "In Brief" copy.
2. Study software documentation to learn to use the indent feature.
3. Set a 60-space line and 5-space paragraph tab stop.
4. Read the copy at right.
5. Key the copy; DS paragraphs, SS indented text, underline and bold where indicated.
6. Proofread and correct your work; then print a copy.

INDENT

A tab stop set in the ruler/format line to mark the position where every line of text (paragraph or column) will begin from the left margin. When word wrap is on, strike a specific key *(such as F4)* and the indent feature remains in effect until the return key is struck.

THE LIFE OF THE PARTY?

Experts assure us that we're all boring people every now and then. Being judged boring makes most people more upset than being judged incompetent! Since boring people are often rejected because of their conversational style, don't let it happen to you. Be aware of these helpful tips:

1. **Behavior that is tedious.** A boring conversationalist drags a two-minute story into a fifteen-minute event.

2. **Preoccupation with one's self.** Often the most boring individual is the one who wants to talk only about herself/himself.

3. **Out to impress others.** Boring people work too hard to be funny and nice. They're always out to impress others. Often they lack a sense of humor resulting in a conversation that is always "serious."

To avoid being a "yawner" who puts others to sleep at a social gathering, give these tips a try:

1. **Help other people get involved.** Always try to involve other persons in conversation by making clear to each of them that they are as valuable as you.

2. **Ask questions.** To find out what another individual wants to talk about, ask questions. How else can you find a topic that interests her or him?

3. **Gain insight into the other person's feelings.** Ask the other person what he or she thinks about a specific topic. Then talk about that person's ideas and thoughts.

4. **Be natural; always be yourself.** Don't attempt to be witty or clever unless you <u>are</u> witty or clever.

5. **Smile!** A smile is the light in your window that tells people you're a caring individual--someone they'll like a lot.

words

and Lake Ontario. As the huge sheets of ice melted, the 85

meltwater from the glaciers helped fill the basins. 96

Physical Feature**S** 103

    Size. The Great Lakes have a combined area of 94,510 162
square miles (244,780 square kilometers). Lake Superior, 173
the largest of the lakes, is only slightly smaller than 185
Maine; and Lake Ontario, the smallest of the lakes, is 196
about the size of New Jersey. 202

    Elevation. The lakes vary *greatly* ~~quite a bit~~ in elevation. 214
Lake Superior, the highest, lies 600 feet (183 meters) 225
above sea level, while Lake Ontario, the lowest, lies just 236
245 feet (75 meters) above sea level. There is a 325-foot 248
difference in elevation between lakes Erie and Ontario. 260
Most of the water from the lakes drains into the St. 270
Lawrence River, which flows into the Atlantic Ocean. 281

    Depth. The depth of the Great Lakes *also* varies widely. 294
The deepest, Lake Superior, is 1,333 feet (406 meters) deep. 306
Lake Erie, the shallowest, is only 210 *feet* (64 meters) deep. 319
Connecting Waterways 327

    Three sets of locks and canals make it possible 336
for ships to sail from one Great Lake to another and *from Lake Ontario* to the 352
Atlantic Ocean, *from which* so they can ~~access~~ *sail to* any port in the world. 366
The canals and the ~~waterways~~ *bodies of water* they connect are listed here. 379

1. Welland Canal--connects Lake Erie and Lake Ontario. 390

    2. Soo Canals--connect Lake Superior and Lake Huron. 401

    3. St. Lawrence Seaway--connects Lake Ontario with 412
the Atlantic Ocean. 416

Significance of the lakes 426

    The five Great Lakes and the canals that link them to- 437
gether make up the most important inland waterway in North 449
America. They provided the *inexpensive* transportation system needed to 463
~~turn~~ *make* the Great Lakes region ~~into~~ one of the most important 474
industrial areas in the United States. 481

Although the Great Lakes were all formed by glacial 113
activity during the same period, they are quite 123
different from one another. The irregular 132
movement of the glaciers created variations in the 142
size, elevation, and depth of the lakes. 150

Document 3
Leftbound Report
Reformat Document 2 as a
leftbound report.

Activity 20
Learn to Use the Hanging Indent Feature

1. Read the "In Brief" copy.

2. Study software documentation to learn to use the hanging indent feature.

3. Set a 60-space line and 5- and 10-space tab stops.

4. Read the drill at right.

5. Key the drill; DS paragraphs, SS hanging indented text; bold where indicated.

6. Proofread and correct your work; then print a copy.

HANGING INDENT

When you enter a specific command *(such as striking the F4 key then holding down on the shift key and striking Tab)*, **this feature positions the first line of a paragraph at the left margin and the remaining lines indented at a specific tab stop from the left margin. Hanging indent remains until the return key is struck.**

GETTING YOUR ACT TOGETHER

Are you involved in the drama club, student council, band, or sports? Have you acquired new interests during the past year? Is your head swimming with new projects? If so, you've probably been asking yourself the same question over and over: "How can I make sure I'll have time to fit everything into my busy schedule?"

The answer: A crash course in time management. Time management skills help you to make the most of each day and to meet your goals almost effortlessly. Consider the following tips for time management.

DAILY TO DOs. Take 10 minutes each morning (when you're fresh and alert) to make a daily "to do" list. Put everything on the list, from feeding the fish and paying a bill to meeting friends for dinner and studying for a test.

"A" AND "B" LISTS. Divide your list into two categories: the "A" items, things that are a must for today; and the "B" items, things that you can put off until tomorrow. When you've completed the lists, rank each item according to its importance, such as A1, A2, B1, B2, etc. This ranking helps you eliminate nonessential, time-consuming tasks from your schedule.

HAVE A MEETING--WITH YOURSELF. Do you let interruptions and distractions get in the way of accomplishing your goals? When the phone rings or a friend stops over to visit, do you stop what you're doing? If that behavior continues, you'll never achieve your objectives. Start setting aside an hour or an hour and a half each day for yourself. Turn off the radio and don't allow interruptions to distract you. Choose a time when your creativity is generally at its peak. Soon you'll find that scheduling a meeting with yourself allows you to accomplish many of your goals.

GET ORGANIZED! Stop spreading yourself thin. If you're like most people, you probably keep information in separate places: a calendar, a phone book, a schedule of appointments, and a datebook. Then you can't find the information when you need it. Purchase a pocket-sized reference folder (the handy, go-anywhere kind) and put all of your information in it. That way you're sure to have what you need when you need it.

223a ▶ 5
Conditioning Practice

each line twice SS
(slowly, then faster);
if time permits, take
1′ writings on line 4

alphabet	1	Jamie expects a high score on every big law quiz if he keeps studying.
figures	2	Mary sold 105 shirts, 28 belts, 94 sweaters, 36 suits, and 47 jackets.
fig/sym	3	Policy #31-407-A paid $26.97 interest and a $47.38 dividend on 3/5/91.
speed	4	The dorm official may name six sorority girls to visit the big social.

| 1 | 2 | 3 | 4 | 5 | 6 | 7 | 8 | 9 | 10 | 11 | 12 | 13 | 14 |

223b ▶ 45 Evaluate Production Skill: Memos/Reports

Time Schedule
Plan and prepare .... 5′
Timed production .... 30′
Proofread; compute *n-pram* .... 10′

1. Arrange 4 full sheets and LP p. 215 for ease of handling.

2. Format and key Documents 1-3 for 30′. Proofread and correct errors before removing each document from the machine.

3. After time is called (30′), proofread again and circle any uncorrected errors. Compute *n-pram*.

Document 1
Simplified Memo
LP p. 215
Key the copy at the right as a simplified memo.

Document 2
Unbound Report
Key the copy at the right and on p. 383 as an unbound report.

words

January 14, 19-- Hilary L. Tribuzio, Marketing Director — 11

SUBJECT: GREAT LAKES COPY FOR PRODUCT BROCHURE — 19

¶ Here is the first draft of the copy on the Great Lakes. Review and return it to me with any changes you recommend. I need it by January 21 in order to complete the brochure describing our new schooner by the date you specified. ¶ I agree with you that general interest topics like this can be included in sales brochures when appropriate. This topic should be of special interest to our customers since most of them sail their schooners on the Great Lakes. ¶ You should consider placing in your next brochure an article on the canals that connect the lakes. — 29 / 37 / 47 / 58 / 67 / 77 / 87 / 97 / 107 / 117 / 127 / 131

Elena J. Harris, Communications Group xx Enclosure — 141

THE GREAT LAKES — 3

QS

The five Great Lakes were formed ~~formed~~ more than 250,000 — 13

years ago during the Ice Age. A Large glaciers moved south across the — 27

land of what is now called the Great Lakes region. The thick — 40

glaciers gouged the land as ~~their way down,~~ scooping out weak rock ~~as~~ — 52

they moved to form the five basins which now ~~form~~ hold the Great — 62

Lakes--Lake Michigan, Lake Erie, Lake Superior, Lake Huron, — 74

Activity 21
Learn to Set Column Tabs

1. Read the "In Brief" copy.
2. Study software documentation to learn to set column tabs.
3. Format the table SS; DS below the main heading.
4. Proofread and correct your work; then print the table.

COLUMN TABS

1. Identify the longest item in each column and determine the number of spaces to be placed between columns.
2. Use the automatic centering feature: key these items and spaces (Step 1) on the line.
3. Move the cursor to the beginning of the first column; note (write down) the cursor position.
4. Repeat Step 3 for each remaining column.
5. Clear all tabs in the ruler line.
6. Set tabs in the ruler line at the positions noted in Steps 3 and 4.
7. Delete the line keyed in Step 2.
8. Key the table.

SPELLING WORDS FOR WEEK OF 01/02/--

accommodate	committee	industrial	participation
appreciate	correspondence	interest	personnel
appropriate	customer	maintenance	possibility
categories	eligible	monitoring	recommend
commitment	immediately	necessary	services

Activity 22
Learn to Set Right Alignment Tabs

1. Read the "In Brief" copy.
2. Study software documentation to learn to set right alignment tabs.
3. Format Drill 1 DS.
4. Proofread and correct your work; then print the table.
5. Repeat Steps 3 and 4 for Drill 2.

RIGHT ALIGNMENT TAB

A tab position set in the ruler line to align a column of text on the right (called "flush right" or "right justified"). A right alignment tab is set in the last position of the longest line in the column.

Often a right alignment tab is set by striking R, which then may display on the ruler line. Copy that is keyed at that tab will "back up" from the tab, ending where the tab is set.

Follow the usual procedure for determining and setting the left margin and for noting (writing down) the position, EXCEPT place right tabs at the end of the column.

Drill 1

WOMEN'S TEAM CAPTAINS

Basketball	Diana Lindsay
Gymnastics	Lili Wong
Soccer	Adia Lopez
Softball	Nancy Brand
Volleyball	Glenda Ford

Drill 2

MEN'S TEAM CAPTAINS

Baseball	Ken Morrison
Basketball	Cy Briggs
Football	Joe Hererra
Gymnastics	Kevin Kwan
Soccer	Bo Simpson

Activity 23
Learn to Set Decimal Tabs

1. Read the "In Brief" copy.
2. Study software documentation to learn to set decimal tabs.
3. Format the table SS.
4. Proofread and correct the table; then print it.

DECIMAL TAB

A tab position set in the ruler line to align numbers at the decimal point. Follow the usual procedure for determining and setting the left margin and for determining tab positions, EXCEPT place decimal tabs at the decimal position, not at the beginning of the column. A decimal tab often is indicated by striking D, which then may display in the ruler line.

Figures entered at a decimal tab "back up" from the tab until the decimal key (.) is struck; then the figures appear aligned at the decimal point. Whole numbers are treated by the decimal tab feature as though a decimal point follows the last figure.

TEST SCORES/AVERAGE SCORE--UNITS 1-3

Adams, R.	75	89.5	82.75	82.42
Ellis, L.	89.25	94	96.25	93.17
Jenkins, Z.	68.75	75.25	71	71.67
Oblinger, S.	85	89	93.5	89.17
Trabel, D.	71.5	68.25	75	71.58
Worrell, K.	82.75	89	75.5	82.42

222b (continued)

Letter 2
LP p. 211
modified block format with indented ¶s, mixed punctuation; address envelope

September 13, 19-- Ms. Roberta L. Davis 212 Seventh Street Bangor, ME 04401-4447 Dear Ms. Davis:

¶ Thank you for conducting the "Personal Productivity" seminar for the executive secretaries and administrative assistants at Berger Insurance Company last week. ¶ I have reviewed the results of the evaluation completed by the participants for our training and development staff. Without exception, the participants ranked each topic as being relevant or highly relevant to their needs. The topic pertaining to dealing with interruptions received the highest ranking.

¶ You should also know that almost all participants rated your presentation style and materials as very good or excellent. Most stated they wanted you back for another seminar.

Sincerely, Mrs. Susan L. Delfiore President xx
c Mr. L. James Walter, Training Director

	11
	20
	31
	41
	53
	62
	73
	85
	96
	106
	114
	124
	134
	144
	149
	159
	167/179

Letter 3
LP p. 213
simplified format; address envelope

Letter 4
plain full sheet
Format Letter 3 in modified block format, mixed punctuation, and address it to

Mr. Samuel T. Ataliotis
820 West Hollis Street
Nashua, NH 03062-3599

Supply other letter parts as needed.
Total words: 132

October 31, 19-- MR ANDREW W HENDERSON 1008 ELM STREET MANCHESTER NH 03101-1716 DAMAGED VALUE PLUS CARD

Your Value Plus electronic banking card was found in the automatic teller ~~when it was used on October 29, 19--~~ at the Landmark's Granite Street branch. Apparently, it was ~~retained~~ your card not returned because it was ~~d while being used on October 29.~~ of damage ~~during the transaction.~~ ¶ Since it the card will no ~~longer~~ t operate ~~the machine~~ an automatic teller any more, it must be replaced. We have ordered a new card, and you will receive it in the mail with in 2 weeks. ¶ You will be able to ~~take advantage of~~ use this convenient form of banking again as soon as you ~~have~~ receive your replacement card.

MISS TRUDI A. PITTS BRANCH MANAGER xx

	11
	21
	33
	39
	53
	67
	81
	93
	102
	117
	125/138

Activity 24
Two-Column Table with Right Alignment Tab

1. Format the table at the right DS. Use the centering feature to center the main and secondary headings; use a right alignment tab for the right-hand column.

2. Proofread and correct errors; then print the table.

Activity 25
Three-Column Table with Column and Right Alignment Tabs

1. Format the table at the right SS. Use the centering feature to center the main and secondary headings; use the bold feature for the main heading. Block the column heads as shown.

2. Use the underline feature to key a line a DS below the table; then DS to the source note. (If your equipment will not display or print the line, insert the line with a pen on the printed table.)

Activity 26
Multi-Column Table with Decimal Tab

1. Format the table at the right DS. Use the centering feature to center the main and secondary headings. To determine the left margin (center the table), use the column heading if it is the longest line in the column. Key the column headings _before_ setting decimal table.

2. Use the underline feature to key a line between the table and source note or use a pen to insert the line on the printed table.

3. Proofread and correct the table; then print.

Riverfront Dinner Show
Week of March 12-16

Dinner Music	Lou Springer
Emcee	Eric Simpson
Dance Demo	Valley School of Dance
Music and Humor	Halcyon Days
Comedy	Fred Hines
Dance Band	Halcyon Days

MOTION PICTURE ACADEMY AWARDS (OSCARS)

1980 - 1989

Year	Movie Title	Studio
1989	Ordinary People	Paramount
1981	Chariots of Fire	Warner Bros
1982	Gandhi	Columbia
1983	Terms of Endearment	Paramount
1984	Amadeus	Orion Pictures
1985	Out of Africa	Universal
1986	Platoon	Orion Pictures
1987	The Last Emperor	Columbia
1988	Rain Main	United Artists
1989	Driving Miss Daisy	Warner Bros.

Source: Information Please Almanac, 1990.

Temperature of Selected Metropolitan Areas
Average Monthly Fahrenheit Degrees

Metro Area	January	April	July	October
Chicago	21.4	48.8	73	53.5
Dallas-Fort Worth	44	65.9	86.3	67.9
Detroit	23.4	47.3	71.9	51.9
Houston	51.4	68.7	83.1	69.7
Los Angeles	56	59.5	69	66.3
New York	31.8	51.9	76.4	57.5
Washington	35.2	56.7	78.9	59.3

Source: Information Please Almanac, 1990.

UNIT 52   LESSONS 222 – 225

Evaluate Document Processing Skills

Measurement Goals

To demonstrate your knowledge and skill in processing
1. Letters
2. Memos and reports
3. Tables
4. Business Forms

Format Guides

1. Paper guide at *0* (for typewriters).
2. LL: 70 spaces for drill copy; as needed for documents.
3. LS: SS drill lines; as needed for documents.
4. PI: 5 spaces, unless otherwise directed.

| Lesson 222 | *Evaluation: Letters in Various Formats* |

222a ▶ 5
Conditioning Practice

each line twice SS
(slowly, then faster);
if time permits, take
1' writings on line 1

alphabet	1	Merv saw my new pilot quickly taxi a jet to the zone by the big field.
figures	2	Their soccer league had 3,650 boys and 2,478 girls in the 1991 season.
fig/sym	3	Expenses increased $82,965 (5%) and net profit decreased $31,470 (6%).
speed	4	The busy neighbor may fix the rifle, bugle, and cycle for the visitor.

| 1 | 2 | 3 | 4 | 5 | 6 | 7 | 8 | 9 | 10 | 11 | 12 | 13 | 14 |

222b ▶ 45 *Evaluate Production Skill: Letters*

LP pp. 209-213
plain full sheet

Time Schedule

Plan and prepare .... 5'
Timed production ....30'
Proofread; compute
   n-pram ....10'

1. Arrange materials for ease of handling.

2. Format and key Letters 1-4 for 30'. Proofread and correct errors before removing each letter from the machine.

3. After time is called (30'), proofread again and circle any uncorrected errors. Compute *n-pram*.

Letter 1

LP p. 209

block format, open punctuation; address envelope

words

April 15, 19--   Mr. Joseph P. Taylor   Taylor's Plumbing and Heating   98 Buell   15
Street   Burlington, VT 05401-3805   Dear Mr. Taylor   Subject   LEASE RE-   27
NEWAL FOR 98 BUELL STREET PROPERTY   34

Enclosed are two copies of your new lease for the property you now lease   48
from Associated Estates Corporation.   56

The enclosed lease is identical to the present one which expires on May 15,   71
19--, except that the new monthly rent ($555.50) has been substituted for   86
the current one ($505). You were notified of this 10 percent increase in my   101
letter of March 15.   105

Before April 30, please return one signed copy of the lease with your signa-   120
ture notarized. Retain the other copy for your files. If you need more in-   135
formation before you sign this lease, call Mrs. Harriet Jamison at 279-4698.   151

Sincerely ASSOCIATED ESTATES CORPORATION Ms. Maryanne E. Shade-   163
Minor Lease Renewal Manager xx Enclosures postscript If you pay the   175
rent for one year before May 15, 19--, you will receive an 8.5 percent dis-   190
count. The discount conditions are the same as those in your current lease.   205/**224**

Begin all tables on line 10 or as directed by your teacher. Clear all preset tabs from the ruler line before setting tabs for a table.

Activity 27
Three-Column Table with Right, Column, and Decimal Tab

1. Format the table at the right DS, setting the appropriate tab for each column. Block the column headings as shown. Key the column headings before setting tabs.

2. Proofread; correct errors; print the table.

Activity 28
Four-Column Table with Varied Tabs

1. Format the table at the right DS, using the appropriate tab for each column. Note (write down) the positions where columns begin and end; on a separate list note the position for each tab.

2. To center column headings, add the numbers representing the beginning and ending positions of the column; divide by 2. (The result is the center of the column.) Count the spaces in the column heading; divide by 2. Subtract the result from the center position. (Begin the column heading in this position.)

3. Proofread your work, checking for format errors as well as misstrokes. Make necessary corrections; then print the table.

Activity 29
Four-Column Table with Decimal and Right Alignment Tabs

1. Format the table at the right SS, using the appropriate tab for each column. Center the column headings (See Step 2, Activity 28).

2. Use the underline feature as you key the last number in each amount column. (If necessary, insert the underlines on the printed table with a pen.)

3. Proofread carefully before printing the table.

PRICE QUOTATION FOR MORTON ASSOCIATES INC.

Item No.	Description	Unit Price
PC-4001A	Microprocessor	$2,895
PC-4031A	Input/Output Units	589
PC-4041A	Dual Disk Drive	416
4050NM	Color Monitor	325
4054M	B/W Monitor	195
840X	Glare Guard	94.94
PC-4024A	Dot Matrix Printer	325
7210X	Printer Stand	194.95
704X	Power Surge Stripe	69.95

CLIENT CONTACTS MADE BY SHEILA SANDERS
Week Ending February 2, 19--

Client	Date	Hours	Site
Swatzky	January 28	1.5	His Office
Grossmane	January 29	.17	Telephone
Schlosser	January 29	.42	Telephone
Wagner	January 30	2	Their Office
Cook	January 30	2.25	Their Office
Washburn	January 31	1.75	Their Office
Murphy	January 31	1	My Office
O'Connor	February 1	.75	Telephone
Daniels	February 1	1.5	Their Office
Miller	February 2	2.5	Their Office

Regional Sales
(In Millions)

Region	This Year	Last Year	% Change
Central	$3.0	$2.8	7% inc.
Northeast	.6	.5	20% inc.
Northwest	2.1	2.0	5% inc.
Southeast	1.8	1.8	0% none
Southwest	1.6	1.4	14% inc.
Total	$9.1	$8.5	

221d ▶ 10
Measure Keyboarding Skill

1. A 3′ writing on both ¶s; calculate *gwam;* circle errors.

2. A 5′ writing on both ¶s; calculate *gwam;* circle errors.

all letters used | A | 1.5 si | 5.7 awl | 80% hfw

	gwam 3′		5′
Taking a major test or examination is very similar to playing an	4	3	46
important game. In both situations, you must control your anxiety level	9	6	49
if you want to achieve the best results. Most people find an increased	14	8	52
anxiety level before a game or test to be normal and helpful. It is im-	19	11	55
portant, however, that the heightened anxiety does not negatively affect	24	14	58
your ability to concentrate on the task at hand. You must focus all	28	17	61
your thoughts and energy on the test questions or game action and not	33	20	63
on the final results to have a good performance.	36	22	65
Another similarity is the need for preparation before taking a test	41	24	68
or playing a game. Coaches and players know they must develop a game	45	27	71
strategy and practice it repeatedly if they expect to achieve desired	50	30	74
results. Similarly, test takers must realize the importance of good	55	33	76
planning and studying. They must plan what, when, where, and how they	59	36	79
will study for a test and then execute the plan. A good routine to fol-	64	39	82
low is to begin studying well in advance of the test and to leave time	69	41	85
for relaxation and reflection before the test is taken.	73	44	87

gwam 3′
5′

221e ▶ 15
Prepare for Measurement

LP p. 207; correct errors

Document 1 Purchase Order

Key the purchase order shown at the right.

Document 2 Invoice

Prepare an invoice from the purchase order at the right. Address it to

SHAEFER RENTALS 1600 MARKET STREET SAN FRANCISCO CA 94105-2186

Date it **September 23, 19--**.
Date Shipped: **9/22/--**
Add 6% sales tax and compute a new total.
Use our order no. **543-85**

Total words: 79

						words
To: **PARK'S BUSINESS PRODUCTS**			Purchase Order No.: **B-45987-A**			7
5704 HOLLIS STREET			Date: **September 5, 19--**			14
OAKLAND CA 94608-2514			Terms: **5/15, n/30**			21
			Shipped Via: **Terner Express**			24

Quantity	Description/Stock Number	Price	Per	Total	
5	Adjustable Hole Punch (P-435)	10.95	ea	54.75	33
4	Office Shear--10″ (S-189)	10.85	ea	43.40	42
10	Push Pins (R-726)	.69	pk	6.90	49
3	Desk Stapler (X-705)	20.95	ea	62.85	56
3	Staples (X-605)	3.55	bx	10.65	63
3	Staple Remover (X-814)	2.75	ea	8.25	72
				186.80	73

Learn About Boilerplate Documents, the Merge Feature, and Stop Codes

1. Read the "In Brief" copy.

2. Study software documentation to learn which specific features are offered by your program.

3. Format the memo (60-space line) at the right below on plain paper. Set a right alignment tab for the colon sequence and a tab for the text in the memo headings. DS between memo headings.

4. Key the document using your program's stop code (or merge code) wherever the @1, @2, @3, etc., symbol appears.

5. Save the document.

6. Print the document three times; insert the following variables in the first printout.

@1 Olivian DeSouza
@2 (yesterday's date)
@3 Ms. DeSouza
@4 crepe hangers
@5 "It won't work"
@6 downers
@7 Ms. DeSouza
@8 Thursday morning

The second document variables:
@1 Maurizio Chuidioni
@2 (today's date)
@3 Mr. Chuidioni
@4 ones with their chins on their shoes
@5 "It's no use trying"
@6 pessimists
@7 Mr. Chuidioni
@8 Wednesday afternoon

The third document variables:
@1 Miyoki Kojima
@2 (tomorrow's date)
@3 Dr. Kojima
@4 ones who think nothing ever goes their way and
@5 "Are you serious?"
@6 negativists
@7 Dr. Kojima
@8 Tuesday afternoon

BOILERPLATE DOCUMENT

A document, such as a form letter or sales contract that is used again and again, in which most of the text remains the same each time. Only names and certain details, such as amounts and dates, are changed here and there within the document.

CONSTANT

The text in a boilerplate document that remains the same for each use of the document.

VARIABLE

The text (names, phrases, dates, etc.) in a boilerplate document that is changed to "personalize" the document.

STOP CODES

A command (or symbol) embedded within a boilerplate document. While printing a document, the printer stops when it recognizes the "stop" command allowing the user to key variable (personalized) information. The user then must strike a designated key to reactivate the printer until the next stop code is recognized.

PRIMARY DOCUMENT

A word processing document made up of the constant and embedded codes.

SECONDARY DOCUMENT

A word processing document consisting only of the variables.

MERGE

Word processing feature that allows the user to combine a primary document and secondary documents to print "personalized" documents.

                TO: @1
              FROM: Dan Henderson
           SUBJECT: Positively! Seminars
              DATE: @2

Although they're often reasonably competent people, negativists can unnerve, devitalize, exhaust, and fatigue the best of us. I'm certain, @3, that you've met at least one or two of them. They're the @4 who respond to anyone else's productive suggestion with @5 or "Forget it, we tried that last year" or "Why waste your time; they'll never let you do it."

What is needed to get the best from @6 in the workplace? An upbeat attitude, that's what! Have you checked yours lately? We all have the potential for being dragged down into despair. @7, is your attitude showing?

This question and many others will be answered for you in the Positively! seminars next week. The seminar presenter, Adele Cook, a nationally known speaker/trainer/consultant, will conduct sessions in Conference Room D.

Sessions are scheduled from 1 to 4 on Monday through Thursday and from 9 to 12 on Tuesday through Friday. The people in your area are to attend the @8 session.

This seminar will pick up where Ms. Cook's sessions ended last year. Distribute the attached materials, please.

Attachments

221a ▶ 5
Conditioning Practice

each line twice SS
(slowly, then faster);
then a 1' writing on
line 4

alphabet	1	Pamela will acquire three dozen red vinyl jackets for the big exhibit.
figures	2	My teacher plans to have 75 test items from pages 289-306 for Unit 41.
symbols	3	Mai-Ling practiced the symbols $, ", %, &, and # in class on 10/25/91.
speed	4	The rich widow is to endow the sorority chapel on a visit to the city.

| 1 | 2 | 3 | 4 | 5 | 6 | 7 | 8 | 9 | 10 | 11 | 12 | 13 | 14 |

221b ▶ 10
Check Language Skills

plain full sheet

1. The memorandum at the right contains errors in spelling, grammar, and punctuation.

2. Key the memo in simplified format. Use **today's date;** address it to **William A. Kurtz, Advertising Manager.** Use **AUTHORIZATION TO ADVERTISE** as the subject; **Leon H. Johnson, Marketing Vice President,** as the writer. Add other memo parts as needed. Correct errors as you key.

words

opening lines 16

Enclosed is the approved advertizing copy for 25
the new line of bridle gowns we are to begin sailing 36
next month. I have authorized $15,000 for the adver- 46
tisements in this series. The controller has been 56
instructed to transfer $15,000 from my contingency 67
account to your advertizing account. 74

Please note that I have indicated that bowled 83
print is to be used to emphasise the deference 93
among the knew line and the old line. The ad 102
is too be run everyday for one week and is too 111
be placed in the daily and weakly news papers 120
so it will be scene by a divers audience. 129

closing lines 140

221c ▶ 10
Improve Keyboarding Speed

1. Each line once as shown; push for speed.

2. A 1' writing on each of lines 8, 10, and 12; calculate *gwam* on each writing.

home/3d rows	1	set pay | low tide | jury duty | quit work | high speed | just that | good futures
	2	Pete said he will work at the pet store this week for his two sisters.
home/1st rows	3	mad dash | can call | hand ax | lack cash | sand bags | black flag | sad jazz band
	4	Hannah and Lana have a small ax, half a banana, a fan, and a gas mask.
3d/1st row emphasis	5	may cut | buy ten | fix bike | new tire | quit my | be quiet | no review | rezone it
	6	Vi is quite sure now is the time to rezone every zoo in the community.
stroke response	7	my mom | my dad | at noon | sad pup | was brave | look up | hilly knoll | water pump
	8	You saw my only pony pull a garage cart uphill at a fast average rate.
word response	9	do half | fix it | pay me | got it | when the | both bowls | giant dog | penalty box
	10	The proficient man is to fix the lane signs when down by the big lake.
combination response	11	no risks | get up | data base | name it | signal them | average pay | minimum wage
	12	The city auditor reacted to the abstract statement with a good answer.

| 1 | 2 | 3 | 4 | 5 | 6 | 7 | 8 | 9 | 10 | 11 | 12 | 13 | 14 |

Activity 31
Applying What You've Learned--Keying a Report

Format the copy at the right as an unbound report, employing the word processing features you have learned.

1. Use the automatic centering and bold text features for the main heading; and, the automatic underline feature for the side headings.

2. For the enumerated items and items at the end of the report, use the hang indent feature.

3. If a widow/orphan feature is available on your software, use it to prevent widows and orphans.

4. After keying the document, turn on the hyphenation feature, if the feature is available on your software, and use it to divide words properly at line endings.

5. Use the page format (automatic page breaks) feature to assure a bottom margin of 1 inch.

6. Using the header/footer feature, create a header on line 6 of the second page; key **TIME MANAGEMENT** at the left margin and the page number flush right.

7. Proofread the document on the screen. Make necessary corrections and format changes; then print the document.

TIME MANAGEMENT: PLAN FOR ATTACK

Do you have time management problems? If so, you belong to a large group with a growing membership. Why should you care about managing your time? Because time is life and when you waste your time, you're wasting your life! Time management revolves around the principle of effectiveness over efficiency. Efficiency refers to how well something is done; effectiveness refers to whether something should be done at all. Effectiveness means making the right choice from all the tasks available and doing it the best way possible. Efficiency is a good trait, but effectiveness should become one of your most important goals.

The Culprits Attack

Culprits surround us every minute of the day. If you look carefully, you'll be able to identify several culprits undermining your efforts toward the best use of your time:

1. Time is a limited, unique commodity. Unfortunately, most people excel at squandering it.

2. It's easy to establish broad goals such as wanting to be healthy, wealthy, and wise, but very rarely do people establish specific goals.

3. Everyone wants some of your time. But if you're busy taking care of everybody else's needs and desires, there's little time left for planning your own time.

4. Does a crisis turn you into an adrenaline junkie? Do you rely on the excuse: "I work best under pressure"?

5. Fear! Regardless of the kind (fear of success, fear of failure, fear of alienating others, etc.), fear often immobilizes a person.

Counterattack

To fight back against these culprits, an individual must devise a plan of action. The following tips serve as a battle plan in the counterattack.

Time is money; therefore, place a dollar value on your time. You're less likely to give up something that costs money.

Determine realistic objectives for yourself. Write them down and specify a date of accomplishment. When you write down your goals, you're less likely to daydream.

Since all objectives are not of equal value, establish priorities. Base your priorities on what is important to you now, not on the ease or your liking for the task.

Learn to say "no." "No" must become a part of a person's vocabulary. Otherwise, time is frittered away at someone else's request.

Set aside a block of time for yourself each day. Use this time to think and plan for immediate and long-range goals.

220b ▶ 10
Language Skills: Word Choice

1. Study the spelling and definition of the words.

2. Key the line number (with period); space twice, then key the **Learn** sentence, noting the correct use of the words.

3. Key the line number (with period); space twice, then key the **Apply** sentences DS, selecting the word in parentheses that makes each sentence correct.

explicit (adj) expressed with precision; clearly defined

implicit (adj) implied or understood although not directly expressed

foul (adj) spoiled; rotten; putrid

fowl (n) any bird used as food or hunted as game

Learn 1. My nod gave implicit agreement; Joe gave explicit agreement.
Apply 2. By starting to weed, she expressed an (explicit/implicit) desire to help.
Apply 3. Please give me (explicit/implicit) directions the next time I need help.
Learn 4. The fowl had a foul odor because it was not refrigerated properly.
Apply 5. Jim, Tom, and Sheila plan to serve (foul/fowl) at the picnic.
Apply 6. Be careful you do not eat (foul/fowl) chicken on the camping trip.

220c ▶ 10
Improve Keyboarding Control

each line twice SS (slowly, then faster); DS between 6-line groups

adjacent keys
1 are oil her pot cash copy rent void past port true worth liquid tickle
2 were there | avoid action | either term | report copy | new trade | fruit juices
3 Sam heard the cheer on the radio as the extra point kick hit the post.

direct reaches
4 many vice cent fund album enemy music brown hence forum manual produce
5 much music|check payment|specific fund|forum audiences|anybody special
6 My music album and brown manual will have a special price at my forum.

one-hand words
7 ace hop bet nil ward lump face puny wear upon treat imply weave poplin
8 are you | best car | extra crew | only hill | water pump | safe starts | was jolly
9 Loni, my greatest pupil, stressed care after my data base was created.

shift keys
10 Pam Sis Zoe Lars Mary Rory Paula Alena Nancy Bobbi Hazel Winnie Vivian
11 Spring Garden|Alabama City|Five Points|Howley Lake|Happy Jack McDowell
12 Will, Mary, Enos, Ozzie, Von, and Karla went to Lower Kalskag, Alaska.

220d ▶ 25
Prepare for Measurement

plain full sheets; correct errors

Document 1
Table with Source Note
Key the table at the right; CS: 8

Document 2
Table with Totals
Rekey Document 1; CS: 12; add amounts in each column; key the total for each column.
Total words: 82

Document 3
Table with Rules
Rekey Document 2; CS: 10; add horizontal rules.
Total words: 122

If necessary, see p. 351.

			words
Crestwood Realty Company			5
Commercial Property Division			11
		Property	13
Property	Assessed Value	Tax Paid	27
517 Locust Place	$ 75,000	$ 12,754	34
5 Merchant Plaza	45,000 (49,765)	9,650	41
St. Clair Building	109,550	14,975	49
Edgar Medical Center	83,600	12,875	56
Allison Park Center	64,500	10,450	64
			67
Source: 19-- Property Tax Invoices.			74

CAPITALIZATION GUIDES

■ Capitalize

1 The first word of every sentence and the first word of every complete direct quotation. Do not capitalize (a) fragments of quotations or (b) a quotation resumed within a sentence.

She said, "Hard work is necessary for success."
He stressed the importance of "a sense of values."
"When all else fails," he said, "follow directions."

2 The first word after a colon if that word begins a complete sentence.

Remember this: Work with good techniques.
We carry these sizes: small, medium, and large.

3 First, last, and all other words in titles of books, articles, periodicals, headings, and plays, except words of four or fewer letters used as articles, conjunctions, or prepositions.

Century 21 Keyboarding   "How to Buy a House"
Saturday Review   "The Sound of Music"

4 An official title when it precedes a name or when used elsewhere if it is a title of distinction.

President Lincoln   She is the Prime Minister.
The doctor is in.   He is the class treasurer.

5 Personal titles and names of people and places.

Miss Franks   Dr. Jose F. Ortez   San Diego

6 All proper nouns and their derivatives.

Canada   Canadian Festival   France   French food

7 Days of the week, months of the year, holidays, periods of history, and historic events.

Sunday   Labor Day   New Year's Day
June   Middle Ages   Civil War

8 Geographic regions, localities, and names.

the North   Upstate New York   Mississippi River

9 Street, avenue, company, etc., when used with a proper noun.

Fifth Avenue   Avenue of the Stars   Armour & Co.

10 Names of organizations, clubs, and buildings.

Girl Scouts   4-H Club   Carew Tower

11 A noun preceding a figure except for common nouns such as *line*, *page*, and *sentence*, which may be keyed with or without a capital.

Style 143   Catalog 6   page 247   line 10

12 Seasons of the year only when they are personified.

icy fingers of Winter   the soft kiss of Spring

NUMBER EXPRESSION GUIDES

■ Use words for

1 Numbers from one to ten except when used with numbers above ten, which are keyed as figures. Note: Common business practice is to use figures for all numbers except those which begin a sentence.

Was the order for four or eight books?
Order 8 shorthand books and 15 English books.

2 A number beginning a sentence.

Fifteen persons are here; 12 are at home sick.

3 The shorter of two numbers used together.

ten 50-gallon drums   350 five-gallon drums

4 Isolated fractions or indefinite amounts in a sentence.

Nearly two thirds of the students are here.
About twenty-five people came to the meeting.

5 Names of small-numbered streets and avenues (ten and under).

1020 Sixth Street   Tenth Avenue

■ Use figures for

1 Dates and time, except in very formal writing.

May 9, 1982   10:15 a.m.
ninth of May   four o'clock

2 A series of fractions.

Key 1/2, 1/4, 5/6, and 7 3/4.

3 Numbers following nouns.

Rule 12   page 179   Room 1208   Chapter 15

4 Measures, weights, and dimensions.

6 ft. 9 in. tall   5 lbs. 4 oz.   8 1/2″ × 11″

5 Definite numbers used with the percent sign (%); but use *percent* (spelled) with approximations in formal writing.

The rate is 15 1/2%.
About 50 percent of the work is done.

6 House numbers except house number One.

1915-42d Street   One Jefferson Avenue

7 Sums of money except when spelled for extra emphasis. Even sums may be keyed without the decimal.

$10.75   25 cents $300
seven hundred dollars ($700)

PUNCTUATION GUIDES

■ Use an apostrophe

1 As a symbol for *feet* in billings or tabulations or as a symbol for *minutes*. (The quotation mark may be used as a symbol for *seconds* and *inches*.)

12' × 16'   3' 54"   8'6" × 10'8"

2 As a symbol to indicate the omission of letters or figures (as in contractions).

can't   wouldn't   Spirit of '76

3 To form the plural of most figures, letters, and words used as words rather than for their meaning: Add the *apostrophe and s*. In market quotations, form the plural of figures by the addition of *s* only.

6's   A's   five's   ABC's   Century Fund 4s

4 To show possession: Add the *apostrophe and s* to (a) a singular noun and (b) a plural noun which does not end in *s*.

a man's watch   women's shoes   boy's bicycle

Add the *apostrophe and s* to a proper name of one syllable which ends in *s*.

Bess's Cafeteria   Jones's bill

Add the *apostrophe only* after (a) plural nouns ending in *s* and (b) a proper name of more than one syllable which ends in *s* or *z*.

boys' camp   Adams' home   Melendez' report

Add the *apostrophe* after the last noun in a series to indicate joint or common possession of two or more persons; however, add the possessive to each of the nouns to show separate possession of two or more persons.

Lewis and Clark's expedition

the manager's and the treasurer's reports

■ Use a colon

1 To introduce an enumeration or a listing.

These are my favorite poets: Shelley, Keats, and Frost.

2 To introduce a question or a long direct quotation.

This is the question: Did you study for the test?

3 Between hours and minutes expressed in figures.

10:15 a.m.   12:00   4:30 p.m.

■ Use a comma (or commas)

1 After (a) introductory words, phrases, or clauses and (b) words in a series.

If you can, try to visit Chicago, St. Louis, and Dallas.

2 To set off short direct quotations.

She said, "If you try, you can reach your goal."

3 Before and after (a) words which come together and refer to the same person, thing, or idea and (b) words of direct address.

Clarissa, our class president, will give the report.

I was glad to see you, Terrence, at the meeting.

4 To set off nonrestrictive clauses (not necessary to the meaning of the sentence), but not restrictive clauses (necessary to the meaning).

Your report, which deals with the issue, is great.

The girl who just left is my sister.

5 To separate the day from the year and the city from the state.

July 4, 1986   New Haven, Connecticut

6 To separate two or more parallel adjectives (adjectives that could be separated by the word "and" instead of the comma).

a group of young, old, and middle-aged persons

Do not use commas to separate adjectives so closely related that they appear to form a single element with the noun they modify.

a dozen large red roses   a small square box

7 To separate (a) unrelated groups of figures which come together and (b) whole numbers into groups of three digits each (however, policy, year, page, room, telephone, and most serial numbers are shown without commas).

During 1991, 1,750 cars were insured under Policy 804423.

page 1042   Room 1184   (213) 825-2626

■ Use a dash

1 For emphasis.

The icy road--slippery as a fish--was a hazard.

2 To indicate a change of thought.

We may tour the Orient--but I'm getting ahead of my story.

3 To introduce the name of an author when it follows a direct quotation.

"Hitting the wrong key is like hitting me."--Armour

4 For certain special purposes.

"Well--er--ah," he stammered.

"Jay, don't get too close to the --." It was too late.

■ Use an exclamation mark

1 After emphatic interjections.

Wow!   Hey there!   What a day!

2 After sentences that are clearly exclamatory.

"I won't go!" she said with determination.
How good it was to see you in New Orleans last
week!

■ Use a hyphen

1 To join compound numbers from twenty-one to ninety-nine that are keyed as words.

forty-six   fifty-eight   over seventy-six

2 To join compound adjectives before a noun which they modify as a unit.

well-laid plans six-year period two-thirds majority

3 After each word or figure in a series of words or figures that modify the same noun (suspended hyphenation).

first-, second-, and third-class reservations

4 To spell out a word or name.

s-e-p-a-r-a-t-e   G-a-e-l-i-c

5 To form certain compound nouns.

WLW-TV   teacher-counselor   AFL-CIO

■ Use parentheses

1 To enclose parenthetical or explanatory matter and added information.

The amendments (Exhibit A) are enclosed.

2 To enclose identifying letters or figures in lists.

Check these factors: (1) period of time, (2) rate of
pay, and (3) nature of duties.

3 To enclose figures that follow spelled-out amounts to give added clarity or emphasis.

The total award is five hundred dollars ($500).

■ Use a question mark

At the end of a sentence that is a direct question; however, use a period after a request in the form of a question.

What day do you plan to leave for Honolulu?
Will you mail this letter for me, please.

■ Use quotation marks

1 To enclose direct quotations.

He said, "I'll be there at eight o'clock."

2 To enclose titles of articles and other parts of complete publications, short poems, song titles, television programs, and unpublished works like theses and dissertations.

"Sesame Street"   "Chicago" by Sandburg
"Laura's Theme"   "Murder She Wrote"

3 To enclose special words or phrases, or coined words.

"power up" procedure   "Murphy's Law"

■ Use a semicolon

1 To separate two or more independent clauses in a compound sentence when the conjunction is omitted.

Being critical is easy; being constructive is not
so easy.

2 To separate independent clauses when they are joined by a conjunctive adverb (*however, consequently,* etc.).

I can go; however, I must get excused.

3 To separate a series of phrases or clauses (especially if they contain commas) that are introduced by a colon.

These officers were elected: Lu Ming, President;
Lisa Stein, vice president; Juan Ramos, secretary.

4 To precede an abbreviation or word that introduces an explanatory statement.

She organized her work; for example, putting work
to be done in folders of different colors to indicate
degrees of urgency.

■ Use an underline

1 With titles of complete works such as books, magazines, and newspapers. (Such titles may also be keyed in ALL CAPS without the underline.)

<u>Superwrite</u>   <u>The New York Times</u>   <u>TV Guide</u>

2 To call attention to special words or phrases (or you may use quotation marks). **Note:** Use a continuous underline unless each word is to be considered separately.

Stop keying <u>when time is called</u>.
Spell these words: <u>steel</u>, <u>occur</u>, <u>separate</u>.

■ Pronoun agreement with antecedents

1 Pronouns (*I, we, you, he, she, it, their,* etc.) agree with their antecedent *in person;* first person, person speaking; second person--person spoken to; person spoken about, third person.

We said we would go when we complete our work.
When you enter, present your invitation.
All who saw the show found that they were moved.

2 Pronouns agree with their antecedents *in gender* (feminine, masculine, and neuter).

Each of the women has her favorite hobby.
Adam will wear his favorite sweater.
The tree lost its leaves early this fall.

3 Pronouns agree with their antecedents *in number* (singular or plural).

A verb must agree with its subject.
Pronouns must agree with their antecedents.
Brian is to give his recital at 2 p.m.
Joan and Carla have lost their homework.

4 When a pronoun's antecedent is a collective noun, the pronoun may be either singular or plural depending on whether the noun acts individually or as a unit.

The committee met to cast their ballots.
The class planned its graduation program.

■ Commonly confused pronoun sound-alikes

it's (contraction): it is; it has
its (possessive adjective): possessive form of it
It's good to see you; it's been a long time.
The puppy wagged its tail in welcome.

their (pronoun): possessive form of they
there (adverb/pronoun): at or in that place/used to introduce a clause
they're (contraction): they are
The hikers all wore their parkas.
Will he be there during our presentation?
They're likely to be late because of the snow.

who's (contraction): who is; who has
whose (pronoun): possessive form of who
Who's been to the movie? Who's going now?
I chose the one whose skills are best.

■ Use a singular verb

1 With a singular subject.

The weather is clear but cold.

2 With an indefinite pronoun used as a subject (each, every, any, either, neither, one, etc.).

Each of you is to bring a pen and paper.
Neither of us is likely to be picked.

3 With singular subjects linked by or or nor. If, however, one subject is singular and the other is plural, the verb should agree with the closer subject.

Either Jan or Fred is to make the presentation.
Neither the principal nor the teachers are here.

4 With a collective noun (*committee, team, class, jury,* etc.) if the collective noun acts as a unit.

The jury has returned to the courtroom.
The committee has filed its report.

5 With the pronouns *all* and *some* (as well as fractions and percentages) when used as subjects if their modifiers are singular. Use a plural verb if their modifiers are plural.

All of the books have been classified.
Some of the gas is being pumped into the tank.

6 When *number* is used as the subject and is preceded by *the;* however, use a plural verb if *number* is preceded by a.

The number of voters has increased this year.
A number of workers are on vacation.

■ Use a plural verb

1 With a plural subject.

The blossoms are losing their petals.

2 With a compound subject joined by *and.*

My mother and my father are the same age.

■ Negative forms of verbs

1 Use the plural verb *do not* (or the contraction *don't*) when the pronoun *I, we, you,* or *they,* as well as a plural noun, is used as the subject.

You don't have a leg to stand on in this case.
The scissors do not cut properly.
I don't believe that answer is correct.

2 Use the singular verb *does not* (or the contraction *doesn't*) when the pronoun *he, she,* or *it,* as well as a singular noun, is used as the subject.

She doesn't want to attend the meeting.
It does not seem possible that winter's here.

■ Word-division guides

1 Divide words between syllables only; therefore, do not divide one-syllable words. **Note:** When in doubt, consult a dictionary or a word-division manual.

through-out	pref-er-ence	em-ploy-ees
reached	toward	thought

2 Do not divide words of five or fewer letters even if they have two or more syllables.

into	also	about	union	radio	ideas

3 Do not separate a one-letter syllable at the beginning of a word or a one- or two-letter syllable at the end of a word.

across	enough	steady	highly	ended

4 Usually, you may divide a word between double consonants; but, when adding a syllable to a word that ends in double letters, divide after the double letters of the root word.

writ-ten	sum-mer	expres-sion	excel-lence
will-ing	win-ner	process-ing	fulfill-ment

5 When the final consonant is doubled in adding a suffix, divide between the double letters.

run-ning	begin-ning	fit-ting	submit-ted

6 Divide after a one-letter syllable within a word; but when two single-letter syllables occur together, divide between them.

sepa-rate	regu-late	gradu-ation	evalu-ation

7 When the single-letter syllable *a, i,* or *u* is followed by the ending *ly, ble, bly, cle,* or *cal,* divide before the single-letter syllable.

stead-ily	siz-able	vis-ible	mir-acle
cler-ical	but	musi-cal	practi-cal

8 Divide only between the two words that make up a hyphenated word.

self-contained	well-developed

9 Do not divide a contraction or a single group of figures.

doesn't	$350,000	Policy F238975

10 Try to avoid dividing proper names and dates. If necessary, divide as follows.

Mary J./Pembroke	not	Mary J. Pem-/broke
November 15,/1995	not	November/15, 1995

■ Letter-placement points

Paper-guide placement

Check the placement of the paper guide for accurate horizontal centering of the letter.

Margins and date placement

Use the following guide:

5-Stroke Words In Letter Body	Side Margins	Date-line
Up to 100	2″	18
101-200	1½″	16
Over 200	1″	14

Letters containing many special features may require changes in these settings. Horizontal placement of date varies according to the letter style.

Address

The address begins on the fourth line (3 blank line spaces) below the date. A personal title, such as Mr., Mrs., Miss, or Ms., should precede the name of an individual. An official title, when used, may be placed on the first or the second line of the address, whichever gives better balance.

Two-page letters

If a letter is too long for one page, at least 2 lines of the body of the letter should be carried to the second page. The second page of a letter, or any additional pages, requires a proper heading. Use the block form shown below, beginning on line 6. Single-space the heading, and double-space below it.

Second-Page Heading

```
Dr. Ronald L. Spitz
Page 2
June 5, 19——
```

Attention line

An attention line, when used, is placed on the first line of the letter address.

Subject line

A subject line, when used, is placed on the second line (a double space) below the salutation. It is usually keyed at the left margin but may be centered in the modified block letter format. A subject line is required in the Simplified Block format; it is placed on the second line below the letter address.

Company name

Occasionally the company name is shown in the closing lines. When this is done, it is shown in ALL-CAPS 2 lines (a double space) below the complimentary close. Modern practice is to omit the company name in the closing lines if a letterhead is used.

Keyed/Printed name/official title

The name of the person who originated the letter and his/her official title are placed a quadruple space (3 blank line spaces) below the complimentary close, or a quadruple space below the company name when it is used. When both the name and official title are used, they may be placed on the same line, or the title may be placed on the next line below the keyed/printed name.

In the Simplified Block format, the name and official title of the originator are placed a quadruple space below the body of the letter.

■ 2-Letter ZIP Code Abbreviations

Alabama	AL	Guam	GU	Massachusetts	MA	New York	NY	Tennessee	TN
Alaska	AK	Hawaii	HI	Michigan	MI	North Carolina	NC	Texas	TX
Arizona	AZ	Idaho	ID	Minnesota	MN	North Dakota	ND	Utah	UT
Arkansas	AR	Illinois	IL	Mississippi	MS	Ohio	OH	Vermont	VT
California	CA	Indiana	IN	Missouri	MO	Oklahoma	OK	Virgin Islands	VI
Colorado	CO	Iowa	IA	Montana	MT	Oregon	OR	Virginia	VA
Connecticut	CT	Kansas	KS	Nebraska	NE	Pennsylvania	PA	Washington	WA
Delaware	DE	Kentucky	KY	Nevada	NV	Puerto Rico	PR	West Virginia	WV
District of Columbia	DC	Louisiana	LA	New Hampshire	NH	Rhode Island	RI	Wisconsin	WI
Florida	FL	Maine	ME	New Jersey	NJ	South Carolina	SC	Wyoming	WY
Georgia	GA	Maryland	MD	New Mexico	NM	South Dakota	SD		

1 Block, open

MERKEL-EVANS, Inc.

1321 Commerce Street • Dallas, TX 75202-1648 • Tel. (214) 871-4400

November 10, 19-- QS (space down
                      4 blank line spaces)

Mrs. Evelyn M. McNeil
4582 Campus Drive
Fort Worth, TX 76119-1835 DS

Dear Mrs. McNeil DS

The new holiday season is just around the corner, and
we invite you to beat the rush and visit our exciting
Gallery of Gifts. Gift-giving can be a snap this year
because of our vast array of gifts "for kids from one
to ninety-two."

What's more, many of our gifts are prewrapped for presentation. All can be packaged and shipped right here
at the store.

A catalog of our hottest gift items and a schedule of
special hours for special charge-card customers are enclosed. Please stop in and let us help you select that
special gift, or call us if you wish to shop by phone.

We wish you happy holidays and hope to see you soon. DS

Cordially yours QS

Ms. Carol J. Suess, Manager DS

rj DS
Enclosures

2 Modified block, open

ASSOCIATION OF OFFICE MANAGERS
518 JUNIPER CIRCLE   GOLDEN, CO 80403-6249   (303) 930-7749

September 26, 19-- QS (space down
                       4 blank line spaces)

Mr. Frank P. Dalton
90 Spring Street
Portland, ME 04101-7430 DS

Dear Mr. Dalton DS

It has come to my attention that several of the publications you
ordered in August may not have arrived as yet. According to the
enclosed copy of your order, Items 3765A, 4890B, and 5021X have
not yet been shipped.

Normally, orders received by the Association of Office Managers
are processed within 10 days of receipt. Because of a computer
problem, however, it appears that some orders in August may not
have been completed.

A copy of Item 3765A is enclosed. Copies of 4890B and 5021X will
be sent priority mail within the next few days by Mrs. Carla F.
Fernandez, chief of special orders.

We appreciate your interest in our publications and thank you for
your patronage. DS

                              Sincerely yours DS

                              ASSOCIATION OF OFFICE MANAGERS QS

                              Brian E. Miller
                              Director of Publications DS

xx DS
Enclosures
    Order
        Item 3765A DS
c Mrs. Carla F. Fernandez DS

If you have received these publications previously, please accept
these copies with our compliments.

3 Simplified block

Communication ✕ Concepts Inc.

178 S. Prospect Avenue ▪ San Bernardino, CA 92410-4567 ▪ (714) 586-7934

September 15, 19-- QS

MISS MICHELLE T LAWSON
DEL AMO SECRETARIAL SERVICE
21200 HAWTHORNE AVE
LOS ANGELES CA 90058-2820 DS

SIMPLIFIED BLOCK LETTER FORMAT DS

This letter illustrates the features that distinguish the
Simplified Block Letter format from the standard block format.

1. The date is placed on line 12 so that the letter address
will show through the window of a window envelope when used.

2. The letter address is keyed in the style recommended by
the U. S. Postal Service for OCR processing: ALL-CAP letters
with no punctuation. Cap-and-lowercase letters with punctuation may be used if that is the format of the addresses stored
in an electronic address file. Personal titles may be omitted.

3. A subject line replaces the traditional salutation which
some people find objectionable. The subject line may be keyed
in ALL-CAP or cap-and-lowercase letters. A double space is
left above and below it.

4. The complimentary close, which some people view as a needless appendage, is omitted.

5. The writer's name is placed on the fourth line space below
the body of the letter. The writer's title or department name
may appear on the line with the writer's name or on the next
line below it. The signature block may be keyed in ALL-CAP or
cap-and-lowercase letters.

6. A standard-length line is used for all letters. A six-inch
line is a common length (60 pica or 10-pitch spaces; 72 elite
or 12-pitch spaces). DS

The features listed and illustrated here are designed to bring
efficiency to the electronic processing of mail. QS

MRS. MARIA T. LOPEZ, DIRECTOR DS

tms

4 Simplified memorandum

henderson associates   INTEROFFICE MEMORANDUM

6623 Mitchell Avenue, Tallahassee, FL 32303-4429

June 12, 19-- QS

Martin F. Jensen, Chief Financial Officer DS

OFFICE RENOVATION DS

All of the furniture ordered for your office has arrived except
for the computer table. It is back ordered, and it should arrive
within the next week.

Arrangements have been made for your new carpet to be installed on
Saturday, June 26. Since your old furniture will be left in the
hallway during the weekend, we will need to take the necessary
security precautions. Mike Jackson has agreed to let you store
your file cabinets in his office over the weekend. Please let me
know by Friday if there are other things you would like stored
along with the files, and I will make the necessary arrangements. QS

Karl L. Hayward, Facilities Manager DS

xx

■ Addressing procedure

Envelope address

Set a tab stop (or margin stop if a number of envelopes are to be addressed) 10 spaces left of center for a small envelope or 5 spaces for a large envelope. Start the address here on Line 12 from the top edge of a small envelope and on Line 14 of a large one.

Style

Key the address in *block style,* SS. Use ALL CAPS and omit punctuation. Key the city name, state abbreviation, and ZIP Code on the last address line. The ZIP Code is keyed 2 spaces after the state abbreviation.

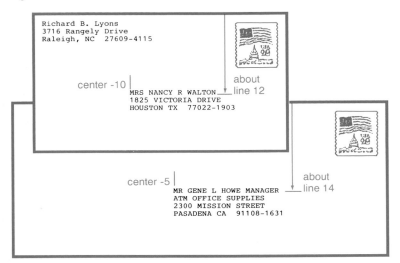
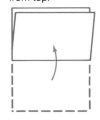

```
Richard B. Lyons
3716 Rangely Drive
Raleigh, NC  27609-4115
```

center -10   about line 12

```
MRS NANCY R WALTON
1825 VICTORIA DRIVE
HOUSTON TX  77022-1903
```

center -5   about line 14

```
MR GENE L HOWE MANAGER
ATM OFFICE SUPPLIES
2300 MISSION STREET
PASADENA CA  91108-1631
```

Addressee notations

Key addressee notations, such as HOLD FOR ARRIVAL, PLEASE FORWARD, or PERSONAL, a double space below the return address and about 3 spaces from the left edge of the envelope. Key these notations in ALL CAPS.

If an *attention line* is used, key it as the first line of the envelope address.

Mailing notations

Key mailing notations, such as SPECIAL DELIVERY and REGISTERED, below the stamp and at least 3 line spaces above the envelope address. Key these notations in ALL CAPS.

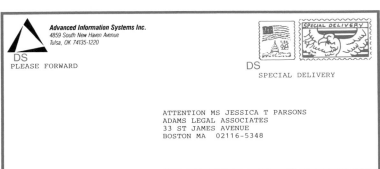

```
Advanced Information Systems Inc.
4859 South New Haven Avenue
Tulsa, OK 74135-1220

DS
PLEASE FORWARD
```

```
DS
SPECIAL DELIVERY
```

```
ATTENTION MS JESSICA T PARSONS
ADAMS LEGAL ASSOCIATES
33 ST JAMES AVENUE
BOSTON MA  02116-5348
```

■ Folding and inserting procedure

Small envelopes (No. 6¾, 6¼)

Step 1
With letter face up, fold bottom up to ½ inch from top.

Step 2
Fold right third to left.

Step 3
Fold left third to ½ inch from last crease.

Step 4
Insert last creased edge first.

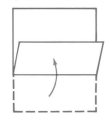

Large envelopes (No. 10, 9, 7¾)

Step 1
With letter face up, fold slightly less than ⅓ of sheet up toward top.

Step 2
Fold down top of sheet to within ½ inch of bottom fold.

Step 3
Insert letter into envelope with last crease toward bottom of envelope.

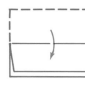

Window envelopes (letter)

Step 1
With sheet face down, top toward you, fold upper third down.

Step 2
Fold lower third up so address is showing.

Step 3
Insert sheet into envelope with last crease at bottom.

---

[1] Unbound, page 1

Main head   THE CHANGING OFFICE

QS   line 10 pica; line 12 elite

A secretary returning to an office job after a 25-year absence
would have a difficult time coping with the changes that have taken
place during that time. Changing technology would best describe
the challenges facing today's office worker. Two "buzzwords" which
are currently being used in the office are electronic desktop publishing and electronic mail. DS

Side head   Electronic Desktop Publishing DS

Desktop publishing is the process of integrating text and
graphics by utilizing computer software to produce professional-
looking documents without using professional services. According
to Winsor (1987, 29): DS

Desktop publishing has a bright future. . . . Desktop publishing enables people and businesses to develop their own brochures, newsletters, and other documents at a fraction of the
cost and time expended sending the work out to a professional
graphics studio. DS

Since today's firms are more concerned than ever about creating
the proper image, it is expected that a greater number of firms will
turn to desktop publishing to enhance their images. DS

Electronic Mail DS

The second "buzzword" being used extensively in the modern office is electronic mail (E-mail). E-mail is the sending, storing,
and delivering of written messages electronically. Reiss and Dolan
(1989, 529) identify two categories of electronic mail services: DS

1. In-house electronic mail. (E-mail which is run on a firm's
computer system.)

at least 1"

---

[2] Unbound, page 2

2 line 6

2. Commercial electronic mail. (E-mail which is supplied by
organizations such as General Electric Information Services
and MCI Communication.)

Summary

Desktop publishing and electronic mail are but two of the
changes which are shaping the future of information processing.
Each year new technology enhances the ability of office personnel
to produce quality information in less time. QS

REFERENCES QS

Reiss, Levi and Edwin D. Dolan. Using Computers: Managing Change.
Cincinnati: South-Western Publishing Co., 1989. DS

Winsor, William M. "Electronic Publishing: The Next Great Office
Revolution." The Secretary, June/July 1987.

---

[3] Leftbound, page 1

Main head   CAREER PLANNING

QS   line 10 pica; line 12 elite

Career planning is an important, ongoing process. It is
important because the career you choose will affect the quality of your life and will help determine the respect and recognition you receive. Throughout your lifetime you are likely
to make three or four career changes.[1] DS

Establish a Career Objective DS

One early, important step in the career planning process
is to define your career objective.

The career objective may indicate your area of interest
(such as finance or sales), the sort of organization you
would like to work for (such as banking or manufacturing), and the level of the position you want.[2]

Complete a Personal Inventory

Another useful step in career planning is to develop a
personal profile of your skills, interests, and values.

Skills. An analysis of your skills is likely to reveal
that you have many different kinds.

1. Functional skills that determine how well you manage time, communicate, motivate people, write, etc.

2. Adaptive skills that determine how well you will
fit into a specific work environment. These skills include personal traits such as flexibility, reliability,
efficiency, thoroughness, and enthusiasm for the job. DS

[1]Susan Bernard, Getting the Right Job, AT&T's College
Series (Elizabeth, NJ: AT&T College Market, 1988), p. 6. DS

[2]William H. Cunningham, Ramon J. Aldag, and Christopher
M. Swift, Introduction to Business, 2d ed. (Cincinnati:
South-Western Publishing Co., 1989), p. 620.

at least 1"

---

[4] Leftbound, page 2

2   line 8   line 6

3. Technical or work content skills that are required
to perform a specific job. These skills may include
such things as keyboarding, accounting, computer operation, and language usage skills.[3]

Interests. "Interests refer to the things that you like
or dislike."[4] By listing and analyzing them you should be
able to identify a desirable work environment. For example,
your list is likely to reveal if you like to work with things
or people, work alone or with others, lead or follow others,
or be indoors or outdoors.

Values. Values are your priorities in life, and you
should identify them early so that you can pursue a career
which will improve your chances to acquire them. Some of the
more obvious values include the importance you place on family, security, wealth, prestige, creativity, power, independence, and glamour. DS

[3]Adele Scheele, "Deciding What You Want To Do," Business
Week Careers, 1988 ed., p. 7. DS

[4]Bernard, Getting the Right Job, pp. 1-2. DS

[5]Cunningham, Introduction to Business, p. 617.

5 Leftbound, contents page

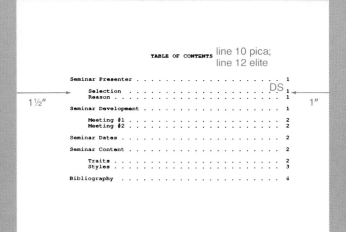

TABLE OF CONTENTS line 10 pica;
line 12 elite

1½″

1″

DS

```
Seminar Presenter . . . . . . . . . . . . . . . . . . . . 1
    Selection . . . . . . . . . . . . . . . . . . . . 1
    Reason . . . . . . . . . . . . . . . . . . . . 1
Seminar Development . . . . . . . . . . . . . . . . . 1
    Meeting #1 . . . . . . . . . . . . . . . . . 2
    Meeting #2 . . . . . . . . . . . . . . . . . 2
Seminar Dates . . . . . . . . . . . . . . . . . . . . . 2
Seminar Content . . . . . . . . . . . . . . . . . . . . 2
    Traits . . . . . . . . . . . . . . . . . . . 2
    Styles . . . . . . . . . . . . . . . . . . . 3
Bibliography . . . . . . . . . . . . . . . . . . . . . 4
```

6 Leftbound, bibliography (references)

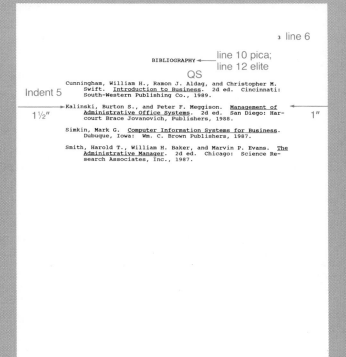

BIBLIOGRAPHY line 10 pica;
line 12 elite

QS

Indent 5

1½″

1″

Cunningham, William H., Ramon J. Aldag, and Christopher M.
    Swift. _Introduction to Business_. 2d ed. Cincinnati:
    South-Western Publishing Co., 1989.

Kalinski, Burton S., and Peter F. Meggison. _Management of
    Administrative Office Systems_. 2d ed. San Diego: Har-
    court Brace Jovanovich, Publishers, 1988.

Simkin, Mark G. _Computer Information Systems for Business_.
    Dubuque, Iowa: Wm. C. Brown Publishers, 1987.

Smith, Harold T., William H. Baker, and Marvin P. Evans. _The
    Administrative Manager_. 2d ed. Chicago: Science Re-
    search Associates, Inc., 1987.

7 Topbound, page 1

Main
head

FINDLEY HIGH SCHOOL BUSINESS CLUB ACTIVITIES line 12 pica;
line 14 elite

QS

1″

1″

The members of the Findley High School Business Club met last
week and decided to conduct the projects listed below. Please consider this document as the club's request for permission to organize and conduct these projects during this school year. The
proposed projects will publicize the business education program
to students, parents, and other members of the community that Findley High School serves. In addition, they will bring recognition
to current business education students.

Fall Semester Projects

The following projects have been suggested for the fall semester. These projects will help to draw students' attention to
the business education program early in the school year.

Poster contest. The club will sponsor a poster contest in
late September to recruit new members into the Business Club. The
posters will be displayed throughout the high school building and
the winner will receive a coupon good for two dinners at George's
Family Restaurant.

Open house. Club members will participate in the Business
Education Department's Fourth Annual Open House. The members will

    1. Greet the guests at the main entrance.

    2. Escort the guests to the Business Education Department
    where the program will be held.

    3. Demonstrate the computer hardware and software that is
    used in the business classes.

at least 1″

8 Formal memorandum

EAGLE & SONS
2299 Seward Highway • Anchorage, Alaska • 99503-4100   INTEROFFICE MEMORANDUM

TO: Warren E. Latouch, Director of Administration

FROM: Carla M. Boniface, Chief of Personnel

DATE: May 2, 19--

SUBJECT: Employee Evaluation Program

DS

1″

1″

As the company continues to expand, it is desirable that we establish an effective program for evaluating the performance of all
our employees. A sound evaluation program offers many advantages
to both the company and our employees, including the following:

1. Assists employees in judging their own value and accomplishments. Ratings should include strong points as well as short-
comings, with suggestions for improvement.

DS

2. Provides managers with information which they may use to determine promotions or lateral reassignments in order to make the
most effective use of each employee's abilities.

3. Provides a basis for determining increases in compensation or
for bonus payments to reward the most efficient employees.

4. Requires supervisors to analyze the work done by their subordinates and to recognize the contribution they make in the accomplishment of their mutual objectives.

5. Promotes an atmosphere of mutual respect and teamwork among
supervisors and employees.

6. Provides an evaluation of the effectiveness of other personnel
programs such as recruitment, selection, orientation, and training.

It is essential that clear-cut policies be established for this
new evaluation program. To insure success, the objectives of the
program must be clearly established, thoroughly understood, and
fully accepted by all concerned. A recommended plan of action to
accomplish these objectives is attached.

As a matter of priority, I recommend that the establishment of a
program to evaluate employee performance be placed on the agenda
of the executive committee for consideration at the earliest possible date.

xx

Attachment

CORRECTION SYMBOLS

■ Proofreader's marks

Sometimes keyed or printed copy may be corrected with proofreader's marks. The keyboard operator must be able to interpret these marks correctly in rekeying the corrected copy or rough draft as it may be called. The most commonly used proofreader's marks are shown below.

≡ or ⫟	Capitalize
⌒	Close up
✗	Delete
∧	Insert
⋎	Insert comma
# or /#	Insert space
⋁	Insert apostrophe
⋎ ⋎	Insert quotation marks
⊏	Move right
⊐	Move left
⌐	Move down; lower
⌐	Move up; raise
lc or /	Set in lowercase
¶	Paragraph
No ¶	No new paragraph
‖	Set flush; align type
⊙	Spell out
stet	Let it stand; ignore correction
~ or tr	Transpose
____	Underline or italics

CENTERING PROCEDURES

1 Horizontal centering

Formula for finding horizontal center of paper

Scale reading at left edge of paper
+ Scale reading at right edge of paper
Total ÷ 2 = Center Point

Example
   0
 102
 102 ÷ 2 = 51

1 Move margin stops to extreme ends of scale.
2 Clear tab stops; then set a tab stop at center of paper.
3 Tabulate to center of paper.
4 From center, backspace once for each 2 letters, spaces, figures, or punctuation marks in the line.
5 Do not backspace for an odd or leftover stroke at the end of the line.
6 Begin to key where backspacing ends.

2 Horizontal centering for machines with automatic center

1 Insert paper with the left edge at 0.
2 Set margins at the extreme right and left edges of the paper.
3 Strike **Return** to move the carrier to the left margin; then press the **Center** key. (If you are using a microcomputer/word processor, refer to your software user's guide for centering.)
4 Key the first line. (Characters will not print as you key the line, but the carrier will move to the left for each character keyed.)
5 Strike **Return** to print the line.
6 Repeat Steps 2-4 to center each line.

3 Vertical centering

Mathematical method

1 Count lines and blank line spaces needed to key problem.
2 Subtract *lines to be used* from *lines available* (66 for full sheet and 33 for half sheet).
3 Divide by 2 to get top and bottom margins. If a fraction results, disregard it.
4 If an even number results, space down that number of times from top of sheet and key the first line. If an odd number results, use the next lower number.

Dropping fractions and using even numbers usually places copy a line or two above exact center-- in what is often called *reading position.*

Formula for vertical mathematical placement

$$\frac{\text{Lines available} - \text{lines used}}{2} = \text{top margin}$$

Backspace-from-center method

Basic rule
From vertical center of paper, roll platen (cylinder) back once for each 2 lines, 2 blank line spaces, or line and blank line space. Ignore odd or leftover line.

Steps to follow:
1 To move paper to vertical center, start spacing down from top edge of paper.
  a half sheet
     down 8 DS (double spaces)
     + 1 SS (Line 17)
  b full sheet
     down 17 DS (Line 34)
2 From vertical center
  a half sheet, SS or DS; follow basic rule, back 1 for 2 lines
  b full sheet, SS or DS; follow basic rule, back 1 for 2; then back 2 SS for reading position.

Prepare

1 Insert and align paper (typewriter).

2 Clear margin stops by moving them to extreme ends of line-of-writing scale. On electronic equipment, set margins as near as possible to the edges of the paper (so that automatic centering may be used for horizontal placement).

3 Clear all tabulator stops.

4 Move element carrier (carriage) or cursor to center of paper or line-of-writing scale.

5 Decide the number of spaces to be left between columns (for intercolumns)--preferably an even number (4, 6, 8, 10, etc.).

1 Plan vertical placement

Follow either of the vertical centering procedures explained on page RG 10.

Spacing headings. Double-space (count 1 blank line space) between main and secondary headings, when both are used. Double-space between the last table heading (either main or secondary) and the first horizontal line of column items or column headings. Double-space between column headings (when used) and the first line of the column entries. On electronic equipment, use the automatic center feature (see RG 10) to center the *key* line (line made up of the longest item in each column plus the number of spaces between columns). Set a tab stop at the beginning of each column; then discard or delete the *key* line.

Spacing above totals and source notes. Double-space between the total rule and the total figures. Double-space between the last line of the table and the 1½" rule above the source note. Double-space between the 1½" rule and the source note.

2 Plan horizontal placement

On an electronic typewriter, backspace from center of paper (or line-of-writing scale) 1 space for each 2 letters, figures, symbols, and spaces in *longest* item of each column in the table. Then backspace once for each 2 spaces to be left between columns (intercolumns). Set left margin stop where backspacing ends.

If an odd or leftover space occurs at the end of the longest item of a column when backspacing by 2's, carry it forward to the next column. Do not backspace for an odd or leftover character at the end of the last column. (See illustration below.)

Set tab stops. From the left margin, space forward 1 space for each letter, figure, symbol, and space in the longest item in the first column and for each space to be left between Cols. 1 and 2. Set a tab stop at this point for the second column. Follow this procedure for each additional column of the table.

Note: If a column heading is longer than the longest item in the column, it *may* be treated as the longest item in the column in determining placement. The longest columnar entry must then be centered under the heading and the tab stop set accordingly.

3 Center column headings (optional)

Backspace-from-column-center method

From point at which column begins (tab or margin stop), space forward once for each 2 letters, figures, or spaces in the longest item in the column. This leads to the column center point; from it, backspace once for each 2 spaces in column heading. Ignore an odd or leftover space. Key the heading at this point; it will be centered over the column.

Mathematical methods

1 To the number on the cylinder (platen) or line-of-writing scale immediately under the first letter, figure, or symbol of the longest item of the column, add the number shown under the space following the last stroke of the item. Divide this sum by 2; the result will be the center point of the column. From this point on the scale, backspace (1 for 2) to center the column heading.

2 From the number of spaces in the longest item, subtract the number of spaces in the heading. Divide this number by 2; ignore fractions. Space forward this number from the tab or margin stop and key the heading.

4 Horizontal rulings

To make horizontal rulings in tables, depress shift lock and strike the underline key.

Single-space above and double-space below horizontal rulings.

5 Vertical rulings

On a typewriter, operate the automatic line finder. Place a pencil or pen point through the cardholder (or the typebar guide above the ribbon or carrier). Roll the paper up until you have a line of the desired length. Remove the pencil or pen and reset the line finder.

On a computer-generated table, use a ruler and pen or pencil to draw the vertical rulings.

```
                MAIN HEADING

             Secondary Heading

   These        Are       Column      Heads

xxxxxx       longest    xxxx        xxxxx
xxxx         item       longest     xxx
xxxxx        xxxxx      item        longest
longest      xxxxxx     xxxxx       item
item         xxxx       xxx         xxx

longest1234longest1234longest1234longest
```

1 Electronic correction

Electronic typewriters, word processors, and computers vary in the way keystroking errors may be corrected. All, however, have a correction key that removes errors from the electronic window/screen and/or paper. Use the User's Manual for your machine to learn the steps for making corrections electronically.

2 Lift-off tape

1 Strike the special backspace/lift-off key to move the printing element (or carrier) to the point of the error.

2 Rekey the error exactly as you made it. In this step, the lift-off tape actually lifts the error off the page. The printing element tape stays in place.

3 Key the correction.

3 Correction fluid

1 Turn the paper up a few spaces to ease the correction procedure.

2 Shake the bottle; remove the applicator; daub excess fluid on inside of bottle opening.

3 Brush fluid sparingly over the entire error by a light touching action.

4 Return applicator to bottle and tighten cap; blow on the error to speed the drying process.

4 Correction paper

1 Backspace to the beginning of the error.

2 Insert the correction tape or paper strip behind the ribbon and in front of the error, coated side toward the copy.

3 Rekey the error exactly as you made it. In this step, powder from the correction paper is pressed by force into the form of the error, thus masking it.

4 Remove the correction paper; backspace to the point where the correction begins and key the correction.

5 Rubber eraser

1 Turn the paper up a few spaces; then move the element carrier (carriage) to the extreme right or left so that eraser crumbs will not fall into the machine.

2 Move the paper bail out of the way. Pull the original sheet forward (if a carbon copy is being made) and place a card (5" × 3" or slightly larger) in front of, not behind, the first carbon sheet to protect the carbon copy from smudges.

3 Flip the original sheet back and make the erasure with a hard eraser. Brush or blow the eraser crumbs off the paper.

4 Move the protective card to a position in front of the second carbon sheet if more than one carbon copy is being made. Erase the error on the first carbon copy with a soft eraser.

5 Remove the card and key the correction.

6 Correcting errors by squeezing/spreading

Letter omitted in a word

1 Remove the word with the omitted letter.

2 Move printing element to second space after preceding word.

3 Pull half-space lever forward (or use electronic incremental backspacer) to move printing element a half space to the left.

4 Hold lever in place as you key the corrected word with the other hand.

5 Release the lever and continue keying.

Letter added in a word

1 Remove the word with the added letter.

2 Move printing element to third space after preceding word.

3 Pull half-space lever forward (or use electronic incremental backspacer) to move printing element a half space to the left.

4 Hold lever in place as you key the corrected word with the other hand.

5 Release the lever and continue keying.

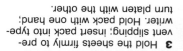

Error   an omitte letter
Correction   an omitted letter

Error   a letter within
Correction   a letter within

7 Carbon-Pack Assembly

1 Assemble letterhead, carbon sheets (uncarboned side up), and second sheets as illustrated above. Use one carbon and one second sheet for each copy desired.

2 Grasp the carbon pack at the sides, turn it so that the letterhead faces away from you, the carbon side of the carbon paper is toward you, and the top edge of the pack is face down. Tap the sheets gently on the desk to straighten.

3 Hold the sheets firmly to prevent slipping; insert pack into typewriter. Hold pack with one hand; turn platen with the other.

4 To keep the carbon pack straight when feeding it into the typewriter, place the pack in the fold of a plain sheet of paper (paper trough) or under the flap of an envelope. Remove trough or envelope when the pack is in place.

Photocopier

Offset Printer

Reprographics refers to the making of multiple copies of all kinds of materials. Numerous items should be considered when planning and organizing material for duplication. One important factor is cost. The objective is to select a duplication process that will provide the material at the lowest possible cost per copy. The appearance of the copy in terms of clarity, attractiveness, format, and size must also be considered. Since time available to do the work may affect quality and cost, time is also an important factor.

The four processes used most often in schools, churches, and business offices are photocopier duplication, offset duplication, spirit duplication, and stencil duplication. Each of these processes is described briefly here.

Photocopier Duplication

Photocopiers have virtually replaced spirit and stencil duplication in the business office. The photocopy process, which produces copies directly from an original electronically, is easier, cleaner, quicker, and even less costly when only a few copies are needed, than the other processes described here.

Copiers are often classified by the kind of paper they require and the number of copies they are designed to produce. Plain-paper copiers, which use the regular paper found in the office, are most popular. Coated-paper copiers require the use of more expensive chemically-treated paper.

Copiers also may be classified by volume of copies produced. Low-volume copiers (which will produce about 20 copies per minute) are designed for no more than 20,000 copies per month. Mid-volume copiers (which produce 40-60 copies per minute) are designed to generate 20,000 to 50,000 copies per month. High-volume copiers (which produce up to 120 copies per minute) are designed to produce more than 50,000 copies per month.

Copiers, especially in the mid- and high-volume range, are available with a variety of special features. These include image reduction/enlargement, color duplication, duplex (two-sided) printing, collating/stapling, and automatic feed. All these features improve the usefulness and efficiency of copiers, but also add to their cost.

Offset Printing

Offset printing (which is done from plates made from camera-ready masters) is primarily a commercial printing process used to make thousands of copies of items containing limited numbers of pages. More sophisticated photocopiers have largely replaced offset printers for within-the-office duplication.

Preparing Master Copies for Photocopying and Offset Printing

Because photocopying and offset printing utilize a photographic process, each method begins with the preparation of a master or model copy of each page. The model or master copy can be generated on a standard or an electronic typewriter, on a computer, or on a word processor. The following steps will result in camera-ready copy usable for either photocopying or offset printing.

1. Be sure that the printing element (type, "ball," or daisy wheel) is clean and free of debris (ink, white-out, etc.).

2. Plan margins, spacing, and space to be left for illustrations (if any) before preparing a rough draft of the model.

3. Prepare a rough-draft model on the same size paper to be used for final printing (unless the copy is to be enlarged or reduced).

4. Proofread and correct the rough-draft copy before keying the final copy.

5. Prepare the final (camera-ready) copy on a smooth-finish paper so that the images are clear and sharp.

6. Correct all errors neatly. Use lift-off tape on typewriters so equipped. On other typewriters, use white-out or cover-up paper strips. On equipment with a display, correct errors on screen before printing a hard copy.

7. Give the master copy a final check to be sure it is error-free and free of smudges, wrinkles, tears, or other blemishes that could be picked up by a camera.

(continued, p. RG 14)

Spirit Duplication

The spirit duplicator, sometimes called a "Ditto" (a trade name), is the least expensive way to reproduce up to several hundred copies. The primary print color used is purple, although pale shades of red, blue, green, and black are also available. These copies are not usually as clear and attractive as those produced by other duplicators. This machine is used primarily by churches, schools, and small business firms.

The spirit master set consists of two basic parts: the master sheet and a sheet of special carbon that can be used only once. A backing sheet also may be used to improve the consistency of the print. If a specially prepared master is not available, simply place the carbon paper between the master sheet and the backing sheet, with the glossy side of the carbon toward you. When you key the copy, the carbon copy will be on the back of the master sheet.

Follow these directions for better masters.

1. Prepare a model copy of the material to be duplicated. Leave at least a one-half inch margin at the top of the master. Proofread the model copy; correct it if necessary.

2. If you do not have a carbon ribbon, you can avoid "fuzzy" type and filled-in characters by preparing the copy with the ribbon indicator in the "stencil" position. This procedure makes it difficult to proofread the copy, however.

3. Insert the open end of the spirit master into the machine first so that you can make corrections easily (see illustration at left). If you make an error, scrape off with a razor blade or knife the incorrect letter or word on the reverse side of the master sheet. Before correcting the error, tear off an unused portion of the carbon and slip it under the part to be corrected. Correct the error and remove the torn portion of carbon as soon as you have done so.

4. On electric and electronic machines, which provide even pressure automatically, key as usual. Use a firm, even stroke to key the master on a nonelectric machine; key capitals a little heavier than usual and punctuation marks a little lighter.

5. Proofread the copy and correct any errors you may have missed before you remove the master from the machine.

6. "Run" the number of copies needed by following the User's Manual that accompanies your spirit duplicator.

Stencil Duplication

Thousands of copies of programs, bulletins, newsletters, and other publications can be reproduced in a short time through the use of the stencil duplication process.

A stencil consists of three basic parts: the stencil sheet, the backing sheet, and the cushion sheet. When a key strikes the cushion sheet, it "cuts" an impression in the stencil sheet. Note: Only a machine having type bars is capable of "cutting" a stencil adequately. A printing element wheel may not actually "cut" the stencil sheet. A cushion sheet is placed between the stencil and the backing sheet to absorb the impact of the type bar. A film sheet may be placed over the stencil sheet if darker print is desired. This film also protects the stencil sheet from letter cutout when the type face is extremely sharp.

Before "cutting" the stencil, follow these steps.

1. Prepare a model copy of the material to be reproduced. Check it for accuracy of format and keying; correct it if necessary.

2. If your machine has a cloth ribbon, clean the printing element thoroughly, paying close attention to the letters where ink tends to accumulate, such as the o and the e. Adjust the ribbon lever to "stencil" position.

3. Insert the cushion sheet between the stencil sheet and the backing sheet. Place the top edge of the model copy at the corner marks of the stencil to see where to position the first line. The scales at the top and sides of the stencil will help you place the copy correctly.

4. Insert the stencil assembly into the machine. On electric and electronic machines, which provide even pressure automatically, key with the usual force. If you are using a nonelectric typewriter, use a firm, uniform touch. Some keys that are completely closed such as d and p must be struck more lightly. Capitals and letters such as m and w must be struck with greater force.

5. If you make an error, it can be corrected easily with stencil correction fluid. If there is a film over the stencil, this must be detached until you resume keying. Use a smooth paper clip to rub the surface of the error on the stencil sheet. Place a pencil between the stencil sheet and the cushion sheet and apply a light coat of correction fluid over the error. Let the fluid dry; then make the correction, using a light touch.

Master Set for Spirit Duplication

Carboned surface toward master
Backing sheet
Master sheet
Regular typewriter ribbon

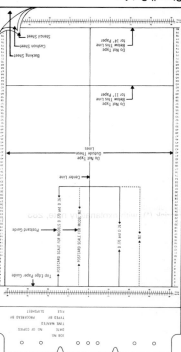

Stencil Set for Stencil Duplication